IFIP Advances in Information and Communication Technology

526

Editor-in-Chief

Kai Rannenberg, Goethe University Frankfurt, Germany

Editorial Board

IFIP – The International Federation for Information Processing

IFIP was founded in 1960 under the auspices of UNESCO, following the first World Computer Congress held in Paris the previous year. A federation for societies working in information processing, IFIP's aim is two-fold: to support information processing in the countries of its members and to encourage technology transfer to developing nations. As its mission statement clearly states:

> IFIP is the global non-profit federation of societies of ICT professionals that aims at achieving a worldwide professional and socially responsible development and application of information and communication technologies.

IFIP is a non-profit-making organization, run almost solely by 2500 volunteers. It operates through a number of technical committees and working groups, which organize events and publications. IFIP's events range from large international open conferences to working conferences and local seminars.

The flagship event is the IFIP World Computer Congress, at which both invited and contributed papers are presented. Contributed papers are rigorously refereed and the rejection rate is high.

As with the Congress, participation in the open conferences is open to all and papers may be invited or submitted. Again, submitted papers are stringently refereed.

The working conferences are structured differently. They are usually run by a working group and attendance is generally smaller and occasionally by invitation only. Their purpose is to create an atmosphere conducive to innovation and development. Refereeing is also rigorous and papers are subjected to extensive group discussion.

Publications arising from IFIP events vary. The papers presented at the IFIP World Computer Congress and at open conferences are published as conference proceedings, while the results of the working conferences are often published as collections of selected and edited papers.

IFIP distinguishes three types of institutional membership: Country Representative Members, Members at Large, and Associate Members. The type of organization that can apply for membership is a wide variety and includes national or international societies of individual computer scientists/ICT professionals, associations or federations of such societies, government institutions/government related organizations, national or international research institutes or consortia, universities, academies of sciences, companies, national or international associations or federations of companies.

More information about this series at http://www.springer.com/series/6102

Marit Hansen · Eleni Kosta
Igor Nai-Fovino · Simone Fischer-Hübner (Eds.)

Privacy and Identity Management

The Smart Revolution

12th IFIP WG 9.2, 9.5, 9.6/11.7, 11.6/SIG 9.2.2
International Summer School
Ispra, Italy, September 4–8, 2017
Revised Selected Papers

 Springer

Editors
Marit Hansen
Unabhängiges Landeszentrum für
  Datenschutz (ULD)
Kiel
Germany

Eleni Kosta
Tilburg Institute for Law, Technology
  and Society (TILT)
Tilburg University
Tilburg
The Netherlands

Igor Nai-Fovino
European Commission - Joint
  Research Centre
Ispra
Italy

Simone Fischer-Hübner
Karlstad University
Karlstad
Sweden

ISSN 1868-4238   ISSN 1868-422X   (electronic)
IFIP Advances in Information and Communication Technology
ISBN 978-3-030-06548-5   ISBN 978-3-319-92925-5   (eBook)
https://doi.org/10.1007/978-3-319-92925-5

Printed on acid-free paper

This Springer imprint is published by the registered company Springer International Publishing AG
part of Springer Nature
The registered company address is: Gewerbestrasse 11, 6330 Cham, Switzerland

Preface

This volume contains the proceedings with selected papers presented at IFIP Summer School 2017 – "The Smart Revolution" – which took place September 4–8, 2017, in Ispra, Italy.

The 2017 Summer School was a joint effort among IFIP Working Groups 9.2, 9.5, 9.6/11.7, 11.6, Special Interest Group 9.2.2, and several European and national projects: The EU H2020 projects CREDENTIAL and PRISMACLOUD, The German project Privacy Forum (Forum Privatheit), and the EU H2020 Marie Curie ITN Privacy&Us. It was hosted and also generously supported by the Joint Research Center (JRC) of the EU Commission in Ispra.

This Summer School brought together more than 45 junior and senior researchers and practitioners from different parts of the world from many disciplines, including many young entrants to the field. They came to share their ideas, build up a collegial relationship with others, gain experience in making presentations, and have the opportunity to publish a paper through these proceedings.

One of the school's goals is to encourage the publication of thorough research papers by students and young researchers. To this end, the school had a three-phase review process for submitted papers. In the first phase, authors were invited to submit short abstracts of their work. Abstracts within the scope of the call were selected for presentation at the school and the authors were encouraged to submit full papers of their work. All papers appeared in the unreviewed online pre-proceedings on the school's website. After the school, the authors received two to three reviews by the Program Committee and were given time to revise and resubmit their papers for inclusion in these proceedings. In total, the school received 29 short paper submissions, from which finally 15 research papers were expanded and submitted in the last review round. Out of these submissions, 12 papers were finally accepted, including the paper by Silvia de Conca, which was judged to be the school's best student paper.

In addition to the submitted papers, this volume also includes reviewed papers summarizing the results of the workshops and a tutorial that were held at the summer school, as well as papers contributed by several of the invited speakers.

We are grateful to all contributors of the Summer School and especially also to the Program Committee for reviewing the abstracts and papers and advising the authors on their revisions. Our thanks to all supporting projects, and especially to the JRC for their support of the school's activities.

April 2018

Eleni Kosta
Marit Hansen
Igor Nai-Fovino
Simone Fischer-Hübner

Organization

General Co-chairs

Simone Fischer-Hübner Karlstad University, Sweden
Jean Pierre Nordvik European Commission - Joint Research Centre, Italy

Program Committee Co-chairs

Marit Hansen Unabhängiges Landeszentrum für Datenschutz (ULD), Germany
Eleni Kosta Tilburg Institute for Law, Technology and Society (TILT), The Netherlands
Igor Nai Fovino European Commission - Joint Research Centre, Italy

Program Committee

Stuart Anderson The University of Edinburgh, UK
David Aspinall The University of Edinburgh, UK
Felix Bieker Unabhängiges Landeszentrum für Datenschutz (ULD), Germany
Michael Birnhack Tel Aviv University, Israel
Jan Camenisch IBM Research – Zurich, Switzerland
Gerard Draper-Gil University of Balearic Islands (UIB), Spain
Penny Duquenoy Middlesex University, UK
Zekeriya Erkin TU Delft, The Netherlands
Hannes Federrath University of Hamburg, Germany
Simone Fischer-Hübner Karlstad University, Sweden
Pedro Freitas University of Minho, Portugal
Michael Friedewald Fraunhofer
Lothar Fritsch Karlstad University, Sweden
Raphael Gellert Vrije Universiteit Brussel (VUB), Belgium
Carlisle George Middlesex University, UK
Gloria Gonzalez-Fuster Vrije Universiteit Brussel (VUB), Belgium
Thomas Gross Newcastle University, UK
Kai Kimppa University of Turku, Finland
Sabrina Kirrane Vienna University of Economics and Business, Austria
Stephan Krenn AIT Austrian Institute of Technology GmbH, Austria
Anja Lehmann IBM Research – Zurich, Switzerland
Alessandro Mantelero Politecnico di Torino, Italy
Jetzabel Maritza Goethe University Frankfurt, Germany
  Serna Olvera
Leonardo Martucci Karlstad Univeristy, Sweden

Joachim Meyer	Tel Aviv University, Israel
Evgeni Moyakine	University of Groningen, The Netherlands
Steven J. Murdoch	University College London, UK
Ricardo Neisse	European Commission, Joint Research Center, Italy
Norberto Patrignani	Politecnico of Torino, Italy
Siani Pearson	UK
Robin Pierce	Harvard University, USA
Jo Pierson	Vrije Universiteit Brussel (VUB), Belgium
Tobias Pulls	Karlstad University, Sweden
Charles Raab	The University of Edinburgh, UK
Kai Rannenberg	Goethe University Frankfurt, Germany
Delphine Reinhardt	University of Bonn, Germany
Arnold Roosendaal	Privacy Company, The Netherlands
Ignacio Sanchez	European Commission, Joint Research Center, Italy
Viola Schiaffonati	Politecnico di Milano, Italy
Daniel Slamanig	AIT Austrian Institute of Technology, Austria
Rosamunde van Brakel	Vrije Universiteit Brussel (VUB), Belgium
Bart Van der Sloot	Tilburg University, The Netherlands
Jozef Vyskoc	VaF, Slovakia
Diane Whitehouse	The Castlegate Consultancy, UK
Tal Zarsky	University of Haifa, Israel/NYU Law School, USA
Harald Zwingelberg	Unabhängiges Landeszentrum für Datenschutz (ULD), Germany
Rose-Mharie Åhlfeldt	University of Skövde, Sweden
Melek Önen	EURECOM, France

Contents

Improving Privacy and Security in the Ear of Smart Environments

Safeguarding Personal Data and Mitigating Risks

Assistive Robots

Mobility and Privacy

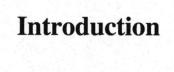

Introduction

The Smart World Revolution

Eleni Kosta[1]([⊠]), Igor Nai Fovino[2], Simone Fischer-Hübner[3],
Marit Hansen[5], Charles Raab[4], Ignacio Sanchez[2],
and Diane Whitehouse[6]

[1] Tilburg Institute for Law, Technology, and Society (TILT), Tilburg Law
School, 90153, 5000LE Tilburg, The Netherlands
e.kosta@tilburguniversity.edu

[2] European Commission, Joint Research Centre (JRC), Directorate for Space,
Security and Migration, Cyber and Digital Citizens' Security Unit, Via E. Fermi
2749, 21027 Ispra, VA, Italy
{igor.nai-fovino,ignacio.sanchez}@ec.europa.eu

[3] Department of Computer Science, Karlstad University, Universitetsgatan 2,
65188 Karlstad, Sweden
simone.fischer-huebner@kau.se

[4] Politics and International Relations, School of Social and Political Science,
University of Edinburgh, Chrystal Macmillan Building, 15a George Square,
Edinburgh EH8 9LD, Scotland, UK
c.d.raab@ed.ac.uk

[5] Unabhängiges Landeszentrum für Datenschutz Schleswig-Holstein,
Holstenstr. 98, 24103 Kiel, Germany
marit.hansen@privacyresearch.eu

[6] The Castlegate Consultancy, 27 Castlegate, Malton, UK
diane.whitehouse@thecastlegateconsultancy.com

Abstract. The explosion of the phenomenon of the Internet of Things and the increasing diffusion of smart living technologies in all the layers of our society – from houses to hospitals, from cities to critical infrastructures such as energy grids – clearly demonstrates the viability and the advantages of a fully interconnected vision of a smart world. Technological advances such as the use of open data, big data, blockchain and sensor development in the Internet of Everything are rapidly changing the societal landscape, raising the question of how to guarantee, in a homogeneous way, the preservation of privacy and other human rights in a completely heterogeneous and cross-sectoral world, without impairing the potentialities of the new smart technologies such as the Internet of Things and big data. The 2017 IFIP Summer School on Privacy and Identity Management was dedicated to the exploration of technical, legal and societal issues relating to the smart revolution. This chapter provides an introduction to the exciting work presented at the summer school.

Keywords: Smart revolution · Summer school · Privacy · Data protection

M. Hansen et al. (Eds.): Privacy and Identity 2017, IFIP AICT 526, pp. 3–12, 2018.
https://doi.org/10.1007/978-3-319-92925-5_1

1   An Introduction to the Summer School on the Smart World Revolution

The world is in the throes of a 'smart' revolution. From smart watches, to smart cars and from smart TV to smart robots, technological developments foster a wide range of smart applications and devices. Digital data is an essential resource for economic growth, competitiveness, innovation, job creation, and societal progress. To be exploited, data needs to flow across borders and sectors. It should be smartly aggregated and should be accessible and reusable by most stakeholders. The explosion of the phenomenon of the Internet of Things and the increasing diffusion of smart living technologies in all the layers of our society – from houses to hospitals, from cities to critical infrastructures such as energy grids – clearly demonstrates the viability and the advantages of a fully interconnected smart world. However, this vision poses concrete concerns related to the potential antagonism between the 'trend to share everything' on the one hand, and the 'citizen's right to privacy and security', on the other. Dilemmas concerning opportunities for discrimination, social profiling, and social exclusion also arise.

The European framework on data protection has been recently reformed. The European Union (EU) General Data Protection Regulation (GDPR)[1] replaces the 1995 Data Protection Directive[2] and becomes applicable as of May 2018, providing an overarching legislative framework that responds to the concerns of processing personal data. Parallel to the adoption of the GDPR, a new Directive was adopted to protect personal data processed for the purpose of criminal law enforcement (LED)[3]. The 2002 e-Privacy Directive[4] regulates issues relating to privacy and data protection in relation to electronic communications services offered over public communications networks. In January 2017, the European Commission published a proposal[5] for the revision of

---

[1] European Parliament and the Council of the European Union, Regulation (EU) 2016/679 of 27 April 2016 on the protection of natural persons with regard to the processing of personal data and on the free movement of such data, and repealing Directive 95/46/EC (General Data Protection Regulation) (Text with EEA relevance) [2016] OJ L 119/1 (4.5.2016).

[2] European Parliament and the Council of the European Union, Directive 95/46/EC of 24 October 1995 on the protection of individuals with regard to the processing of personal data and on the free movement of such data [1995] OJ L281/31 (23.11.1995).

[3] European Parliament and the Council of the European Union, Directive (EU) 2016/680 of 27 April 2016 on the protection of natural persons with regard to the processing of personal data by competent authorities for the purposes of the prevention, investigation, detection or prosecution of criminal offences or the execution of criminal penalties, and on the free movement of such data, and repealing Council Framework Decision 2008/977/JHA [2016] OJ L 119/89 (4.5.2016).

[4] European Parliament and the Council of the European Union, Directive 2002/58/EC of 12 July 2002 concerning the processing of personal data and the protection of privacy in the electronic communications sector (Directive on privacy and electronic communications) [2002] OJ L201/37 (31.07.2002).

[5] European Commission, Proposal for a regulation of the European Parliament and of the Council concerning the respect for private life and the protection of personal data in electronic communications and repealing Directive 2002/58/EC (Regulation on Privacy and Electronic Communications) {COM(2017) 10 final}.

that Directive as well. The Commission proposed the replacement of the Directive by a Regulation that may eventually provide an instrument to enforce not only the privacy, but also, to some extent, the security of the upper layers of the telecommunication services relevant for implementing a smartly interconnected world. One of the novelties of the proposed e-Privacy Regulation is the extension of its scope to include new functionally equivalent electronic communications services offered by Over The Top (OTT) players i.e., with no involvement of multi-system operators. The goal of the expansion of the scope of the Regulation to OTTs is to ensure respect for the principle of confidentiality and the protection of fundamental rights in those types of services[6].

While these legislative instruments define the principles to be respected and enforced, not a lot has been said about the *way* in which these principles should be deployed technically in different industrial and societal sectors. Technological advances such as the use of open data, big data, blockchain and sensor development in the Internet of Everything are rapidly changing the societal landscape. Questions arise about who holds what data, and where and how that data may be used. These advances challenge the way in which privacy and data protection should be handled, because current national regulatory mechanisms were not devised with these new technologies and possibilities in mind. What is also clear, from discussions in the general press, media and social media, is that there are also huge societal, social, and ethical concerns with regard to the implications of these emerging technologies both in theory and in their practical deployment.

Here, indeed, lies a major scientific and social challenge: how to guarantee, in a homogeneous way, the preservation of privacy and other human rights in a completely heterogeneous and cross-sectoral world, without impairing the potentialities of the new smart technologies such as the Internet of Things and big data. Such questions, as well as many other current and general research issues surrounding privacy and identity management, were addressed by the 2017 IFIP Summer School on Privacy and Identity Management.

The Summer School welcomed contributions from PhD students from various disciplines (e.g., computer science, informatics, economics, ethics, law, psychology, sociology, history, political and other social sciences, surveillance studies, business and public management). These contributions were supplemented by invited talks from experts in the field, as well as tutorials and workshops. This volume reflects the outcome of the exciting work presented at the summer school and mirrors the sparkling interdisciplinary debates that took place during and around the event. The submissions are divided into six categories, each dealing with a concrete aspect of the 'smart revolution': privacy engineering, privacy in the era of smart revolution, improving privacy and security in the era of smart environments, safeguarding personal data and mitigating risks, assistive robots, and finally, mobility and privacy.

---

[6] European Commission, Proposal for a Regulation of the European Parliament and of the Council concerning the respect for private life and the protection of personal data in electronic communications and repealing Directive 2002/58/EC (Regulation on Privacy and Electronic Communications), Brussels, 10.1.2017 COM(2017) 10 final, p. 4.

2   Privacy Engineering

Privacy engineering is a key topic that aims at the development of methodologies, tools and techniques that contribute to ensuring privacy in engineered systems. Given the importance of privacy engineering in the era of 'smart revolution', the Summer School organisers invited three groups of distinguished researchers to cover various aspects of this topic.

Privacy and data protection by design are important principles embraced by the privacy and data protection community: they were recently captured in the content of the GDPR. The notion of "by design" implies that the privacy and data protection dimension should be considered at the inception of new projects and taken into account all the way during the projects' design and development.

In Chap. 2, Del Alamo, Martín and Caiza, in their invited paper, provide an introduction to the emerging field of privacy engineering, which aims to bridge the gaps among the legal, the academic and the engineering dimensions with the goal of providing engineers with tools and methods to address data protection and privacy during the software development process. In this work, the authors describe a conceptual metamodel that can be used to organise and structure knowledge in this domain in a way that can be more easily used and integrated into engineering practice. They elaborate on privacy design patterns as means to gather systematic reusable knowledge.

The topic of data protection by design is also at the core of the chapter authored by Rommetveit, Tanas and van Dijk. This invited paper presents results from recent empirical investigations on privacy by design and privacy engineering (the H2020 CANDID project), in which social science methods such as written consultations, questionnaires, interviews and focus groups were used to research the existing approaches, perceptions, imaginations and expectations in regard to privacy engineering. Tensions and frictions discovered during these investigations are described in the chapter, such as lessons learnt relating to the limits of privacy by design that should not be passed – the impossibility of "law becoming code" in the strict sense of the word.

In Chap. 4, Marx, Sy, Burkert, and Federrath focus on the heavily debated issue of ensuring anonymity in the online world. Their contribution starts with an overview of relevant terminology particularly in the field of computer science, points to data protection regulation on the European level, and shows their work on formalising anonymity. Furthermore, the authors give an overview of different techniques and solutions providing anonymity on the application level as well as on the network level, protecting against adversaries of different strengths. They conclude that the protection of users' privacy on the Internet becomes increasingly difficult and discuss risks such as those involved in fingerprinting as well as storage-based and behaviour-based tracking. Finally, they identify open research questions, in particular with respect to practical and usable anonymity on the Internet.

3   Privacy in the Era of the Smart Revolution

Issues revolving around conceptualisation of privacy and principles relating to privacy protection could not but be in the focus of numerous contributions to the Summer School. The increased popularity of interconnected devices puts privacy and data protection at the centre of the cyber-arena even more than in the past. However, the debate is not only around technologies, but also around their users and how they perceive privacy.

Kitkowska, Wastlund, Meyer and Martucci performed an empirical investigation on the perception of privacy harm. In their work they identify differences in privacy concerns related to information disclosure, protection behaviour and demographics. Additionally, their results suggest that there are some general tendencies in privacy concerns. Their findings show that people create simplified models of privacy harms, such as worries about security, unlawful use of data, disclosure or exposure.

Three co-authors (Patrignani, Whitehouse and Gemo) investigate the changes that have taken place in the concept of privacy, due to both societal and technological advances, based on a 1999 consideration that one should forget about data privacy. This topic was discussed during one of the workshops held at the Summer School, through the prism of disciplines such as ethics, philosophy, and education. The goal of the workshop was to stimulate reflection and discussion among attendees by assessing a broad set of questions. Examples follow: Is privacy still a human right? What are the implications of data collection and the cloud for privacy? What will become of the concept of privacy in the future? What kinds of education will be needed in the future to inform children and young people particularly about notions of privacy and future technological developments? Each of four main questions/topics are handled, analysed and discussed in a separate section of Chap. 6. The co-authors then lay out tentative conclusions, emerging both from and after the workshop.

In their invited paper, Sabelli and Tallacchini approach the principle of fairness as a core principle in privacy protection in the era of algorithms and big data. The authors provide an overview of the historical evolutions of privacy legislation in the United States (US) and the European Union (EU). They further discuss how the legal and ethical debates on the digital world in the two continents have significantly opened up to include new dimensions other than privacy, particularly in connection with machine learning algorithms and big data. While acknowledging that privacy and data protection remain essential interpretive constructs in the information and communication technology (ICT) domain, they can no longer be seen as capable of capturing all relevant normative issues in the digital space. Issues of discrimination, equal opportunity, fairness and, more broadly, models of justice, are gradually entering the picture, requiring novel approaches. The authors offer concrete examples of the inadequacy of privacy and data protection to cover new normative concerns related to big data and machine learning, such as the broadly known anti-spam filters. According to the authors, however, attempts to grant algorithmic fairness represent just the first step in solving new digital normative issues. The wider question about what models of justice people are willing to take into account and apply still needs to be addressed.

The topic of the next chapter is closely related to the general question about fairness and the role of individuals. Consent – what it means, how it can be implemented, what part it plays in legitimising data processing – is a central topic and focus of debate in the communities of scholars, regulators and practitioners of data protection. Whether it is possible for consent to be 'freely given, specific, informed and unambiguous' (GDPR, Art. 11(4)) in all the contexts in which it is sought engages many complex forms of behaviour in terms of law, communication processes, cognitive processes and power relationships that provide the conditions that must be satisfied if consent is to be more than a rhetorical or ideological gesture in the idiom of informational self-determination. Bergemann's discussion is timely and contributes to an understanding of consent by examining a large body of existing literature and exploring what he calls the 'consent paradox': 'How can we account for the prominent position of consent despite critique?'. This is set within the long-running German debate about consent, which the author analyses using the tools of discourse analysis rather than those of philosophy and law. He casts light on how the 'paradox' is sustained through the very critique of consent, and not despite it. The critique emphasises the larger social issues and conflicts that come to the fore in and around the idea and practice of consent across many fields of data processing. His conclusion points to a rethinking of data protection in terms of a more comprehensive critique of power.

The notion of the Internet of Things has gained in prominence, reaching public attention over the past decade. Devices are now on the market and are being increasingly used. In Chap. 9, Railean and Reinhardt conduct a questionnaire survey on Internet of Things products: their acquisition, use and eventual discarding/de-commissioning, and the implications that these three activities have for privacy. Implicit in the authors' investigation of the devices – many of which may be embedded or hidden – is a lifecycle approach. This chapter raises concerns with regard to 'digital literacy' or, perhaps, the 'privacy literacy', of people in contemporary society, especially users who – for various reasons – may be relatively vulnerable. The end focus of the paper is, however, on a set of nine recommendations made to the vendors of Internet of Things devices, which may individually or collectively improve the companies' privacy practices. Replication of the work by the same (or different) researchers in other settings and/or on the larger scale than the 110 completed responses achieved by this research may be encouraged by the fact that the 30+ survey questions are laid out in an annex to the paper.

4 Improving Privacy and Security in the Era of Smart Environments

The third set of contributions aimed at proposing solutions or approaches that will contribute to the improvement of privacy and security.

Chapter 10 summarises the workshop that two H2020 projects jointly held at the Summer School: the CREDENTIAL project and the PRISMACLOUD project. Both projects employ cryptographic primitives for cloud services that aim at improving security and privacy features. The workshop organisers presented several concepts and pilots of privacy-preserving solutions that enable storing, sharing, and processing of potentially sensitive data in untrusted clouds environments. The vivid discussion that followed encompassed junior and senior researchers from multiple disciplines and resulted in some new aspects that may help the further evolution of the concepts and implementations as well as ways to demonstrate their advantages.

Sakpere and Kayem address, in Chap. 11, the need for re-designing existing applications under privacy-based-service-oriented principles. In particular, in their paper, they present a solution for anonymising streaming crime data using k-anonymity, l-diversity and t-closeness approaches.

In line with some of the considerations that motivated the previous work, Shulman, with a completely different approach, argues that to address privacy-related decisions it is necessary to consider aspects of human cognition, employing, for instance, methods used in Human-Computer Interaction (HCI) and Information Science research. In his contribution, Shulman analyses findings and contributions of existing privacy decision-making research and suggests filling gaps in current understanding by applying a cognitive architecture framework to model privacy decision-making.

5 Safeguarding Personal Data and Mitigating Risks

Closely linked to the previous session of the school are contributions that focus on the safeguarding of personal data and the mitigation of risk, especially in view of the new principles and rights introduced in the GDPR.

In Chap. 13, Bieker, Martin, Friedewald and Hansen report on their interactive workshop that dealt with Data Protection Impact Assessment (DPIA), which plays an important part in the GDPR as an instrument for assessing and mitigating data processing's potential risk to rights and freedoms. DPIA builds on decades of practice that was shaped around Privacy Impact Assessment (PIA), of which there have been many varieties and levels of quality around the world. The GDPR, however, is unclear about what is expected in a DPIA, and how to perform it, although it is mandatory in many cases. The workshop aimed to enable participants to become more familiar with DPIA, how it can be carried out, and what issues are likely to arise in this process. It did this through expounding a diagrammatic Standard Data Protection Model, explaining the inventory of data protection goals derived from legal requirements, and involving the workshop attendees in examining two case studies in terms of risks to rights and freedoms: smart surveillance in train stations, and emotional coding for in-store advertising. The authors conclude that more research and refinement is needed to improve the ability to implement DPIA in complying with the GDPR, and that a multidisciplinary perspective is required to identify and mitigate risks.

In Chap. 14, Raschke, Küpper, Drozd and Kirrane focus on designing a GDPR-compliant and Usable Privacy Dashboard. The chapter outlines the design, implementation and first expert user evaluation of a Privacy Dashboard that was developed in the scope of the EU H2020 project, SPECIAL, for enabling data subjects to exercise their data subject rights in compliance with the GDPR. A specific focus, in contrast to previous related work on privacy dashboards, is on consent review and withdrawal.

Neisse, Steri and Nai Fovino provided an invited contribution in the form of an extended abstract on blockchain-based identity management and data usage control. The authors discuss the approach for a blockchain-based solution based on smart contracts, which helps to enforce the transparency and accountability principles of the GDPR. In particular, their solution allows end users to track how their data were processed by data controllers and data processors and whether the processing of their data is compliant with their provided consent. Controllers and processors can in turn prove that they have rightfully obtained consent and are not violating data protection obligations. Three different solutions for provenance and accountability tracking models using blockchains are analysed and compared in regard to privacy, performance and scalability.

The invited extended abstract of Ferrari follows, focusing on Identification Services for Online Social Networks (OSNs). Given that digital identities are a key element of OSNs, their users become more reliant on online identities with often no means of knowing who really is behind an online profile. The problem of fake accounts and identity-related attacks in OSNs has attracted considerable interest from the research community. In her short paper, Ferrari provides an overview of the Sybil attack problem, briefly discussing the research proposals aimed at empowering users with tools that can help them to identify the validity of the online accounts with which they interact.

Chapter 17 summarises a workshop given at the Summer School on a design and reporting toolkit for experimental HCI research related to privacy and cyber security that was presented and practically applied to exemplary publications. Coopamootoo and Gross present a set of 'completeness indicators' for the quality of experimental research that can support researchers in the design phase of a user study and provide a structure for writing and reviewing research papers in that area.

6   Assistive Robots

A book on today's 'smart revolution' would be incomplete without contributions on robots and their ethical implications.

Based in Germany, Heuer, Schiering and Gerndt have begun to explore some of the ethical concerns, especially around privacy, implied by the use of socially assistive robots. Their almost 60-item literature search – a meta-study – has permitted them to structure the problem area. Not only did the authors categorise socially assistive robots into four types – ranging from the more functional to the most human-like – but they also explored how three categories of users – children, families, and older adults – might experience privacy concerns. Ultimately, their research shows that relatively little attention has been paid to date to the ethics of socially assistive robots. This conclusion appears especially surprising when one considers the vulnerability of the parties involved. The ethics of robot design and robot use is clearly a domain to watch. One should anticipate more in-depth investigations of the ethical, social, and societal implications of robot use in a range of fields, especially over the life-course of human beings.

In Chap. 19, De Conca presents a theoretical model called the Aggregated Privateness Model, inspired by the structure of snowflakes, to explain a change in the 'positioning' of the home with regard to its role as place of expression and protection of the private sphere. The change is connected to the presence of robotic intelligent assistants such as Google Home and Amazon Echo inside the home, and in particular with the constant fluxes transferring information in and out of the private sphere. The data collected and transferred by such devices creates several detailed profiles and predictive models that overlap with the individuals inside the home, creating an entire informational ecosystem around them while maintaining certain aspects of 'private-ness' and seclusion. This projects the home and the private spheres of individuals into a dense informational structure, a hive of data (described by De Conca's model as an interaction of clusters of nodes and aggregates of privateness) whose connections spread in different directions. In this way, De Conca's model sheds light on a more collective dimension of privacy, a context in which mathematical rules gain norma-tivity. The model highlights how the behaviour of individuals can influence the other private spheres in the clusters and the aggregation itself due to a network effect, and how Diffused Network Liability could help compensate for such influences without becoming practically impossible.

7 Mobility and Privacy

It has been more than 20 years since mobile phones became an integral part of the everyday life of individuals, a phenomenon that intensified with the introduction and exponential growth of smartphone devices. This collection of chapters on mobility and privacy contains texts that are focused on mobile phones and the vast capabilities they offer.

Kununka, Mehandjiev and Sampaio present the results of a study in which they analyse the privacy policies of a dataset of Android and IOS apps to determine to what extent these policies reflect the actual behaviour of the apps in terms of collection and flows of personal data to third parties. Their results show that there are a substantial numbers of apps, both in Android and IOS, that collect, manage and disseminate personal data in a way that does not match the description and requirements provided in their privacy policies. These results highlight the need to put in place mechanisms to ensure the enforcement of privacy policies and secure their alignment with the actual behaviour of the apps. The authors suggest that privacy policy specification languages could be used for the automatic enforcement of privacy policies, facilitating the development of technological solutions that could assist in the monitoring of the compliance of apps with their policies and the provision of an opt-out for users in cases of non-compliance.

In their paper, Harborth and Pape examine the privacy-related behaviour of players of Pokémon Go – a location-based augmented reality game available on mobile phones – in Germany. The two researchers have conducted an online two-part survey to study both the attitudes and the behaviour of players. Their focus is chiefly around the privacy paradox. They examine the extent to which players express their concerns about privacy and whether they then behave in a privacy-preserving way. Three highlights of the paper are: the examination of the differences in attitude/behaviour dependent on the age and the gender of the Pokémon Go players; the wealth of the literature explored; and the availability of the survey questions in an annex. As a result, other researchers may be tempted to replicate the study in different cultural settings and with the same (or extended) augmented reality applications. Will the dilemmas surrounding the gap between expressed concern and actual behaviour remain? And will utilitarian trade-offs continue?

Data processing in the health sector is based on sensitive data. It is of the utmost importance that privacy risks are detected and mitigated. This is the starting point for the contribution from Gabel, Schiering, Müller and Ertas. The authors focus on mobile health applications and analyse the scenario of neuropsychological training after brain injuries. Employing privacy protection goals and privacy design strategies, they model privacy requirements such as the pseudonymity of patients, data minimisation and transparency. Finally, the authors suggest technical and organisational measures to implement those requirements.

Near Field Communication (NFC) is being used for payments. In the contribution from Kumar, Bechinie and Tscheligi, the authors investigate the gaps between user perception and reality, in particular concerning privacy and security aspects. They conducted a study that showed that users have different mental models about NFC. The authors propose to modify NFC payment systems in such a way that users can gain experience not only in their usage, but also better understand privacy and security concepts.

In Chap. 24, digital identities are discussed as a key element of the future digital society. Today there is already a broad range of existing electronic identity (eID) systems, which provide methods to sign documents or authenticate online services. Quite often, however, these identities lack appropriate techniques so that they can be used as regular identity cards to digitally authenticate an eID holder to a physical person in the real world. Starting from this assumption, Hölzl, Roland and Mayrhofer explore a new way of implementing mobile eID taking into consideration this requirement in a privacy-preserving fashion.

8 Outlook to the Future

The annual IFIP Summer Schools offer a wonderful platform for PhD students and experienced researchers alike, to present their work and to benefit from the exchange and cross-fertilisation of ideas during an intensive week of lectures, presentations, tutorials and workshops. The contributions to the 2017 IFIP Summer School that were presented either as PhD papers, invited talks or workshops, all cover different aspects of privacy and security in the era of the smart revolution: from privacy engineering to risk mitigation and from assistive robots to mobile applications.

The 2017 IFIP Summer School offered an exciting journey through the challenges that are raised by recent technological developments and the rethinking and novel conceptualisations of traditional issues in the scholarly debates on privacy and identity management. It is our aspiration that research in this field will continue, and that answers to some of the questions that were raised during the Summer School and that are included in chapters of this volume will be answered in the coming years. And – why not? – maybe in one of the following IFIP Summer Schools.

Privacy Engineering

Towards Organizing the Growing Knowledge on Privacy Engineering

Jose M. del Alamo[1](✉) [iD], Yod-Samuel Martín[1] [iD],
and Julio C. Caiza[1,2] [iD]

[1] Universidad Politécnica de Madrid, 28040 Madrid, Spain
jm.delalamo@upm.es
[2] Escuela Politécnica Nacional, Quito 170517, Ecuador

Abstract. Regulation asks engineers to stick to privacy and data protection principles and apply them throughout the development process of their projects. However, in spite of the availability of technological solutions to identify and address different privacy threats these have not seen widespread adoption in the engineering practice, and developers still find difficulties in introducing privacy considerations in their new products and services. In this context, privacy engineering has emerged as an inter-disciplinary field that aims to bridge legal, computer science and engineering worlds, as well as concepts from other disciplines. The goal is to provide engineers with methods and tools that are closer to their mindset, and allow them to systematically address privacy concerns and introduce solutions within the workflow and environment they are accustomed to. This paper provides an introduction to Privacy Engineering, describing a conceptual metamodel useful to organize the increasing knowledge in this emergent field and make it more accessible to engineers. We exemplify some of this knowledge focusing on privacy design patterns, a set of privacy engineering elements that distill best-practices available.

Keywords: Privacy · Data protection · Software engineering

1 Introduction

The European Union (EU) General Data Protection Regulation (GDPR) [1], in force since 2016 and mandatory in May 2018, sets an array of binding data protection principles, individuals' rights, and legal obligations to ensure the protection of personal data of EU citizens. But the legal approach is not enough if it does not come along with technical measures to protect privacy and personal data in practice. As it is often said, "*[software] code is law*": the technological support regulates what we do by favoring, imposing or precluding specific actions, as much as the legal framework does so by allowing, enforcing or banning them.

Indeed, the notion that privacy and data protection must be proactively considered since the onset of a project and during the design and development of information systems is captured by the principles of Privacy by Design (PbD) [2]. This approach

M. Hansen et al. (Eds.): Privacy and Identity 2017, IFIP AICT 526, pp. 15–24, 2018.
https://doi.org/10.1007/978-3-319-92925-5_2

was openly embraced by Data Protection Authorities in Europe [3] and worldwide [4], and afterwards it has explicitly become legally required by GDPR (rec. 78 and art. 25).

While there seems to be consensus on the benefits of the privacy and data protection by design approach its realization in engineering processes remains limited due to the divergent approaches taken so far from different disciplines. First, privacy is a multi-dimensional [5], plural [6] and essentially contested concept [7], which can thus be subject to multiple reference frameworks e.g. [8, 9]. If engineers find difficulties to deal with abstracts principles coming from regulations, having several different privacy conceptualizations just worsens the problem. From the purely technological arena, solutions have long been researched and elaborated to create Privacy-Enhancing Technologies (PETs) that foster data protection and respond to privacy concerns [10]. However, PETs remain unknown for most engineers, due to the uncoupling between these technologies and the practice of systematic engineering and development, which makes engineers unaware or unknowledgeable of the proper applicability of such solutions. On top of that, software and systems engineering practices are also varied regarding e.g. the type of information system targeted and the development process followed, and thus preclude having a one-size-fits-all engineering approach for privacy.

In this context, Privacy Engineering is the nascent field of research and practice that aims to address these challenges by reconciling the different approaches and deliver methods to systematically identify and address privacy and data protection concerns throughout the software development process.

This paper describes our proposal for the organization and progress of this emerging field. In particular, we introduce a methodological framework to describe the concepts and elements that underlie the various contributions subsumed under the Privacy Engineering field, following a common model and an agreed vocabulary. We further detail one of such elements that exemplify the knowledge available in practice i.e. privacy design patterns.

2 From Privacy by Design to Privacy Engineering

For PbD to be viable, engineers must be effectively involved in the loop, as they are ultimately responsible for conceiving, elaborating, constructing and maintaining the systems, services, and software products. Indeed, Data Protection Authorities around the world have also recognized developers and engineers overall as key stakeholders to achieve effective data protection [11].

However, despite the interest sparked by PbD in the regulatory arena, it has not yet gained widespread, active adoption in the engineering practice [12]. This responds to a mismatch between the legal and the technological mindsets [13]. Indeed, regulations tend to provide abstract guidance and provisions which are independent of specific technological contexts and can remain applicable as these evolve. However, technical requirements need be more concrete and anticipate the specific scenarios that may unfold. Unfortunately, this mismatch has caused privacy and data protection to be neglected or simply overlooked by most relevant works on data engineering. As a consequence, from the engineers' mindset [12], privacy and data protection are usually considered just from the perspective of data security, if any; and they tend to rely for compliance on privacy policies rather than on the technical designs and architecture, which they chose instead depending on requirements and constraints other than privacy and data protection.

Furthermore, academic research has consistently shown [14, 15] that developers and engineers (who usually are not privacy-savvy at all), find privacy and data protection alien to their work and, most importantly, seldom use privacy management tools, as they find these are more oriented to the legal arena rather than to the engineering activities. Same research has encountered that they will be more akin to take decisions that protect privacy and data protection when the process is embedded within their usual development workflow and tools.

Nonetheless, privacy and data protection regulatory innovations do have an impact on the engineering process. As a matter of example, the right to be forgotten or the right to data portability, besides entitling individuals to request data controllers to honor those rights, entail that the products need to implement any functionalities needed to support the user requests. This has a real impact throughout the development cycle of the product, as it implies, introducing the operational requirements to enforce those rights, modelling the categories of personal data affected, determining the functions and behavior of the system upon the users' requests, and implementing and validating those behaviors. Other regulatory innovations affect directly the process, such as accountability or data protection impact assessment.

We have identified the greatest impact in the following software and systems engineering disciplines:

- *Risk management*, which supports the execution of privacy and data protection impact assessments from the engineering perspective to identify, assess, evaluate and mitigate risks for the data subjects that may arise from processing activities dealing with their personal data.
- *Requirements engineering*, which supports the operationalization of high-level privacy and data protection goals (e.g. privacy principles, data subjects' rights, obligations of controllers and processors) into design requirements (privacy controls), and their overall systematic specification, management, analysis, traceability, validation and verification.
- *Modelling*, which supports engineers to analyse the systems under development from the perspective of privacy and data protection, and the appropriate choice of solutions (e.g. architecture, privacy patterns, PETs).
- *Assurance*, which supports the demonstration of compliance with the regulation and the observance of the principle of accountability through systematic capture of evidences, their association to requirements and artefacts, traceability to the regulation, and argumentation of compliance derived from those evidences.

The privacy engineering community have proposed dozens of novel contributions fitting in some of these engineering disciplines [16, 17]. Even engineering methodologies have been developed [18–21] which define activities that deal with privacy aspects at different stages of the development process. Yet each proposal targets specific aspects of the privacy problem, using different techniques, and following diverse methodologies to suit its own situation. This makes difficult to grasp the adequacy and assess the benefits of any such solution.

To overcome this problem, there is a need to deliver a comprehensive privacy engineering metamodel able to encompass and organize all the components available in the privacy engineering realm, including the different privacy conceptualizations as well as engineering methodologies and their elements. It can be thought of as a labelled rack, to each of whose compartments the contributions on privacy engineering can be anchored. This metamodel will further facilitate:

- The description of the different types of concepts and elements involved in existing privacy engineering methods, following a common model and agreed, shared vocabulary.
- The comparison, assessment, interoperability and integration of the distinct elements, both within and outside of the context of the method where they were originally defined, thanks to enrich descriptions of method elements that include well-defined connection hooks.
- The communication among privacy engineers, and with the other roles involved in the development process.

Method Engineering is the discipline dealing with these issues as it focuses on "*the design, construction and evaluation of methods, techniques and support tools*" [22]. Different conceptual frameworks have been historically developed for method engineering. All share a set of concepts that allow defining methodologies in compatible terms: processes, activities and tasks that can be executed, people carrying them out, products resulting from their application, and guidelines or constraints that tell how all those should be related in practice. The Software Engineering Metamodel for Development Methodologies (SEMDM), standardized as ISO/IEC 24744 [23], has perhaps been able to best capture all these concepts in its entirety, covering processes, producers (including people) and products, as well as given resources that are applied in a methodology as is (rather than instantiated or enacted). Thus, we build on SEMDM to elaborate our privacy engineering metamodel.

3   A Privacy Engineering Metamodel

Research has shown that, oftentimes, systems development activities concentrate on delivering the required functionalities at the expense of dismissing other, non-functional requirements (NFRs) [24] —such as those dealing with privacy properties. This phenomenon has been observed even in the presence of sizeable academic corpuses that deal with those requirements. Moreover, when NFRs are only considered as an afterthought, if any, to remediate blatant infringements, the correct application of Privacy by Design is eventually hindered. Nonetheless, method engineering has been proposed by same research as an approach to make existing knowledge attractive for practitioners, whose systematic application is cost-effective, whose benefits can be appraised, whose application can be customized, and which can leverage the help of computer-aided software and systems engineering tools. Thus, we propose the systematic application of method engineering to privacy engineering methods so as to facilitate their adoption by engineers. Method engineering allows arranging the different concepts that usually underlie privacy engineering methodologies into a controlled vocabulary of methodological elements and a normalized set of connection points and relationships to organize those.

All in all, even though different privacy engineering methodologies exist, all of them can be modelled in terms of the above mentioned SEMDM metamodel. For instance, a given privacy engineering methodology may define:

– *Tasks*, which specify what must be done when enacting the methodology, e.g. mapping the types of personal data processed by the system, designing the appropriate architecture, etc. Each methodology will define its own set of tasks.
– *Techniques*, which describe procedures that tell how the tasks are to be completed; e.g. analyze a database model, apply a formal architecture analysis method, etc. Depending on the methodology, such techniques can be mandatory, recommended, optional or discouraged.
– *Processes* that group related tasks into larger units of work, within a common area of expertise, e.g. privacy impact assessment, application of PETs, etc.
– *Phases* of the software and systems application lifecycle where the tasks are applied e.g. inception, analysis, maintenance, operation, etc.
– *Work Products* that are consumed as inputs by the tasks and/or produced as their result. Different types of work products include *Models* (e.g. a dataflow diagram, a misuse case, etc.), *Documents* (a requirements specification, a risk assessment document), *Software* products, or even *Hardware* products.
– *Roles* that perform or take part in some of those tasks, e.g. a Data Protection Officer, a systems analyst, a software architect, an external auditor, etc.

It shall be noted that, in any case, a privacy engineering methodology need not be all-encompassing (specifying all the tasks, techniques, etc.). They may also require inputs (e.g. a system's architecture) that depend on the results of external tasks, refer engineers to external resources, leave unspecified techniques for some tasks, or even focus only on specific processes or phases. A detailed example of how a particular privacy engineering methodology (LINDDUN) can be described in terms of the SEMDM metamodel may be found at [25].

Even though the SEMDM metamodel may cater for a large variety of method-ologies, non-functional requirements may entail the addition of new elements into the metamodel. In our case, and in order to deal with privacy NFRs, we have extended SEMDM with a set of Resources that are usually encountered in privacy engineering methods. In SEMDM, a Resource is a methodology element to be used 'as is' at the project level, without requiring any instantiation. In particular, and in order to take privacy into account when designing systems, engineers can be provided with four kinds of Resources, each of them dealing with privacy from different, complementary perspectives (Table 1).

A *Privacy Conceptual Model (PCM)* deals with privacy from an ontological perspective. Any privacy engineering method is framed by and grounded on a particular, underlying theory of privacy (even if different, competing theories currently exist). That theory describes the essential concepts of privacy in terms of principles, harms, goals, etcetera; as well as it defines the subject and the object of privacy itself. Often (but not always) the concept of privacy is partitioned into a list of unitary concepts. For instance, ISO29100 privacy framework [9] provides a list of fundamental, privacy

Table 1. Types of resources provided by privacy engineering methodologies.

Resource	Privacy Conceptual Model (PCM)	Privacy Normative Framework (PNF)	Privacy Engineering Code (PEC)	Privacy Knowledge Base (PKB)
Perspective	Ontological	Deontological	Situational	Epistemological
Source	Theory of privacy	Binding regulations, non-binding best practices	Codes of conduct, codes of practice	Community of practice, repositories
Purpose	Describes	Prescribes	Refines, clarifies, documents	Compiles, arranges, endorses
Contents	Essential concepts	Method constraints and product requirements	Guidelines	Applicable knowledge models

principles, besides defining personal information, actors involved and their interactions, etc. Or, LINDDUN [21] methodology defines nine privacy properties in opposition to seven threat categories.

A *Privacy Normative Framework (PNF)* deals with privacy from a deontological perspective. Many privacy engineering methods claim to abide by some binding regulations (established by e.g. laws, quasi- and co-regulations, binding policies, etc.) or non-binding recommended best practices. These prescribe both constraints that refer to the application of the method itself (e.g. impose the existence of specific method elements, or that they be applied according to a precise temporal order), and requirements that refer to the products created when the method is enacted. For example, the EU GDPR requires (in certain cases, and among others) that:

- a Data Protection Officer (DPO) is nominated who performs specific tasks (e.g. monitoring compliance, training, etc.);
- an impact assessment process is carried out before processing any personal information;
- technical measures are implemented so as to ensure confidentiality, integrity, availability and resilience of processing systems and services.

Note that GDPR defines as well a set of principles for personal data processing which are not part of the PNF, but rather of a PCM, even if defined within the same document.

A *Privacy Engineering Code (PEC)* deals with privacy from a situational perspective. There exist many codes of conduct and codes of practice which provide different sets of guidelines that document how normative requirements can be better applied on specific contexts or situations, thus refining or clarifying the application of the corresponding PNF. The compliance with such codes can be usually subject to audits.

A *Privacy Knowledge Base (PKB)* deals with privacy from an epistemological perspective. The community of practice and research of privacy engineering has developed an amount of generally recognized knowledge, whose value and usefulness are collectively endorsed for their application by privacy engineering practitioners. This knowledge is sometimes compiled into repositories, modelled according to a homogeneous template, and arranged into a structure that facilitates their systematic application. Such PKBs have been defined which gather e.g. privacy design strategies [26], privacy threats [21], and privacy design patterns [27].

Indeed, the PKBs of privacy design patterns particularly illustrate the usefulness of having systematic, reusable knowledge at hand, as advocated by method engineering proponents. A privacy design pattern (privacy pattern for short) provides a commonly applied, well-proven design solution to common privacy problems in particular contexts. Further, privacy pattern repositories gather patterns endorsed by the community and provide navigation mechanisms that allow engineers to easily choose the most appropriate design solution(s) to apply whenever they need to cope with privacy issues in a specific context. Next section elaborates in detail into privacy patterns and their repositories.

4 Privacy Design Patterns

Patterns researchers have defined a path to improve their applicability in system's development: patterns collections can evolve from being mere patterns catalogs, through patterns systems, until achieving a pattern language level [28]. Each provides more operationalization benefits than the previous one. A pattern catalog maintains together and classifies a set of design patterns. A pattern system goes further and presents a set of patterns with a uniform structure, some relationships between them, and as sufficient base to build the foundations of an information system. Finally, a pattern language should eventually support the complete construction of an information system, but in a very specific domain.

The state of the art already includes different contributions on privacy design patterns. Some authors have identified single patterns [29, 30]; other have proposed catalogs of privacy patterns classified by different approaches [27]; and there has been even a pattern language proposal revolving around anonymity [31].

The existing privacy pattern catalogs have remained isolated and approached from different perspectives for classification and implementation. For instance, Colesky et al. classify patterns according to strategies and tactics [32], while Drozd uses ISO 29100 privacy principles [33]. In an attempt to generate a uniform knowledge base for privacy engineering practice, some authors have joined efforts to set up a common repository of privacy patterns, which could be used as a toolbox to help system designers. The efforts of this community have concentrated in gathering the privacy patterns together, describing them according to an agreed template, and using a common categorization schema for their classification [27].

As part of this community, we have evolved a part of this catalogue into a system of patterns. To this end we have (1) proposed a taxonomy of types of relationships to describe the patterns connections [35], (2) dug into the available patterns to identify these connections, and (3) built a patterns system out of the individual patterns [34]. Table 2 enumerates and describes a sample of patterns focused on the selective disclosure of personal data. Figure 1 further shows the relationships identified.

Table 2. Patterns supporting the selective disclosure of personal information.

Pattern name	Pattern description
Buddy list	Use a short list of close and trusted contacts for the user and allow the expansion of the list
Enable/Disable functions	Allow the users to define which functions (and provided data) they require inside an application
Decoupling content and location	Allow the users to configure the privacy level of location to be disclosed associated to a content depending on the context
Discouraging blanket strategies	Give the users a range of possibilities to select the privacy level associated to a content to be shared
Negotiation of privacy policy	Allow the users opt-in and opt-out in the privacy configuration since the beginning of the service use
Reasonable level of control	Give the users a selective control on the information they provide and to whom. Explore push and pull mechanisms for achieving this goal
Selective access control	Allow the users to specify (granularly) the audience for the content during and after sharing
Support selective disclosure	Instead of the massive collection of personal data, even before the use of a service, allow the users to configure the privacy level they feel comfortable with before, during and after sharing content

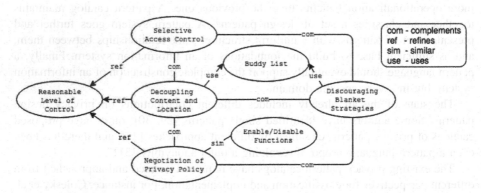

Fig. 1. Privacy patterns for the selective disclosure of personal information.

5 Conclusion

Regulation asks engineers to stick to Privacy by Design principles and apply data protection solutions throughout their projects. However, to accomplish that, engineers demand methodological elements that are closer to their mindset, and allow them to systematically introduce such solutions within the workflow and environment they are accustomed to. This paper has introduced a conceptual model to organize the growing number of methodological elements already available for privacy engineering, and has further elaborated on privacy pattern systems as means to gather systematic, reusable knowledge.

Our next steps point towards introducing some of these privacy engineering methodological elements into existent mainstream software engineering methods and tools, so as to ease their adoption by engineers even when they are not savvy in the privacy field. This is aligned with the recommendations issued by the EU Agency for Network and Information Security (ENISA) [36]: "Providers of software development tools and the research community need to offer tools that enable the intuitive implementation of privacy properties.".

Acknowledgements. This work has received funding from the European Union's Horizon 2020 research and innovation programme under grant agreement No 731711 and from the Spanish Government's Agencia Estatal de Investigación under grant agreement No EUIN2017-87180.

References

1. Regulation (EU): 2016/679 of the European Parliament and of the Council of 27 April 2016 on the protection of natural persons with regard to the processing of personal data and on the free movement of such data, and repealing Directive 95/46/EC (General Data Protection Regulation)
2. Cavoukian, A.: Privacy by design: the 7 foundational principles. Implementation and mapping of fair information practices. Information and Privacy Commissioner of Ontario, Canada (2009)
3. Article 29 Data protection working party: the future of privacy: joint contribution to the consultation of the European commission on the legal framework for the fundamental right to protection of personal data (WP168)
4. Data Protection and Privacy Commissioners: Resolution on Privacy by Design, 32nd International Conference of Data Protection and Privacy Commissioners (2010)
5. OHara, K.: The seven veils of privacy. IEEE Internet Comput. **20**(2), 86–91 (2016)
6. Solove, D.J.: A taxonomy of privacy. U. Pa. L. Rev. **154**, 477 (2005)
7. Mulligan, D.K., Koopman, C., Doty, N.: Privacy is an essentially contested concept: a multi-dimensional analytic for mapping privacy. Philos. Trans. R. Soc. A **374**(2083) (2016). https://doi.org/10.1098/rsta.2016.0118
8. Nissenbaum, H.: Privacy in CONTEXT: TECHNOLOGY, POLICY, and the Integrity of Social Life. Stanford University Press, Palo Alto (2009)
9. ISO/IEC JTC 1/SC 27: ISO/IEC 29100:2011. Information technologies – security techniques – privacy framework. Geneva (CH) (2011)
10. Heurix, J., et al.: A taxonomy for privacy enhancing technologies. Comput. Secur. **53**, 1–17 (2015)
11. Data Protection and Privacy Commissioners: Warsaw declaration on the "appification" of society. In: 35th International Conference of Data Protection and Privacy Commissioners (2013)
12. Hadar, I., et al.: Privacy by designers: software developers' privacy mindset. Empir. Softw. Eng. **23**(1), 259–289 (2018)
13. Birnhack, M., Toch, E., Hadar, I.: Privacy mindset, technological mindset. Jurimetrics **55**, 55–114 (2014)
14. Balebako, R., Cranor, L.: Improving app privacy: nudging app developers to protect user privacy. IEEE Secur. Priv. **12**(4), 55–58 (2014)

15. Van Der Sype, Y.S., Maalej, W.: On lawful disclosure of personal user data: what should app developers do? In: 7th International Workshop on Requirements Engineering and Law (2014)
16. IWPE homepage. http://iwpe.info. Accessed 25 Nov 2017
17. ESPRE homepage. http://espre2017.org/. Accessed 25 Nov 2017
18. Notario, N., et al.: PRIPARE: integrating privacy best practices into a privacy engineering methodology. In: IEEE Security and Privacy Workshops (2015)
19. Shapiro, S., et al.: Privacy Engineering Framework. The MITRE Corporation, McLean (2014)
20. Brooks, S. et al.: An Introduction to Privacy Engineering and Risk Management in Federal Systems. National Institute of Standards and Technology Internal Report 8062 (2017)
21. LINDDUN homepage. https://linddun.org/. Accessed 27 Nov 2017
22. Brinkkemper, S.: Method engineering: engineering of information systems development methods and tools. Inf. Softw. Technol. **38**(4), 275–280 (1996)
23. ISO/IEC JTC 1/SC 27: ISO/IEC 24744:2014. Software engineering – metamodel for development methodologies. Geneva (CH) (2014)
24. Franch, X., et al.: Bridging the gap among academics and practitioners in Non-Functional Requirements management: Some reflections and proposals for the future. In: Essays Dedicated to Martin Glinz on the Occasion of His 60th Birthday, pp. 267–274. Monsenstein und Vannerdat (2012)
25. Martin, Y.S., Del Alamo, J.M.: A metamodel for privacy engineering methods. In: 3rd International Workshop on Privacy Engineering, pp. 41–48. CEUR workshop proceedings, San Jose (2017)
26. Hoepman, J.-H.: Privacy Design Strategies. In: Cuppens-Boulahia, N., Cuppens, F., Jajodia, S., Abou El Kalam, A., Sans, T. (eds.) SEC 2014. IAICT, vol. 428, pp. 446–459. Springer, Heidelberg (2014). https://doi.org/10.1007/978-3-642-55415-5_38
27. PrivacyPatterns homepage. https://privacypatterns.org/. Accessed 27 Nov 2017
28. Buschmann, F., et al.: Pattern-Oriented Software Architecture: A System of Patterns. John Wiley & Sons, Hoboken (1996)
29. Romanosky, S., et al.: Privacy patterns for online interactions. In: Proceedings of the 2006 Conference on Pattern Languages of Programs - PLoP 2006. ACM (2006)
30. Fernandez, E., Mujica, S.: Two patterns for HIPAA regulations. In: Proceedings of AsianPLoP (Pattern Languages of Programs) 2014 (2014)
31. Hafiz, M.: A pattern language for developing privacy enhancing technologies. Softw. Pract. Exp. **43**(7), 769–787 (2013)
32. Colesky, M., Hoepman, J.-H., Hillen, C.: A critical analysis of privacy design strategies. In 2016 IEEE Security and Privacy Workshops (SPW), pp. 33–40. IEEE (2016)
33. Drozd, O.: Privacy Pattern Catalogue: A Tool for Integrating Privacy Principles of ISO/IEC 29100 into the Software Development Process. In: Aspinall, D., Camenisch, J., Hansen, M., Fischer-Hübner, S., Raab, C. (eds.) Privacy and Identity 2015. IAICT, vol. 476, pp. 129–140. Springer, Cham (2016). https://doi.org/10.1007/978-3-319-41763-9_9
34. Colesky, M., et al.: A system of privacy patterns for user control. In: Proceedings of the 33rd ACM Symposium on Applied Computing. ACM, Pau (2018)
35. Caiza, J., et al.: Organizing design patterns for privacy: a taxonomy of types of relationships. In: Proceedings of the 22Nd European Conference on Pattern Languages of Programs EuroPLOP 2017. ACM, Germany (2017)
36. Danezis, G., et al.: Privacy and data protection by design-from policy to engineering. European Union Agency for Network and Information Security (2014)

Data Protection by Design: Promises and Perils in Crossing the Rubicon Between Law and Engineering

K. Rommetveit[1(✉)], A. Tanas[2], and N. van Dijk[2]

[1] SVT, Centre for the Study of the Sciences and Humanities,
University of Bergen, Bergen, Norway
kjetil.rommetveit@uib.no
[2] LSTS, Law Science, Technology and Society Studies,
Vrije Universiteit Brussel, Brussels, Belgium
alessia.tanas@vub.ac.be, Niels.Van.Dijk@vub.be

Abstract. This article reports some main findings from a study of recent efforts towards building privacy and other fundamental rights and freedoms into smart ICT systems. It mainly focuses on the concept of 'Data Protection by Design and by Default' (DPbD), recently introduced by EU legislation, and as implemented through the new field of privacy engineering. We describe the new constellations of actors that gather around this legislative and engineering initiative as an emerging 'techno-epistemic network'. The article presents the empirical findings of a broad consultation with people involved in the making of this network, including policy makers, regulators, entrepreneurs, ICT developers, civil rights associations, and legal practitioners. Based on the findings from our consultations, we outline how DPbD is subject to differing, sometimes also conflicting or contradictory, expectations and requirements. We identify these as three main points of friction involved in the making of data protection by design: organisations versus autonomous data subjects; law versus engineering, and local versus global in the making of standards and infrastructures.

Keywords: Privacy and data protection by design · Privacy engineering
Techno-epistemic network · Organisations · Law · Engineering
Socio-technical infrastructures

1 Introduction

The explosion of digital developments such as the internet of things, big data, and radically enhanced interconnectedness and sensoring capacities, have placed privacy and other fundamental rights and freedoms under strong pressure. The recently adopted EU General Data Protection Regulation (GDPR, that will take effect in May 2018) recognises these developments, and introduces a number of new tools for protecting and upholding fundamental rights and freedoms, such as data protection by design and by default (DPbD). DPbD consists in designing and building privacy and data protection into the emerging systems, technologies and infrastructures themselves, a move that is seen as necessary in order to handle the ubiquity, complexity and general

© IFIP International Federation for Information Processing 2018
Published by Springer International Publishing AG 2018. All Rights Reserved
M. Hansen et al. (Eds.): Privacy and Identity 2017, IFIP AICT 526, pp. 25–37, 2018.
https://doi.org/10.1007/978-3-319-92925-5_3

unpredictability of digital innovations and technologies. This design-based approach is not new. It has developed over time, (i.e. since the mid 1990s), in various sites and by various actors, initially focusing on Privacy Enhancing Technologies (PETs) and Privacy by Design. It has now become mandatory in EU legislation under the DPbD designation, for entities controlling and processing personal data ("data controllers"). This development has catalysed the evolution of the technological field of practice devoted to its realisation, frequently referred to as 'privacy engineering' [4, 9, 11, 19].

The introduction of DPbD comes along with other related developments, such as a risk-based approach towards fundamental rights and freedoms, where significant future risks to the rights of individuals, ("data subjects"), are to be mapped, and turned into organisational measures as well as technological and engineering ones (Art. 35 GDPR). Another related trend is a gradual reinforcement of self-regulation, or (in Europe) co-regulation, where greater responsibility for the safeguarding of privacy and data protection is placed on the data controllers (Art. 24). These developments must therefore be seen as parts of a concerted package [6] encapsulated by the GDPR, and representative of broad developments at the intersections of technology, markets and society.

That such transformations take place should come as no surprise to observers of the fields of privacy and personal data protection. Some 20 years ago, the privacy activist Simon Davis noted how privacy had *metamorphosed from an issue of societal power relationships to one of strictly defined legal rights* [7, p. 143]. Implied in Davis diagnosis was the claim that the notion of privacy was changing: an issue that had started as a social and political project, driven and shaped by civic activism [see 1] was gradually transformed into a consumer and rights issue subject to regulatory and bureaucratic requirements and means, and moving closer to the (German) notion of data protection (*Datenschutz*). Now, with the turn towards a design-based approach to privacy and personal data we observe a next stage in the evolution of these concepts, one strictly dependent on engineering, and with outcomes still uncertain. On the one hand, digital technologies have strong impacts on fundamental rights and freedoms such as privacy and data protection, and regulation is extending into these areas in order for technology not to become too invasive. On the other hand, in order to deal with these issues, regulation is increasingly relying upon the contributions of engineers, technologists and other practitioners. These new entanglements raise serious questions about the ways in which rights' protections become conceptualised and implemented: the case is not simply one of law formulating the principles, and engineers adapting them to new practices; as we describe, quite fundamental changes to rights and principles take place through these new exchanges and collaborations. The notion of the Rubicon in the title refers to an existing divide between legal and engineering methods and to questions on whether, when and how such divides should be crossed.

In this brief article, we recount some results from recent empirical investigations[1] into the turn towards privacy-by-design, including the introduction of risk-based approaches [27]. Using social science methods such as written consultations,

[1] CANDID – *Checking Assumptions and promoting responsibility in smart Development* – was an EU Horizon 2020 project, Grant no—732561. The project aimed to critically appraise smart technologies and to explore their prospects. For a presentation of the project, see: https://candid.w.uib.no.

interviews and focus groups, we have conducted an 'extended peer consultation'[2] and mapped out different existing logics, but also perceptions, imaginations and expectations related to privacy engineering. We extended invitations to representatives from DPAs, universities, the standardisation field and the business sector, but also technology developers and software engineers. We also included other peers with experience in articulating privacy like legal practitioners and judges in European high courts, civil rights organisations, technology prosumers, ethical hackers, social science and humanities scholars, and practitioners of value sensitive design. Peers were presented with issues concerning data protection by design and by default and data protection impact assessment, to which they provided written responses. In a next round, we also carried out face-to-face interviews, focusing on more in-depth issues discovered during the first stage of consultation. The findings from the consultations were validated through a workshop that included some representatives from the prior consultation. Throughout this process, we wanted to understand what constitutes privacy and personal data protection rights in design, and how design-based techniques relate to notions such as fundamental rights, freedoms and legal protections.

A main outcome from our investigation is that, within the overall network, different ways of imagining, understanding and articulating these rights occur. We mapped various modes of articulation invoked by the different peers, and related these to their occupational, organisational or civic backgrounds. Important here is how, what we term a 'techno-epistemic network' of professionals dedicated to the engineering of rights and for this purpose work to exchange knowledge and create collaborations across boundaries that were previously kept largely separate. Involved in this work are practitioners from engineering, regulation and managerial practices and more, favoring the emergence of the technical and regulatory field of privacy engineering for (D)PbD[3]. Based on this, we have elaborated upon different networked modes [28] in which rights become (re-)articulated and implemented by actors situated within the techno-epistemic network, or claimed by actors situated outside the network, like legal practitioners, civil rights organizations, ICT prosumers, ethical hackers, etc. We observe and describe how these different modes converge or not, when seen in relation to the shared objective of designing rights and legal principles in technological infrastructures and artefacts. It is here, in the comparison between the various approaches and positions taken, that we point to tensions or contradictions. As argued elsewhere [22], we think that such tensions are not to be overlooked, but clarified in their practical and theoretical implications. The argument is a shortened version that complements a larger paper,

---

[2] We draw inspiration from the notion of 'extended peer review' elaborated by Funtowicz and Ravetz [10]. An extended peer review is the process of including people and groups that have experience and knowledge beyond academic science when trying to assure the quality of research, thus increasing the reliability of results. Here we apply the concept within a regulatory context, also with the aim of stretching towards other sources of knowledge. In this text we refer variously to 'peers' and to 'informants', as the agents providing such sources.

[3] We use the DPbD concept in association with that of Privacy by Design (PbD) although we realize that the two are not identical. This is because many professionals consulted tend to use these notions interchangeably.

which traces the formation of the techno-epistemic network and the way it has so far aligned and unaligned different articulations of privacy [27].

2 Requirements and Expectations on Data Protection and Privacy

Privacy and data protection change due to complex reasons, simultaneously technological, legal, political and cultural. Within the recent paradigmatic shift [cf. 2] towards privacy engineering, the major driving forces may be seen to be technological, or 'data-driven' [14]. Yet, data protection and privacy are not shaped by technology only, and belong within dynamically evolving clusters of principles, practices, institutions, means and technologies. As to the EU regulatory framework, this can be clearly seen in preparatory documents for the GDPR, where DPbD was described as beneficial for a variety of reasons: it enhances the protection of individual rights *and* the efficiency and security of processing; it was also argued to increase oversight and accountability, significantly through its firm focus on data processors and (large) organisations. And, DPbD was invoked as a fundamental tool in the building of the European digital market, since *European industries could become world leaders in privacy enhancing technology or privacy by design solutions* [23]. Hence, the drivers and rationales that enter into data protection by design are composite and incorporate differing policy and digital market goals, interests and logics.

In our consultations with actors involved (in different ways) with the making of data protection by design, we observe how differing logics [cf., 3] are at work in the project to implement data protection (and privacy) by design. There is dedication within the GDPR to the *legal* logic of *fundamental rights and freedoms of individuals*, but this logic cannot be fully detached from the *economic* goals of creating and enhancing the internal digital market. In the claims for enhanced accountability and efficiency, we detect a *bureaucratic or regulatory* logic at work. All of these approaches are now to be integrated with *engineering* ways of doing things, following engineering logics. Finally, hovering above (or underneath) all of this, there is the original *civic* goal of protecting public values of autonomy, dignity, freedom of thought and expression. We can observe the continued reality of this civic approach in public actions against privacy-invasive projects and technologies in Europe, such as the privacy class-action against Facebook by *Europe vs. Facebook*, protests in the Netherlands against mandatory introduction of smart metering devices, or initiatives in the UK to take the Government Communications Headquarter's (GCHQ) surveillance initiatives to court.

3 Designing Data Protection: Articulations and Frictions

During our research, we observed that these logics re-occur in new modes within networked practices dedicated to operationalise DPbD, although we point to different visions and practices still in the making. As part of this we indicate tensions, gaps, limits and perhaps even contradictions at work. In the next section, we point to three overarching points of tension, where different modes and visions of rights and engineering are at work: (1) *individual versus organisational autonomy*; (2) *law versus engineering*, and (3) *global versus local* in the making of infrastructures. Articulating and describing some of these require contributions from social scientists, social actors, philosophers and legal scholars, since the challenges involved with DPbD are not merely technical, but importantly also social, practice-based and disciplinary. They crucially depend on the possibilities of establishing cross-institutional, disciplinary and experiential collaborations between the various actors.

To reiterate, insofar as real tensions or contradictions exist among logics or modes of articulating rights to privacy, we believe that constructive approaches can only come from a proper formulation of these tensions, since we agree with the constructive proposition (from philosophical pragmatism) that "a problem well put is half-solved" [5]. DPbD requires careful consideration of limits (technical, legal, civic, etc.), and due appreciation of the various values, interests, regimes and logics at work. Spelling out some of these can help improve actors' mutual understandings, and possibly also overcome some misunderstandings. As for the limitations involved, becoming clear about what can and what cannot be done, can direct practitioners towards searching for other solutions where necessary. In what follows, we briefly introduce some tensions in practice, as discovered in our consultations.

3.1 Organisations Versus Autonomous Data Subjects?

Data protection law relies decisively upon large organisations for the attainment of its goals. As such the rights and principles themselves take on characteristics and logics typical of work inside organisations. Here, we have learnt about several challenges.

First, managerial and cultural issues pertain to the accustomed workings of the organisations that implement DPbD: today's large corporations, public institutions, or small and medium enterprises are not really trained or geared towards considering people's privacy concerns, or towards thoroughly understanding their own data flows in terms of the threats they could pose to the rights of natural persons. One problem here has to do with the very nature of the alleged contemporary 'information economy' or 'surveillance economy'. There is a proliferation and over-production of ('big') data, and many actors are getting involved in the hope of extracting value from the data. Yet, there are still great uncertainties about how to do this [16], or whether indeed data turns out to be the 'new oil'. Therefore, the chosen strategy is often to generate as much data as possible, then work out the necessary business strategies afterwards. From the point of view of data protection, however, this place the activities of the organisations in a difficult position with regard to data protection principles, such as data minimisation, purpose limitation and specification. As expressed by one of our informants, a data protection consultant to the private sector, businesses and corporations *are not promoting privacy by design, because data are of high value and if you apply privacy by design techniques the amount of data you would collect would diminish and therefore you have impact on your business model* (data protection consultant). A second, and related, problem, has to do with a lack of understanding of the data processing operations taking place within the organisations, since some of these may indeed have become 'too big to understand': *My experience is that in order to understand this, organisations have to analyse in depth their data flows and most organisations haven't done that. Most of them actually do not know what kind of processing is taking place in their organisations (ibid.).* This is problematic, since major presuppositions of data protection and privacy by design rest upon the assumption that data flows are properly mapped and understood in the first place [cf. 4, 30].

Secondly, even if these challenges would be tackled, new challenges arise, since the implementation of personal data protection becomes dependent on the operational logics of organisations. As stated, organisations work according to their own goals, means, and strategies when also having to take into account the needs and concerns of single individuals, users, and data subjects. Our informant systematically refers to privacy breaches as possible risks to 'an asset'. But an 'asset' is something typically belonging to the world of business as a resource that can be owned or controlled by a company to produce economic value. This is at odds with the spaces and processes in which notions of privacy normally arise (the home, family life, correspondence, browsing habits, etc.) and that have become legally acknowledged. To an actual person concerned with privacy, such spaces and processes are not economic 'assets' but often pose definite limits that cannot be so easily traded away.[4] Yet this talk about privacy rights as assets is no mere slip of the tongue, but rather representative of a steady development in which privacy is increasingly being conceived as a risk to the reputation of organisations [27].

Similarly, a person working as a DPA described how *IT people are good at thinking about risks, but it is usually the risks to the organisation.* Whereas some have argued that this makes for a win-win situation [4] for both organisations and data subjects, the interview points to several possible conflicting interests: organisations may want to produce and retain maximum amounts of information on individuals, often without their knowledge; they may combine data in new ways, thus producing sensitive data from non-sensitive sources; organisations may create representations of data subjects that do not correspond with the self-image of the subject, they may hold data secret and without the knowledge of the subject, and so on.

Therefore, whereas the transformation of data protection into 'technical and organisational measures' (GDPR, Art. 24, 1) seems like a necessary step for effectively protecting privacy (as it may contribute to bring organisations on board), this mode of operationalisation may come at the expense of certain trade-offs with the autonomy of individuals (natural, data subjects, etc.).

Furthermore, this happens in a situation where the entitlements through which data subjects could oppose such developments and influence decisions (*ex ante*, prior to processing) are limited. Article 35 of the GDPR on data protection impact assessments, provides in its point 9 that the controller *'shall seek the views of data subjects or their representatives on the intended processing'*. However, this should happen only where *'appropriate'* and *'without prejudice to the protection of commercial or public interests*

---

[4] Our informant talks about risk as 'the probability of damage to the fulfilment of an asset', namely a human right. An asset is defined as 'an item of property owned by a person or company, regarded as having value' (Oxford dictionary). Hence, privacy becomes something that can be owned or controlled (through risk and design approaches) to produce economic value for a company. That privacy articulation is thus linked to trust and reputation. This conception is very different from the Continental European law tradition, in which fundamental rights like privacy are considered to be 'inalienable', not to be owned or sold.

or the security of processing operations', all of which are aspects that the controller is given the full mandate to decide upon. The entitlement of data subjects to influence decisions over protection of their rights during assessment procedures is thus limited and it does not correspond to a duty on the side of the controller to take these views on board. One of our informants, a member of a prominent civil rights privacy organisation, expressed dissatisfaction with this general state of affairs: *Privacy by Design and Privacy Impact Assessments are used as an excuse for innovation. Once it is written they have been done, no one opposes (...) them and no one checks the quality of the process. Politicians have no notice of the contents* (civil rights activist). When introduced together with other measures of the GDPR, such as privacy seals and data protection certification, impact assessments and data protection by design could be used to deflect the expectations of individual right-holders, activists and publics, *de facto* excluding them.[5] Expectations are that such early interventions will enable controllers, data subjects and society at large, to avoid right infringements before they materialise [cf. 26]. However, the informant from the privacy NGO argued that these practices can also be used pre-emptively in order to avoid public opposition to privacy-infringing projects and technologies.

3.2   Law Versus Engineering

At the heart of design-based approaches to personal data protection, privacy and other fundamental rights and freedoms, we find expectations about new and innovative interactions between the practices of law and engineering. This could be described as the main instantiation of the imperative to cross the 'Rubicon' of data protection by design, since legal principles related to personal data protection and other fundamental rights and freedoms as spelled out by lawyers and judges, should be implemented by engineers and designers.[6] Yet, there are huge differences between lawyers and engineers: in terms of their basic assumptions and methods; in terms of the medium through which they work; in terms of the procedural checks and balancing exercises they are subject to, and in terms of the scope of their interventions. Again, we single out a few major issues as encountered in our empirical data.

Firstly, we find decisive differences and limitations in terms of the practices of law and engineering, where legal principles cannot so easily be translated into something that can be rendered operable by engineers. Whereas a paradigmatic statement holds

---

[5] This is not to say that the present proposals are not improvements on the situation existing prior to the GDPR; we are merely pointing to ways in which the new mechanisms could be misused.

[6] In ordinary parlance, 'crossing the Rubicon' refers to a risky undertaking. But the underlying story of how Julius Caesar crossed the river Rubicon and took Rome is instructive for yet another reason: at the time (49 BC), Caesar was a promagistrate of the province Cisalpine Gaul, and his authority (*Imperium*) to command troops was only valid within that area. Only elected magistrates of Rome had the authority to command troops on Roman land. Upon crossing the Rubicon, Caesar overstepped his authority, under threat of death penalty for himself and his troops. Therefore, in transgressing the territorial and legal boundary, he took the first step towards changing the nature of authority on that territory (the final change occurring as he won the civil war). Similarly, data protection and privacy by design may start a transfer of authority, from law to engineering.

that 'law is code' [17], people trying to turn this into practice easily end up perplexed.[7] We already know this problem from the privacy design literature, where bridging efforts have been made through articulations of 'privacy goals' and 'design strategies' [15, 19]. A fundamental problem here is that legal principles and texts are by definition and nature polysemic, i.e. they have multiple possible meanings and interpretations, without which they lose much of their meaning and function *as legal principles* [8]. The GDPR only provides few general instructions, and these are not sufficient to perform the necessary translations. One of our informants, working in interaction design, expressed this as follows: *There is a difference between the moral reasoning linked to human rights and the attempt of solving an engineering problem, which is technically and mathematically specified* (human-computer interaction practitioner). In contradistinction to law, engineering goals and means are usually dependent on uni-lateral, non-ambiguous meanings, on reducing the design space, in order for coding operations to be able to proceed. Even small changes to the original parameters may be highly demanding, in terms of work and resources:

Data Protection by Design and by Default can be costly in terms of computations, speed, and accuracy of models. In many cases this can be alleviated, but it usually requires very substantial research and work to achieve a good outcome. It can also be less flexible since the approach is often tailored to a particular goal and algorithm, and a small change can require a lot of work (privacy engineer).

Secondly, this difference of law and engineering may put a spanner in the wheels of technically oriented efforts towards 'prospective adjudication', whereby legal princi-ples are invoked by designers and risk assessors before the fact of the infringement of a right.[8] As explained to us by a judge, engineers *do not think about human rights when they work*. This is why law *must play a role which is of course posterior* to that of technical design. It should not be the role of legislation to foresee all possible breaches of rights: *situations are so different (…) even if you provide for detailed rules in law, in certain cases they will not be applicable or their application would create a bad result (…) this is the task of law, of doctrine, of case law to find in a concrete case a justified solution"* (judge, European Court of Justice). The Rubicon of law and engineering is, for such reasons, not to be crossed, according to the judge. The judge's statement is about the proper role and domain of law. Nevertheless, in a situation of broad dis-cretion currently afforded by organisations as to self-restriction on how to ensure rights' protections, some bridging towards engineering and technology is needed. This applies especially when data protection by design becomes itself a legal obligation.

First, this might require attuning design processes where engineers have to come up with specific privacy solutions by applying generic legal principles to concrete techno-logical contexts, to the ways in which law practitioners apply such principles within

---

[7] Hence, we agree with the statement 'law is code' as a *description* of the fact that technologies, (artefacts, algorithms, code) influence social and cultural norms, some of which also enjoy legal protection. We question that this description can easily be turned into a *prescription* for design and engineering, when based on safeguarding the specific requirements of social norms and legal rights and principles.

[8] As in assessments of prospective and possible 'risks to rights' [27], as well as the general anticipatory and future-oriented orientation of privacy by design [4].

specific legal cases. Second, procedural checks could be introduced, to enhance oversight of decisions to be made within design processes and inspired by the long-standing procedural guarantees enjoyed by fundamental rights within institutional settings and courts.

Finally, even if such aspects (hermeneutics, procedural) could be worked out, we encounter differing ideas about what design is and what specific role it could play in the process of translation. According to a classical image, design is a uni-directional process in which the designer oversees and integrates an impressive amount of knowledge, building it into the material artefact. This image conveys the process as linear, and based upon neat separations between designers, producers and consumers, whereas in actual software development, these roles are much more blurred [25]. Within the incipient field of privacy engineering, we hear talk about an 'agile turn' [12] as replacing previous modes ('waterfall'), in which the main emphasis is placed upon shorter development cycles, user centricity, constant updates and developments. Indeed, such changes in design processes seem necessary, since they follow and replicate what is going on anyway in software developments more generally [12].

We think these novel approaches, along with other related developments such as 'values in design' are highly interesting and relevant to the challenges at hand. Here, privacy engineering ceases to be a 'science', and turns towards 'artfulness' and creativity in the process possibly becoming more of a craft [11]. In so doing they possibly open up towards the broader meanings, interpretations and methods required by law (as just described), and concerned social actors, since the process goes beyond classical applications of scientific or engineering principles deemed as objective and beyond discussion. Yet, we can also see how this may run up against other main principles of data protection, such as the basic requirement that data subjects give their informed consent to a processing operation. This becomes difficult in processes of agile design, where a software product may be seen as in a permanent state of flux: 'permanently Beta', under constant development.[9] The old linear modes of design would have offered some assurance here, since there would be a decisive body of stabilised knowledge on the basis of which data subjects could make up their minds and provide their consents (or not). Yet, in the current design modes, other options must be sought out, since there is little consensus or technical guidance as to how this could happen. Therefore, we maintain that 'privacy engineering' remains an interesting field where valuable experimental efforts have already taken place, but this field should not be institutionally and politically overcharged.

3.3   Global Standards Versus Local Requirements

As implied in the above section, solutions for how to carry out DPbD are simultaneously being sought on various levels, from single technologies (PETs) to practices (law, engineering, design), at single organisational level and beyond. Yet, the overarching reference is at the level of standards and infrastructures, since this is where interventions must be made in order to render the internal digital market a reality, and to technically connect the various systems involved, for instance for the making of the Internet of

---

[9] This point was conveyed to us by an interactional computing practitioner. The term 'permanently Beta' was coined by Gina Neff and David Stark [18].

Things. Here, we encounter another mode, which we have termed 'privacy by network' [28]. If market actors are to place their trust in the digital value chains, data protection should be safeguarded across all levels of infrastructures, and also include basic information security. Yet, here the challenges increase, since now the focus is on whole value chains, and incorporating all actors involved in the making of IoT products: devices, applications, IoT semantics and other services, or in processing of data. Several of our informants mention issues of 'systemic risk', according to which weaknesses in one part of the chain transmit to other parts, rendering the whole chain vulnerable.[10] Yet, the GDPR places the main responsibility for the protection of personal data on 'data controllers'. This responsibility does not seem to symmetrically extend to other actors in the chain, such as the designers and producers of the hard- and software used by the data controllers.[11] Hence, a privacy and security advisor involved in EU activities aimed at the implementation of smart grids, told us how existing approaches are insufficient, and how *the discussion should have been taken from the chain point of view. In this way the transparency of the smart meter would have been discussed in an early stage with all the stakeholders that are related in the chain* (privacy and security officer – energy utility).[12] From an infrastructural point of view this makes sense, and triggers the question of how personal data protection and privacy could be implemented across all actors involved. Our informants also referred to the notion of privacy and data protection as 'transversal concerns', meaning 'cross-cutting' matters of concern to be implemented across the entire infrastructural chain by all actors:

When we want to take into account privacy and other concerns, we have to take them into account as transversal concerns…: security, privacy, safety, energy consumption or taking into account ethical aspects and things like that. … we need to be able to engineer transversal concerns and "capabilities" in things (privacy and security consultant).

However, in order to be able to build privacy, security and data protection as 'capabilities', there is a need to first establish interoperability. In the case of the Internet of Things, to which the quote refers, this is a long-standing effort of digital-physical engineering that has turned out to be more complicated than previously expected. Indeed, there are too many formats and standards in play, and global efforts to reduce the huge plurality have so far not succeeded in establishing interoperability across regions or sectors, or between different producers [29]. This means that there is no stable technical base from which to start, in relation to which privacy concerns could be assessed and communicated. Therefore, the project to implement rights and values as transversal 'concerns' of engineering in large-scale infrastructures and systems, exists more as a promise than as real intervention according to known principles and standards. Yet, similarly to what we have seen in relation to organisations and individuals, this promise may end up having real effects since it becomes central to the organisation

---

[10] In security research these aspects are referred to by grading systems and value chains according to different security maturity levels.

[11] Instead, the impression is that, according to GDPR, responsibility will somehow 'trickle down' to other actors. This is so, even as it is becoming harder by the day to define who is really a data controller, who is a processor, and who is a user.

[12] To illustrate: with 'all stakeholders' our informant referred to: grid operator, data processor, energy retailer, customer, regulator, policy maker, energy service provider company.

and coordination of large-scale engineering and regulatory efforts. Here, the dangers are even greater that the scale and complexity of these infrastructural efforts have the side-effect of disregarding crucial inputs from users and from societal actors on what they expect from IoT applications.

This problem is also replicated in the case of privacy and personal data protection, in the tension between how legal principles should be invoked, and how the semantic spaces and design spaces should be compressed to enable standardisation. Here, we can draw an analogy to the arguments of the judge, and the limits to how legal principles and reasoning can be translated into engineering principles. In order to enable standardisation efforts to go ahead, an overall problem pertains to the level of generality and scale of implementation. If some IoT application or system is to be rendered functional, and to include legal principles and privacy concerns, they also need to make intuitive sense to the people using and operating them, including ordinary users and lawyers/judges. As stated in a major work on the social dimensions of information infrastructure, 'an infrastructure occurs when local practices are afforded by a larger-scale technology, which can then be used in a natural, ready-to-hand fashion' [24, p. 381]. Here, there are huge challenges pertaining to the kind of language that could be used to communicate privacy concerns and how to translate these into design, where such concerns are frequently of a local, personal and singular character, and not global and standardisable. Indeed, we could say that many privacy concerns of people arise in the face of efforts to build increasingly globalised and centralised systems, and that what they implicitly or explicitly seek is to recapture and bring powers back to local levels. Furthermore, the technical challenges are immense, since many devices, applications, interoperability services and platforms are built by different companies, using different standards: *Many efforts currently go into putting technical complexity at work...99% focus of technical people is about solving that* (DPbD and standardisation consultant). As in the case of the organisations, this points to the dual requirement of making something that works within highly complex, heterogeneous networks. Here, privacy becomes infrastructurally articulated and co-articulated with other transversal concerns, especially security, safety, trust and interoperability. Adequacy of the protections is associated to degrees of users' trust. The connotation of privacy and personal data protection as fundamental rights does not seem to play a determining role in the legitimation of the system. As the peer explains, *'trust is about psychology'*. The challenges here are rather huge, and chances are that only very thin, and minimal conceptions of rights can be integrated within this narrowed-down semiotic and infrastructural space.

4 Concluding Remarks

In this article, we have pointed to some tensions and frictions as discovered during consultations with actors within and around the emerging field of privacy and data protection engineering. Some of these, such as lack of public and organisational awareness, may be temporary, and subject to change. A few of the tensions, such as working out the proper relations and design spaces for engineers and lawyers to communicate in better ways, may be eased, given time and spaces for learning. However, we also think that some of the lessons learnt point to decisive limits that should not be transgressed: here we include the impossibility of 'law becoming code' in the strict sense of the word. This would effectively turn law into a mere instrument in a mix aimed at technocratic regulation (which was actually Lessig's prescription) [17]. Hence, law needs to retain its own autonomy in articulating privacy and data protection rights, including judgments about (un)successful privacy design, as was also implied by the above quotes from the ECJ judge. In spite of this, legal practices (both legislative, adjudicative and procedural) crucially also need to understand these new design practices and interact with them, and their fast-changing technological and social realities. Here, we argued that the new and emerging field of privacy engineering is interesting. We also argued that design practices will remain bound to intrinsic constraints, to what can realistically be made subject to engineering approaches, to the interests of those involved in their making and should not be overcharged with political promises as to what can realistically be achieved or guaranteed. This points at a need for a firmer embedding of design-based approaches to rights within 'extended' ecologies of practice, in which mutual checks can be exercised: between different epistemic and normative commitments and as provided for by robust public and legal guarantees. Furthermore, our empirical materials demonstrated that there are real tensions involved in the project to turn personal data protection into organisational principles, and into standards for global engineering of infrastructures. Whereas infrastructures, and the markets enabled by them, are increasingly global, people's privacy concerns and legal data protection implications, remain stubbornly attached to the local and singular. The meanings of data protection and privacy, therefore, cannot be detached from questions about where, by whom and through what methods, they are enacted.

References

1. Bennett, C.: The Privacy Advocates. Resisting the Spread of Surveillance. MIT Press, Cambridge (2008)
2. Bennett, J., Raab, C.D.: The Governance of Privacy: Policy Instruments in a Global Perspective. MIT Press, Cambridge (2006)
3. Boltanski, L., Thevenot, L.: On Justification. Economies of Worth. Princeton University Press, Princeton (2006)
4. Cavoukian, A.: Privacy by design: the 7 foundational principles. Inf. Priv. Comm. Ont. Can. (2009)
5. Dewey, J.: Logic: The Theory of Inquiry. The Later Works: 1938, at 112 (Jo Ann Boydston ed. 1991) (1938/1991)
6. De Hert, P., Papakonstantinou, V.: The new general data protection regulation: still a sound system for the protection of individuals? Comput. Law Secur. Rev. **32**(2), 179–194 (2016)
7. Davies, S.G.: Re-engineering the right to privacy: how privacy has been transformed from a right to a commodity. In: Agre, P.E., Rotenberg, M. (eds.) Technology and Privacy: The New Landscape. MIT Press, Cambridge (1998)
8. Dworkin, R.: Taking Rights Seriously. Duckworth, London (1977)
9. Danezis, G., et al.: Privacy and data protection by design – from policy to engineering. ENISA (2014)
10. Funtowicz, S.O., Ravetz, J.R.: Science for the post-normal age. Futures **25**, 735–755 (1993)
11. Gürses, S., Del Álamo, J.M.: Privacy engineering: shaping an emerging field of research and practice. IEEE Secur. Priv. **14**(2), 40–46 (2016)

12. Gürses, S., van Hoboken, J.V.: Privacy after the agile turn. In: Polonetsky, J., Tene, O., Selinger, E. (eds.) Cambridge Handbook of Consumer Privacy. Cambridge University Press, Cambridge (2017)
13. Gutwirth, S., De Hert, P., De Sutter, L.: The trouble with technology regulation from a legal perspective. Why Lessig's "optimal mix" will not work. In: Brownsword, R., Yeung, K. (eds.) Regulating Technologies, pp. 193–218. Hart Publishers, Oxford (2008)
14. Hildebrandt, M.: Smart Technologies and the End(s) of Law: Novel Entanglements of Law and Technology. Edgar Elgar Publishers (2015)
15. Hoepman, J.-H.: Privacy design strategies. In: Cuppens-Boulahia, N., Cuppens, F., Jajodia, S., Abou El Kalam, A., Sans, T. (eds.) SEC 2014. IAICT, vol. 428, pp. 446–459. Springer, Heidelberg (2014). https://doi.org/10.1007/978-3-642-55415-5_38
16. Kitchin, R.: The Data Revolution. Big Data, Open Data, Data Infrastructures and Their Consequences. SAGE Publishers, Thousand Oaks (2014)
17. Lessig, L.: Code: Version 2.0. Basic Books, New York (1999/2006)
18. Neff, G., Stark, D.: Permanently beta: responsive organization in the internet era. In: Howard, P. N., Jones, S. (eds.) Society Online: The Internet in Context. Sage, Thousand Oaks (2004)
19. Notario, N., et al.: PRIPARE: integrating privacy best practices into a privacy engineering methodology. In: IEEE CS Security and Privacy Workshops, pp. 151–158 (2015)
20. Oliver, I.: 2014 Privacy Engineering: A Dataflow and Ontological Approach. CreateSpace Independent Publishing Platform
21. Rommetveit, K., Van Dijk, N., Gunnarsdottír, K.: Integrated assessments in technoepistemic networks. EPINET discussion paper (2015). http://www.epinet.no/sites/all/themes/epinet_bootstrap/documents/wp1_cross_cutting_report.pdf
22. Rommetveit, K., et al.: Working responsibly across boundaries? Some practical and theoretical lessons. In: von Schomberg, R. (Ed.) Handbook of responsible Innovation. Edgar Elgar Publishers (forthcoming 2018)
23. European Commission 2012 SEC(2012) 72 final COMMISSION STAFF WORKING PAPER Impact Assessment Accompanying the document Regulation of the European Parliament and of the Council on the protection of individuals with regard to the processing of personal data and on the free movement of such data (General Data Protection Regulation) and Directive of the European Parliament and of the Council on the protection of individuals with regard to the processing of personal data by competent authorities for the purposes of prevention, investigation, detection or prosecution of criminal offences or the execution of criminal penalties, and the free movement of such data (2012)
24. Star, S.L., Ruhleder, K.: Steps toward an ecology of infrastructure: design and access for large information spaces. Inf. Syst. Res. 7(1), 111–134 (1996/2015)
25. Stewart, J., Williams, R.: The wrong trousers? Beyond the design fallacy: social learning and the user. In: Rohracher, H. (ed.) User Involvement in Innovation Processes. Strategies and Limitations from a Socio-Technical Perspective. Profil-Verlag, Munich (2005)
26. van den Hoven, J.: Value sensitive design and responsible innovation. In: Owen, R., Bessant, J., Heintz, M. (eds.) Responsible Innovation. Managing the responsible emergence of science and innovation in society, pp. 75–83. Wiley, Chichester (2013)
27. Van Dijk, N., Gellert, R., Rommetveit, K.: A risk to a right? Beyond data protection impact assessments. Comput. Law Secur. Rev. 32(2), 286–306 (2016)
28. Van Dijk, N., Tanas, A., Rommetveit, K.: Right engineering? The redesign of privacy and personal data protection. International Review of Law, Computers and Technology (forthcoming)
29. Vermesan, O., et al.: Visions and challenges for realizing the internet of things. CERP-IoT, Cluster of European Research Projects on the Internet of Things (2010)
30. Wright, D., De Hert, P.: Introduction to privacy impact assessment. In: Wright, D., De Hert, P. (eds.) Privacy Impact Assessment, vol. 6. Springer, Dordrecht (2012). https://doi.org/10.1007/978-94-007-2543-0_1

Anonymity Online – Current Solutions and Challenges

Matthias Marx, Erik Sy, Christian Burkert, and Hannes Federrath(✉)

University of Hamburg, Hamburg, Germany
federrath@informatik.uni-hamburg.de

Abstract. Internet communication, regardless whether it is encrypted or not, comes with an abundance of protocol metadata. Web browsers reveal plenty of information to web applications. Additionally, web service operators have a great interest in their users' preferences and behaviour, leading to the development and deployment of several sophisticated tracking mechanisms. Therefore, the protection of the user's privacy on the Internet becomes increasingly difficult. Helpful privacy enhancing tools and techniques, which are often free of charge, are available to everyone, although have not reached widespread adoption yet. In this paper, we discuss different techniques of tracking as a challenge to online anonymity. Furthermore, we present current solutions on the application level as well as on the network level to provide anonymity, and finally we point out avenues for future research in the field of online anonymity. We find security-hardened operating systems promising to protect personal data against relatively strong adversaries on the user side. On the network side we consider lightweight network-based techniques like IPv6 pseudonymisation as promising technologies for future practical and usable anonymity on the Internet.

Keywords: Privacy · Anonymity · Tracking · Fingerprinting

1 Introduction to Anonymity

Anonymity online is the effort to communicate over the Internet while disclosing no or as little as possible of directly or indirectly identifying information unless explicitly wanted. Identification happens directly if someone discloses his or her own name accidentally or deliberately, e.g., when registering an account or signing a message. Indirect ways of identification emerge when disclosed information can be combined with additional knowledge containing sufficiently identifying information. When communicating over the Internet, being literally anonymous could mean that neither a communication partner, any intermediary, nor an outside observer is able to identify a communicating person.

This paper provides an overview of past and contemporary efforts to provide anonymity throughout different technology layers involved in online communication. Section 1 provides the legal background on online anonymity, the

M. Hansen et al. (Eds.): Privacy and Identity 2017, IFIP AICT 526, pp. 38–55, 2018.
https://doi.org/10.1007/978-3-319-92925-5_4

definition of important terms and a motivation for doing research in the field of online privacy. Section 2 discusses the problem of and countermeasures against application-level tracking, followed by a discussion of network-level anonymisation techniques in Sect. 3. Section 4 concludes with an overview of the presented challenges regarding anonymity online.

1.1 Anonymity from a Legal Perspective

From a legal perspective, the term anonymity is known in association with privacy and data protection regulations. In this section, we focus on EU regulations and court decisions, i.e. the General Data Protection Regulation (GDPR), the ePrivacy Regulation, and a fundamental decision by the European Court of Justice regarding the identifiability of personal data.

EU General Data Protection Regulation (GDPR). The GDPR mentions anonymity only in its recitals. Recital 26 defines data as anonymous when it is either not related to an identified or identifiable natural person or it has been rendered anonymous such that the data subject is not or no longer identifiable. Therefore, anonymous data is not considered as personal data. Its processing does not fall within the material scope of the GDPR as defined in Article 2.

Whether given data is anonymous or not comes down to the question of how much effort is needed by an attacker to identify a person and how likely it is that the attacker undergoes such efforts, e.g., by linking several attributes of an anonymized dataset with a priori information held by the attacker. Recital 26 lists aspects that should be taken into consideration if one assess which means are likely to be used by an attacker. Aspects to be considered are the costs and the amount of time required for identification as well as the available technology at the time of the processing and technological developments.

EU ePrivacy Regulation. As part of the amendment of EU data protection regulations, the ePrivacy Regulation (ePR) is developed to repeal the current ePrivacy Directive and to complement the GDPR as a lex specialis for electronic communication services.

Article 10 of the Commission's draft [1] proposes the obligation for software manufacturers to provide privacy settings that allow end-users to prevent third parties from storing or processing information on their devices. Third parties are components and services that are used by the first party services to fulfill a specific task like customer research or advertisement. Recital 22 of the Commission's proposal describes the proposed privacy settings as a more user-friendly approach to express consent to website cookies compared to the overwhelming numbers of consent requests currently prompted by individual websites. Recital 23 sees such privacy settings as an implementation of the principles of data protection by design and by default as defined in Article 25 of the GDPR and suggests differentiated cookie settings that should be prominently and intelligibly presented to end-users.

Regardless of the explicit reference to cookies in the recitals, Article 10's opt-out of processing information already stored on end-user devices could also be interpreted as a prohibition of techniques that utilise stored device information, e.g. device fingerprinting. Such a wider interpretation of Article 10 would require software manufacturers to further confine the capabilities of third parties to query device or user-specific information. As a consequence, web browser manufacturers could be obliged to put code from third parties into a sandbox environment and deny unredacted access to sensitive APIs.

Identification Through IP Addresses. In October 2016, the European Court of Justice (ECJ) ruled in case C-582/14 [2] with regard to the nature of dynamically assigned IP addresses, that such addresses, when registered by an online media service provider, constitute personal data, provided that the online media service provider has the legal means to identify a user behind the IP address by consulting additional data stored e.g. by the Internet Service Provider (ISP) of that person. This decision clarifies the fundamental dispute between the relative and the absolute approach to the identification of data subjects [3]. While the relative theory states that the question of identification depends on the individual processing context and the knowledge of the processor, the absolute theory considers data as identifiable as long as anyone has the means to attribute that data to a natural person [3]. ECJ followed the relative approach, but additionally used a wide interpretation of means of identification such that also information and capabilities of third parties should be taken into consideration if the processor has the legal means to utilise them.

1.2 Formalising Anonymity

Legal definitions of anonymity and identifiability are designed to be adaptable to future technological developments. Additionally, there is also a demand for more formalised and objective notions to facilitate compliance or to objectify scientific efforts. This section presents various formal definitions of anonymity and of algorithmic properties, which limit the disclosure of potentially personal data.

Anonymity Set. Pfitzmann and Hansen [4] define anonymity as not being identifiable within a set of subjects, the anonymity set. Not being identifiable means that the subject is not distinguishable from other subjects within the anonymity set. Pfitzmann and Hansen describe the ability to distinguish subjects as a function of the attacker, its knowledge and capabilities. Thus, they state anonymity as a property relative to an attacker. A subject can be considered as being identified, if an attacker can attribute a given action to that subject with a probability exceeding a certain threshold. Pfitzmann and Hansen differentiate between anonymity of individual users of a system and global anonymity provided by the system. The level of global anonymity increases by a more even distribution of attribution probabilities. Consequently, a high global anonymity does not guarantee a high anonymity of each individual subject. Ensuring individual anonymity would require enforcing a uniform behaviour within a set of subjects, which Pfitzmann and Hansen consider both very difficult to enforce and not desirable from a human rights perspective.

If a subject is known to be part of multiple anonymity sets, e.g. due to repeated interactions over time, the effective anonymity set is reduced to the intersection of all known anonymity sets. This is known as an *intersection attack*.

k-Anonymity. Sweeney [5] defines a set of data records as k-anonymous, if every record is indistinguishable from at least $k - 1$ other records in terms of identifiability. Such an indistinguishable group of records is called a bucket and corresponds to Pfitzmann and Hansen's anonymity set. Sweeney uses the term quasi-identifiers to denote a subset of record fields or attributes that are sensitive to linking attacks, i.e. attributes that are likely to appear in other data collections. Therefore, such quasi-identifiers can be used to correlate data collections and possibly disclose the identity of subjects. Given a data collection, Sweeney assumes, it is possible to find attributes that qualify as quasi-identifiers. Based on that assumption a data holder wishing to release an anonymised version of its data collection could redact values of quasi-identifiers until an acceptably large bucket size is reached. Under Sweeney's quasi-identifier assumption, variations within non-quasi-identifier attributes of the same bucket are not considered problematic.

ℓ-Diversity. Machanavajjhala et al. [6] proposed ℓ-diversity as an enhancement of k-anonymity. Two attacks against k-anonymity are presented which utilise potentially low diversity within non-quasi-identifier attributes, denoted as sensitive attributes. The *homogeneity attack* shows that the size of a bucket is insignificant if a sufficiently high proportion of records within a bucket share the same sensitive attribute. A subject known to be part of that bucket can be assumed to share that value with reasonable likelihood, too. The *background knowledge attack* demonstrates that background knowledge about a subject can be used to single out the corresponding bucket and to reduce the anonymity set of that bucket by eliminating records that are incompatible with the attacker's background knowledge. As a countermeasure, ℓ-diversity requires ℓ different values for each sensitive attribute within a bucket.

t-Closeness. Li et al. [7] demonstrate that the sensitive values within each bucket need to be distributed closely to the distribution of the overall data collection to avoid two kinds of attacks that are still possible with ℓ-diverse data. The *skewness attack* utilises a potential mismatch between the relative frequency of a stigmatising sensitive value within a bucket and that within the overall data collection. Based on that mismatch, an attacker can infer that subjects within that bucket are more likely to share the sensitive value than subjects in other buckets. The *similarity attack* shows that ℓ-diversity is not sufficient to protect against the homogeneity attack, if the diverse values are semantically similar and thus fall within the same category rendering the bucket homogeneous. Li et al. introduce the notion of t-closeness which requires the value distributions of each bucket to differ no more than t from the distribution of the overall data collection.

Differential Privacy. Dwork [8] introduces Differential Privacy not as a metric for the degree of anonymity of sanitised data collections, but as a property of data processing algorithms. An algorithm is considered ϵ-differentially private if it processes similar inputs into outputs which are only distinguishable with a certainty that is bound by ϵ. As a consequence, the probability is limited that such an algorithm exposes discernible information after adding or removing a subject from the input data. Differential Privacy does neither limit the amount nor the sensitivity of the information which is exposed within the tolerance of the ϵ boundary.

Summary. While the definition of Pfitzmann and Hansen mostly conforms with legal notions of anonymity and is less formal, the other metrics aim at providing a provable property that allows an unambiguous reasoning about the sensitivity of data or algorithms. Such formalisation necessarily comes at the cost of simplification. Focusing on quasi-identifiers neglected that practically any information can be used in background knowledge attack to single out individuals or at least reduce the anonymity set. Regardless of the size of an anonymity set, information about subjects is disclosed if the anonymity set as a whole is abnormal and this abnormality reflects on all subjects within this anonymity set. For an analysis of the aforementioned notions and anonymisation techniques in the context of EU regulations we refer to the opinion paper of the Article 29 data protection working party [9].

1.3   Profiling and Unlinkability

Striving for anonymity and for less disclosure of personal data is not sufficient to protect individuals against a non-transparent and potentially malicious data processing. Even if a subject might not be identifiable by a processor, his or her data can be linkable and thus aggregated over time to build a profile of that subject. Consider a system in which each user is only represented and re-identified by a unique token, that is only meaningful in the context of that processor and not linkable to any external data. Profiles of such users would be considered legally anonymous if the processor had no likely means to identify the natural person behind that profile. For example, consider a news aggregation service, which knows neither its users' names nor e-mail addresses, IP addresses, or any other identifying information that has any meaning to third parties. The service recognises its users by a randomly chosen unique token and records their news preferences to provide a targeted selection of news to each user. This service could plausibly argue, that due to the lack of identifiability, no personal data is handled and therefore data protection regulations do not apply. Consequently, this service could legally sell those profiles or use them for different purposes like targeted advertising without any restrictions.

Unlinkability is defined by Pfitzmann and Hansen [4] as the property of two or more items to be indistinguishable regarding their relation from the perspective of an attacker. Applied to the example of a news aggregation service, unlinkability of users' news consumption demands that two news requests by the same user appear indistinguishable from requests which were made by two different users. With unlinkability, profiling of users is impossible, since each profile comprises one item only. Unlinkability is a strong privacy guarantee which in turn comes at the cost of losing the ability to personalise services.

1.4 Lightweight Anonymity and Privacy

In 2012, Hsiao et al. proposed a setting for anonymous communication networks (ACNs) called Lightweight Anonymity and Privacy [10]. In this setting, the attacker model is relaxed, packets travel near-optimal routes, and only an intermediate level of privacy can be achieved. Lightweight anonymisation techniques can achieve higher efficiency compared to other anonymisation techniques. They can be a tool for so-called zero-effort privacy [11].

2 Anonymity on the Application Level

This section provides an introduction to tracking mechanisms on the application level and discusses their threat to anonymity online.

2.1 Tracking

Useful and legitimate applications for online tracking include the provision of personalised services, the distribution of personalised advertisements, and the measurement of website or application utilisation in order to derive patterns from the collected data. However, the collection and aggregation of this data can provide deep insights into online activities of a single user [12].

Tracking does not only influence the privacy of a user, it additionally introduces a high risk of discrimination based on the collected data. Findings by Hannak et al. [13] show that some e-commerce sites offer their products with different prices based on individual user profiles, which is also known as price discrimination.

In the following, we consider common tracking mechanisms (such as storage-based tracking and fingerprinting) which are capable to uniquely identify a computer system. Furthermore, we present behaviour-based tracking as an approach to identify a specific user instead of a computer system. Tracking mechanisms are a field of active research and development. Thus, countermeasures are required to continuously adapt protection mechanisms to the technical progress.

We consider the attacker to be a remote entity such as an online service with the privilege to store data or execute code on the victims machine (Fig. 1). However, we assume the attacker is not capable of compromising the operating system of the host device. This assumption applies to website operators who run their code in the user's browser or to application providers, whose software is installed on the user's machine.

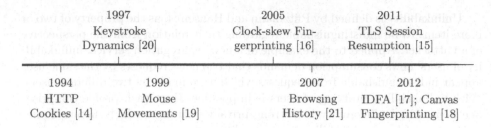

Fig. 1. Timeline of tracking mechanisms based on their first documented occurance.

Storage-Based Tracking. With storage-based tracking mechanisms, users can be uniquely identified through information stored on their device. Among others, these mechanisms include HTTP cookies [14], session identifiers stored in hidden fields, Apple's advertising identifier (IDFA) [17], and the TLS session resumption cache [15]. For trackers, it might be attractive to access stored information which can persist on the user's device and is available within different sessions or even different applications such as the IDFA. For this group of tracking mechanisms, the user has at least theoretically the option to delete the stored tracking information and thus, thwart the creation of profiles.

Fingerprinting. Fingerprinting mechanisms collect information about the user's computer system with the aim to discriminate the system among an anonymity set. Preferably, the collected information is difficult or unlikely to be changed by the user, thus, fingerprints can be used to recognise the user's computer system for long periods of time. However, if the fingerprint can extensively aggregate information about the user's computer system, the user might be recognised even after a partial modification of his or her system. Examples for fingerprinting are clock-skew measurements [16] and canvas fingerprinting [18].

Behaviour-Based Tracking. Behaviour-based tracking mechanisms aim to identify a user by characteristic traits such as mouse movements [19], keystroke dynamics [20], and browsing history [21]. While storage-based tracking and fingerprinting is capable to identify a specific device or application, the mechanism of behaviour-based tracking targets to identify a specific user. Research indicates, that the precision of identification for behaviour-based tracking decreases for large sample sizes [22]. In comparison, storage-based tracking can be used to store unique information with a high entropy on a user's device and therefore has a negligible error rate when used for tracking purposes.

2.2 Current Challenges for Anonymity on the Application Level

Tracking does not only occur in the context of web browsing. Empirical studies show that many popular mobile applications connect to services on the Internet [23]. Half of the Top 100 mobile applications under iOS, Android and Windows Phone transfer personal information to online services [24]. Therefore, every application on a computer system needs to be regarded as a potential leak of personally identifying information. In the following we describe challenges and solutions for the prevention of tracking on the application level.

Access Control for Runtime Environments. To restrict applications in their ability to collect, process, store and transfer personally identifying information access controls for runtime environments can be used. Therefore, this approach can enforce restrictions onto applications that reduce their functionality and thus limit their capabilities to track the user. For example, an application without access to network interfaces has no means to directly transfer collected data to a tracking service.

Unification of System Configurations. The unification of system configurations aims to make tracking by fingerprinting more difficult by reducing the number of possible system configurations which are visible to an application, or by reducing the probability that a system deviates from the standard configuration. A naive utilisation of this approach is to reset the system configuration to the standard configuration after a period of time. However, a malicious application might still deduce differences in systems hardware or user specifics characteristics usage. It remains a challenge to address this issue and to reduce the capabilities of trackers.

Disguise User Behaviour. This approach addresses the problem of behaviour-based tracking and aims to reduce the exposure of characteristic user behaviour towards malicious applications. For example, a system might use keystroke dynamics or mouse movements by randomly modifying the latency between two mouse or keyboard events. Characteristic user behaviour can also be deduced from contextual information such as browsing histories. Research by Herrmann et al. [25] indicates that datasets containing browsing sessions of 24 h have 85.4% accuracy of finding and matching the sessions of the same users, while shorter sessions of 5 min yield only an accuracy of 30.4%. Besides such temporal schemes to disguise characteristic user behaviour, also contextual schemes could be applied, where sessions are separated when a new website is visited.

2.3 Current Solutions for Anonymity on the Application Level

The presented challenges point out, that current solutions, and popular operating systems in particular, do not sufficiently protect against tracking. We now investigate operating systems such as Tails [26], Qubes OS [27] with Whonix [28], and Subgraph OS [29] in terms of their ability to prevent tracking. These operating systems assume a stronger attacker model compared to popular operating systems and aim to solve the current challenges for anonymity online. A brief comparison of these operating systems is given in Table 1 and afterwards.

Tails. Tails is designed as a live operating system, which is directly bootable from an external medium and aims to leave no traces of its usage on the computer used. As a security feature, the Tails OS provides high barriers for subsequently installed potentially malicious applications to persist after a system reboot. The drawback of this design decision is the limited usability of the system for users who want to install additional applications or to personalise their operating systems with an individual configuration. Tails uses the AppArmor [30] Linux kernel security module for access control policies of installed applications.

Qubes OS. Qubes OS with a Whonix virtual machine aims at providing anonymous Internet access as well as strict security by confinements. In this context confinements describe security mechanisms to separate running programs. All applications are installed in virtual machines, and the host utilises the Xen hypervisor [31]. This architecture reduces the trusted code base of the host in comparison to typical monolithic operating systems such as the Linux kernel and therefore the attack surface is diminished. Single virtual machines can be configured with specific security configurations such as a restricted filesystem access, usage of ACNs, or firewall rules. However, the design of Qubes OS comes along with high hardware requirements for the execution of multiple parallel virtual machines.

Subgraph OS. Subgraph OS provides anonymous Internet access and a design for strict application confinement. This operating system includes a hardened Linux kernel which is patched with Grsecurity/Pax [32] to provide additional memory protection and enhanced local access control. Subgraph allows a fine-grained confinement of individual applications by, among other mechanisms, application specific firewall rules, control of filesystem access, seccomp filter to restrict permitted system calls, isolation of some drivers such as audio, control of desktop access or process visibility.

Table 1. Comparison of operating systems with support for online anonymity.

System properties	Tails	Qubes OS + Whonix	Subgraph OS
Live USB OS	Yes	No	No
Firewall rules	Entire OS	Per VM	Per App
Filesystem isolation	Per App	Per VM	Per App
Hardware compatibility	High	Limited	High
ACN usage	Default	Per VM	Per App
Host architecture	Debian-based	Xen hypervisor	Debian-based
Seccomp filter	No	No	Yes, per App
Isolate devices and drivers	No	Yes	Yes
GUI isolation	Yes	Limited, per VM	Limited, per App
Process visibility	Yes	Limited, per VM	Limited, per App

2.4   Usability and Security

We tested whether a Tor Browser is able to collect hardware information on Qubes OS with Whonix, Subgraph OS, or Tails. We noticed that the default privileges of the Tor Browser on these systems are sufficient to collect detailed hardware information. These information could be used for device fingerprinting.

Tails, Subgraph OS, and Qubes OS with Whonix provide the Tor Browser within their standard configuration, which provides the features of tab isolation and stream isolation [33] in order to protect against identification based on contextual information such as browsing habits of a user.

Furthermore, Qubes OS and Subgraph OS implement GUI isolation towards the restriction of applications in observing user behaviour in the context of other applications. However, the investigated operating systems do not provide functionalities to protect user tracking based on mouse movements or keystroke dynamics.

As a live operating system, Tails implements the unification of system configurations by resetting the system after each reboot. Consequently, storage-based tracking methods do not persist a restart of the system. Hence, this approach makes it more difficult for fingerprinting mechanisms to collect personally identifying information. However, malicious applications can still retrieve information about the hardware of the system.

Within Qubes OS the feature of disposable VMs supports the approach of a unification of system configurations. In this way, the user installs a potentially malicious application in a separate VM, which can be disposed after its usage. Thus, storage-based tracking over multiple sessions of application usage becomes more difficult, since the VM can be easily disposed in the meantime. Disposable VMs also improve the defence against fingerprinting mechanisms, since modifications of the VM by the user are removed with every disposal of the VM.

Tails and Subgraph OS are based on the Debian Linux distribution and provide a similar usability as Debian. However, as a live operating system, which returns to its initial state after each reboot, Tails has limited use cases. In Qubes OS, it is the responsibility of the user to isolate applications from each other by installing them in different virtual machines. Thus, Qubes OS requires a higher security awareness of the user which limits its usability. As a negative side effect on usability, Qubes OS has higher hardware requirements in comparison to the other operating systems.

3   Anonymity on the Network Level

This section provides a chronology of techniques which have been used to prevent tracking on the network level. Furthermore, we will present selected applications that are in use today. Finally, we discuss current challenges.

3.1   Chronology

In 1978, Rivest, Shamir and Adleman presented a method for obtaining digital signatures and public key cryptosystems that became known as RSA cryptosystem [34]. The cryptosystem had the novel property that a public encryption key does not reveal the corresponding decryption key. A sender encrypts the message to be sent with the receiver's public key and transmits it via a potentially insecure channel. Only the receiver could decrypt the message with his or her secret private key. Similarly, messages can be signed [34]. The RSA cryptosystem serves as building block for various privacy enhancing techniques until today.

A technique based on public key cryptography that allows unlinkability of sender and recipient was presented by Chaum in 1981. The basic idea makes use of so-called mixes, which sample messages of same length in a batch, change their appearance and forward all of them at the same point of time but in a different order [35]. Unlinkability can be achieved if more than one mix is used, if the mixes are operated by different operators and if at least one mix operates trustworthy and honestly. In the same paper, Chaum introduced digital pseudonyms. A digital pseudonym is a public key with which digital signatures of an anonymous holder of the corresponding private key can be verified. A combination of mixes and digital pseudonyms enables electronic elections in which any party can verify that the votes have been properly counted [35]. In 1991, Pfitzmann et al. presented ISDN-MIXes, a combination of Chaum's mixes, dummy traffic and broadcasts. ISDN-MIXes allow untraceable communication with low communication overhead [36]. Federrath et al. presented mixes in mobile communication systems in 1991. Their mix-based system utilises untraceable return-addresses to hide routing information and achieves location privacy [37]. In 1998, Kesdogan et al. introduced Stop-and-Go-MIXes that provide probabilistic anonymity. Unlike other mixes, Stop-and-Go-MIXes do not collect a fixed number of messages in a batch [38].

Blind signatures were introduced by Chaum in 1983. As traditional digital signatures, blind signatures can guarantee authenticity of a message. However, blind signatures allow signing of a message without revealing the message itself to the signer [39]. Blind signature schemes are utilised in electronic cash and electronic voting systems.

Tracking organisations use personally identifiable information, such as name, date and place of birth, or address, to match or link records with those provided by other organisations. With Chaum's credential system, presented in 1985, an individual could use unlinkable pseudonyms to interact with different organisations. For instance, a one-time-use pseudonym may be used to purchase goods from a shop and a persistent pseudonym may be used to open an account with a bank. The credential system ensures that individuals are held accountable for abuses created under their pseudonyms. Also, organisations could limit the number of pseudonyms per individual and individuals are able to authenticate ownership of their pseudonyms [40].

A communication protocol that achieves unconditional sender and recipient untraceability was published by Chaum in 1988. In contrast to mix networks, the Dining Cryptographers Network (DC-Net) relies on secure multi-party computation [41].

In a privacy preserving value exchange (e.g. unobservable and anonymous exchange of digital money) over a network, the main problem is the lack of simultaneity. It gives a temporary advantage to one party who can stop the communication midway through the value exchange process. In 1990, Bürk and Pfitzmann compared two approaches that utilise third parties to overcome this problem [42].

In 1995, Cooper and Birman introduced a service that allows reading from a shared memory without revealing which piece of information is being read. Those so-called blind message services can be used as an alternative to mixes to build a message service that achieves location privacy [43].

Goldschlag, Reed and Syversen introduced onion routing in 1996 [44], a lightweight approach to the dissemination of mixes.

Figure 2 shows a timeline of development of the aforementioned privacy enhancing technologies.

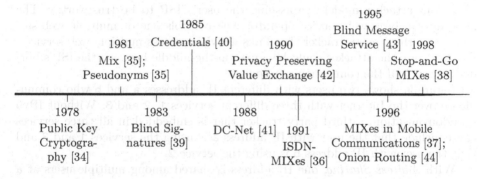

Fig. 2. Timeline of development of privacy enhancing technologies.

3.2 Current Solutions

JAP, formerly known as Java Anon Proxy, is a mix-based solution for anonymous Internet access. A first test version was launched in October 2000 and was developed by the research project *AN.ON – Anonymity.Online* [45]. The full service is running since February 2001 and has been outsourced to JonDos GmbH [46]. JAP is currently used by 5000 paying and several thousand non-paying users [47]. The research project named *AN.ON-Next – Anonymity Online for the next Generation* [48] aims to further develop JAP's mix-based anonymisation techniques.

Tor is the most widely used anonymisation network. It was presented by Dingledine et al. in 2004 and is based on onion routing [49]. Today, Tor has millions of users [50]. The servers that are used to relay traffic are mainly run by volunteers. One noteworthy product of the Tor project is the Tor Browser. It combines

Tor's protection on the network level with a modified Mozilla Firefox Browser in order to thwart tracking based on fingerprinting on the application level [51]. JAP and Tor protect against relatively strong adversaries. Other solutions focus on weaker adversaries.

IPv6 Pseudonymisation. Long-lived IP addresses are one of the easiest ways for tracking. Daily changing IP addresses (on reconnect or through IPv6 Privacy Extensions) are not sufficient [25]. As long as unlinkability of actions against ad networks and websites based on an IP address is intended and sufficient, ISPs can offer anonymity with a new approach to IP address assignment. Multiple users could share the same IP address (*Address Sharing*) or a single user could frequently change his or her IP address (*Address Hopping*). The anonymisation functionality can be implemented on the router or in the datacenter of the ISP. An advantage of this solution is that users are not required to make any changes to their operating system or client software and hardware. As a positive side effect, also devices, whose network configuration can not be changed, can be protected.

In our attacker model, we assume the user's ISP to be trustworthy. The attacker can be a web service operator who controls one or multiple web services, or a third party tracker that links activities across multiple web services. Furthermore, the attacker could be a man-in-the-middle between the ISP's border routers and the connection's endpoint.

Figure 3a shows two users with different IP addresses a and b who communicate over the Internet with three different services 1, 2 and 3. Without IPv6 pseudonymisation, a third party tracker that is embedded in all three services can conclude that the user with IP address a is using the services 1 and 3 and that the user with IP address b is using the service 2.

With *Address Sharing*, one IP address is shared among multiple users at a given point in time. All users are using the same IP address and thus form an anonymity group, implying that trackers cannot distinguish users based on their IP address anymore. *Address Sharing* can be implemented with state-of-the-art techniques such as Network Address Translation (NAT) has been deployed on Internet gateways for decades. Figure 3b shows three users who communicate via a router through the Internet with different services. Each user has his or her own IP address a, b or c. The router replaces the IP addresses on its public network interface, with the result that all users share the same public IP address d. The third party tracker cannot discriminate between the users based on their IP addresses. From the viewpoint of the tracker, it appears to be a single user with IP address d who is using services 1, 2 and 3.

Address Hopping means that each user distributes his or her traffic over multiple IP addresses within a short period of time. Web services or third party trackers can link activities for which the same IP address is used. However trackers cannot link activities based on IP addresses, when the IP address is changed frequently. Figure 3c shows a single user with IP address a who communicates via a router through the Internet with different services. The router replaces the

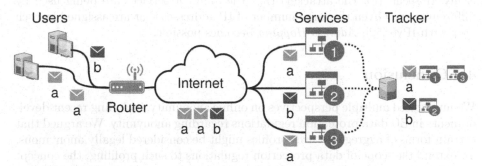

(a) Without IPv6 pseudonymisation, a third party tracker can conclude that the user with IP address a is using the services 1 and 3 and that the user with IP address b is using the service 2.

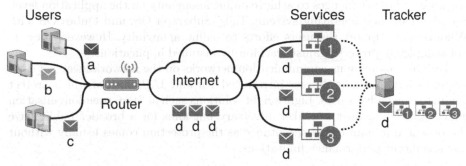

(b) With *Address Sharing*, one IP address is shared among multiple users. The third party tracker cannot discriminate between the users based on their IP addresses.

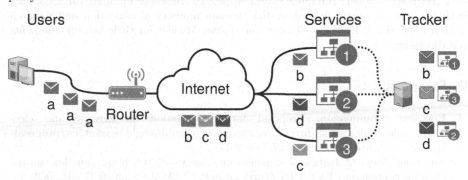

(c) With *Address Hopping*, each user distributes his or her traffic over multiple IP addresses. It seems that the different services are being used by different users.

Fig. 3. IPv6 pseudonymisation.

IP address, with the result that the different services 1, 2 and 3 see different IP addresses b, c and d. A third party tracker cannot link the user's IP addresses easily. It seems (for the attacker) that the different services are being used by different users. Given the large number of IP addresses that are assigned to each user with IPv6 [52], *Address Hopping* becomes possible.

4   Conclusion

We introduced multiple perspectives on online anonymity, including recent developments in EU data protection regulations regarding anonymity. We argued that certain forms of aggregated user profiles might be considered legally anonymous. To extend the scope of data protection regulations to such profiling, the concept of linkability needs to be incorporated into legal interpretations of identifiability and personal data.

We discussed fingerprinting as well as storage-based and behaviour-based tracking and the challenges to achieve online anonymity on the application level. Security hardened operating systems Tails, Subgraph OS, and Qubes OS with Whonix may support the users efforts to online anonymity. However, they do not completely protect against tracking by installed applications.

Building anonymous communication networks on the network level is a challenging effort. As examples, we introduced Tor and JAP, both of which protect against strong adversaries. Lightweight solutions such as IPv6 pseudonymisation which protects against a weaker adversary but aims for a broader public have the potential to gain broad acceptance as the protection comes usually without any significant performance limitations.

Acknowledgement. Part of this work has been developed in the projects AN.ONnext (reference number: 16KIS0368) and AppPETs (reference number: 16KIS0381K). Both projects are partly funded by the German ministry of education and research (BMBF). We thank Ephraim Zimmer and Tobias Mueller for their helpful comments and discussion.

References

1. European Commission: Proposal for a regulation on privacy and electronic communications. https://ec.europa.eu/digital-single-market/en/proposal-eprivacy-regulation. Accessed 27 Nov 2017
2. European Court of Justice: Judgement on Case C-582/14. http://eur-lex.europa.eu/legal-content/en/TXT/PDF/?uri\=uriserv\%3AOJ.C_.2016.475.01.0003.01.ENG. Accessed 27 Nov 2017
3. Reid, A.S.: The European court of justice case of Breyer. J. Inf. Rights Policy Pract. **2**(1) (2017)
4. Pfitzmann, A., Hansen, M.: A terminology for talking about privacy by data minimization: anonymity, unlinkability, undetectability, unobservability, pseudonymity, and identity management (2010)

5. Sweeney, L.: k-anonymity: a model for protecting privacy. Int. J. Uncertainty Fuzziness Knowl.-Based Syst. **10**(05), 557–570 (2002)
6. Machanavajjhala, A., Gehrke, J., Kifer, D., Venkitasubramaniam, M.: l-diversity: privacy beyond k-anonymity. In: Proceedings of the 22nd International Conference on Data Engineering (ICDE 2006), p. 24. IEEE (2006)
7. Li, N., Li, T., Venkatasubramanian, S.: t-closeness: privacy beyond k-anonymity and l-diversity. In: Proceedings of the 23rd International Conference on Data Engineering (ICDE 2007), pp. 106–115. IEEE (2007)
8. Dwork, C.: Differential privacy. In: Bugliesi, M., Preneel, B., Sassone, V., Wegener, I. (eds.) ICALP 2006. LNCS, vol. 4052, pp. 1–12. Springer, Heidelberg (2006). https://doi.org/10.1007/11787006_1
9. Article 29 Data Protection Working Party: Opinion 05/2014 on Anonymisation Techniques (2014)
10. Hsiao, H.C., Kim, T.H.J., Perrig, A., Yamada, A., Nelson, S.C., Gruteser, M., Meng, W.: LAP: lightweight anonymity and privacy. In: Security and Privacy, pp. 506–520. IEEE (2012)
11. Herrmann, D., Lindemann, J., Zimmer, E., Federrath, H.: Anonymity online for everyone: what is missing for zero-effort privacy on the internet? In: Camenisch, J., Kesdoğan, D. (eds.) iNetSec 2015. LNCS, vol. 9591, pp. 82–94. Springer, Cham (2016). https://doi.org/10.1007/978-3-319-39028-4_7
12. Bujlow, T., Carela-Español, V., Solé-Pareta, J., Barlet-Ros, P.: A survey on web tracking: mechanisms, implications, and defenses. Proc. IEEE (2017)
13. Hannak, A., Soeller, G., Lazer, D., Mislove, A., Wilson, C.: Measuring price discrimination and steering on e-commerce web sites. In: Proceedings of the 2014 Conference on Internet Measurement Conference, pp. 305–318. ACM (2014)
14. Schwartz, J.: Giving Web a Memory Cost Its Users Privacy. http://www.nytimes.com/2001/09/04/business/giving-web-a-memory-cost-its-users-privacy.html. Accessed 27 Nov 2017
15. Perry, M.: Disable TLS session resumption and session IDs. https://trac.torproject.org/projects/tor/ticket/4099. Accessed 27 Nov 2017
16. Kohno, T., Broido, A., Claffy, K.C.: Remote physical device fingerprinting. IEEE Trans. Dependable Secur. Comput. **2**(2), 93–108 (2005)
17. Edwards, J.: Apple has quietly started tracking iPhone users again, and it's tricky to opt out. http://www.businessinsider.com/ifa-apples-iphone-tracking-in-ios-6-2012-10. Accessed 27 Nov 2017
18. Mowery, K., Shacham, H.: Pixel perfect: fingerprinting canvas in HTML5. In: Proceedings of W2SP, pp. 1–12 (2012)
19. Goecks, J., Shavlik, J.: Automatically labeling web pages based on normal user actions. In: Proceedings of the IJCAI Workshop on Machine Learning for Information Filtering (1999)
20. Monrose, F., Rubin, A.: Authentication via keystroke dynamics. In: Proceedings of the 4th ACM Conference on Computer and Communications Security, pp. 48–56. ACM (1997)
21. Padmanabhan, B., Yang, Y.C.: Clickprints on the web: are there signatures in web browsing data? (2007)
22. Banerjee, S.P., Woodard, D.L.: Biometric authentication and identification using keystroke dynamics: a survey. J. Pattern Recogn. Res. **7**(1), 116–139 (2012)
23. Sy, E., Mueller, T., Marx, M., Herrmann, D.: AppPETs: a framework for privacy-preserving apps. In: SAC 2018 Symposium on Applied Computing, 9–13 April 2018, Pau, France (2018)

24. Ren, J., Rao, A., Lindorfer, M., Legout, A., Choffnes, D.: Recon: Revealing and controlling PII leaks in mobile network traffic. In: Proceedings of the 14th Annual International Conference on Mobile Systems, Applications, and Services, pp. 361–374. ACM (2016)
25. Herrmann, D., Banse, C., Federrath, H.: Behavior-based tracking: exploiting characteristic patterns in DNS traffic. Comput. Secur. **39**, 17–33 (2013)
26. The Tails Project: Tails. https://tails.boum.org. Accessed 27 Nov 2017
27. The Qubes OS Project: Qubes OS. https://www.qubes-os.org. Accessed 27 Nov 2017
28. Whonix developers: Whonix OS. https://www.whonix.org. Accessed 27 Nov 2017
29. Ahmad, D.M.: Subgraph OS. https://subgraph.com. Accessed 27 Nov 2017
30. AppArmor developers: AppArmor. http://wiki.apparmor.net. Accessed 27 Nov 2017
31. Xen developers: Xen Project. https://www.xenproject.org. Accessed 27 Nov 2017
32. Open Source Security Inc: Grsecurity. https://grsecurity.net. Accessed 27 Nov 2017
33. Appelbaum, J.: Description of Tor Stream Isolation. http://archives.seul.org/or/dev/Jul-2010/msg00021.html. Accessed 27 Nov 2017
34. Rivest, R.L., Shamir, A., Adleman, L.: A method for obtaining digital signatures and public-key cryptosystems. Commun. ACM **21**(2), 120–126 (1978)
35. Chaum, D.L.: Untraceable electronic mail, return addresses, and digital pseudonyms. Commun. ACM **24**(2), 84–90 (1981)
36. Pfitzmann, A., Pfitzmann, B., Waidner, M.: ISDN-mixes: untraceable communication with very small bandwidth overhead. In: Effelsberg, W., Meuer, H.W., Müller, G. (eds.) Kommunikation in verteilten Systemen. Informatik-Fachberichte, vol. 267, pp. 451–463. Springer, Heidelberg (1991). https://doi.org/10.1007/978-3-642-76462-2_32
37. Federrath, H., Jerichow, A., Pfitzmann, A.: MIXes in mobile communication systems: location management with privacy. In: Anderson, R. (ed.) IH 1996. LNCS, vol. 1174, pp. 121–135. Springer, Heidelberg (1996). https://doi.org/10.1007/3-540-61996-8_36
38. Kesdogan, D., Egner, J., Büschkes, R.: Stop-and-go-MIXes providing probabilistic anonymity in an open system. In: Aucsmith, D. (ed.) IH 1998. LNCS, vol. 1525, pp. 83–98. Springer, Heidelberg (1998). https://doi.org/10.1007/3-540-49380-8_7
39. Chaum, D.: Blind signatures for untraceable payments. In: Chaum, D., Rivest, R.L., Sherman, A.T. (eds.) Advances in Cryptology, pp. 199–203. Springer, Heidelberg (1983). https://doi.org/10.1007/978-1-4757-0602-4_18
40. Chaum, D.: Security without identification: transaction systems to make big brother obsolete. Commun. ACM **28**(10), 1030–1044 (1985)
41. Chaum, D.: The dining cryptographers problem: unconditional sender and recipient untraceability. J. Cryptol. **1**(1), 65–75 (1988)
42. Bürk, H., Pfitzmann, A.: Value exchange systems enabling security and unobservability. Comput. Secur. **9**(8), 715–721 (1990)
43. Cooper, D.A., Birman, K.P.: Preserving privacy in a network of mobile computers. In: Security and Privacy, pp. 26–38. IEEE (1995)
44. Goldschlag, D.M., Reed, M.G., Syverson, P.F.: Hiding routing information. In: Anderson, R. (ed.) IH 1996. LNCS, vol. 1174, pp. 137–150. Springer, Heidelberg (1996). https://doi.org/10.1007/3-540-61996-8_37
45. AN.ON: Anonymität.Online. https://anon.inf.tu-dresden.de. Accessed 27 Nov 2017
46. JonDos GmbH: JonDonym. https://www.anonym-surfen.de. Accessed 27 Nov 2017

47. JonDos GmbH: Status der Mixkaskaden. https://www.anonym-surfen.dc/status/. Accessed 27 Nov 2017
48. AN.ON-Next: Anonymität Online der nächsten Generation. https://www.anon-next.de. Accessed 27 Nov 2017
49. Dingledine, R., Mathewson, N., Syverson, P.: Tor: the second-generation onion router. Technical report, Naval Research Lab, Washington DC (2004)
50. Tor Project: Tor Metrics. https://metrics.torproject.org. Accessed 27 Nov 2017
51. Perry, M., Clark, E., Murdoch, S., Koppen, G.: The Design and Implementation of the Tor Browser (2017). https://www.torproject.org/projects/torbrowser/design/
52. Narten, T., Huston, G., Roberts, L.: IPv6 Address Assignment to End Sites. Technical Report 157, RFC Editor (2011)

Privacy in the Era of the Smart Revolution

Is It Harmful? Re-examining Privacy Concerns

Agnieszka Kitkowska[1]([✉]), Erik Wästlund[1], Joachim Meyer[2],
and Leonardo A. Martucci[1]

[1] Karlstad University, Karlstad, Sweden
agnieszka.kitkowska@kau.se
[2] Tel Aviv University, Tel Aviv, Israel

Abstract. The increased popularity of interconnected devices, which we
rely on when performing day-to-day activities expose people to various
privacy harms. This paper presents findings from the empirical investigation of privacy concerns. The study revealed that people, regardless
of their diversity, perceive privacy harms as generic and simplified models, not individually as suggested in Solove's framework. Additionally,
the results identified differences in privacy concerns related to information disclosure, protection behavior, and demographics. The findings may
benefit privacy and system designers, ensuring that policies and digital
systems match people's privacy expectations, decreasing risks and harms.

Keywords: Privacy · Human factors · Attitudes · Decision making

1 Introduction

The widespread Internet availability and access to various devices, from PCs,
through mobile to smart devices, enabled the establishment of an ecosystem of
interconnected applications. People adapt these technologies and feed them with
a large amount of data. Such applications assist people with performing most
of their daily activities, including socializing, healthcare, financial transactions,
work and more. People voluntarily, and sometimes unknowingly contribute data
to Internet-based applications, and that may expose them to privacy risks, violations, and harms.

Due to the increasing amount of security breaches, digital privacy became a
subject of public debate. The news about data leakages and their potential effects
frequently appear in media, informing the audience about the potential privacy
risks. Since privacy violations are in the center of interest, governments and
policymakers introduced legal guidelines and regulations aiming to protect personal data, such as the General Data Protection Regulation (GDPR) in Europe
[42] or FTC requirements in USA [49]. Simultaneously, the academic research
resulted in multiple studies about online privacy, demonstrating that people are

M. Hansen et al. (Eds.): Privacy and Identity 2017, IFIP AICT 526, pp. 59–75, 2018.
https://doi.org/10.1007/978-3-319-92925-5_5

concerned about their data, nevertheless, they trade them for potential benefits arising from applications [4,16,55]. Despite the efforts of researchers and policymakers, as well as increased privacy awareness raised in media, people's attitudes and behaviors remain unchanged. Regardless of their concerns, people provide personal information to online companies to use their services, ensure social interactions, improve well-being and more.

The aim of this study is to investigate privacy perceptions and to re-examine some of the privacy behaviors. The primary contribution of this research is a novel instrument to measure privacy attitudes, Privacy Harms Concerns (PHC) scale. Following the recommendation of the past research [28], we used *privacy harms* identified by Daniel Solove as a foundation for the scale's development [48] (Table 1). The goal of this research was to identify how people perceive privacy concerns relevant to harms (to ensure consistency labeled privacy concerns throughout the article). The results confirmed that people, in spite of their diversity, tend to have rather comprehensive and simplified view of privacy concerns, perceiving their severity and importance in a similar manner. Regardless of this general tendencies, we identified differences in privacy perceptions, information disclosure, and protection behaviors. Additionally, the findings demonstrate a potential for demographic differences in privacy concerns. Overall, the results contribute to further understanding of people's privacy attitudes and behaviors.

Table 1. Typology of privacy harms according to the Solove's framework.

Information collection	Information processing	Information dissemination	Invasions
Surveillance	Aggregation	Breach of confidentiality	Intrusion
Interrogation	Identification	Disclosure	Decisional interference
	Insecurity	Exposure	
	Secondary use	Increased accessibility	
	Exclusion	Blackmail	
		Appropriation	
		Distortion	

2   Related Work

2.1   Privacy Attitudes: Concerns and Harms

According to Westin, privacy concern is the intention to protect personal information from others [10]. Thus it carries a negative weight and should result in preventive or protective actions. As defined by Campbell, the information privacy concern is a subjective notation concentrated around the *input, use and control of data* [32]. Therefore, the information concern is related to the flow of data between the user and involved data processors. The online privacy research recognized various antecedents of privacy concerns such as trust, risk perception, previous privacy experience, privacy awareness, personality traits and demographic differences [8,21,26,31,46,52]. Some of this research investigated the influence of concerns on privacy behaviors but the results are inconsistent. Some studies show that despite concerns, people disclose information, however, it is a natural consequence of being a part of community [31]. On the other hand, there is a large volume of research illustrating, that regardless of privacy concerns, people tend to share their information, and their decisions are based on cost and benefit trade-off [2,18,44]. This so-called *privacy paradox* is frequently explained by factors such as information asymmetry [1,2,5] or psychological biases and heuristics [9,12,20,25,29].

To the best of our knowledge, privacy concerns have not been investigated from the perspective of privacy harms. Similarly to the notion of privacy itself, there is no clear definition of privacy harm. However, scholars from legislative sector tried to provide a coherent explanation of the term. For instance, Solove identified a privacy problem as a result of harm, claiming that harms do not have to be physical or emotional, they *can occur by chilling socially beneficial behavior (for example, free speech and association) or by leading to power imbalances that adversely affect social structure (for example, excessive executive power)* [50]. Similarly, Calo defines harm as a conceptualized negative consequence of privacy violation [11]. Nevertheless, the most comprehensive definition of privacy harms we found was provided by researchers investigating smart grids privacy, De & Métayer. They defined harm as *the negative impact on a data subject, or a group of data subjects, or the society as a whole, from the standpoint of physical, mental, or financial well-being or reputation, dignity, freedom, acceptance in society, self-actualization, domestic life, freedom of expression, or any fundamental right, resulting from one or more feared events* [15]. In this research, we follow this definition and consider harms as a multidimensional notion.

The previous research resulted in multiple scales measuring privacy concerns. Such measuring scales are constructed in various ways, for example by asking people directly about their concerns, treating concerns as latent variables or as moderators [38]. For instance, Smith et al. [47] developed Concerns for Information Privacy (CFIP) scale aiming to explore the concerns' structure. The study identified four dimensions of privacy concerns: improper access, unauthorized secondary use, error, and collection. Malhotra et al. developed Internet Users Information Privacy Concern (IUIPC) scale identifying three dimensions: collection, control, and awareness of privacy practices [32]. According to their research consumers perceive as the most important awareness and control over their data stored by online companies. The IUIPC scale can be applied to privacy research in various contexts. Regardless of the coherent nature of this scale, it seems to be an organization- and consumer-oriented, as authors put it, IUIPC is *representation of online consumers' concerns for information privacy*. Buchanan et al. developed another privacy concerns scale, measuring individual privacy issues, asking directly about concerns, for instance regarding personality theft, access to medical records etc. [10].

Considering the definitions of privacy harms and the past research, we want to improve understanding of attitudes and re-examine dimensionality of privacy concerns. Hence, the first research question:

RQ1   How do people perceive privacy harms concerns?
RQ1.1 What are the main dimensions of privacy concerns?
RQ1.2 Are some concerns perceived as more severe than others?

2.2 Privacy Behaviors

In order to cross-validate findings of privacy concerns, some research examined their relations with other attitudinal or behavioral factors, such as information disclosure or protection behavior.

According to the research, the information disclosure behavior varies, depending on psychological states [40], risk perceptions [14,56], trust and more. Several studies explored the relationship between privacy concerns and information disclosure. For example, research showed significant effects of privacy concerns on information disclosure, influenced by psychological biases, such as optimism bias, over-disclosure and others [29,39,52]. Similarly, the researchers found evidence of irrational behavior, when people tend to disclose data knowingly about the potential risks [17].

In this research, we will not examine factors influencing privacy concerns or the direction of the relationship between attitude and behavior. Instead, we focus on a variance of privacy concerns among people who disclose (or not) sensitive or non-sensitive information. Hence, our next research question:

RQ2   Is there a relationship between privacy concerns and privacy behavior?
RQ2.1 Do privacy concerns vary among people disclosing and not-disclosing non-sensitive information?
RQ2.2 Do privacy concerns vary among people disclosing and not-disclosing sensitive information?

The past privacy research identified control as an important factor influencing privacy behaviors [5,19]. To achieve control over online information disclosure people apply different protection measures. Some use technical protections, such as anti-malware or anti-virus software, add blockers, or other privacy enhancing technologies. Others may be more careful about their physical privacy (hiding PIN, shredding documentation), limit information provided to social networks (such as reduction of the posts' audience, limited profile visibilities etc.), decrease number of online profiles or even entirely resign from the online presence. The relationship between privacy concerns and protection is unclear. There is some research claiming, that such relationship exists, however, the correlations are low and people less concerned about privacy use more of protective measures [3,37]. Considering the past research demonstrating that the relationship between concerns and behavior exists, we ask following questions:

RQ2.3 Is there a relationship between people's privacy concerns and general privacy caution?
RQ2.4 Is there a relationship between people's privacy concerns and technical privacy protection?

2.3   Demographics

To assess individual differences in privacy concerns some of the researchers used demographics, such as geographic/cultural differences, age, education or gender [13,41]. However, the results of studies investigating demographic dependencies are inconclusive. For instance, there are studies claiming that gender impacts privacy perceptions and females are more concerned about their data than males. However, some of these findings show that the impact of gender on privacy attitudes and behaviors is indirect or insignificant [6,23,36]. Regarding the age, there seems to be a general tendency that older generations are more concerned about their privacy than the younger ones [34,51]. Nevertheless, it does not mean that younger people ignore it. In contrary, the research demonstrates that younger people use technical protection measures to better manage their privacy [33].

The previous research associated privacy concerns with geographic/cultural background [7,54]. The geographic divide was confirmed in the qualitative study of seven European countries, identifying main privacy concerns influencing information disclosure and a variety of privacy fears among different nationalities [34]. Similarly, other studies showed differences among respondents from North America and Europe [45], and France and Hong Kong [22]. Such differences were accredited to cultural dimensions, for instance, assertiveness or gender egalitarianism [41,53].

Considering the previous research's findings, we aim to examine whether there are any significant demographic differences in privacy concerns and behaviors among the participants of our study. Hence, our last research question:

RQ3 Do privacy concerns differ depending on the demographic background?

3   Method

The online survey was created to answer the research questions. It contained 80 questions, divided into thematic sections, such as participants' demographics, opinions related to data collection and processing, security, identity, and personal questions. To measure the responses, we used mixed design, including questions collecting responses on the scale ranging from 0 to 100 (strongly disagree/strongly agree; never/always) and multiple choice questions.

Before participating in the survey, respondents were presented with informed consent, explaining what type of information will be requested during the survey, what is the study purpose and who should be contacted in case of any questions. Each participant had to agree to the informed consent and confirm that he/she is over 18 years old.

3.1   Instrument

The online survey consisted of three major sections: the new scale to measure privacy concerns, and two scales acquired from the past research, measuring privacy behaviors. Due to the thematic division of the survey and to ensure the instrument's consistency, some of the questions from the PHC were mixed with questions from the scale measuring protection behavior.

To create the new scale, we applied the privacy harms framework defined by Solove [48]. We developed the 48 items scale derived from Solove's 16 privacy harms. Solove categorized 16 privacy harms into four groups, which are presented in Table 1. Solove's work addresses privacy harms from the legal perspective, however, in the past it was used in the information privacy research [27]. Additionally, we believe that privacy harms may be recognizable and meaningful, since the framework origins from court cases and real-life examples. Originally we aimed to measure each individual privacy harm, hence we used three items for each of them. The instrument collected continuous data, scores ranging from 0 to 100 (strongly disagree/strongly agree). After all data were collected, some of the items were modified, to ensure scores' consistency.

The scale measuring information disclosure was acquired from Joinson et al. [24]. It consisted of 11 items, asking respondents questions of personal nature. To ensure consistency, the information disclosure scale was modified and did not include two questions requiring respondents to type answers in the text boxes. The scale aimed to measure disclosure of sensitive and non-sensitive information. The sensitive items were measured by asking intimate questions, such as 'How many different sexual partners have you had?'. The non-sensitive items contained less invasive questions, for instance 'Are you right or left handed?'. The disclosure level was measured by providing respondents with option 'I prefer not to say', which if chosen was coded as 1 (don't disclose). All other responses were coded 0. In a result participants who do not disclose scored 5 per sensitive and 4 per non-sensitive items. All other participants were treated as disclose group. This resulted in division of respondents to two groups: disclosing sensitive information ($N = 273$) and non-disclosing sensitive information ($N = 109$), and disclosing non-sensitive ($N = 325$) and non-disclosing non-sensitive information ($N = 57$).

The second scale acquired from the previous research aimed to measure protection behavior [10]. It consisted of 12 items, 6 measuring a general privacy caution and 6 measuring technical protection [10]. To ensure consistency we modified the scale, and instead of Likert scale, we applied range scores. In a result, we collected continuous data with scores ranging from 0 to 100 (never/always).

3.2 Data Collection

The online survey was distributed on two platforms, Microworkers and CallForParticipants (CFP). Participation in the survey was voluntary. Microworkers' participants received financial compensation \$1–\$1.50 per response, while CFP respondents did not receive any compensation. The total number of participants reached 437 (375 from Microworkers, 62 from CallForParticipants), however, only 382 responses were valid. On Microworkers the response validity was checked automatically. Additionally, all responses were monitored manually, one by one. Furthermore, any surveys completed in less than five minutes or longer than four hours were removed. Participants had to respond to all questions and in a result, there was no missing data; the survey allowed respondents to backtrack and amend responses. Each respondent could participate in the survey only once.

Furthermore, to decrease the possibility of statistical bias, the data set was scanned for outliers. As recommended in the literature, instead of using a standard method for detecting extreme cases, such as the mean plus/minus two or three standard deviations [30], we applied $3x$ Inter-quartile Range. All responses that contained outliers were removed from the analysis, which left the sample of 382 responses.

To assess the desired demographics, we used a geographic cluster sampling, with cluster sizes aiming to reach 100 respondents each. Choice of geographic areas was based on the results from the Data Protection Eurobarometer [35]. We focused on four geographic areas: UK, USA, Italy and Nordic countries (Sweden, Norway, Finland, Denmark, and Germany). Among the respondents 57.9% ($N = 221$) were males and 42.1% ($N = 161$) females; the average age was 32 years ($Min = 18; Max = 70$). The full demographics beak-down is presented in Table 2.

Table 2. Participants demographics

Demographic	N	Percent
Country		
Italy	91	23.8
Nordic countries	76	19.9
UK	113	29.6
USA	102	26.7
Gender		
Male	221	57.9
Female	161	42.1
Education		
High school	70	18.3
Higher education	203	53.1
Still studying	109	28.5
Age		
18–24	98	25.7
25–34	153	40.1
35–44	76	19.9
Over 44	55	14.4
Total	382	

4 Results

4.1 Dimensions of Privacy Concerns

To assess the answer to the RQ1 we commenced with investigating its sub-question: *What are the dimensions of privacy concerns?* (RQ1.1). We created the PHC and used the Exploratory Factor Analysis (EFA) to assess dimensions of privacy concerns.

The EFA was used because it allows to ascertain factors that may explain correlations between variables, but it does not require underlying theoretical structure [43]. The Kaiser-Meyer-Olkin measure (.903) and Bartlett test for sphericity (significant at the level $p < .001$) confirmed EFA's suitability. We used orthogonal rotation, varimax presuming that the correlations between the variables are weak.

To extract factors, we used the principal axis factoring (PAF) allowing to measure the latent structure of variables and their relationships [43]. From the original 48 items 30 items remained, after removing factors with communalities $< .3$, item loadings $< .3$ and factors consisting of less than three loaded items.

After applying the solution and scree plot analysis, we extracted seven factors, identifying people's perceptions of privacy concerns: *unauthorized access, misuse of data, secondary use of data, insecurity, exposure, interrogation, distortion*. When computing the internal consistency for the scale based on the factors, the Cronbach alpha scores for the identified factors were all above .7 (Table 3).

Additionally we computed the means for each dimension of the privacy concerns as demonstrated in Table 4. We used the means in further analysis, to assess the relationship with behavior and investigate demographics.

Table 3. The results of Exploratory Factor Analysis; $N = 382$.

Extracted factors	Cronbach alpha
Factor 1: *unauthorized access to data*	.865
Factor 2: *misuse of data*	.836
Factor 3: *secondary use of data*	.811
Factor 4: *insecurity*	.736
Factor 5: *exposure*	.745
Factor 6: *interrogation*	.721
Factor 7: *distortion*	.735

4.2 Information Disclosure

To asses the differences in concern between respondents who disclose sensitive/non-sensitive items (RQ2.1 and RQ2.2) we performed the independent-sample t-Test. We checked the outcomes of Levene's test that were significant at level $< .05$, hence we report the results for equal variances not assumed.

Table 4. Means of the privacy concerns dimensions, $N = 382$.

Dimension	M	SD
Insecurity	90.02	10.4
Exposure	77.82	17.7
Unauthorized access	72.75	17.2
Secondary use of data	72.42	20.0
Misuse of data	71.23	16.1
Distortion	63.75	21.5
Interrogation	45.89	21.2

We found a significant difference among respondents that disclose (M = 70.5, SD = 20.6) and do not disclose (M = 77.1, SD = 17.5) sensitive information about the *secondary use of data*, $t(380) = -2.9, p = .002$; and *interrogation* (M = 42.9, SD = 21.4; M = 53.3, SD = 18.8 respectively), $t(380) = -4.4, p < .001$.

We identified the same type of concerns among participants disclosing non-sensitive information. The respondents who did not disclose information (M = 77.6, SD = 19) were significantly more concerned about the *secondary use of data* than those who disclose it (M = 71.5, SD = 20.1), $t(380) = -2.1, p = .029$; the same behavior was observed regarding *interrogation* (M = 52.9, SD = 21.9; M = 44.6, SD = 20.9 respectively), $t(380) = -2.7, p = .010$.

4.3   Protection Behavior

To determine the relationship between privacy concerns and protection behaviors (RQ2.3 and RQ2.4) we performed Pearson Correlation tests, and examined scatter plots for the correlated variables (Table 5).

Table 5. Correlations between privacy concerns and protection behaviors; $N = 382$.

	General caution	Technical protection
Unauthorized access	.318**	.290**
Misuse of data	.404**	.357**
Secondary use	.024	.184**
Insecurity	.201**	.346**
Interrogation	−.243**	−.027
Exposure	.215**	.233**
Distortion	.358**	.246**

** Correlation is significant at the .001 level (2-tailed)

We identified significant correlations between general caution and technical protection behavior, and privacy concerns, ranging between $r = .184$ and

$r = .404$ (Table 6). The results demonstrate positive correlations for general caution and concerns about *unauthorized access, misuse of data, insecurity, exposure* and *distortions*, and a negative correlation for *interrogation*. Similarly, positive correlations were found for technical protection behavior and *unauthorized access, misuse of data, secondary use of data, insecurity, exposure* and *distortions*. However, we did not identify a relationship between general caution and *secondary use*, as well as between technical protection and *interrogation*.

4.4 Demographics

We conducted One-Way Analysis of Variance (ANOVA), t-Tests and Chi-Square to analyze whether there are significant differences in privacy concerns among people from various demographics (RQ3).

First, we analyzed responses of participants from different geographic locations (Table 7). There were significant effects for *secondary use of data* $(F(3, 381) = 5.010; p = .002)$, *interrogation* $(F(3, 381) = 3.241; p = .022)$ and *distortion* $(F(3, 381) = 2.885; p = .036)$. The post-hoc Tukey test results confirmed significant differences $(p = .001)$ between Italy (M = 77.2; SD = 19.9) and the UK (M = 77.2; SD = 17.9) regarding the *secondary use of data*. Similarly, there was a significant difference $(p = .038)$ between Italy (M = 40.3; SD = 20.5) and the Nordic Countries (M = 49.8; SD = 19.7), and Italy and the UK (M = 48.3; SD = 20.7), $(p = .034)$ in concerns related to *interrogation*. Additionally, we found a significant difference $(p = .017)$ between the USA (M = 68.4; SD = 20.1) and Nordic Countries (M = 60.6; SD = 19.7), and the USA and Italy (M = 60.4; SD = 23.0) about *distortion* $(p = .010)$.

Table 6. Differences in privacy concerns among participants from different geographic areas; $N = 382$, $p < .05$ (One-Way ANOVA).

Source	SS	df	MS	F	P
Secondary use					
Between	5857.7	3	1952.5	5.0	.002
Within	147327.7	378	389.7		
Total	153185.4	381			
Interrogation					
Between	4311.6	3	1437.2	3.2	.022
Within	167642.2	378	443.4		
Total	171953.8	381			
Distortion					
Between	3974.4	3	1324.8	2.8	.036
Within	173576.6	378	459.1		
Total	177551.0	381			

We performed One-way ANOVA and the post-hoc Tukey test to asses whether there are potential differences in privacy concerns, protection behavior and information disclosure among participants from different age groups. For this purpose we divided our sample to four age groups: 18–24, 25–34, 35–44 and over 45 years old. We found a significant effect of age on concerns about the *unauthorized access* ($F(3, 378) = 4.860, p = .002$), *misuse of data* ($F(3, 378) = 3.094, p = .027$), *secondary use of data* ($F(3, 378) = 3.162, p = .013$), *insecurity* ($F(3, 378) = 4.710, p = .003$) and *exposure* ($F(3, 378) = 3.759, p = .011$). The participants belonging to 35–44 and 18–24 years old groups differed in perception about *unauthorized access* and *misuse of data*; *over* 45 and 18–24 differed in perceptions of *exposure*; over 45 differed from 18–24 and 25–34 years old in perception of *secondary use* of data. Lastly, participants belonging to 35–44 and *over* 45 years old differed from the 18–24 years old in concerns about *insecurity*. We did not find any significant differences among participants from different age groups in relation to protection behavior and information disclosure.

Lastly, we used the independent *t*-Test to see whether there are significant gender differences about privacy concerns, but we did not find any $p < .05$. Similarly, we did not identify any gender dependencies in regards to both general caution and technical protection. Furthermore, we used Chi-Square test to determine whether the sensitive and non-sensitive information disclosure differed among males and females, however, once again the results were insignificant.

5 Discussion

To improve understanding of privacy perceptions we investigated privacy harms by creating the new scale measuring privacy concerns (RQ1). As we wanted to achieve a greater understanding of people's attitudes, we used the legal framework as a basis for the study design. The results demonstrated, that privacy perceptions vary from those identified by Solove. However, there are some resemblances. While Solove proposed to consider harms at the individual level, the results showed that people express privacy concerns differently. They tend to perceive concerns as comprehensive and simplified models. Possibly, such perception is related to the cognitive information processing, intending to decrease the cognitive effort and use affect heuristics.

We identified seven dimensions of privacy concerns: *insecurity, exposure, unauthorized access, secondary use of data, misuse of data, distortion* and *interrogation*. The analysis of the means suggests that people express high concerns about *security*. They want to be informed about data security breaches and in general, they expect that online services will guarantee safety. According to the findings, people worry about *exposure*, which may suggest that they care about online presence and information visibility. They want to be in control of personal information, ensuring that none of it is used without their knowledge or permission. The findings show general worries about the *secondary use of data*, such as selling or sharing data with external organizations, and about *misuse of data*, such as blackmail or malicious use of information by strangers to reach their own goals. *Distortion* seems to be less important, and *interrogation* is perceived as the least severe. Considering *interrogation*, paradoxically, respondents expressing concerns about secondary use or misuse of information did not find the information probing important. Overall, the new dimensions show similarities to Solove's findings. The results show that almost all of the harms defined by Solove are subject to concern, however, not at the individual level and not accordingly with the process of information flow. Additionally, it seems that invasions are the one group of harms which is perceived as less severe than others.

The identified dimensions of privacy concerns relate to findings from the past research. For instance an improper access and secondary use of data, the two of four dimensions defined by CFIP [47]. Similarly, our findings relate to the factors identified by IUIPC: collection (*interrogation* and *insecurity*) and control (*exposure, distortion*) [32]. The seven dimensions of PHC add to the previous scales by identification of wider range of concerns. Our findings origin from participants with broad demographics, while CFIP was based on students and professionals from business environment, IUIPC was customer oriented. Furthermore, the PHC uncovers issues related to the *self* (me as a person and as a part of the society), such as *distortion* or *exposure*, showing that personal image, online reputation, fear of the damages, which could be caused by disclosed data are important factors causing privacy concerns.

Additionally, we investigated whether privacy perceptions differ among people who disclose sensitive and non-sensitive information (RQ2). The findings demonstrate that privacy concerns of participants who do not disclose both sensitive and non-sensitive information differ from those who disclose information. Respondents who do not disclose information expressed concerns about their data being sold to third parties and about providing feedback related their online activities. This result suggests that people concerned about their data ownership use preventive methods, such as non-disclosure, to ensure that none of their information, whether it has sensitive or non-sensitive nature, is provided to the online companies. Additionally, the results found that people's privacy concerns are the same among those who disclose/non-disclose sensitive and non-sensitive information. Presumably, if one worries about the privacy, he/she will behave in the same way regardless of information sensitivity.

Further, the study identified relationships between protection behaviors and privacy concerns (RQ2). Despite the low correlations between protection behaviors and privacy concerns, scatter-plots' analysis confirmed the relationships. Respondents with higher technical protection behavior seemed to have high concerns about the *unauthorized access, misuse* and *secondary use of data, insecurity, exposure* and *distortions*. The same applies to general caution, except there is no correlation with *secondary use of data*. Instead, the higher general caution, the higher *interrogation* concerns. Interestingly, our results did not find any correlation between technical protection and *interrogation*. This may suggest, that people using different technical protections may feel confident that data will not be sold or transferred to unknown organizations, because of users' preventive measures. On the other hand, it may be related to the fact, that people do not perceive *interrogation* as a very severe concern.

The demographic results indicate possible differences in privacy perceptions among respondents from different geographic locations, education and age groups (RQ3). We identified differences between respondents from different countries. This could imply the role of cultural diversity in shaping people's concerns. However, due to the small sample size, our findings are only an indication of possible cultural dependencies, which require further studies.

Considering other demographics, our results show that people from older generations express more concerns about privacy than the younger generations, confirming findings from the previous research [51]. The age divide may be explained by the fact that older people have more experience, awareness, and knowledge related to privacy violations. Also, the younger population may use internet as a tool for communications, to develop social relationships or as a source of leisure activities, while older people may use it to cope with day-to-day activities, such as work, financial transactions, information source. For that reason, older generation may add more value to their online information, and in a result express stronger privacy concerns. On the other hand, as demonstrated in the past research, the younger generation may express fewer concerns due to their protection behaviors.

Limitations. There is a number of limitations in this study. The method: self-reported survey, may decrease validity and reliability of the results. However, as the study was designed to reach international respondents within a short time, this method was the most effective. Similarly, the enlarged sample size could improve the results, especially the demographic assumptions. Furthermore, the research explored general privacy concerns and did not investigate whether they would change considering specific context, for instance, different technologies. The collected data did not allow to model causal relationships between concerns and behaviors. The investigation of causal relations could provide a better overview on the role of privacy concerns in the decision making.

6 Conclusion

This study contributes a new measurement instrument for privacy concerns. To differentiate it from the existing privacy scales, we aimed to shift the focus of privacy concerns to privacy harms, based on the framework developed by Solove. We demonstrated that identified privacy concerns vary among individuals, by analyzing self-reported behavior and demographics. The new instrument can be used in future studies assessing privacy attitudes.

Additionally, the results suggest that there are some general tendencies in privacy concerns. The findings show that people create simplified models of privacy harms, such as worries about security, unlawful use of data, disclosure or exposure. All of these concerns can be addressed by developers and designers to ensure privacy. Due to the similarities among people from different demographics, we can assume that there is a potential to build systems with 'privacy for all' or 'privacy with no borders'.

Future Work. Our privacy scale requires further validation in qualitative and quantitative studies. For instance, to improve the scale it is recommended to implement it in experiments of the actual privacy behavior, using the PHC as pre- and/or post-questionnaire. Our results will be fundamental to develop models for instruments influencing peoples' behavior, nudging people's privacy choices and improving their privacy risk awareness. Similarly, further studies of PHC could result in the set of guidelines for developers and designers of privacy enhancing technologies (PET). Such guidelines could enable easier assessment of people's privacy needs, improving usability of PETs and in a result increasing users' satisfaction.

Acknowledgment. This work has received funding from the European Unions Horizon 2020 research and innovation programme under the Marie Skłodowska-Curie grant agreement No 675730.

To obtain more information about the study or to gain access to the original questionnaire, please contact the corresponding author.

References

1. Acquisti, A., Brandimarte, L., Loewenstein, G.: Privacy and human behavior in the age of information. Science **347**(6221), 509–514 (2015)
2. Acquisti, A., Grossklags, J.: Privacy attitudes and privacy behavior. In: Economics of Information, Security, pp. 1–15 (2004)
3. Acquisti, A., Grossklags, J.: Privacy and rationality in individual decision making. challenges in privacy decision making. the survey. IEEE Secur. Priv. **3**(1), 26–33 (2005)
4. Acquisti, A., Taylor, C.: The Economics of privacy. J. Econ. Lit. **52**, 1–64 (2016)
5. Adjerid, I., Acquisti, A., Brandimarte, L., Loewenstein, G.: Sleights of privacy: framing, disclosures, and the limits of transparency. In: Symposium on Usable Privacy and Security (SOUPS), p. 17 (2013)
6. Sheehan, K.B.: An investigation of gender differences in on-line privacy concerns and resultant behaviors. J. Interact. Market. **13**(4), 24–38 (1999)
7. Bellman, S., Johnson, E.J., Kobrin, S.J., Lohse, G.L.: International differences in information privacy concerns: a global survey of consumers. Inf. Soc. **20**(5), 313–324 (2004)
8. Bergström, A.: Online privacy concerns: a broad approach to understanding the concerns of different groups for different uses. Comput. Hum. Behav. **53**, 419–426 (2015)
9. Brandimarte, L., Acquisti, A., Loewenstein, G.: Misplaced confidences: privacy and the control paradox. Soc. Psychol. Personal. Sci. **4**(3), 340–347 (2013)
10. Buchanan, T., Paine, C., Joinson, A.N., Reips, U.-D.: Development of measures of online privacy concern and protection for use on the internet. J. Assoc. Inf. Sci. Technol. **58**(2), 157–165 (2007)
11. Calo, R.: The boundaries of privacy harm. Indiana Law J. **86**(3), 1131 (2011)
12. Camp, L.J.: Mental models of privacy and security. IEEE Technol. Soc. Mag. **28**(3), 37–46 (2009)
13. Cho, H., Rivera-Sánchez, M., Lim, S.S.: A multinational study on online privacy: global concerns and local responses. New Media Soc. **11**(3), 395–416 (2009)

14. Coventry, L., Jeske, D., Briggs, P.: Perceptions and actions: combining privacy and risk perceptions to better understand user behaviour. In: Symposium on Usable Privacy and Security (SOUPS) (2014)
15. De, S.J., Le Métayer, D.: Privacy harm analysis: a case study on smart grids. In: Security and Privacy Workshops (SPW), pp. 58–65. IEEE (2016)
16. Dinev, T., Hart, P.: Internet privacy concerns and their antecedents - measurement validity and a regression model. Behav. Inf. Technol. **23**(6), 413–422 (2004)
17. Egelman, S.: "My profile is my password, verify me!": the privacy/convenience tradeoff of facebook connect. In: Proceedings of the SIGCHI Conference on Human Factors in Computing Systems, pp. 2369–2378. ACM (2013)
18. Fagan, M., Khan, M.M.H.: "Why do they do what they do?": a study of what motivates users to (not) follow computer security advice. In: Proceedings of the Symposium On Usable Privacy and Security (SOUPS) (2016)
19. Fogel, J., Nehmad, E.: Internet social network communities: risk taking, trust, and privacy concerns. Comput. Hum. Behav. **25**(1), 153–160 (2009)
20. Gambino, A., Kim, J., Sundar, S.S., Ge, J., Rosson, M.B.: User disbelief in privacy paradox: heuristics that determine disclosure. In: Proceedings of the 2016 CHI Conference Extended Abstracts on Human Factors in Computing Systems, pp. 2837–2843. ACM (2016)
21. Harbach, M., Hettig, M., Weber, S., Smith, M.: Using personal examples to improve risk communication for security & privacy decisions. In: Proceedings of the 32nd Annual ACM Conference on Human factors in Computing Systems, CHI 2014, pp. 2647–2656 (2014)
22. Ho, K.T., Li, C.: From privacy concern to uses of social network sites: a cultural comparison via user survey. In: Proceedings - 2011 IEEE International Conference on Privacy, Security, Risk and Trust and IEEE International Conference on Social Computing, PASSAT/SocialCom, pp. 457–464 (2011)
23. Hoy, M.G., Milne, G.R.: Gender differences in privacy-related measures for young adult facebook users. J. Interact. Advert. **10**(2), 28–45 (2010)
24. Joinson, A.N., Paine, C., Buchanan, T., Reips, U.D.: Measuring self-disclosure online: blurring and non-response to sensitive items in web-based surveys. Comput. Hum. Behav. **24**(5), 2158–2171 (2008)
25. Kehr, F., Wentzel, D., Kowatsch, T.: Privacy paradox revised: pre-existing attitudes, psychological ownership, and actual disclosure. In: IS Security and Privacy, pp. 1–12 (2014)
26. Kehr, F., Wentzel, D., Kowatsch, T., Fleisch, E.: Rethinking privacy decisions: pre-existing attitudes, pre-existing emotional states, and a situational privacy calculus. In: ECIS 2015 Completed Research Papers (2015)
27. Knijnenburg, B.P., Kobsa, A.: Making decisions about privacy: information disclosure in context-aware recommender systems. ACM Trans. Interact. Intell. Syst. **3**(23), 1–23 (2013)
28. Kokolakis, S.: Privacy attitudes and privacy behaviour: a review of current research on the privacy paradox phenomenon. Comput. Secur. **7**(2), 1–29 (2015)
29. Krasnova, H., Kolesnikova, E., Guenther, O.: "It won't happen to me!": self-disclosure in online social networks. In: AMCIS 2009 Proceedings, p. 343 (2009)
30. Leys, C., Ley, C., Klein, O., Bernard, P., Licata, L.: Detecting outliers: do not use standard deviation around the mean, use absolute deviation around the median. J. Exp. Soc. Psychol. **49**(4), 764–766 (2013)
31. Lutz, C., Strathoff, P.: Privacy concerns and online behavior - Not so paradoxical after all? Multinationale Unternehmen und Institutionen im Wandel Herausforderungen für Wirtschaft, Recht und Gesellschaft, pp. 81–99 (2013)

32. Malhotra, N.K., Kim, S.S., Agarwal, J.: Internet users' information privacy concerns (iuipc): The construct, the scale, and a causal model. Inf. Syst. Res. **15**(4), 336–355 (2004)
33. Marwick, A.E., Boyd, D.: Networked privacy: how teenagers negotiate context in social media. New Media Soc. **16**(7), 1051–1067 (2014)
34. Miltgen, C.L., Peyrat-guillard, D.: Cultural and generational influences on privacy concerns: a qualitative study in seven European countries. Eur. J. Inf. Syst. **23**(2), 103–125 (2014)
35. T. Opinion and Social. Special Eurobarometer 431 'Data Protection'. Technical report, European Union (2015)
36. Park, Y.J.: Do men and women differ in privacy? gendered privacy and (in)equality in the internet. Comput. Hum. Behav. **50**, 252–258 (2015)
37. Park, Y.J., Campbell, S.W., Kwak, N.: Affect, cognition and reward: predictors of privacy protection online. Comput. Hum. Behav. **28**(3), 1019–1027 (2012)
38. Preibusch, S.: Guide to measuring privacy concern: review of survey and observational instruments. Int. J. Hum. Comput. Stud. **71**(12), 1133–1143 (2013)
39. Preibusch, S., Krol, K., Beresford, A.R.: The privacy economics of voluntary over-disclosure in web forms. In: Böhme, R. (ed.) The Economics of Information Security and Privacy, pp. 183–209. Springer, Heidelberg (2013). https://doi.org/10.1007/978-3-642-39498-0_9
40. Raij, A., Ghosh, A., Kumar, S., Srivastava, M.: Privacy risks emerging from the adoption of innocuous wearable sensors in the mobile environment. In: Proceedings of the SIGCHI Conference on Human Factors in Computing Systems, pp. 11–20. ACM (2011)
41. Reed, P.J., Spiro, E.S., Butts, C.T.: "Thumbs up for privacy?": Differences in online self-disclosure behavior across national cultures. Social Science Research (2016)
42. G.D.P. Regulation: Regulation (eu) 2016/679 of the European parliament and of the council of 27 April 2016 on the protection of natural persons with regard to the processing of personal data and on the free movement of such data, and repealing directive 95/46. Off. J. Eur. Union (OJ) vol. 59, pp. 1–88 (2016)
43. Reio, T.G., Shuck, B.: Exploratory factor analysis: implications for theory, research, and practice. Adv. Dev. Hum. Res. **17**(1), 12–25 (2015)
44. Roback, D., Wakefield, R.L.: Privacy risk versus socialness in the decision to use mobile location-based applications. ACM SIGMIS Database **44**(2), 19 (2013)
45. Sheth, S., Kaiser, G., Maalej, W.: Us and them: a study of privacy requirements across North America, Asia, and Europe. In: Proceedings of the 36th International Conference on Software Engineering, pp. 859–870 (2014)
46. Slyke, C.V., Shim, J.T., Johnson, R., Jiang, J.: Concern for information privacy and online consumer purchasing. J. Assoc. Inf. Syst. **7**(6), 415–444 (2006)
47. Smith, H., Milberg, S., Burke, S.: Information privacy: measuring individuals' concerns about organizational practices. MIS Q. **20**(2), 167–196 (1996)
48. Solove, D.: A taxonomy of privacy. Univ. Pa. Law Rev. **154**(477), 477–560 (2006)
49. Solove, D., Hartzog, W.: The FTC and the new common law of privacy. Columbia Law Rev. **114**(3), 583–676 (2014)
50. Solove, D.J.: I've got nothing to hide and other misunderstandings of privacy. S.Diego Law Rev. **44**, 745 (2007)
51. Steijn, W.M., Schouten, A.P. Vedder, A.H.: Why concern regarding privacy differs: The influence of age and (non-) participation on facebook. Cyberpsychology: J. Psychosoc. Res. Cyberspace, **10**(1) (2016)
52. Stutzman, F., Capra, R., Thompson, J.: Factors mediating disclosure in social network sites. Comput. Hum. Behav. **27**(1), 590–598 (2011)

53. Sun, Y., Wang, N., Shen, X.L., Zhang, J.X.: Location information disclosure in location-based social network services: privacy calculus, benefit structure, and gender differences. Comput. Hum. Behav. **52**, 278–292 (2015)

54. Lim, S.S., Cho, H., Rivera-Sanchez, M.: A multinational study on online privacy: global concerns and local responses. New Media Soc. **11**(3), 395–416 (2009)

55. Taddicken, M.: The 'Privacy Paradox' in the social web: the impact of Privacy concerns, individual characteristics, and the perceived social relevance on different forms of self-disclosure. J. Comput.-Mediated Commun. **19**(2), 248–273 (2014)

56. Trepte, S., Dienlin, T., Reinecke, L.: Risky behaviors: How online experiences influence privacy behaviors. Von Der Gutenberg-Galaxis Zur Google-Galaxis, From the Gutenberg Galaxy to the Google Galaxy (2014)

Forget About Privacy … or Not?

Norberto Patrignani[1,2(✉)], Diane Whitehouse[3(✉)],
and Monica Gemo[4]

[1] Politecnico of Torino, Turin, Italy
norberto.patrignani@polito.it
[2] Uppsala University, Uppsala, Sweden
[3] The Castlegate Consultancy, Malton, UK
diane.whitehouse@thecastlegateconsultancy.com
[4] European Commission - Joint Research Centre (JRC), Ispra, Italy
monica.gemo@ec.europa.eu

Abstract. This book chapter reflects the content of one of the 2017 IFIP summer school's workshops. This workshop's focus was chiefly around whether one should forget about privacy as a basic human right. The workshop was co-led by members of the International Federation of Information Processing (IFIP)'s working group on social accountability and computing. The challenge was proffered that today's commercial push for free trade in people's data, supported by information technologies, requires counterbalancing efforts to be made from the public interest point of view. During the workshop, this preoccupation with the public interest was addressed through a number of different questions, which in turn inspired in-depth discussions. Each of the four questions/topics covered is handled here in a separate section of the book chapter. The four points are illustrated through images and illustrations that have often been drawn from works from the fields of art, education, ethics, film, literature, and philosophy.

Note: Many of these themes are among the core subjects of the conference entitled *This Changes Everything* [1], which is the thirteenth in a series of Human Choice and Computers (HCC) (HCC13) to be held in Poznan, Poland, on 19–21 September 2018, and run by IFIP.

Keywords: Cloud · Data · Education · IFIP · Onlife · People
Privacy · Protection

1 Introduction

"Forget about privacy" is a message that grew in popularity throughout the past two decades (for its origins, see [2], referring to the words of Sun Microsystems co-founder, Scott McNealy). This book chapter investigates in a broad way the changes that have taken place in the concept of privacy due to both societal and technological advances. These topics were raised in a workshop, held at the 2017 International Federation of Information Processing (IFIP) summer school, through the prism of disciplines such as ethics, philosophy, and education. The content of the workshop is described in sequence throughout this book chapter.

© IFIP International Federation for Information Processing 2018
Published by Springer International Publishing AG 2018. All Rights Reserved
M. Hansen et al. (Eds.): Privacy and Identity 2017, IFIP AICT 526, pp. 76–85, 2018.
https://doi.org/10.1007/978-3-319-92925-5_6

The goal of the workshop was to stimulate reflection and discussion among attendees by assessing a broad set of questions. Examples follow: Is privacy still a human right? What are the implications of data collection and the cloud for privacy? Has techno-determinism already conquered the younger generation's mindshare through its 'forget about privacy' mantra? What kinds of consequences will these different attitudes to privacy have on the design of information systems? What will become of the concept of privacy in the future, e.g., by 2030? What kinds of education will be needed in the future to inform children and young people particularly about notions of privacy and future technological developments? Thus, the focus of these questions was on the well-known debate around the possible obsolescence of the concept of privacy in a fully interconnected society obsessed with information-sharing.

Each of the four sections of the book chapter that follow is dedicated to a specific question or questions: the issues covered have been adapted and fine-tuned in response to the workshop attendees' comments and criticisms. The main points of the workshop are drawn together in a brief conclusion, together with some reflections that have emerged over the latest months since the workshop was held.

2 With the Growth in Data Collection, Is Privacy Still a Human Right?

Rapid technological advances are being made. The evolution in the design and use of information and communication technologies (ICT) is growing in speed. The amount of information stored, analysed, and visualised is a 'tsunami' of bits, handling data related to huge volumes of human beings. The typical 18+ year-old user in the United States of America (USA) spends more than three hours a day online, using a combination of mobile devices and apps [3]. The amount of data (which can be called the "digital universe") is doubling every two years; by 2020, it is estimated that it will have reached 44 Zettabytes (44 $\times$ 10^{21} bytes) [4]. This information deluge contains not only data produced by sensors, but also the digital traces left by human beings – the logs of their digital lives.

Human lives are becoming transparent: easy to see, perceive, or detect. In the most extreme scenario, somewhere every human gesture is logged and there is someone (or some authority or corporation) who may have access potentially to all of these movements or behaviours. Some authors described this new era – of an environment totally populated by information – as one characterised by the end of privacy [5, 6]. One of the most well-known philosophical explorers of this new kind of infosphere is Floridi [7, 8].

A somewhat 'poetic' view of the end of privacy was presented by director, Peter Weir, in the 1998 movie, *The Truman Show* [9]. Set at the end of the 20th century, the film highlights the imagined degree of intrusion possible into people's lives. In this film, a broadcasting television channel offers as regular viewing the whole of an unwitting person's life to audience of viewers; the cast of television actors colludes in hiding this lie from the show's protagonist.

A decade later, around 2009–2010, data was increasingly being perceived either purely as commerce or at least a trade of which to be wary [10, 11]. Information – once viewed as the source of knowledge and wisdom – was becoming a commodity to trade. As Peter Sondergaard famously said, *"information is the oil of the 21st century"* [10], when he echoed the earlier, somewhat more critical, speech of European Commission commissioner, Meglena Kuneva, in which she formulated the outlook that, *"Personal data is the new oil of the internet and the new currency of the digital world"* [11].

By 2010, corporations that are sometimes referred to as the Titans of the Web (among them, such well-known examples as Amazon, Apple, Facebook, Google, and Microsoft) were among the top ten companies in the world in terms of market value [12]: this economic positioning was due, in part, probably to the immense storage and processing capabilities of their data centres and capabilities to collect large data sets. They are among the few organisations on the planet with the capability of mining and distilling big data (the level of data: reserved to machines).

This collection/collation of data ('big data') enables the uncovering of interesting facts among the data bits that result from smart visualisations or images (available at the level of information). They result in a third level which is reserved for human beings only (the level of knowledge). This 'lift' or hierarchy (which provides the opportunity to move from level-to-level or stage-to-stage) has been much adopted in the world of information science and computing science since it was adapted from its origins in the work of poet and playwright, Eliot [13]. What is most conspicuous today is the increasing visual representation of the data or information involved, used in fields that range from research to commerce.

Vision and sound can be combined to be used in what are basically surveillance techniques, occasionally made more impressive by the fact that they are described as attempts to provide efficient or sophisticated services. The wording of the 2015 guidelines designed for the viewers of a smart television could be compared all too closely with an imaginary, fictional text published some 65 years earlier [14, 16]. Although they were later removed [14], Samsung TV privacy guidelines were originally reputed to state these instructions [15]: *"Please be aware that if your spoken words include personal or other sensitive information, that information will be among the data captured and transmitted to a third party through your use of voice recognition"*. A similar text in the first chapter of George Orwell's 1949-published novel, *Nineteen Eighty-Four* [16] reads: *"Any sound that Winston made, above the level of a very low whisper, would be picked up by it, moreover, so long as he remained within the field of vision which the metal plaque commanded, he could be seen as well as heard. There was of course no way of knowing whether you were being watched at any given moment"*. The similarities between these two sentences, written some sixty years apart, were shocking to both direct consumers and general commentators.

The risks underpinning these various privacy-related scenarios are that humans may shift steadily, as entities, from being organic, living beings to becoming sensors that simply produce data streams. These streams of data could be stored and analysed to sell goods and services: out of bits, human beings will produce merely therefore the visualisations of useful hints for future technological, scientific or commercial developments. This data could be intimately related to information stored in people's brains and bodies. Ultimately, therefore, while privacy has long been considered a human right [e.g., 17], it could appear that this perceived right is being worn down through leaps in available technologies, the attitudes of commercial companies and of designers, the variety of stances on privacy globally, and generational behaviours and attitudes.

3 With the Expansion of the Cloud, What Kinds of Systems Will Be Designed?

The technological infrastructure that enables the data collection ('big data') scenarios, described in the previous section of this chapter, is that of cloud computing. Users connect their mobile devices to information services where the data and the processing power are located in the cloud, an expression developed some 20 years ago [18]. The cloud provides a global infrastructure with a number of characteristics: It is a network based on broadband that has computing servers which act as shared platforms. It is typified by resource pooling and multi-tenancy, rapid scalability and elasticity, and – for billing purposes – uses either measured or metered services. It is available on-demand and is therefore 'self-service' in orientation [19].

Society is now entering the cloud computing era. Today, for many users – such as people who have started to use computing technology most recently or younger generations – it can seem absolutely natural to hold just a touchscreen in their hands: everything else, such as storage space and computing power, can be based 'in the cloud'.

In terms of computing architecture, there is a shift that can be termed 'back to the future' which can be envisioned as a repeat of an earlier era of centralised computing infrastructure. The term is adapted from the Californian 1985 adventure movie, in which a young protagonist travels backwards in time with consequences that will alter his family's future [20]. It is argued that people will lose the computing freedom of members of recent or past generations, a freedom available at the phase when personal computing was first introduced [19, 21]. Thus, there is a reaction to the phase of the autonomy of personal computers – when input, storage, processing, output and networking were all in the hands of the end-users – to the heteronomy of the cloud: this forms a leap back in time to the pre-personal computer era of 'dumb terminals' [19, 21] that possessed no processing capabilities. These two aspects of independence and self-control as opposed to external control can be directly contrasted with each other.

What impact will the revival of such a sequence of events have on society? What kind of relationship is there, in reality, between technology and society? According to Deborah Johnson [22], it is co-shaping that typifies the relationship between technology and society: *"The belief that technology develops independently from society is wrong; social factors steer engineers in certain directions and influence the design of technological devices and systems; on the other direction, technology shapes society, society and technology shape each other (co-shaping); adoption of a particular technology means adoption of a particular social order; systems are infused with social and moral values"*. Cloud computing can be viewed as simply one example of a socio-technical system that involves co-shaping.

With this vision of co-shaping, it would be wise to scrutinise other upcoming generations of technologies and ICT systems that will be designed by 2030, including robotics and artificial intelligence and their successors such as quantum computing. As a result of developments in the cloud and other future technologies, further questions will arise, such as: What kind of society will be shaped by these new directions in ICT? Are people losing the status of digital citizens so that they become simply digital consumers? Will human beings lose even the status of 'human' beings?

It is for these reasons, among others, that the workshop explored various ways and means of dealing with an obsessive onlife environment (see the next section of this chapter), the historic and developing notions of privacy in society, the kinds of educational developments that might help to alleviate the predominance of technology use as well as how to handle data privacy and data protection specifically.

4   Onlife, and What Can One Do to Get Back to Real Life?

By 2018, people are now entering an onlife age [23] which is typified by what has been called the *"persistent, visible, searchable, and spreadable nature of online social environments"* [24]: more and more aspects of people's existences are becoming digital and are reshaped through their increasingly relentless online interactions. Onlife real and virtual dimensions are becoming intertwined. Attention and focus has shifted from entities (such as organisations or machines and devices) to connections.

Compulsive applications ('apps') are deliberately designed that keep users tethered i.e., tied or restricted to their mobile devices and, as a result, they are constantly prompted to consume their own intellect, time, and attention while they generate floods of personal trails that feed various online business models [25]. Data has increasingly been monetised, and people are encouraged either not to give data-sharing any thought whatsoever or simply to think about the release of data as a transactional (commercial) procedure. Profound transformations are altering people's relationships with themselves, with others, and how they experience the world around them: older values are becoming obsolete.

As users instant-message, e-mail, text, and tweet, they develop new 'alone together' behaviours that show a reliance on, and preference for, technology rather than real social relationships, first documented in 2011 [26]. In 2015, in *Reclaiming Conversation*, scholar Sherry Turkle [27] reported on the electronic erosion of conversational attention at both work and home. At many face-to-face encounters or meetings, although people are physically in the same space, they cannot refrain from turning away from each other to their phones/online connections [28]. These common societal trends, in which technology overuse increasingly diminishes human relationships, was illustrated visually in 2014 in a highly symbolic way by street artist, Banksy [29]: called *Mobile Lovers*, the mural features a pair of lovers in the dark, checking busily their smartphones for new messages rather than kissing.

There is the potential that this predominance of the influence of technology over meaningful relationships and conversations will lead to an unlearning of human values and an impoverishment in human capacities like empathy, self-reflection, creativity, and productivity. Hence, Turkle [27] called for a re-taking of control in response to a disenchantment with technology. She suggested a series of first steps towards the self-regulation of one's personal onlife world, and a set of disengagement strategies so that people might learn to start and, most importantly, to close or end their digital interactions. Since 2013, the Center for Humane Technology – founded by early members of a number of high-tech firms – has focused on forms of humane technology design, ways of re-focusing attention, and tips to enhance a more self-controlled use of mobile phones [29, 30]. More and more people are attempting to escape from technology by looking towards completely different ways of living [31, 32]. Conversely, there are also currently shifts taking place towards the sharing of data for more publically altruistic purposes [33]. One interpretation of good ICT [34] might also be that it should include 'privacy for good' or good forms of privacy.

In addition to these suggestions, the next section of the chapter explores other concrete interventions that have a more direct linkage to the notion of data privacy and data protection, particularly in the fields of education and training.

5 Privacy Past, Present, and Future: What Are the Educational Trends?

Part of this workshop looked at privacy past, present, and future. The attendees explored past meanings of the term 'privacy', what changing views of privacy mean in current terms with regard to the development and implementation of the General Data Protection Regulation [35], and where privacy may head in the future – particularly in terms of either the trading of data and/or consideration of the use of data to assist with commitments to the public good e.g., in relation to health or well-being or sustainability [33].

When exploring the meanings of the term privacy, there are many different views of the same term, developed over more than a century and a half, that can be identified. Contributors to an event like this summer school are among the most eminent and informed of researchers and practitioners in the privacy field and are at the leading edge of developments in this domain. Therefore, in this case, simply five of the most well-known perspectives on privacy, past and present, were cited. They ranged from the historical *"right to be let alone"* [36], which dates back to 1890, to the *"right to control the use that others make of information about myself"* [37]", to the more recent *"protection of life choices against any form of public control and social stigma"* [38] to the noteworthy definition Stefano Rodotà, of the *"right to do NOT know, right to keep control of our information and determine the modality of construction of our private sphere"* in which the lawyer proclaimed the shift from the legal term of *habeas corpus* to *habeas data* [39]. This right is indeed available in several countries around the globe, including a number in Latin America. Probably the most concise statement about privacy is associated with the utterance attributed to Hollywood actor, Greta Garbo (1905–1990): *"I never said 'I want to be alone!' I only said, 'I want to be let alone.'"* [40].

Ultimately, in the workshop, the date of 2030 was selected as a specific point in time, for reflection, in order to cover both millennials who originated in the early 1980s (who will be aged around 50 years old at that point) and those born in the early years of the 21st century (who will by then be adults shifting from one stage of maturity in their lives to another). However, the workshop attendees did not have the time or opportunity to explore this futures-related thinking in detail. Instead, the focus was more on the current present and on May 2018.

In 2018, the General Data Protection Regulation will come into force during the month of May [34]: this new over-arching regulation has tremendous importance for the meaning of data protection and data privacy. As the introduction to this book (see:

'The Smart World Revolution') points out, there can be fundamental contradictions between the pressures (even if simply implied or perceived) to share all forms of personal data, and the individual rights of citizens to privacy and security.

While the introduction of regulations is crucial, the need for education and training about what such legislation means for ordinary human beings of all ages, but especially for young and ever younger children, is equally important. Teachers have themselves been highly critical of the lack of thinking and planning they are giving to privacy and security while they are introducing children to digital technologies and managing school resources. Some current data privacy, data protection, and cybersecurity education initiatives have been focused on coping and/or resilience narratives that attempt to counter threats rather than offer mechanisms for positive self or community empowerment [41]. Hence, there is an urgent requirement for data protection governance in educational settings combined with robust teacher training. Teaching aids in cybersecurity, online safety, data protection awareness, data literacy and skills development should be brought to the attention of teachers, educators and parents as 'ready-for-use' resources.

This is nevertheless a favourable time-period, in the sense that there are a number of positive actions taken in recent years to fill digital skill gaps, especially in the fields of data protection and data privacy. There are several materials that it is worthwhile citing. One is a handbook published by researchers from the Vrije Universiteit Brussel [42]. it is a compilation of work undertaken by three eastern European data protection authorities that identifies leading examples of schools-based education about data privacy and data protection. Another has a more international perspective: it is a training framework on data protection intended for young people at school [43]. Designed for educators by a wider set of data protection authorities, it outlines nine basic principles, each of which is enhanced by a description of the competences needed in this field. A third example, for children and adults interacting together, Happy Onlife is a quiz or game that can be used to construct Internet safety and security [44]. More generically, research sponsored by the European Commission's Joint Research Centre, focusing on research and skills for the digital era, has led to the production of a fundamental set of needed digital competences [45]. Five competence areas are supported by eight levels of proficiency that can be taught and assessed – these are often more pertinent to adults than children, however. Examples of how these proficiencies can be observed and used in both employment and education settings are described. Of most interest in the context of this summer school is likely to be the field of safety, which is taken in this booklet [45] to relate also to privacy and security.

As a result of contemporary developments, an opportunity arises to ride on the back of the need for awareness of data privacy, data protection, and cybersecurity, to shift to other awareness-raising approaches. In the education field, training about data protection and data privacy could be bundled together with education about digital competences more generally. As legislation, regulation, and technologies change, such materials need to be designed for both child and adult populations; materials need to be refined and upgraded continuously; they need to be valid for international contexts as well as European settings; and they need to be relevant to a range of technologies and not be limited simply e.g., to the use of mobile phones.

6 A Discussion that Leads Towards a Conclusion

It is feasible to merge both the opinions expressed at the end of this summer school workshop and those of the authors themselves.

As often in times past, a growth in emerging technologies poses ethical and societal challenges that may be old as well as new or revived or revised. Among technological developments are those related in particular to big data and cloud computing. Today, the use of technology is becoming ultra-pervasive: technologies have entered many different aspects of the lives of human beings, to the extent that they are encroaching on spheres of great intimacy. They are no longer present solely in places of isolation such as outer space or theatres of war, but in people's places of employment, communities and residences and increasingly near to their bodies, brains, and minds.

Society as well as technology changes. As the series of IFIP summer schools shows, over the past decade and more, the notion of data privacy has also been changing and developing. Many aspects of privacy are being modified: through the attitudes of commercial companies and designers; resulting policies and legislation; and generational and inter-generational behaviours and attitudes. These challenges are paralleled by the posing of many challenging and provocative questions about the past, present, and the future.

Taking a view that merges both the social and the technical, through processes like co-shaping, encourages people to group together to consider, on the one hand, what kinds of technologies they wish to see designed and advanced and, on the other hand, to determine not only what kinds of data privacy they desire for themselves, but also what forms of data they wish to share with others (including commercial companies and services) and how this data-sharing can be used to help wider communities of people. These discussions form part of wider questioning and debates about social responsibility and societal accountability. They enable also a re-thinking of educational and training needs. Both sets of challenges, and suggestions of solutions to them, formed part of this summer school workshop's discussions.

Opportunities like the introduction of the General Data Protection Regulation [35] can act as enablers for opportunities to re-explore certain approaches to education and training. Ultimately, events such as this summer school can benefit from increasing coverage of the educational and training needs required to prepare people at large, and young people in particular, for new ways of handling data protection and data privacy. Options can be taken up that encourage practical application and assessment of these challenges.

Considering developments that have taken place since the summer school itself was held, it is unlikely – given contemporary socio-political circumstances – that people at large will forget about data privacy and data protection. They are much more likely to desire to reinforce their own individual competences in this field, but also demand that organisations and institutions take greater responsibility for their use of data and actions pertaining to data-sharing too. People may begin to consider not only what can they themselves gain or obtain from data-sharing, but also what they can do to benefit themselves, their families, communities, and societies e.g., by way of 'data donoring'. It may ultimately be that a much more international perspective is taken on these challenges than a purely European approach.

References

1. Human Choice and Computers Conference (HCC13). http://hcc13.net/. Accessed 02 Jan 2018
2. Springer, P.: Sun on Privacy: 'Get Over It', Wired, 16 January 1999 (1999)
3. Average Time Spent per Day with Mobile Internet. www.emarketer.com. Accessed 02 Jan 2018
4. The Digital Universe of Opportunities, IDC (2014)
5. Enserink, M., Chin, G.: The End of Privacy. Science 347(6221), 490–491 (2015)
6. Whitaker, R.: The End of Privacy. New Press Publishing, New York (1999)
7. Floridi, L.: Philosophy and Computing: An Introduction. Routledge, Abingdon (1999)
8. Floridi, L.: The Fourth Revolution: How the Infosphere is Reshaping Human Reality. Oxford University Press, Oxford (2014)
9. The Truman Show, British Board of Film Classification. http://www.bbfc.co.uk/releases/truman-show-1970-5. Accessed 02 Jan 2018
10. Sondergaard, P.: Gartner Symposium/ITxpo, 16–20 October 2011, Orlando, USA. https://www.gartner.com/newsroom/id/1824919. Accessed 02 Jan 2018
11. Kuneva, M.: Keynote Speech. Roundtable on Online Data Collection, Targeting and Profiling, 31st March 2009, Brussels, Belgium. http://europa.eu/rapid/press-release_SPEECH-09-156_en.htm. Accessed 02 Jan 2018
12. The World's Biggest Public Companies. https://www.forbes.com/global2000/list/. Accessed 02 Jan 2018
13. Eliot, T.S.: Collected Poems 1909–1962. London (2002)
14. Samsung SmartTV Privacy Policy. http://www.samsung.com/sg/info/privacy/smarttv/. Accessed 02 Jan 2018
15. BBC TV, Not in front of the telly: Warning over 'listening' TV, 9 February 2015. http://www.bbc.co.uk/news/technology-31296188. Accessed 02 Jan 2018
16. Orwell, G.: Nineteen Eighty-Four. Harvill Secker, London (1949)
17. United Nations, United Nations Declaration of Human Rights (1948). http://www.un.org/en/universal-declaration-human-rights/. Accessed 02 Jan 2018
18. Regalado, A.: Who coined 'cloud computing'. MIT Technol. Rev. (2011). https://www.technologyreview.com/s/425970/who-coined-cloud-computing/. Accessed 02 Jan 2018
19. Patrignani, N., Whitehouse, D.: Slow Tech and ICT – A Responsible, Sustainable and Ethical Approach. Palgrave Macmillan, Basingstoke (2018)
20. Back to the Future. http://www.backtothefuture.com. Accessed 02 Jan 2018
21. Patrignani, N., Kavathatzopoulos, I.: The brave new world of socio-technical systems: cloud computing. In: Bynum, T.W., Fleischman, W., Gerdes, A., Nielsen, G.M., Rogerson, S. (eds.) The Possibilities of Ethical ICT. Proceedings of ETHICOMP 2013 - International Conference on the Social and Ethical Impacts of Information and Communication Technology, Print & Sign University of Southern Denmark (2013)
22. Johnson, D.: Computer Ethics. Prentice Hall, Upper Saddle River (2009)
23. Floridi, L. (ed.): The Onlife Manifesto: Being Human in a Hyperconnected Era. Springer, Heidelberg (2015). https://doi.org/10.1007/978-3-319-04093-6
24. Youth Tech Health (Youth-centred Health Design): Teen Privacy & Safety Online: Knowledge, Attitudes, and Practices. http://yth.org/research/teen-privacy-safety-online-knowledge-attitudes-practices/. Accessed 02 Jan 2018
25. Solon, O.: Ex-Facebook president Sean Parker: site made to exploit human 'vulnerability', 9 November 2017. https://www.theguardian.com/technology/2017/nov/09/facebook-sean-parker-vulnerability-brain-psychology. Accessed 02 Jan 2018

26. Turkle, S.: Alone Together: Why We Expect More from Technology and Less from Each Other. Basic Books, New York (2011)
27. Turkle, S.: Reclaiming Conversation: The Power of Talk in a Digital Age. Penguin Press, London (2015)
28. Bradley, G.: The Good ICT Society: From Theory to Actions. Routledge, Abingdon (2017)
29. Barnes, S.: Banksy's New Mural Mocks Smart Phone Distracted Lovers, 15 April 2014. http://mymodernmet.com/banksy-mobile-lovers-street-art/. Accessed 02 Jan 2018
30. Center for Humane Technology. www.humanetech.com. Accessed 02 Jan 2018
31. Lapowsky, I.: Ethical Tech will Require a Grassroots Revolution, Wired, 8 February 2018. https://www.wired.com/story/center-for-humane-technology-tech-addiction/. Accessed 07 Apr 2018
32. Hendricks, J.: Be a Little Analog. Thiele Verlag, München (2016)
33. Laszlo, M.: Own it. Personal data trading as an alternative model. In: George, C., Whitehouse, D., Goodman, K., Duquenoy, P. (eds.) Developments in ICT & Healthcare: Legal, Ethical & Social Aspects, pp. 15–16. Middlesex University, 8/9 March 2018 (2018)
34. Patrignani, N., Whitehouse, D.: Slow Tech and ICT – A Responsible, Sustainable and Ethical Approach. Palgrave Macmillan, Basingstoke (2018)
35. Regulation (EU) 2016/679 of the European Parliament and of the Council of 27 April 2016 on the protection of natural persons with regard to the processing of personal data and on the free movement of such data, and repealing Directive 95/46/EC (General Data Protection Regulation). https://eur-lex.europa.eu/legalcontent/EN/TXT/PDF/?uri=CELEX:32016R0679&from=EN. Accessed 02 Jan 2018
36. Warren, S.D., Brandeis, L.D.: The right to privacy. Harvard Law Rev. **4**(5) (1890)
37. Westin, A.: Privacy and Freedom. Atheneum (1967)
38. Friedmann, L.M.: The Republic of Choice. Law Authority, and Culture. Harvard University Press, Cambridge (1990)
39. Rodotà, S.: Tecnologie e Diritti. Il Mulino (1995)
40. Bainbridge, J.: Garbo (1955). Holt, Rinehart and Winston (1971)
41. Smahel, D., Wright, M.F.: The meaning of online problematic situations for children: results of qualitative cross-cultural investigation in nine European countries. EU Kids Online. London School of Economics and Political Science (2014)
42. González Fuster, G., Kloza, D. (eds.): The European Handbook for Teaching Privacy and Data Protection, 28 July 2016. EAP (2016)
43. International Working Group on Digital Education. Personal Data Protection Competency Framework for School Students Intended to help Educators. International Conference of Privacy and Data Protection Commissioners, Personal Data Protection Competency Framework for School Students by International Conference of Privacy and Data Protection Commissioners, October 2016 (2016)
44. Happy Onlife. https://ec.europa.eu/jrc/en/scientific-tool/happy-onlife-game-raise-awareness-internet-risks-and-opportunities. Accessed 02 Jan 2018
45. Carretero, S., Vuorikari, R., Punie, Y.: The Digital Competence Framework for Citizens with Eight Proficiency Skills and Levels of Use. DigComp2.1, Luxembourg (2017). http://publications.jrc.ec.europa.eu/repository/bitstream/JRC106281/web-digcomp2.1pdf_(online).pdf. Accessed 02 Jan 2018

From Privacy to Algorithms' Fairness

Chiara Sabelli[1] and Mariachiara Tallacchini[2(✉)]

[1] Milan, Italy
chiara.sabelli@gmail.it
[2] Facoltà di Economia e Giurisprudenza, Università Cattolica S.C.,
Via Emilia Parmense 84, 29100 Piacenza, Italy
mariachiara.tallacchini@unicatt.it

Abstract. This article aims to show how the legal and ethical debate – as far as ethics has become an indispensable complementary normative tool within legal frameworks – on the digital world in the United States (US) and the European Union (EU) has significantly opened up to include new dimensions other than privacy, particularly in connection with machine learning algorithms and Big Data. If privacy still remains the main interpretive construct to normatively forge the digital space, increasingly issues of discrimination, equal opportunity, fairness and, more broadly, models of justice, are entering the picture. While offering some examples of the inadequacy of privacy to cover new normative concerns related to Big Data and machine learning, the article also argues that attempts to grant algorithmic fairness represent just the first step in addressing the wider question about what models of digital justice we are willing to apply.

Keywords: Privacy · Law · Ethics · Fairness · Equal opportunities
Models of justice

1 Introduction

The soft and hard normative framework built around the concept of privacy and data protection has been critical in regulating ICT and the Internet development. The right to privacy has been early identified as having a unique potential to represent and solve the new challenges coming from information technologies. Indeed, it has been depicted not only as the major area of concern surrounding the digital world, but also as an incredibly fruitful notion in the attempt to capture and protect several aspects of human life. Due to its flexibility in making sense of a variety of human expressions, privacy has been envisioned as capable, and then charged with the role, of encompassing and responding to most issues related to the information society [25,43].

Moreover, the attempt to shape and convey the majority of ICT ethical and legal implications through privacy and data protection has appeared (and appealed) as an effective strategy to simplify and normalize normative issues.

M. Hansen et al. (Eds.): Privacy and Identity 2017, IFIP AICT 526, pp. 86–110, 2018.
https://doi.org/10.1007/978-3-319-92925-5_7

For a long time this strategy has been successful. Only in the last decade, at first with the problems created by the Internet of Things (IoT) and then even more with the fast rise and ubiquitous presence of Big Data, the normative landscape has appeared more complex, and new normative issues irreducible to privacy and data protection have started attracting attention.

This has been true especially in the US, where issues of equality, equal opportunity and, more generally, fairness of algorithms have become a major concern. In the EU context, also in conjunction with the broad effort to create an all-encompassing regulatory environment through the GDPR (Regulation (EU) 2016/679), until recently algorithms' fairness has emerged in very few documents.

In the current debate the US (soft law) principle of 'equal opportunity by-design' is pairing with the EU (hard law) principle of 'privacy by-design' as a new main regulatory focus for Big Data and machine learning. While privacy relates to individuals, fairness has both an individual and a collective, social dimension: namely it creates the space for a broad discussion on social choices and change.

This article aims to show how, in the United States (US) and in the European Union (EU), the legal and ethical debate – as far as ethics has become an indispensable complementary normative tool within legal frameworks – after having unified all issues under the umbrella of privacy, has significantly opened up to include new dimensions, particularly in connection with machine learning algorithms and Big Data.

If privacy still remains the main interpretive construct to normatively forge the digital space – especially in the EU –, increasingly, issues of discrimination, equal opportunity, and fairness are calling for a normative response. Some examples are offered of the inadequacy of privacy to cover situations triggered by new digital developments.

While the EU idea of fair processing of data is not entirely adequate to address algorithms' fairness, and the US concept of fairness - though providing a better account of the problems involved– is mostly based on soft law measures, an important effort is devoted to designing algorithms more responsive to fairness. The article ends with the suggestion that algorithmic fairness should be coupled with democratic awareness and discussion of models of digital justice as the fundamental value towards change.

The article is structured as follows. Section 2 provides an overview of the historical evolutions of privacy legislation in the US and the EU. Section 3 shows how the notion of privacy as autonomy has become increasingly relevant when dealing with digital data and communications. In Sect. 4 we illustrate the crucial role of algorithms designed to analysing digital data and how they raise issues related to discrimination and equality of opportunity. In Sects. 5 and 6 we look at how the US and the EU have taken into account the concept of fairness in regulating personal data processing. Finally, in Sect. 7 we argue that, in order to design fair algorithms, more institutional, expert and public debate about a shared model of justice is needed.

2   Legal 'Privacies' in the US and the EU

Privacy should be properly referred to in the plural form of 'privacies'. Indeed, it has been widely recognized that privacy meanings and contents are multifaceted and filled with semantic ambiguities and developments - that have also led to the splitting of what relates to private individual life, family and correspondence, from what concerns private or sensitive data. Widely diverging meanings concern what is felt as private at individual and collective level as well as what refers to individual and collective identities, ethical systems, and cultures [23].

In building the concepts of privacy in relation with their structures and ways of functioning, legal rules have actually increased the variety of 'privacies', as heterogeneous notions characterize different legal systems. While it is already difficult to generalize in mentioning a single European idea of privacy and while past and current debates on what is privacy and how to protect it in the US are still broadly open, the prism of the legal framework surrounding privacy and data protection allows to capture at least some relevant discrepancies. What follows is a very brief summary of some major differences between the European and US notions of privacy and their current interactions[1].

As known, privacy has been framed as a right in the US in connection with technological development in terms of being let alone [52], namely primarily as a right to autonomy[2]. After a few US Supreme Courts landmark decisions establishing limits and criteria for public authorities to enter the private sphere[3], at the beginning of the 1970s ICT, and later the Internet, shed new light on privacy [16]. Data, and especially personal data, has rapidly become not only a separate, new reality, but also a commodified entity connecting different aspects of social life (from consumption to credit to health). Even more, in the construction of the information society, data has emerged as a new transversal language through different disciplines and technologies, from the life sciences to the sciences of the artificial [6]. These changes have triggered the enactment of some soft law principles, together with some case-by-case binding legislation in sectors where consumers/users' rights appeared more vulnerable[4].

---

[1] As the shift from the Safe Harbor to the Privacy Shield shows.

[2] Warren and Brandeis 1890, 194: "Recent inventions and business methods call attention to the next step which must be taken for the protection of the person, and for securing to the individual what Judge Cooley calls the right 'to be let alone'.".

[3] Such as, e.g., Olmstead v. United States 277 U.S. 438 (1928) and Katz v. United States 389 U.S. 347 (1967).

[4] These laws include: Fair Credit Reporting Act, 15 U.S.C. 1681 et seq.; Privacy Act of 1974, 5 U.S.C. 552a, as amended; Family Educational Rights and Privacy Act of 1974, 20 U.S.C. 1232g; Electronic Communications Privacy Act of 1986, 18 U.S.C. 2510-22; Video Privacy Act of 1988, 18 U.S.C. 2710; Children's Online Privacy Protection Act of 1998, 15 U.S.C. 6501-6506; Gramm-Leach-Bliley Act of 1999, the Financial Services Modernization Act (Public Law 106-102, 106th Congress); the Genetic Information Nondiscrimination Act of 2008 (Public Law 110-233, 122 Stat. 881).

The first main policy document on privacy, proposed by the Federal Trade Commission [28] – which content was later endorsed by the OECD [39] – enounced five essential components for privacy protection: consumers should be given notice of an entity's information practices before any personal information is collected from them; consumers should express their choice through consent; they should be able to access information concerning them and to contest data accuracy and completeness; data should be accurate and secure; privacy protection can only be effective if an enforcing mechanism is in place. These principles, known as the Fair Information Practice Principles (FIPPs) became the basis for the Privacy Act of 1974 and widely inspired several legislations.

Though not a constitutional right, privacy has been constitutionally rooted primarily in Amendment 4 of the US Constitution, stating "the right of the people to be secure in their persons, houses, papers, and effects, against unreasonable searches;" and also, as to the procedural aspects, in Amendment 14, according to which States will not "deprive any person of life, liberty, or property, without due process of law; nor deny to any person within its jurisdiction the equal protection of the laws."

Notwithstanding these constitutional foundations, a lot of room has been left for self-regulatory measures, voluntary adopted by corporations in their privacy policies; and a widely shared feeling, both within institutions and scholarly literature, surrounds the idea that privacy – which still remains the prevailing way to refer to both privacy and data protection – should not be pervasively regulated. While some documents suggest that "regulatory parsimony" should remain the rule, namely "only as much oversight as is truly necessary to ensure justice, fairness, security, and safety while pursing the public good" [43, p. 25]; various new approaches to privacy point at new solutions. Some recommend that data, at least in research, should be regulated under property and autonomy models of privacy [36,46]. Other approaches, concerned about preserving private life together with public goods, call for more empowerment and control for users in order to promote altruism and to leverage "inequity aversion, reciprocity, and normativity to lessen exploitation among group members", in [26, p. 396] and [47]. Others warn about a new "tragedy of the commons," but there is no shared view about which commons are at stake. Some authors think of the tragedy of the social "trust commons", diminished by corporate misbehaviors and requiring new business models [31]; others see it as the data commons, threatened by people removing their data (especially in research) -as they do not believe in anonymization and ignore that "the collective benefits derived from the data commons will rapidly degenerate if data subjects opt out to protect themselves" [54, p. 4]. In many ways the current US debate on privacy reflects the fluctuations between an individualistic culture and the increasing tendency towards forms of solidarity, sharing, and even a new philanthropic anthropology [4, pp. 2–3][5].

Compared to the US context, the European Union regulatory landscape has been much more dependent on formal legislation and on the strong foundation of privacy as a fundamental right. In the immediate aftermath of World War II – and in the light of Hannah Arendt philosophical reflections on privacy as the main tenet for allowing individuals to emerge as unique persons in the world [2] – the Council of Europe (CoE) Convention on Human Rights (1950) has established privacy as everyone's right "to respect for his private and family life, his home and his correspondence" (Article 8). This right was split into two separate dimensions related to the person and their personal data in the Charter of Fundamental Rights of the European Union at Articles 7 and 8. While Article 7 recalls the respect for private and family life, home and communications; Article 8 establishes the protection of personal data as fundamental, and introduces the criteria of fair processing for specified purposes, consent of the person or some other legitimate basis laid down by law.

The CoE Convention of 1981 on the Automatic Processing of Personal Data[6] – currently under amendment[7] – and Directive 1995/46/EC[8], together with other directives, have provided harmonized legislation on data protection in a constantly changing sociotechnical scenario, that the new GDPR is meant to address through new constructs, requirements, sanctions[9].

While the GDPR is built around a bundle of traditional and new principles (the major are lawfulness, fairness and transparency) – interactively used to cover the many detailed aspects of a complex regulation – the principle of

---

[5] As Benkler has pointed out, "(f)or decades economists, politicians and legislators, business executives and engineers have acted as though all systems and organizations had to be built around incentives, rewards, and punishments in order to get people to achieve public, corporate, or community goals (...). And yet all around us we see people cooperating and working in collaboration, doing the right thing, behaving fairly, acting generously, caring about their group or team, and trying to behave like decent people who reciprocate kindness with kindness" [4, pp. 2–3].

[6] Convention for the Protection of Individuals with regard to Automatic Processing of Personal Data, ETS No. 108, Strasbourg, 28/01/1981. Convention 108 was the first and is still today the only binding international legal instrument in the field of data protection.

[7] Parliamentary Assembly of the Council of Europe, Committee on Legal Affairs and Human Rights, Draft Protocol amending the Convention for the Protection of Individuals with regard to Automatic Processing of Personal Data (ETS No. 108) and its Explanatory Report, Doc. 14437, 15 November 2017.

[8] Directive 95/46/EC of the European Parliament and of the Council of 24 October 1995 on the protection of individuals with regard to the processing of personal data and on the free movement of such data, Official Journal L 281, 23/11/1995, 31–50.

[9] Regulation (EU) 2016/679 of the European Parliament and of the Council of 27 April 2016 on the protection of natural persons with regard to the processing of personal data and on the free movement of such data, and repealing Directive 95/46/EC (General Data Protection Regulation), Official Journal of the European Union, 4.5.2016 L 119/1.

Privacy by Design (PbD), or, in the GDPR, Data Protection by Design (DPbD) (Article 25), can be at least metaphorically identified as the unifying symbol that synthesizes the EU regulatory approach. In fact, it refers to protection embedded in the entire cycle of data processing, "to integrate the necessary safeguards into the processing in order to meet the requirements of this Regulation and protect the rights of data subjects" (Article 25).

Within this increasingly articulated European legal framework, populated by a variety of specific directives – and with all the national implementations – for a long time soft law and ethics have been playing a modest role in 'data legal protection' – the main European expression for citizens' personal information in the digital age. With a remarkably different approach as to the biotechnological domain, law had the primacy over ethics in privacy matters [8,50,51]. In the past few years, and primarily in relation to ICT fast developments and pervasive implications for people's lives (e.g. social networks and the Internet of Things), other ethical aspects (e.g. identity, agency, surveillance) have emerged. In 2012 for the first time the European Group on Ethics in Science and New Technologies (EGE) was asked to address the ethical issues raised by ICT, which were essentially identified (again) in privacy and the (traditionally bioethical) protection of individual dignity [25].

Most interpretive and often 'ethical' institutional reflection has been performed through Art.29 Working Party (Art.29 WP) and the European Data Protection Supervisor (EDPS) opinions. Only in 2015 a dedicated ethics committee was established within the EDPS to explore privacy and data protection ethics [22]. The Advisory Group is deemed to help define a "new digital ethics" that should combine the benefits of technology for society and the economy with a reinforcement of individual rights and freedoms. However, a general rise of soft law as an active complements to binding regulation is taking place worldwide [23], "a supplementary approach" where "regulators should encourage businesses to adopt new business models" [45], see also [5] on binding corporate rules]. This 'ethical turn' in privacy matters comes from the awareness that "in today's digital environment adherence to the law is not enough; we have to consider the ethical dimension of data processing" [Buttarelli 2016]. Indeed, also in Europe the impression is growing that development such as Big Data is exceeding the GDPR reform efforts. However, the attempt to show that privacy remains an all-encompassing concept, the main concern and the answer, is still strong. As the EDPS pointed out in 2015, because privacy is now more than ever connected to human dignity, and human dignity is the most fundamental human value and right, privacy and data protection are becoming immediate synonyms for dignity ([21], p. 4; see also [9]).

3   The Renewed Relevance of Privacy as Autonomy: The Facebook Case and the 'Filter Bubble'

As said, while in a very distinct way 'data protection' is the main EU construct related to personal information and ICT, in the US 'privacy' has remained the broad term to refer also to individual data protection in the digital domain.

Indeed, even though no 'consensus definition' exists, in the US legal context privacy is multidimensional and includes physical, informational, decisional, proprietary, associational, and intellectual aspects [1]. Therefore, privacy is "a general concept that includes confidentiality, secrecy, anonymity, data protection, data security, fair information practices, decisional autonomy, and freedom from unwanted intrusion" [43, p. 25].

This is why the right to personal autonomy and self-determination has been protected for a long time through the concept of privacy. In the famous case *Roe v. Wade* (410 U.S. 113 (1973)), where the US Supreme Court had to legally frame abortion, privacy was called in as the foundation for an autonomous private decision. While recognizing that the right to privacy was not explicitly mentioned in the US Constitution[10], the Court stated that "the right of privacy, whether it be founded in the Fourteenth Amendment's concept of personal liberty and restrictions upon state action, as we feel it is, or, as the District Court determined, in the Ninth Amendment's reservation of rights to the people, is broad enough to encompass a woman's decision whether or not to terminate her pregnancy" (at VIII, 153).

Privacy as the entitlement to autonomous decisions, however, is not foreign to the European legal context and had a remarkable application by the European Court of Human Right (ECHR) in 1998. While the ECHR has intervened on the right to privacy in a number of cases, the Case of Guerra and Others v. Italy remains quite unique in the way respect for private life (Article 8) has been interpreted. The controversy followed an industrial accident in Manfredonia where the population, exposed to the effects of toxic chemical substances, accused Italian institutions of having infringed their right to privacy by not providing people with sufficient information about the situation.

In rejecting the arguments of the Italian Government, the Court not only recognized the applicability of Article 8, but also stated that this was not a merely negative right of non-interference, but instead should be seen as a positive right. "(A)lthough the object of Article 8 is essentially that of protecting the individual against arbitrary interference by the public authorities, it does not merely compel the State to abstain from such interference: in addition to this primarily negative undertaking, there may be positive obligations inherent in effective respect for private or family life. (...) The Court holds, therefore, that the respondent State did not fulfil its obligation to secure the applicants' right to respect for their private and family life, in breach of Article 8 of the Convention" (Sects. 58; 60).

---

[10] Both courts and scholars have shown that the US Constitution implicitly recognizes the value of privacy and rights of privacy through provisions guaranteeing: (1) freedom of speech, freedom of religious, political and personal association, and related forms of anonymity (First Amendment); (2) freedom from government appropriation of one's home (Third Amendment); (3) freedom from unreasonable search and seizure of one's body and property (Fourth Amendment); (4) freedom from compulsory self-incrimination (Fifth Amendment); (5) freedom from cruel and unusual punishment, including unnecessarily extreme deprivations of privacy (Eight Amendment); and (6) other personal freedoms (Ninth Amendment).

If the original meaning of the right to privacy as autonomy and integrity of the personal sphere belongs to the US legal landscape, and is not foreign to the European context – even more as a positive right –, this dimension is acquiring a renewed relevance in the light of the digital interferences in human life. And, in this respect, it is quite interesting that, in their Opinion 7/2015 on the challenges of Big Data, the EDPS has observed that "(t)he right to be let alone is indeed the beginning of all freedom" [21, p. 1].

The renewed relevance of privacy as the right to preserve the 'integrity' of the personal and intimate sphere, has become evident, even when personal data are not at stake, as, e.g., in the Facebook-Cornell case of psychological contagion and in what is called the 'filter bubble'.

In 2014 a group of researchers, from the Data Science Team of Facebook Inc. and the Information and Communication Departments of Cornell University, published the results of an experiment conducted on 689,000 subjects using Facebook in English [35]. During one week in January 2012, researchers manipulated the extent to which users were exposed to 'emotional' communication in their News Feed in order to understand whether emotions can be transferred to others without any direct contact. Two separate experiments were conducted, one for positive emotions and the other for negative ones. In each experiment the users were divided into an experimental group and a control group. Each post was analyzed by a text mining algorithm which classified its content in three categories (positive emotion, negative emotion, not emotional) and, with some probability, deleted it if it contained a positive (negative) emotion in the experimental group, whereas it was deleted completely at random for the users in the control group. The researchers found that users with reduced exposure to 'positive' posts produced less 'positive' posts, and in turn wrote more 'negative' posts. The opposite happened for the users with reduced exposure to 'negative' posts.

The participants were completely unaware of having been enrolled in an experiment. When the results appeared in the Proceedings of the National Academy of Science (PNAS) questions were raised about the principles of informed consent and opportunity to opt out, in line with the rules on Human Research Subjects.

PNAS published an Editorial Expression of Concern where, while recognizing that the experiment "involved practices that were not fully consistent" with the relevant principles, it was argued that, being Facebook a private company, the agreement to the Data Use Policy, to which all users agree prior to creating an account on Facebook, constituted informed consent for the research. Moreover, according to PNAS, users' privacy was never violated since the posts were never analyzed by researchers, but processed by a text mining system which kept the whole process blind to humans. However, despite these explanations, it became apparent that, as users' personal sphere of emotions had been violated, privacy was at stake.

Something similar, even outside the research context, is happening constantly with Google search engine and personal accounts on social network platforms.

The contents users are exposed to are selected based on their past preferences, with the aim of offering them the most appropriate and enjoyable content. This process gradually encloses everyone inside a 'filter bubble' [41] where they are mostly exposed to opinions similar to those they already have. Search engines and news feed algorithms are acting as editors, they design the information diet, and this has a big influence on the way users see the world and on the related choices they make.

4 How Algorithms Learn from the Past

The huge quantity of data produced by users, mostly digital data, would be of no use without algorithms capable of analyzing them to extract valuable information. When dealing with large quantity of data coming from different sources, some specific types of algorithms, namely machine learning programs, are needed. Unlike conventional computer programs, these algorithms are only partially pre-programmed. Indeed the most common ones learn from examples offered by historical data. By using previous examples, they produce predictions about the future. This feature of machine learning algorithms is one of the most relevant in this context: algorithms processing historical data detect patterns inside them. These patterns, for example correlation between variables, often incorporate the prejudices and inequalities of our societies. Once the algorithms have learned these patterns, they will use them to make future decisions, thus perpetuating the biases on a much larger scale.

The idea that computer-based decisions would be more objective than human decisions in solving controversial issues has already proved not only fallacious, but often also shortsighted. This is why the attempt to disentangle algorithms and data is neither possible nor meaningful in order to understand how Big Data are changing social life and threatening democratic values.

A simple example of a machine learning algorithm, namely a naive Bayesian filter, may help clarifying what learning 'from historical data' means and implies; and it helps ask whether this use of the term 'learning' is appropriate to what machine learning algorithms do.

4.1 A Simple Example of Machine Learning Algorithm: The 'Anti-spam' Filter

Email spam filters represent a specific type of machine learning systems, called *classifiers*. Each time new email message arrives, the classifier decides if it is 'spam' or 'ham', *i.e.* legitimate email. This a very simple case of classifier, which discriminates between only two categories. More complex classifiers are used, for example, to identify the blood type, where the categories are four: 'A', 'B', 'AB' or '0'. The spam filters cannot be pre-programmed, as there is no complete agreement about what an undesired message is and also because the characteristics of spam messages evolve in time. For this reason the program is designed so that it learns by continuously analyzing the user's message flow, helped also by the users when they explicitly mark a message as 'spam' or 'ham'.

Anti-spam filters work with probabilities. The classifier computes the probability of a message being 'spam' and, if it is above some predefined threshold, e.g. 95%, it places the message in the 'spam' folder or deletes it.

Machine learning is used exactly to compute these probabilities, as the case of a naive Bayesan filter shows. After having checked the sender and other attributes of the new incoming message M, the anti-spam filter analyzes the text T with the objective of computing

$$P(\text{M is spam}|T) : \text{probability that M is 'spam' if it contains the text T.} \quad (1)$$

In order to evaluate this probability, the filter will look for words frequently used in spam emails. For the sake of simplicity we can interpret the text T of a new incoming message as a list of words: $T = (W_1, W_2, \ldots, W_N)$, and assume that we can factorize the probability above as the product of the single probabilities associated to each word:

$$P(\text{M is spam}|T) \sim P(\text{M is spam}|W_1) \times P(\text{M is spam}|W_2) \times \cdots \times P(\text{M is spam}|W_N),$$
$$(2)$$

where

$$P(\text{M is spam}|W_i) : \text{probability that M is 'spam' if it contains the word } W_i$$
$$i = 1, \ldots, N. \quad (3)$$

It is important to stress here that in this simple example the semantic structures connecting the words inside a text are being neglected. We are oversimplifying the problem with the aim of obtaining simple mathematical expressions whose meaning should appear as clear as possible.

Thanks to the spam reporting activities of all the users of the same email provider, an estimate can be obtained of the probability that W_i appears in a spam message: $P(W_i|\text{M is spam})$. A very simple estimate of this quantity is the frequency of the word W_i appearing in the messages reported as spam by the users:

$$P(W_i|\text{M is spam}) = \frac{\text{number of spam messages containing the word } W_i}{\text{total number of spam messages}} \quad (4)$$

What we are looking for, however, is the probability that the incoming message is 'spam' given that it contains the word W_i, defined in Eq. (3). To do this one can resort to Bayes theorem:

$$P(\text{M is spam}|W_i) = \frac{P(W_i|\text{M is spam}), P(\text{M is spam})}{P(W_i)} \quad (5)$$

where $P(\text{M is spam})$ is the *a priori* probability that an incoming message is 'spam' and $P(W_i)$ is the *a priori* probability that the word W_i appears in email messages. Every time a user reports a message as 'spam', the filter will first compute a new value of $P(W_i|\text{M is spam})$ according to Eq. (4), then it will substitute this new estimate inside Eq. (5). This is the *learning* phase of the algorithm: as soon as new data is recorded, the algorithm will update the probabilities.

After having repeated this procedure for each word in the text, and having combined the results in Eq. (2), the algorithm will finally compute $P(\text{M is spam}|T)$ and, depending on the chosen threshold, it will classify the new incoming message. However, even if $P(\text{M is spam}|T)$ is high, e.g. 98%, the chance still exists for the message to be 'ham'. In this case the classifier will return a so called 'false-positive', a legitimate message marked incorrectly as 'spam'. This simple example shows that machine learning algorithms commit errors, because they work with probability and statistics and, as long as this approach is applied, these errors are implicitly accepted.

4.2 Machine Learning in the Social Realm

Machine learning algorithms are at work in many sectors of our society: credit access, finance, insurance, health, policing, justice, human resources management [10], access to education[11].

Two relevant examples illustrate the potential negative effects that algorithms can have when used to assist decision making on very delicate issues.

More than fifty US Police Corps currently use a *predictive policing* software called PredPol, an algorithm designed by the consultancy company PredPol, founded in 2011 by two researchers at the University of California Los Angeles. The software is adapted from an earthquake prediction model: it takes only three variables about each crime committed in a certain area (location, time, type of the crime). It then aggregates crimes committed in the past and predicts the areas where is more likely that a crime will be committed in the near future. These predictions are used to optimize the patrolling strategy of the police officers.

The overall accuracy of the software has never been evaluated by an independent party, but in 2016 the Human Rights Data Analysis Group published a research [37] on the risk of racial discrimination in software outputs. The study compared the predictions on illegal drug consumption in the city of Oakland, California, made, respectively, by PredPol and by the Department of Health and Human Services (DHHS). While according to Health and Human Services illegal drug consumption is homogeneously distributed among neighbourhoods, PredPol estimated a higher risk in the areas inhabited by African Americans.

The point here is that geography in many American cities is a good proxy for race. Even though ethnicity as an explicit variable is not included in the data about past crimes, the system is able to reconstruct it because it is highly correlated with home address.

In many other countries, including Europe, Police Corps are experimenting these kinds of software despite the lack of rules on how to assess their efficacy,

---

[11] Existing literature in the fields illustrates a variety of cases [40,42].

fairness and their economic value. In most cases this software is related to scientific research projects, that start working with institutions in order to obtain real world data to test their systems, and later develop products for the market.

The second example is the evaluation program of public school teachers in Washington D.C.. Called IMPACT, the program started in 2011 and led, only after the first year, to nearly 200 teachers fired by the Department of Education. The program bases its decisions partly on the feedback given by experts' observation during school classes, partly on the outcome of the *Value Added Model*, in the version devised by the consultancy company Mathematica Policy Research. The model is quite ambitious: it has the objective to estimate how big is the contribution of the teacher to the progress of his/her students from one year to the next one. The algorithm takes as input the outcomes of end-of-year tests which students receive in the different subjects, and some information about their socioeconomic and psychological background. To take into account the students' socioeconomic status, the model considers if he/she is eligible for free meals at school, whereas the psychological condition is approximated by possible learning disabilities.

The outcome of the program have been criticized by many teachers, in particular the case of Sarah Wysocki received extensive media coverage[12]. Wysocki was fired in the summer of 2011, and did not agree with this decision. She tried to understand the functioning of the algorithm, but she did not have the chanche to look at the code or to receive an exahustive explanation, neither by the Department of Education nor by the company which provided the software. This story shows how difficult is in practice to know the logic behind algorithms. This is because on the one hand the institutions that run the software do not know and master its details, and on the other because of the intrinsic complexity of some mathematical models.

Some months later an investigation of the newspaper USA Today[13] revealed that at least 70 schools in the district cheated on the end-of-year test results, thus questioning the robustness of the entire program. This is another dangerous implications of algorithmic decision-making: it depends strongly on the input data and if the subjects of the decision understand this vulnerability they will try to game the system.

5   The Limits of De-identification and the Differential Privacy Framework

Since 1990s, a big effort has been devoted by information and data science research to designing privacy preserving algorithms, *i.e.* data analysis processes

---

[12] Turque, B., "'Creative ... motivating' and fired", *The Washington Post*, March 6, 2012. https://www.washingtonpost.com/local/education/creative--motivating-and-fired/2012/02/04/gIQAwzZpvR_story.html?utm_term=.602a90cfd863 (accessed 8 January 2018).

[13] Toppo, G., "Memo warns of rampant cheating in D.C. public schools", *USA Today*, April 11, 2013. https://www.usatoday.com/story/news/nation/2013/04/11/memo-washington-dc-schools-cheating/2074473/ (accessed 8 January 2018).

able to extract valuable knowledge from a database without violating the privacy of the subjects who contributed their personal information. Some examples are provided here below.

5.1   The Limits of De-identification

The first works in this field have focused on data de-identification, but the approach has quickly revealed its limits.

The case of Netflix Prize is quite famous. In 2006 Netflix launched a contest to improve the design of a 'recommendation system', an algorithm for personalized advice on movies.

The algorithm used by Netflix belongs to the *nearest neighbour* class. When users log in into their account, Netflix will provide them with some recommendations. In order to define these recommendations the system compares your rating history with other Netflix customers' history and identifies which resembles you most. Once the algorithm has identified your *nearest neighbour*, it looks for movies or TV series they rated highest and recommend them to you (these algorithms are also called *collaborative rating algorithms*).

The accuracy of the algorithm is measured by its ability to predict your next rating. The better the software can predict how you will rate different movies, the higher will be your satisfaction and thus your willingness to purchase more products. In 2006 Netflix launched a contest among developers and data scientists to improve the accuracy of its recommendation algorithm. The team that could predict customers' ratings better than the Netflix's recommender system would have been awarded one million dollars.

The training data set included 100,480,507 ratings given by 480,189 users to 17,770 movies. The dataset form's entry was ⟨user, movie, date, rating⟩ and the rating was an integer number from 1 (lowest rating) to 5 (highest rating). Once the competitors had designed the algorithm, they had to train it on the training data set, and then test it on a set containing 1,408,342 entries in the form ⟨user, movie, date, ?⟩. 'Testing' means that the algorithms run over the sample predicting the users' ratings to movies at different points in time. In order to protect privacy, both users and movies were labeled with integer numbers.

A concern for users' privacy was raised some time later, when a scientific article by two data scientists from the University of Texas at Austin [38] showed that anonymized users in the Netflix Prize dataset could be identified through the Internet Movie Database. Following this publication Netflix ended the Netflix prize.

This episode revealed the limits of de-identification procedures: are these strong enough to resist re-identification, given the large amount of redundant data people produce and make available on the Internet?

Another interesting case of privacy violation has been raised in Genome Wide Association Studies (GWAS). Sharing sequencing data sets without identifiers has become a common practice in genomics, even though in 2008 David Craig and collaborators showed that, notwithstanding the fact that GWAS released only summary statistics about their participants, information from an individual's DNA sample could determine if he/she had contributed to the study [32].

A bigger concern was raised by Gymrek and collaborators in 2013 regarding the possibility of re-identifying participants to a GWAS, using information publicly available on the Internet through surname inference [29]. Surnames are paternally inherited in most human societies and thus one can find a correlation between surnames and Y-chromosome haplotypes (the non-recombining portion of the Y-chromosome which is passed, almost unchanged, from father to son). Based on this fact, a number of genetic genealogy projects have flourished, with the aim of reconnecting distant patrilineal relatives. Currently there are at least eight databases, containing hundreds of thousands of surname-haplotype records. These databases are publicly available on the Internet and some are free-of-charge. Using these records researchers have positively matched 12% of male genomes with the exact person they originated from.

5.2   Differential Privacy and Beyond

The GWAS example shows that, if data controllers release too much statistical information about a sample or if redundant information is publicly available on the same subject, re-identification is possible and the privacy of the subjects who contributed to the study will be violated.

Differential privacy has been proposed to answer the question "How can a curator release only the information about a population which does not compromise participants' privacy?". As Dwork and others have explained, the basic idea in differential privacy is that the statistical information disclosed should not change if a single individual is or is not included in a data set. A survey of the results about differential privacy can be found in [17].

However, as said, even differential privacy falls short when dealing with cases such as illegal drug use in the city of Oakland, where privacy, as protection of private data, cannot prevent discrimination from machine learning algorithms. This is because even if sensible variables are not included, other variables can reconstruct them.

A further and more profound reason exists to say that preserving privacy alone will not solve the problem of unfair algorithms. Cynthia Dwork has made this point very clear[14]. If a clinical study on 1,000 subjects founds that smoking is associated with increased risk of lung cancer, every smoker will be affected by these findings, even if he/she neither participated in the study nor disclosed any personal information. The insurance premium will rise for all smokers because the study finds that they are more exposed to the risk of developing lung cancer. Whenever we can be identified as members of a certain population, we will be affected by the findings of the algorithms analyzing a sample which is considered representative of that population.

---

[14] Research seminar given in Novembre 2016 at the Institute of Advanced Studies, Princeton during the "Differential Privacy Symposium: Four Facets of Differential Privacy", "The Definition of Differential Privacy", November 12, 2016. https://www.youtube.com/watch?v=lg-VhHlztqo (accessed 17 December 2017).

6   From Privacy to Fairness: The Challenges of Machine Learning

Already in 1980, in "Do Artifacts Have Politics?" Langdon Winner highlighted that all machines, structures and technical systems should be assessed "for the ways in which they can embody specific forms of power and authority" [53, p. 21]. These early observations have raised awareness about the choices implicitly embedded, packed, and black-boxed in programs and devices, showing that "architecture matters" [Kroes 2011], namely that ICT structures do not only have ethical and policy impacts, but have built-in values and choices that should be opened-up and unpacked. In other words, digital architectures embody rules and values in their hard and soft structures as "factual normativity," norms written as digital instructions [30].

The renewed relevance of privacy as autonomy and integrity of the personal sphere has revealed that the pervasive 'virtual' dimensions in human life call for more diversified and complex ways of capturing and humanizing the digital. Big Data and machine learning have strongly impacted the capability of extending privacy towards further meanings and frontiers. While this awareness started quite early in the US, EU institutions, also due to their regulatory effort, only quite recently have become active on the subject. In the US, at both the institutional and academic level, the awareness that some new issues raised by digital transformations could not be framed in terms of privacy began in the early 2010s, with the social applications of algorithms combining Big Data and machine learning. The discriminatory results produced by supposedly neutral artefacts became increasingly apparent, triggering institutional concern, academic conferences[15], and science journalism analyses and responses[16].

In the field of genomic research, in 2012 the Presidential Commission for the Study of Bioethical Issues (PCSBI) added new principles to privacy, namely (1) public beneficence, (2) responsible stewardship, (3) intellectual freedom and responsibility, (4) democratic deliberation, and (5) justice and fairness [43, p. 28].

In 2013 Dwork and Mulligan highlighted that both the computer scientists and policy makers, while acknowledging concerns about discrimination, were still maintaining a narrow vision of the issues at stake, tending to position privacy as the dominant problem. However, and regrettably, they noted, "privacy controls and increased transparency fail to address concerns with the classifications and segmentation produced by Big Data analysis" ([19], p. 36; see also [18,20]). In the past few years the literature on algorithms' justice and fairness has vastly

---

[15] See, e.g. the series of conferences started in 2013 by NYU, Steinhardt School of Culture, Education, & Human Development, Governing Algorithms: A Conference on Computation, Automation, and Control (May 16–17, 2013), available at http://governingalgorithms.org (accessed 3 January 2017).

[16] Gillespie, T.: Can an Algorithm Be Wrong? Twitter Trends, the Specter of Censorship, and Our Faith in the Algorithms Around Us, Culture Digitally, October 19, (2011), available at http://culturedigitally.org/2011/10/can-an-algorithm-be-wrong (accessed 3 January 2017).

grown, consistently showing that algorithms are already governing our lives and that privacy and transparency are no longer the effective response, e.g. [40,42].

6.1   The US (Obama) Policy Framework: Big Data Challenges and 'Equal Opportunity by Design'

The most relevant US initiatives of 'institutional awareness' stemmed from the Council of Advisors on Science and Technology (CAST) of the Executive Office of President Obama that, between 2014 and 2016, published a series of policy reflections and recommendations ([11–14]; see also [15]).

In analyzing opportunities and challenges of Big Data and machine learning, the reports clearly showed that, while the benefits of digital new developments are manifold, several risks need to be addressed, mostly dealing with the potential for discriminatory treatments and perpetuations of biases affecting decisions in several social, economic, and health sectors.

The challenges are primarily identified at two levels: the data used as inputs to an algorithm; and algorithm design, namely how an algorithm works and how knowable it is by the user – both for computational or proprietary reasons. Problems with data may consist of: poorly selected data; incomplete, incorrect, or outdated data; selection biases (data inputs not representative of a population); unintentional perpetuation and promotion of historical biases. Problems with algorithms' design can refer to: poorly designed matching systems; personalization and recommendation services narrowing instead of expanding user's options; decision-making systems assuming that correlation necessarily implies causation; data sets lacking information or disproportionately representing certain populations.

While data systems should remove inappropriate human biases, the risk exists that use of Big Data can contribute to systematically disadvantaging certain groups by encoding forms of discrimination into technological systems.

In order to fight against these outcomes, CAST has proposed a principle of 'equal opportunity by design' – somehow the US response to 'privacy by design'. This principle aims at designing data systems that promote fairness and safeguards against discrimination from the first step of the engineering process throughout their lifespan.

According to CAST, the framing of algorithms in the light of equal opportunity should be also accompanied by a number of policy actions, from support to research and the market to inventing better systems, to development of algorithmic auditing and external testing of Big Data systems, to mechanisms for transparency and accountability, to considering the roles of the government and private sector in setting the rules, to civic participation and education in computer and data science.

What is peculiar to the CAST approach is that it does not focus – at least not primarily – on the remedies and protection offered to users/citizens in dealing with data driven decision-making. Instead, it takes an upstream look at the 'politics of algorithms' as a complex and diversified involvement and recombinations of institutional, corporate, and civil society actors.

6.2 Fairness and Data Protection in the EU

As said, the European single normative language in dealing with the digital
world has been and remains data protection; and, even though the term "fair"
has been inhabiting privacy legislation for a long time, it does not seem to
adequately apply to algorithmic discrimination, as it primarily refers to "fair
data processing". Indeed, only recently fairness, meant as designing technologies
that fully respect human rights, has started been taken into account in very few
soft law European documents.

Moreover, the term "fair", having a variety of meanings, is very ambiguous.

"Fair" appears only one time in the 1981 CoE Convention at Article 5 ("Quality of data") establishing that data shall be "obtained and processed fairly and
lawfully"[17]. In Directive 46/95 the "fair processing" of data is defined at Whereas
28 and 38 through several practices, that the GDPR has further elaborated in
a detailed and complex set of requirements, often repeated, overlapping, and
mixed with transparency. Indeed, a variety of requirements are listed (primarily
at Whereas 39, 60 and 71, and Article 5) that range from the data subject's
awareness of the processing and of risks and rights related to it, to the clarity
and accessibility of information, the limits to purposes, the storage time, the
right to erasure; from the legitimate grounds for data collection and the absence
of unjustified adverse effects, to appropriate notice, transparent intention of use,
reasonable handling, accuracy of data and rectification of errors; compliance with
the law; and more. In many ways, "fair" broadly covers all GDPR provisions, but
still leaves some room for further interpretation, as a sort of open interpretive
clause.

However, that "fair processing" of individual personal data does not fully
respond to the issues raised by Big Data and machine learning algorithms is
revealed by Article 22(1)[18], "Automated individual decision-making, including
profiling" - where "automated individual decision-making" concerns all activities exclusively performed by a machine, while "profiling" (as defined in Article
4) refers to data collection, automated analysis to identify correlations, and the
inference from these correlations towards an individual's present or future behavior [3, p. 7].[19]. Article 22(1) establishes for the data subject the "right not to
be subject to a decision based solely on automated processing, including profiling, which produces legal effects concerning him or her or similarly significantly
affects him or her."

A guideline published in late 2017 by Art.29 WP has clarified how to interpret
and apply Article 22, also admitting that the new provisions on the risks arising
from profiling and automated decision-making still concern, but are "not limited
to, privacy" [3, p. 4]. According to Art.29 WP, in order to be effective, the right

---

[17] Directive 46/95 mentions "fair" 5 times and "fairly" 2. In the GDPR "fair" has 14
occurrences, "fairly" 2, "fairness" 1, "unfair" 2.

[18] In Directive 46/95 at Article 15, "Automated individual decisions.".

[19] See also: CoE, Recommendation CM/Rec(2010)13 of the Committee of Ministers to
member states on the protection of individuals with regard to automatic processing
of personal data in the context of profiling (adopted on 23 November 2010).

granted at Article 22 has to translate into several other rights. First of all, it includes the right to be informed (Articles 13(2) (f) and 14(2) (g)), namely to "receive meaningful information about the logic involved," "simple ways to tell the data subject about the rationale behind" the algorithm [3, pp. 9; 12]. Also, it involves the right to understand the significance of the envisaged consequences for the data subject, the right to obtain human intervention and the right to challenge the decision (Article 22(3)).

The effectiveness of these rights should result from the application of transparency and fairness requirements: greater accountability obligations; specified legal bases for the processing; rights to oppose profiling; and, under certain circumstances, to carry out a data protection impact assessment. Further safeguards should come from other general provisions listed at Article 5(1), namely lawful, fair and transparent processing, purpose limitation, data minimization, accuracy and storage limitation.

The credibility of all this complex narrative, and more simply its feasibility, has been strongly challenged by some commentators who argued that the complexity of algorithms – sometimes opaque even to programmers –, as well as their proprietary protection, make these promises quite unrealistic [24].

While recognizing that other measures introduced by the GDPR – such as the right to erasure, the right to data portability, privacy by design, Data Protection Impact Assessments, certification and privacy seals – can be helpful, Edwards and Veale see restrictions introduced at Article 22 as problematic in many respects: the non-enforceability of statements appearing in the recitals and not in the GDPR text, substantial legal uncertainty, the practical difficulty in knowing when or how decisions are being made, etc. [24, p. 21].

Art.29 WP guideline does not convincingly overcome these objections, and keeps suggesting that transparency is the answer, claiming that "the controller should find simple ways to tell the data subject about the rationale behind (...) without necessarily always attempting a complex explanation of the algorithms used or disclosure of the full algorithm" [3, pp. 9; 14]

However, if Article 22 (with all its ramifications) can be hardly seen as the adequate framework towards "more responsible, explicable, and human-centered" algorithms [24, p. 19], the very concept of data protection has its own limits: a culture of better algorithms requires taking into account a full range of individual and collective rights. Moreover, within the perspective of the GDPR, most measures concern *ex-post* remedies for individuals who have undergone unfair automated processing, while Big Data and machine learning call for early, upstream analysis of digital architecture and algorithms in terms of fairness.

In this respect, the most open perspectives come from some non-legally binding documents issued in 2017 by the Parliamentary Assembly of the Council of Europe and the European Parliament. In its Resolution on the fundamental rights implications of Big Data[20], the European Parliament, after having provided a wide landscape of the digital era and of its challenges to traditional regulatory instruments, has shown that "it is not just a question of data protection"[21]: not only many fundamental rights, but also relevant collective values such as public trust, media freedom and pluralistic information are at stake. In the context of the Council of Europe, the Parliamentary Assembly[22] Recommendation on technological convergence, artificial intelligence and human rights – also touching on machine learning and Big Data – has evoked Article 2 of the Convention on Human Rights and Biomedicine[23], establishing the primacy of the human being "over the sole interest of society or science" as a key right; and has pointed out that "safeguarding human dignity in the 21st century implies developing new forms of governance, new forms of open, informed and adversarial public debate, new legislative mechanisms and above all the establishment of international co-operation" (at point 3).

6.3 Designing Fair Algorithms

Data scientists who are convinced that data protection will not prevent algorithms from having negative effects on the weaker members of our societies, have gradually moved their research towards *algorithmic fairness*[24]. An example of efforts in this new direction is the "Fairness, Accountability, Transparency in Machine Learning" Conference series started in 2014[25].

A first and very general attempt to define a 'fair algorithm' has indeed been made by Cynthia Dwork and collaborators in 2011 [18]. The basic idea they proposed is to "treat similar individuals similarly", namely to interpret fairness as 'equality'. A fair algorithm is formulated as a constrained optimization problem. The constraint is written in terms of a metric, a mathematical definition of distance. According to Dwork and collaborators (referring to Rawls [44]), the choice

---

[20] European Parliament Resolution of 14 March 2017 on fundamental rights implications of big data: privacy, data protection, non-discrimination, security and law-enforcement, P8_TA(2017)0076, (2016/2225(INI)).

[21] Parliament's rapporteur Ana Gomes, available at http://www.europarl.europa.eu/news/en/press-room/20170314IPR66586/big-data-ep-calls-for-better-protection-of-fundamental-rights-and-privacy (accessed 5 January 2018).

[22] Parliamentary Assembly of the Council of Europe, Recommendation 2102 (2017)1, Technological convergence, artificial intelligence and human rights, adopted by the Assembly on 28 April 2017.

[23] Convention for the Protection of Human Rights and Dignity of the Human Being with regard to the Application of Biology and Medicine: Convention on Human Rights and Biomedicine (ETS No. 164, "Oviedo Convention").

[24] This gradual shift is well described by Cynthia Dwork herself in an interview published by Quanta Magazine. Hartnett, K. "How to Force Our Machines to Play Fair", *Quanta Magazine*, November 26, 2016. https://www.quantamagazine.org/making-algorithms-fair-an-interview-with-cynthia-dwork-20161123 (accessed 17 December 2017).

[25] Fairness Accountability and Transparency of Machine Learning: research group website https://www.fatml.org/.

of the metric should be made by a regulatory body or a civil rights organization and should be public and open to debate. This framework is designed to enforce 'individual fairness', not 'group fairness'. As seen in previous examples, unfairness is mostly connected to a collective dimension, not only to an individual one. Members of minority groups are more likely to be discriminated by algorithms designed by members of the majority, who are not necessarily 'aware' of their existence and in some cases are not inclined to listen to their needs.

The difficulty in designing algorithms which are fair towards different social groups became apparent in the case of the recidivism risk model called COMPAS, used by many federal courts in the US and sold by the private company NorthPointe. COMPAS takes as inputs the answers given to a standard questionnaire by defendants and policemen and gives as output the risk that the defendant will commit another crime in the near future. This risk estimate helps the judge to decide the length of the sentence, whether the arrested has to be imprisoned until the beginning of the process, and the possible enrollment in some support programs.

In May 2016 ProPublica published a thorough investigation[26] stating that COMPAS fails differently for black and white defendants. In particular in order to assess the accuracy of the algorithm, they studied more than 10,000 criminal defendants in Broward County, Florida, and compared their predicted recidivism rates with the actual rate on a two-year period. The results showed that the percentage of defendants labeled as high risk who did not commit further crimes was 23.5% among white defendants and 44.0% among black defendants. Similarly, the percentage of defendants labeled as low risk who did commit further crimes was 47.7% and 28.0%, respectively for white and black defendants[27].

The ProPublica investigation has triggered academic attempts to 'fix' the COMPAS algorithm, *i.e.* to remove its discriminatory behavior against the black population. However, for the time being these efforts have proved unsuccessful[28]. The problem is still open. In a recent contribution [55], Zafar and co-authors introduce a notion of fairness based on group's preference for being assigned one

---

[26] Julia Angwin, Jeff Larson, Surya Mattu, and Lauren Kirchner, "Machine Bias. There's software used across the country to predict future criminals. And it's biased against blacks", *ProPublica*, May 23, 2016. https://www.propublica.org/article/machine-bias-risk-assessments-in-criminal-sentencing (accessed 7 December 2017).

[27] Julia Angwin, Jeff Larson, Surya Mattu, and Lauren Kirchner, "Machine Bias. There's software used across the country to predict future criminals. And it's biased against blacks", *ProPublica*, May 23, 2016. https://www.propublica.org/article/machine-bias-risk-assessments-in-criminal-sentencing. Accessed on 7 December 2017.

[28] Julia Angwin, Jeff Larson, Surya Mattu, and Lauren Kirchner, "Bias in Criminal Risk Scores Is Mathematically Inevitable, Researchers Say", *ProPublica*, December 30, 2016. https://www.propublica.org/article/bias-in-criminal-risk-scores-is-mathematically-inevitable-researchers-say?utm_source=suggestedarticle&utm_medium=referral&utm_campaign=readnext&utm_content=https%3A%2F%2Fwww.propublica.org%2Farticle%2Fbias-in-criminal-risk-scores-is-mathematically-inevitable-researchers-say (accessed 7 December 2017).

set of decision outcomes over another, as opposed to the notion of fairness based on parity (equality) of treatment.

The high degree of complexity and specificity of the problems related to algorithmic discrimination has led many to propose the development of some forms of auditing for algorithms. During 2017 the French commission for digital rights[29] has organized a public debate on the ethical aspects of algorithms, called "Éthique Numérique". In the final recommendations, which originated from the discussions held among professionals of different sectors as well as among citizens, one concerns the "creation of a national platform in order to audit algorithms"[30]. The idea is that not only engineers and programmers, but policy makers and citizens should become more aware of the difficulties involved.

7   Whose Vision of Fairness?

As a proxy for justice, equity, equality, and appropriateness, fairness opens up an umbrella of meanings and problems even wider than privacy, as visions of justice have animated philosophical, legal, and political debates of different cultural traditions since their origins. What is now at stake is that diverging visions of fairness can be opaquely and disorderly be embedded in all sort of digitalized decision making. The attempts to design fair algorithms, though controversial [27], still represent a promising way forward and may facilitate a better understanding of how to approach fairness and what it involved [49].

However, while new dialogues between the languages of justice and computer and data science need to be framed, some issues should be clarified.

A first point is the following. Attention should be paid to the fact that fair algorithms have already revealed an inclination towards privileging specific visions of fairness, namely those where the model itself (or some of its components) can be more easily quantified and translated into mathematical terms. For instance, even though Rawls's theory remains a powerful vision of justice [44], its adoption in several software mostly depends on the possibility to convert it in algorithms [34]. In other words, the appeal of visions of justice having the potential for an algorithmic definition is higher compared to other lacking this adaptability.

Already in 1979 Nobel laureate Amartya Sen, in discussing the ambiguities of equality (The Equality of What?), noted that "(t)he recognition of the fundamental diversity of human beings does, in fact, have very deep consequences, affecting not merely the utilitarian conception of social good, but (...) even the Rawlsian conception of equality. If human beings are identical, then the application of the prior-principle of universalizability in the form of 'giving equal weight

---

[29] Commission nationale de l'informatique et des libertés (CNIL).

[30] "Comment permettre à l'homme de garder la main? Les enjeux éthiques des algorithmes et de l'intelligence artificielle", Summary of the public debate organized by the CNIL as established by The Digital Republic Bill (Loi pour une rèpublique numèrique). https://www.cnil.fr/sites/default/files/atoms/files/cnil_rapport_garder_la_main_web.pdf (accessed 8 January 2017).

to the equal interest of all parties' simplifies enormously" [48, p. 202]. And again, in its "The Idea of Justice," Sen has shown how the fundamental axioms about justice are incommensurable. Though all legitimate within their own assumptions, the choices about how to characterize individuals, how to define their similarities and how to prioritize our choices need wider and public reasons to be debated. Who is going to choose the relevant axioms? Principle of justice are plural, criteria need democratic discussion and assessment through the worlds that are generated.

And this leads to a second point. As said, ethics as a non-legally binding regulatory tool has become increasingly relevant in the digital domain, even though there is no agreement about how to implement it. While some authors suggest, for instance, private ethical auditing for algorithms [40], others point at institutional ethics committees (as in the biomedical field) [9], and others, while calling for the "adoption of a normative definition of fairness within the machine learning community", argue in favor of dialogues between machine learning experts and vulnerable populations [49]. Adequate discussion of fair algorithms requires legitimacy and should avoid both the tensions between experts and non-experts and the bureaucracy of ethics committees. The concept of Participatory Design (PD) may be helpful here as an important exploratory tool. Theories of PD, originated in the domain of Human-Computer Interactions (HCI), information systems and socio-informatics, reflect on building digital architectures through participatory procedures, with the aim of making knowledge and values embedded in technological systems more open and democratically shared. In PD users are "co-designers during all stages of the design process;" which "means that decisions about possible design trajectories should .... be open to the possibility of change and in ways that enable choices to be unmade or changed" [7, pp. 3; 6].

Indeed, digital architectures should not deterministically impose their own structures, ontologies, mechanisms, explanations over social normativity [36]; instead, in the complex evolution between technoscience and normativity, new spaces for choice and scrutiny in technosocial architectures should be made available to citizens as a matter of democracy and participation [33].

References

1. Allen, A.: Privacy Law and Society, 2nd edn. Thomson Reuters, St. Paul (2011)
2. Arendt, H.: The Human Condition. University of Chicago Press, Chicago (1958)
3. Article 29 (Data Protection Working Party): Guidelines on Automated individual decision-making and Profiling for the purposes of Regulation 2016/6799, 17/EN, WP 251, Adopted on 3 October (2017). Accessed 20 dicembre 2017
4. Benkler, Y.: The Penguin and the Leviathan: The Triumph of Cooperation over Self-Interest. Random House, New York (2011)
5. Bowman, J., Gufflet, M.: Meeting the challenge of a global GDPR and BCR programme. Eur. Data Prot. Law Rev. 3(2), 257–261 (2017)
6. Boyle, J.: Shamans, Software and Spleens: Law and the Construction of the Information Society. Harvard University Press, Cambridge (1996)

7. Bratteteig, T., Wagner, I.: Disentangling Participation: Power and Decision-making in Participatory Design. Springer, Dordrecht (2014)
8. Busby, H., Hervey, T., Mohr, A.: Ethical EU law?: The influence of the European group on ethics in science and new technologies. Eur. Law Rev. **33**, 803–842 (2008)
9. Buttarelli, G.: Ethics at the Root of Privacy and as the Future of Data Protection. Address given at event hosted by Berkman Center for Internet and Society at Harvard University and the MIT Internet Policy Initiative and the MIT Media Lab, 19 April 2016. Accessed 23 Dec 2017
10. Cantoni, F., Mangia, G. (eds.): Human Resource Management and Digitalization. Routledge, London (2018)
11. CAST (Council of Advisors on Science and Technology of President): Big Data and Privacy: a Technological Perspective, May 2014. Accessed 4 Jan 2018
12. CAST: Big Data: seizing opportunities, preserving values, May 2014. Accessed 4 Jan 2018
13. CAST: Big Data: Seizing Opportunities and Preserving Values: Interim Progress Report, February 2015. Accessed 4 Jan 2018
14. CAST: Big Data: A Report on Algorithmic Systems, Opportunity, and Civil Rights, May 2016. Accessed 4 Jan 2018
15. Council of Economic Adviders: Big Data and Differential Pricing, February 2015. Accessed 4 Jan 2018
16. DHEW (U.S. Department of Health, Education, and Welfare): Records, Computers, and the Rights of Citizens. Report of the Secretary's Advisory Committee on Automated Personal Data Systems, July 1973. Accessed 22 Dec 2017
17. Dwork, C.: Differential privacy: a survey of results. In: Agrawal, M., Du, D., Duan, Z., Li, A. (eds.) TAMC 2008. LNCS, vol. 4978, pp. 1–19. Springer, Heidelberg (2008). https://doi.org/10.1007/978-3-540-79228-4_1
18. Dwork, C., Hardt, M., Pitassi, T., Reingold, O., Zemel, R.S.: Fairness through awareness. arXiv.org/abs/1609.07236v1 [**cs.CC**] (2011). Accessed 3 Jan 2017
19. Dwork, C., Mulligan, D.K.: It's not privacy and it's not fair. Stanford Law Rev. Online **66**, 35–40 (2013)
20. Dwork, C., Roth, A.: The algorithmic foundations of differential privacy. Found. Trends® Theoret. Comput. Sci. **9**(3–4), 211–407 (2014)
21. EDPS (European Data Protection Supervisor): Meeting the challenges of big data. A call for transparency, user control, data protection by design and accountability. Opinion 7/2015, November 2015. Accessed 4 Jan 2018
22. EDPS: European Data Protection Supervisor Decision of 3 December 2015 establishing an external advisory group on the ethical dimensions of data protection ('the Ethics Advisory Group'), Brussels, December 2015. Accessed 4 Jan 2018
23. EDPS: Debating ethics: Dignity and respect in data driven life. In: 40th International Conference of Data Protection and Privacy Commissioners, December 2017. Accessed 2 Jan 2018
24. Edwards, L., Veale, M.: Slave to the algorithm? Why a 'Right to an explanation' is probably not the remedy you are looking for. Duke Law Technol. Rev. **16**, 18–84 (2017)
25. EGE (European Group on Ethics in Science and New Technologies): Opinion 26. Ethics of Information and Communication Technologies (2012)
26. Fairfield, J., Engel, C.: Privacy as a public good. Duke Law J. **65**(3), 385–457 (2015)
27. Friedler, S., Scheidegger, C., Venkatasubramanian, S.: On the (im)possibility of fairness. arXiv.org/abs/1609.07236v1 [**cs.CY**] (2016)

28. FTC (Federal Trade Commission): Fair Information Practice. The United States Federal Trade Commission's Fair Information Practice Principles (FIPPs) (1973)
29. Gymrek, M., McGuire, A.L., Golan, D., Halperin, E., Erlich, Y.: Identifying personal genomes by surname inference. Science **339**(6117), 321–324 (2013)
30. Hildebrandt, M.: Legal and technological normativity: more (and less) than twin sisters. TECHNE **12**(3), 169–183 (2008)
31. Hirsch, D.: Privacy, public goods, and the tragedy of the trust commons: a response to professors Fairfield and Engel. Duke Law J. Online **65**, 67–93 (2016)
32. Homer, N., Szelinger, S., Redman, M., Duggan, D., Tembe, W., Muehling, J., Pearson, J.V., Stephan, D.A., Nelson, S.F., Craig, D.W.: Resolving individuals contributing trace amounts of DNA to highly complex mixtures using high-density snp genotyping microarrays. PLOS Genet. **4**(8), 1–9 (2008)
33. Jasanoff, S.: Science and Public Reason. Routledge, New York (2012)
34. Joseph, M., Kearns, M., Morgenstern, J., Roth, A.: The authority of "fair" in machine learning. **Research Gate** (2016) Presented as a talk at the 2016 Workshop on Fairness, Accountability, and Transparency in Machine Learning (FAT/ML 2016) (2016)
35. Kramer, A.D.I., Guillory, J.E., Hancock, J.T.: Experimental evidence of massive-scale emotional contagion through social networks. Proc. Natl. Acad. Sci. **111**(24), 8788–8790 (2014)
36. Lessig, L.: Code - Version 2.0. Basic Books, New York (2006)
37. Lum, K., Isaac, W.: To predict and serve? Significance **13**(5), 14–19 (2016)
38. Narayanan, A., Shmatikov, V.: Robust de-anonymization of large sparse datasets. In: Proceedings of the 2008 IEEE Symposium on Security and Privacy, SP 2008, Washington, DC, USA, pp. 111–125. IEEE Computer Society (2008)
39. OECD (Organization for Economic Cooperation and Development): Guidelines on the Protection of Privacy (1980, updated 2013). Accessed 24 Dec 2017
40. O'Neil, C.: Weapons of Math Destruction: How Big Data Increases Inequality and Threatens Democracy. Crown Publishing Group, New York (2016)
41. Pariser, E.: The Filter Bubble: How the New Personalized Web Is Changing What We Read and How We Think. Penguin Group, New York (2012)
42. Pasquale, F.: The Black Box Society: The Secret Algorithms that Control Money and Information. Harvard University Press, Cambridge (2015)
43. PCSBI (Presidential Commission for the Study of Bioethical Issues): Privacy and Progress in Whole Genome Sequencing, Washington, D.C., October 2012
44. Rawls, J.: A Theory of Justice. Harvard University Press, Cambridge (1971)
45. Rubinstein, I.S.: Big Data: The End of Privacy or a New Beginning? New York University Public Law and Legal Theory Working Papers, Paper 357 (2012). http://lsr.nellco.org/nyu_plltwp/357
46. Schwartz, P.: Property, privacy, and personal data. Harvard Law Rev. **117**(7), 2056–2128 (2004)
47. Searls, D.: The Intention Economy: When Customers Take Charge. Harvard Business Review Press, Cambridge (2012)
48. Sen, A.: Equality of what? The Tanner Lecture on Human Values. Delivered at Stanford University, 22 May 1979
49. Skirpan, M., Gorelick, M.: The authority of "fair" in machine learning. arXiv.org/abs/1706.09976v2   [cs.CY] (2017). Presented as a talk at the 2017 Workshop on Fairness, Accountability, and Transparency in Machine Learning (FAT/ML 2017)

50. Tallacchini, M.: From biobanks to genetic digital networks: why official pre-identified values may not work. In: Guimaraes Pereira, A., Funtowicz, S. (eds.) "Science, Philosophy and Sustainability. The End of the Cartesian Dream", pp. 98–111. Routledge, London (2015)
51. Tallacchini, M.: To bind or not bind? European ethics as soft law. In: Hilgartner, S., Miller, C., Hagendijk, R. (eds.) Science and Democracy. Making Knowledge and Making Power in the Biosciences and Beyond, pp. 156–175. Routledge (2015)
52. Warren, S.D., Brandeis, L.D.: The right to privacy. Harvard Law Rev. 4(5), 193–220 (1890)
53. Winner, L.: Do artifacts have politics? Daedalus 109(1), 121–136 (1980)
54. Yakowitzas, J.: Tragedy of the data commons. Harvard J. Law Technol. 25(1), 1–67 (2011)
55. Zafar, M.B., Valera, I., Rodriguez, M.G., Gummadi, K.P., Weller, A.: From Parity to Preference-based Notions of Fairness in Classification. arXiv.org/abs/1707.00010 [stat.ML] (2017). To appear in Proceedings of the 31st Conference on Neural Information Processing Systems (NIPS 2017)

The Consent Paradox: Accounting for the Prominent Role of Consent in Data Protection

Benjamin Bergemann[(⊠)]

WZB Berlin Social Science Center, Berlin, Germany
benjamin.bergemann@wzb.eu

Abstract. The concept of consent is a central pillar of data protection. It features prominently in research, regulation, and public debates on the subject, in spite of the wide-ranging criticisms that have been levelled against it. In this paper, I refer to this as the consent paradox. I argue that consent continues to play a central role not despite but because the criticisms of it. I analyze the debate on consent in the scholarly literature in general, and among German data protection professionals in particular, showing that it is a focus on the informed individual that keeps the concept of consent in place. Critiques of consent based on the notion of "informedness" reinforce the centrality of consent rather than calling it into question. They allude to a market view that foregrounds individual choice. Yet, the idea of a data market obscures more fundamental objections to consent, namely the individual's dependency on data controllers' services that renders the assumption of free choice a fiction.

Keywords: Commodification · Data protection · Discourse analysis
Informed consent · Information control · Power

1 Introduction: The Consent Paradox[1]

Despite criticism, consent enjoys a massive and ongoing presence in data protection. I refer to this counterintuitive observation as the *consent paradox*. Consent is omnipresent in policy making, regulatory practice, and scholarly debates. Yet, the prominent role ascribed to consent in data protection is puzzling given the sustained critique from data protection professionals and average users alike [2, p. 171]. Both groups argue that it is hard for users to comprehend what they are consenting to. Moreover, they criticize that users often do not have a choice but to consent because they rely on products such as social network services or smartphones. In data protection parlance, lay people and specialists criticize that consent is, in many cases, neither *informed* nor *freely given*. Nevertheless, consent continues to be an essential part of data protection both in theory and practice. The aim of my paper is to account for this consent paradox: How is it that consent is ascribed such a prominent role in data protection while at the same time being subject to numerous criticisms?

---

[1] This paper refines several arguments that I have developed in my master's thesis [1].

© IFIP International Federation for Information Processing 2018
Published by Springer International Publishing AG 2018. All Rights Reserved
M. Hansen et al. (Eds.): Privacy and Identity 2017, IFIP AICT 526, pp. 111–131, 2018.
https://doi.org/10.1007/978-3-319-92925-5_8

I set out to explain the consent paradox in data protection by analyzing the nexus between criticizing consent and keeping it in place. In other words, I assume that the consent paradox does not exist *despite* but *due to* the criticisms of consent. Thus, I do not discuss in how far consent *is* a meaningful instrument of data protection. Instead, I analyze how this very discussion *makes* consent a fitting solution to today's data protection problems. At first glance, assuming a productive, rather than a destructive relationship between critique and its object appears counter-intuitive. However, the idea is not unfamiliar in political sociology [3, p. 27] and, more importantly, seems to tie in well with others' observations regarding consent in data protection.

Several scholars have repeatedly pointed to what I term a consent paradox. They emphasize that consent continues to be an essential part of data protection policies despite its perceived limits [see 4–6]. Koops, criticizing a "mythology of consent", wonders why "the conclusion is too seldom drawn that consent is simply not a suitable approach to legitimate data processing in online contexts" [6, p. 251]. For Koops and others the consent paradox is manifested in the new General Data Protection Regulation (GDPR), which, according to them, has a strong focus on consent and individual information control in general [see 7, p. 313].

Some authors have already suggested a connection between criticizing consent and keeping it in place. Zanfir notes that the modifications made to consent in the GDPR "are responses to the critiques of the provisions in the [Data Protection Directive]" [5, p. 241]. Arguing in the same direction, Schermer et al. state that "the crisis of consent" has led to regulatory attempts to reform consent [2, p. 172]. A similar observation has been made by Barocas and Nissenbaum from an US perspective [8, p. 58]. According to them, questioning consent prompts an "urgent need" to fix it. Elaborating further on the nexus between critique and reform, Rouvroy and Poullet suggest that certain kinds of critique can be addressed by reforming consent, while more fundamental objections, resulting from "socio-economic and other structural inequalities," seem to question consent in general [9, p. 74]. One issue with consent that falls into the former category of perceived 'solvable' problems is ensuring that individuals consent in an *informed* manner. As authors on both sides of the Atlantic observe, enhancing individual information provision seems to be the most common suggestion for mitigating the problems with consent [6, p. 252, 7, p. 318, 9, p. 74, 10, p. 5, 11, p. 3].

Yet, the studies mentioned make these observations in the course of other arguments, thus only touching upon the question I want to answer in this paper: How can we account for the prominent position of consent despite critique? To answer this question, I develop these arguments further, proceeding in two steps. I first review the scholarly critiques of consent. In a second step, I complement this literature review by analyzing the debate on consent among German data protection professionals between 2000 and today.

Drawing on this analysis, I claim that it is the emphasis on *informedness* that keeps consent in place. Criticizing consent in terms of information asymmetries makes reforming consent not only a feasible but also a valuable project. As I will show in the following, this is because problematizing consent in terms of information asymmetries goes along with the idea of seeing data protection through a market lens. From the data market viewpoint, consent is a key instrument for consumers to exchange "their data" in order to benefit from the services provided by internet companies. However, for the consumer to understand that she is benefiting from the transaction of "her data," it must be clear to her what is in the deal. This ties the data market narrative to the legal requirement of *informed* consent, making it the yard stick for proper consent. The focus on informedness, I argue, comes at the expense of an understanding of data protection in terms of power. Approaching consent from the perspective of power asymmetries calls into question whether consent can be *freely given*, thus challenging the case for consent more profoundly.

My contribution takes a discourse analytical perspective. It differs from most of the literature on consent in that it does not argue from a legal or philosophical standpoint. I try to show how the debate on consent in data protection, although being legal in nature, is shaped by greater societal debates and conflicts. My goal is to map the discussion on consent in data protection, to understand its inner workings and the effects it produces. One such effect, I suspect, is the consent paradox.

The paper is structured as follows. The second part introduces the consent approach in data protection and its respective critiques. Looking at the critical debate about consent as the assumed source of the consent paradox, I argue that a closer, more empirical, view is needed to understand how exactly criticizing consent leads to the consent paradox. Third, I briefly introduce discourse analysis as my methodology. Then I present the debate on consent among German data protection professionals between 2000 and today as my object of analysis, explaining the case selection and the steps taken to come to my findings. The results are presented in section four. In the concluding section, I reflect on the implications of my argument for data protection research and practice.

2   Consent in Data Protection and Its Discontents

The aim of this section is to present the basics of the consent debate in data protection and linking it to the idea of the consent paradox. In line with the scope of my paper, this section will focus on the literature about consent in data protection, excluding other important work on the role of consent, most notably in the medical field [12, 13].[2] As the field of data protection is traditionally dominated by legal scholars [15, p. 76], I often refer to legal scholarship and documents. Yet, I do not provide a legal analysis of consent in data protection.

2.1   The Consent Paradox in European Data Protection Law

Legally speaking, consent is just one of the six legal grounds that authorize the processing of personal data in European data protection legislation [5, p. 237]. This has been true since the 1995 Data Protection Directive (DPD) and has been continued in the new General Data Protection Regulation (GDPR). Here, consent is defined as "any freely

---

[2] Works on consent in the medical field have considerably influenced the academic debate on consent in data protection. Kosta [14] as well as Barocas and Nissenbaum [8] rely on arguments from the literature on consent in the medical field. From a discourse analytical perspective, linking two distinct fields is interesting in its own right. One could ask what implications such an analogy has for data protection and consent, in contrast to borrowing from other analogies such as the rule of law [4].

given, specific, informed and unambiguous indication of the data subject's wishes by which he or she, by a statement or by a clear affirmative action, signifies agreement to the processing of personal data relating to him or her" (art 4). There are other legal grounds to base processing on, most importantly, the performance of a contract, legal provisions and the legitimate interest of the data controller. According to European data protection law, consent also does not change the fact that every data processing, regardless of its legal basis, is "subject to 'suitable safeguards'" [5, see also 16]. As Zanfir [5] describes, suitable safeguards encompass the principle of purpose limitation, data subject's rights and organizational and enforcement measures to hold data controllers accountable. In short, consent is always embedded in an environment of other data protection rules and principles. Yet, the degree to which data protection rules should focus on consent—in law as well as in practice—has been disputed among specialists.

The new GDPR, as several authors have noted, keeps with the directive's emphasis on consent, which is in line with my argument of a consent paradox [5–7, 17]. Yet, Quelle has convincingly argued that consent's and user control's role in the GDPR is a matter of interpretation [18].[3] What, however, speaks in favor of reading the GDPR in terms of a consent paradox is that it not only keeps with consent, but it does so *through* the process of reforming it. Most of those reforms address the requirements of freely given and informed consent.[4] The GDPR, in other words, speaks to the criticisms of consent that I will introduce in the paragraphs ahead.

Finally, I do not intend to imply that the GDPR is the only instance of the consent paradox. The preoccupation with consent and its improvement manifests itself in research and development projects, campaigning and litigation activities or privacy literacy efforts, just to name a few. Yet, legal instruments such as the GDPR are especially important since—on the one hand—they are a product of professional and societal debates. On the other hand, they are also a guiding source for new discussions, regarding laws' interpretation and future reform. To better understand the consent paradox, the following section will turn from one of its empirical manifestations to one of its assumed sources: the critical debate about consent among specialists.

2.2   Consent and Its Critics: Neither Freely Given, nor Informed?

Despite its stable and prestigious position in European data protection, consent has faced critique by practitioners and scholars alike. While criticisms of consent are as old as consent in data protection itself[5], the last decade has seen an increasing number of

---

[3] Lynskey provides an in-depth discussion of data protection law's understanding of individual information control [19].

[4] Discussing the reforms made to consent in the GDPR is outside the scope of this paper. They have been described elsewhere [see 17, p. 9, 18, p. 142].

[5] Tellingly, it was only after a heated debate that the first German data protection act of 1977 included consent as a legal ground for processing personal data. Early adopters of automatic data processing argued that only consent alone could provide for the legal certainty required to implement the new means of data processing. Critics, on the other side, claimed that the consent provision would constitute a potential loophole, allowing data controllers to depart from stricter data protection obligations [20].

critical engagements with the consent approach, especially in academia. There are different ways to map this vast literature. In line with the previous section, I will concentrate on those accounts that criticize consent regarding the requirements of freely given and informed consent.[6]

Several voices doubt that there are many examples of *freely given* consent *in practice*. The practice they usually refer to is the use of notice and consent by digital platforms [see 6, p. 251]. Here, they lament, the individual is not free to authorize the processing of her data for three major reasons. First, for the individual there is "little to no room for negotiation" [2, p. 177] as she can only consent to standardized privacy policies [see also 4, p. 143]. She is thus not expressing her free choice. She merely reacts to a "take it or leave it" deal. Second, the data subject often has no choice but to consent since they are no alternatives among the quasi-monopolies of internet plat-forms, let alone more data protection-friendly ones [6, p. 252]. Third and related, users increasingly depend on the usage of digital platforms [21, p. 297], reflecting the fact that they became private infrastructures, necessary to exist in our digital societies. In sum, all three arguments state that consent does not live up to its promise of free choice due to power imbalances between users and platforms. What sets these criticisms apart from the next line of arguments is that they consider power imbalances as distinct from information asymmetries. This implies that properly informing the data subject will not suffice to redress consent's shortcomings [see 19, p. 260].

Among those critiques based on the notion of freely given consent, there is a general tendency to raise doubts about the reformability of consent, at least in the narrow sense proposed in the GDPR. Most contributions in this camp advocate, although often rather vaguely, for regulating the behavior of data controllers to ensure the fairness of data processing [2, 4, 6, 21]. Focusing on controllers and their opera-tions, they argue, would allow for reducing the burden the user. More specifically, Koops suggests relying on other legal grounds than consent in "online contexts" [6, p. 252]. Rhoen proposes to address power asymmetries between data subjects and controllers by evaluating "privacy contracts", by which he means the legal grounds of both consent and contract, with the help of consumer law's notion of "unfair terms" [22]. He thus advocates to complement the "formal requirements" of data protection law with consumer law, regulating what can fairly be consented to by the consumer in the first place [22]. However, the bigger point among those critics seems to be that the emphasis on consent should be reduced, which speaks against my hypothesis that the consent paradox stems from reforms induced by consent's critics.

The second, and apparently more common, criticism of consent concerns its *in-formedness*. Again, I will focus on the three major lines of reasoning in the literature [for comprehensive accounts see [2, 23, 24]. The first critique addresses the fact that most people do not read privacy policies [see 23, p. 1883]. The most often-cited reason for this is that reading privacy policies takes too long ("information overload) while at the same time there are too much of them ("consent overload") [2, p. 177]. The

---

[6] This excludes several serious objections, for instance that, even under perfect conditions, consent cannot ensure privacy and data protection due to the technical possibility of making inferences—even about those who do not disclose their data [7, p. 322, 8, p. 61].

objective amount of time that would be needed to read, or even skim, the privacy policies presented to data subjects by far exceeds the time that can be reasonably expected to be invested by the average user [see 2, p. 177]. Schermer et al. argue further that information and consent overload lead to "consent desensitization", that is, people giving their consent blindly, thereby devaluing consent and lowering the level of data protection in the long term [2, p. 178]. A second line of objections raises doubts over the possibility of understanding privacy policies and data processing more generally. To begin with the latter, modern data processing operations in general are difficult to comprehend for the average data subject and the specialist alike [8, p. 59, 23, p. 1888]. As Solove points out, the same is true for the consequences caused by a lack of privacy/data protection as they often remain "abstract" [23, p. 1885]. Privacy policies, in turn, need to translate these complexities ensuring informed consent.[7] As a result, privacy policies turn out to be difficult to understand. This is only aggravated by the highly standardized and often legalistic language used in privacy policies [see 23, p. 1884]. The problem with understanding privacy policies is often discussed in terms of a "transparency paradox" as Barocas and Nissenbaum put it [8, p. 58]. While it seems obvious that privacy policies could be simplified to ease the users' understanding, the loss of complexity necessarily involves a loss of information [see 6, p. 252, 23, p. 1886]. Third and lastly, it is far from clear whether better information also leads to better decisions by data subjects. In fact, people's decision-making, is "skewed" [23, p. 1886], since it is largely decoupled from the quality of information provided to them. Rather than by information provisions, users are influenced by their own biases and the immediate context of their decisions, for example, what their perceived short-term gains are [see 25, p. 6].

The problem of how to improve the informedness of users has motivated numerous researchers and practitioners. Ideas on how to improve users' ability to notice, read, understand and decide abound [for an overview see 24]. Most of them involve visualizing (images, icons) as well as simplifying and condensing information into different degrees of complexity. Often, this is combined with rating the privacy policies' content [24, 26]. Rating can take the forms of warnings (mostly from third-parties) but also comes in more positive forms such as official labels and certificates where the quality of processing conditions is granted by a certification authority [see 24, p. 39].[8] Others seek to improve the user's informedness by personalizing privacy policies and notices in accordance with her level of knowledge [see 24, p. 44]. Last but not least, with the rise of behavioral research that brought to fore users' irrational decision making, the idea of nudging people into better privacy decisions, for instance through designing applications and small notices in particular ways, has gained credibility in recent years [see 25]. Finally, it is important to note that the literature does not claim that improved

---

[7] For a more general critique on this reduced understanding of how humans process information see Barocas and Nissenbaum [8] who refer to Manson and O'Neill's *Rethinking informed consent in bioethics* [12]. Manson and O'Neill provide an in-depth discussion of how human information processing works and the consequences of these insights for informed consent.

[8] Interestingly, procedural and substantial measures overlap in the latter case, situating certification approaches in-between so-called "paternalistic", that is, organizational measures addressing the behavior of data controllers, and improving user choice.

information provisions will solve all of consent's problems. Rather, it is regarded as a first step to reform [see 24, p. 62].

Summing up the literature review, it becomes clear that criticizing the informedness of consent is linked to a more profound interest in reforming consent. Thus, criticizing consent in terms of informedness seems to re-emphasize rather than to call into question consent in data protection, which is in line with the consent paradox hypothesis. However, the evidence gained from the scholarly accounts cannot explain the consent paradox satisfactorily. First, while the literature review can provide initial evidence for the consent paradox, it fails to account for the fact that criticizing consent in terms of information asymmetries appears more prominent than the objections regarding power asymmetries. What is it that makes the information camp's arguments so compelling and amenable to the consent discussion? Second, foregrounding either freely given *or* informed consent, the critiques discussed do not explain how to—technically—deal with the fact that both requirements need to be fulfilled for consent to be lawful. Another legal-technical but important aspect that most criticisms of consent do not address, concerns the distinction between the legal grounds of consent and contract. When criticizing consent, both EU and US authors often refer to a practice that is commonly known as "notice and consent" (agreeing in exchange for getting a service on the internet) but that does not necessarily constitute consent in the sense of EU data protection law, since it could also be regarded as "necessary for the performance of a contract" from a controller's perspective. Thus, what can be learned from the literature review is both too broad, omitting the legal complexities of consent, and too narrow, passing over the embeddedness of these critiques in wider professional and societal discourses. The remainder of this paper seeks to address these two points by analyzing the consent paradox in a more empirical fashion, zooming into the consent debate among German data protection practitioners.

3 Study and Methods: Analyzing the Consent Paradox Through the Lens of German Data Protection Specialists

3.1 Case Selection: The German Consent Debate

To reconstruct the consent paradox in more detail, I conducted a discourse analysis of the consent debate among German data protection professionals between 2000 and early 2017. Before discussing how this analysis can help to address the broader issue of the consent paradox, it should be noted that the rationale for this kind of analysis comes from political sociology, which assumes that professionals shape important political questions in their respective areas of expertise [see 27]. Thus, I assume data protection professionals and their debates influential for the development of consent and, consequently, worth analyzing.

Why is it worth looking at German data protection specialists in particular? First, the German tradition of data protection, informational self-determination, and consent has been influential in data protection at the European level [14, p. 54]. Second, it can be argued that the German discussion on consent was shaped by European and international debates, and therefore reflects the wider debate on consent to some extent. The most notable example of this mutual influence is the development of the EU legal framework for data protection as it has developed over time. Further, perhaps less obvious examples include transnational discussions on topics such as the "economics of privacy" [28], a theme that has made its way into the German debate in recent years. Third, the *form* of the German consent debate is distinct in that it has evolved as a hybrid of a scholarly, a societal, and a technical debate, involving academics, members of data protection authorities, and lawyers and data protection officers working in the private sector. However, I neither argue that the German debate has been decisive for the European field of data protection in general, nor do I claim that it merely reflects European or transnational developments. Rather, I want to demonstrate that the German debate, as a piece of the consent puzzle, can provide a useful starting point to understand the consent paradox. In particular, I expect these discussions to provide a more nuanced perspective on the technical details of consent in data protection law, which, as I have argued above, are notably absent from the scholarly debate on consent.

My analysis focuses on a period extending from the beginning of 2000 to March 2017. The research material consists of 27 written contributions to the consent debate, most of them taking the form of articles in professional journals (n = 23), some contributions to edited volumes (n = 3), and one research report. Due to the time-consuming interpretative method used (see below), it was not possible to include entire monographs.

The process of selecting these texts involved multiple stages. I first identified a series of influential, that is, frequently cited, articles on consent in data protection journals by compiling references from the authoritative legal commentary on the Germany Federal Data Protection Act (BDSG) [29, p. 432]. In addition, I compiled all of the references from the literature review chapters of recent dissertations on consent, assuming that they include the most important and recent work on the topic [30, 31]. In a second step, I systematically searched a major German database[9] as well as Google scholar for German-speaking articles on consent in data protection. This was necessary to avoid reproducing potential citation bias from the first round of selection.[10] After sorting out those articles that dealt primarily with consent in the medical field, I arrived at 92 texts, two-thirds of them from the period between 2000 and 2017.[11] The increasing number of articles on consent reflects a growing interest in the issue among data protection specialists since the turn of the millennium. This can be read as evidence of the consent paradox. Most of the articles published since 2000 discuss the importance of consent in the dawning age of commercial Internet usage and the associated business model of offering services in exchange for monetizing user data. As this discussion seems to be at the core of the consent debate, I decided to focus on these articles and exclude texts written before 2000[12]. I further excluded the few texts since 2000 that dealt with consent in the offline world, for instance, in the case of loyalty

---

[9] Database of the Berlin State Library: http://staatsbibliothek-berlin.de/en/.

[10] A likely citation bias in this case could consist of authors who do not cite each other because they belong to different schools of thought.

[11] The exact numbers of texts for the respective decades are: 1970s (n = 9), 1980s (n = 9), 1990s (n = 13), 2000s (n = 27), 2010s (n = 34).

[12] I allowed for a tolerance of one year, assuming that a text published in 1999 was written around the turn of the millennium.

programs [see 14, p. 195]. This left a total of 37 articles for the document analysis. This number was further reduced to 27 in the process of interpretation, which I turn to in the following.

3.2 Method: Making Sense of the Consent Debate with the Help of Discourse Analysis and Grounded Theory

To analyze the material selected, I conducted a *discourse analysis*. Discourse analysis does not rely on a prescribed theory or method, but rather denotes a methodological standpoint. Discourse analysis encompasses different schools of thought, sharing the premise that reality is shaped by *discourse*. Discourse can be defined as "ideas, concepts, and categories through which meaning is given to social and physical phenomena" [32]. In short, discourses are knowledge orders, underlying arguments and debates. At the same time, discourses often come with certain narratives, which, as Gottweis put it, have the "power to create order" [33, p. 468]. Thus, in discourse analysis, knowing and telling blend into each other. Even the most technical debates rely on certain views and assumptions to make sense of what they are doing. Most discourse analyses aim at identifying discourses in spoken and written language. The role of discourse in data protection has not been studied sufficiently in the research to date. A notable exception[13] is Bennett and Raab's argument that the field of data protection and privacy has been shaped by a discourse they call the "privacy paradigm," which links actors' "agreed understanding of the nature and the scope" of privacy to the values of liberal democracy and the autonomous individual [34, p. 13]. Bennett and Raab have shown that these assumptions are not merely rhetoric but have substantial and wide-ranging implications, including the focus on *personal data* in data protection law [34, p. 16].

Applying discourse analysis to a complex legal issue such as data protection involves going beyond the analysis of law itself. As Klein et al. argue in the area of copyright law, legal arguments rely on non-legal justifications that in turn are connected to broader narratives, making them appear as compelling arguments [35]. It is important to note that competing justifications or discourses are often rooted in fundamentally different understandings of what is "good, right, and just" [35, p. 4]. This also implies that there can be no single understanding of, in our case, data protection or their respective aims. Rather, there are different and conflicting ways of thinking about data protection and the role of consent therein. As Bennett and Raab have shown, these different ways of meaning making, in turn, lead to different (interpretations of) the legal framework and regulatory options. Discourse analysis goes further than a literature review that merely summarizes the arguments made: It aims at explicitly identifying the worldviews and assumptions underpinning those arguments. I consider those underpinnings an important part of the consent paradox, since they can help to explain why certain views of consent persist while others are rejected or, at least, less prominent.

---

[13] Bennett and Raab's work is not the only exception. I refer to other recent works on data protection's discourses in the conclusion.

Since discourse analysis does not prescribe a specific method to identify *discourses* in the research material, I employed *grounded theory*, a framework for qualitative data analysis. Grounded theory aims at deriving a "theory" from a recursive interpretation of data [36, p.12]. In this context, "theory" means abstracting underlying concepts "that can be used to explain or predict phenomena" [15, 36]. As others have shown, grounded theory ties in well with discourse analysis since both share the aim of discovering explanations that are not manifest in the data [see 37, p. 237]. In the case of texts, this means that reading and summarizing them is not enough: they need to be interpreted instead. Grounded theory provides the tools for such an interpretation. It allows for "reading between the lines" in a controlled manner.[14] Thus, I consider grounded theory a helpful tool to identify the discourses shaping the consent paradox.

Grounded theory is based on a multi-staged interpretation process. It begins with "breaking down" the data "into discrete parts", that is, single words and sentences [36, p. 102]. These parts are examined, shedding light on specific terms and connections that remain invisible in the usual approach of reading and summarizing. From these newly discovered meanings, hypotheses for interpretation are developed and tested against the material. This recursive process is supported by techniques such as asking generative questions (who, what, why, how), making comparisons in the data, and placing the data into categories and sub-categories. The aim of grounded theory is to "open up the text" [36, p. 102] in order to develop ideas about underlying concepts, refine them in the light of the material, and test them against old and newly added material. The goal of this exercise is to "reassemble" the material in a new and illuminating way [36, p. 102]. New texts are added until a point of saturation has been reached, which means that nothing new is brought to the fore by adding more material [36, p. 214]. In my case, I reached this point after interpreting 27 texts. To organize the interpretation process, I used the qualitative data analysis software MAXQDA, which makes it possible to visualize and perform the procedure of assigning attributes to text segments, referred to as "coding" in qualitative and interpretative research [39, p. 3]. As findings from interpretative research and discourse analysis take the form of narratives and rationales, they cannot be presented as graphs and numbers. They are usually presented first as a comprehensive, evidence-rich analysis, allowing the reader to clearly understand the interpretation derived from the material [see 40, p. 113].

As I will discuss in the following, I was able to reconstruct two different discourses on consent from the material: the *world of data protection rules* and *the data market world*[15]. These two discourses correspond to the two major critiques of consent: *freely given* and *informed consent*. Furthermore, I argue that my findings complement the literature review in Sect. 2. First, they provide a more nuanced understanding of the technical details of the consent debate and the relationship between freely given and informed consent. Second, and at the same time, they provide a broader picture by

---

[14] However, interpretative studies do not and cannot aspire to the same goals and evaluative standards as positivist research [see 38].

[15] The term "world" is widely used in constructivist social science to foreground the fact that discourses produce different "realities" [see 41, p. 125]. In the following, I use the term interchangeably with discourse.

linking the technical arguments to broader societal discourses, thus explaining their influence (or their lack thereof).

4   The Two Worlds of Consent in Data Protection

In the following I discuss the two predominant discourses of consent that I have identified among German data protection professionals: the *world of data protection rules* and the *data market world*.[16] I use these terms as a kind of shorthand to distinguish the two most common ways of discussing consent in data protection among German data protection specialists. I introduce both worlds in their own words—to the extent possible in an English-speaking publication drawing on German texts. Presenting both worlds in their own language allows the reader to grasp each one's own reality [see 41, p. 153]. For example, whereas the *data market* appears as profit-driven to the critical observer, it produces mutual benefits from its own perspective.[17] I argue that each world's stance on consent depends on these kinds of narratives, which makes it important to present each in its own right.

I distinguish both worlds based on their different (1) understanding of data protection's aims and rationales, (2) their view on the relationships between and responsibilities of data controllers and data subjects, and (3) their approach to consent in the Internet age. In accordance with my methodology, these categories emerged from the interpretation process. Consequently, the material also revealed which text and which author belongs to which camp. Discourse theory, however, assumes that discourses reach beyond their authors, embodying broader worldviews that authors make use of and modify but do not create on their own [see 42, p. 11]. Thus, while referring to specific texts, I foreground the competing ideas and worldviews on consent and data protection instead of their authors. These discursive patterns, I argue, can provide insights beyond the specificities of the German case. The main tenets of each world are summarized in Table 1.

4.1   The World of Data Protection Rules

The first discourse I identified in the German consent debate is the *world of data protection rules*. The world of data protection rules emphasizes *informational self-determination* as its higher aim [43, see 44, 45], but in a relatively formalistic manner that does not explain well the rationale behind this camp's stance on data protection and consent. The world of data protection rules' way of thinking and arguing can be characterized more accurately as a bureaucratic or regulatory one.[18] It is

---

[16] In my master's thesis, I made a more fine-grained distinction of discourses on consent, resulting in four different worlds. For this paper, I reduced complexity by leaving out one discourse and merging two others. This also explains why, in the following, I do not cite all 27 texts analyzed.

[17] I thank one of the anonymous reviewers for the question that led to this clarification.

[18] I thank Kjetil Rommetveit who suggested these terms to me.

Table 1. Discourses on consent among German data protectionists between 2000 and 2017.

	World of data protection rules	Data market world
Higher aim of data protection	Right to informational self-determination	Beneficial data economy
Logic of argumentation	Bureaucratic (compliance)	Evidence-based (correspondence with reality)
Relations between data subjects and data controllers	Power asymmetry	Information asymmetry
Operationalization of consent	Freely given consent Consent $\neq$ contract Linkage prohibition	Informed consent Consent $\sim$ contract Ensuring informed choice
Future of consent	Uncertain (*whether*)	Reformist (*how*)
Emblematic texts	[43–49]	[51–56, 58, 59]

concerned with the rigorous application of a hierarchical set of rules, instruments, and criteria. It values rules that are "explicit"[19], "comprehensive", and "precise" [see 44, 46, 47]. Adhering to the logic of *functionality*, data protection rules are both means and ends. Consent is "good right and just" when it fulfills the criteria laid out in data protection rules. This is a challenging task because, as one author has noted, "a number of substantial, formal and other requirements must be met" [47, p. 727]. These requirements are set out in general and specific data protection laws[20] and elaborated further through the decisions of courts and data protection authorities and in legal commentary. In sum, the world of data protection rules understands data protection as a complex set of regulations—a machinery that needs to be put to work.[21]

In the world of data protection rules, it is the data controller who bears the burden of compliance [see 46]. Consequently, the world of data protection rules refers to the data controller as the *verantwortliche Stelle*, which literally translates as "responsible authority" [see 45, p. 725]. The data subject, in turn, is addressed as "affected person" (*Betroffener*). The assumption behind these terms is that controllers' data processing practices can have negative effects on data subjects. More generally, the world of data protection rules assumes a certain imbalance between data subjects and controllers [43, p. 404, 46, p. 91]. Meaningful consent needs to reflect this imbalance.

The asymmetry between data subjects and controllers is addressed through the requirement that any consent must be freely given. While, in fact, all requirements for valid consent must be met, it is the issue of freely given consent that dominates the world of data protection rules' discussions. The world of data protection rules holds that consent cannot be freely given in situations where the data subject is confronted

---

[19] All direct quotations from German sources are my translations.

[20] The laws those texts mainly refer to are the German Federal Data Protection Act (BDSG) and the German Telemedia Act (TMG).

[21] This characterization is inspired by Boltanski and Thévenot's description of an industrial way of thinking and acting [41, p. 203].

with the "coercive power of the state", "irresistible incentives", or "legal and factual dependencies" [46, p. 92]. In those instances, the data subject's decisional autonomy is limited.

German data protection law's concept of "linkage prohibition" (*Koppelungsverbot*) specifies the requirement of freely given consent in certain situations of factual dependencies. It forbids that data controllers "depend the conclusion of a contract on the consent of the data subject for advertising or for marketing/opinion research purposes, when the data subject does not have alternative access to comparable contractual services without the consent or such an alternative is not possible in a reasonable way" [translation by Kosta, see 14, p. 194]. In other words, denying consent for marketing purposes will not lead to a denial of access to a particular service [see 45, p. 709]. From this viewpoint, freely given consent differs from a contract, in which one party imposes certain conditions upon the other. The linkage prohibition thus offers a litmus test for assessing whether consent has been freely given. It relies upon the purpose limitation principle as well as an assessment of the data controller's market position.[22] The linkage prohibition and its underlying principles are key in understanding the world of data protection rules' critique of consent in the Internet age.

The world of data protection rules holds that the practice of "paying with data" for online services is difficult to reconcile with the requirement of freely given consent. Its advocates arrive at this conclusion based on the ideas expressed in the linkage prohibition. First, they argue that consent in the context of information society services (*Telemediendienste*) need to be assessed by asking whether their users can access the service without consenting to the usage of data for advertising purposes. A second and related, question is whether there are alternatives that fulfill this criterion [43, p. 405, see 44, p. 648]. Since major online services or platforms do not offer this possibility or can be considered monopolies [see 48, p. 113], the linkage prohibition is often violated. Thus, there are very few situations where consent can be deemed freely given: only those in which consent and contract have been unbundled from each other [49, p. 82]. In the majority of situations, data processing must be based on other grounds than consent, such as contracts, sector-specific laws, or codes of conduct and certification schemes as a more flexible alternative [see 49, p. 82]. Consequently, it is only in those rare situations where consent can be considered freely given that the issue of informed consent eventually becomes relevant [see 43, p. 408, 50, p. 145].

To summarize, the world of data protection rules calls into question *whether* data protection in the Internet age can continue to rely on consent. However, its operationalization of the imbalance between individuals and data controllers presents a kind of quiet critique of power, embodying bureaucratic rather than fundamental rights-related values. Put differently, consent appears problematic for the modest reason that it does not tick the box on freely given consent. The world of data protection rules appears rather self-referential, lacking a compelling narrative of why power asymmetries endanger freely given consent.

---

[22] Interestingly, the new GDPR introduces a linkage prohibition in its Article 7(4). In contrast to the older German linkage prohibition, the provision in the GDPR is not limited to situations of using personal data for marketing purposes.

4.2   The Data Market World

The second discourse among German data protectionists is the *data market world*. From the data market viewpoint, data protection serves the higher goal of creating *mutual benefits* by facilitating the exchange of personal data between data subjects and controllers. Its advocates claim that data markets present a win-win-situation, asserting that it is not just companies but also their customers who benefit from data driven business models [see 51 p. 18]. The fact that data subjects do benefit from the data market becomes visible when observing users' behavior: Users do not refrain from using services, but deliberately give their data to benefit from data processing. The data market provides them with a number of useful and indispensable services such as social networks [see 52, p. 635]. The principle of "paying with data" has become an accepted part of users' lived reality [see 53, p. 499].

The data market's thesis is that data protection should be more *evidence-based*. Its advocates call for an empirically informed understanding of modern data processing and user behavior. While earlier works mention those new realities in a rather anecdotal manner [see 51, 54], more recent contributions build their arguments on actual scientific evidence, referring to works on the "economics of privacy" [see 55, 56]. These insights, whether anecdotal or empirical, need to be reflected in data protection law and, in turn, in its operationalization of consent. Articulating this fact-based rationale, the data market world distinguishes itself from the world of data protection rules. Some of its earlier contributions, in particular those from before 2010, refer directly to the contributions from the world of data protection rules [see 54, 57]. As one data market advocate puts it, the other side, that is, the world of data protection rules, "understands self-determination as an end in itself" [54, p. 1622]. They criticize that the world of data protection rules' understanding of data protection is detached from actual harms and in ignorance of individuals' deliberate choices to decide for themselves on the risks and benefits of data processing.

The data market world understands data subjects as "customers" [see 53, 54]. More recent works refer to data subjects as "users" [see 55, 56]. The notions of "customer" and "user" suggest a more active role for the data subject—compared to the "affected person" in the world of data protection rules. Further, the terms imply that data subjects have commercial interests reaching beyond the mere expectation of having their data protected. In more technical terms, the data market world argues that the right to informational self-determination includes the idea of granting data subjects a commercial interest and, going even further, a certain leverage in commercializing their personal data [see 52, p. 639]. The German general right to personality has been increasingly interpreted in favor of a commercialization of the personality [see 57, p. 43]. Since the right to informational self-determination is also based on the right to personality, it is "only a small step" [52, p. 639] from understanding the commercial exchange of personal data as an expression of informational self-determination. Against this backdrop, consent is considered not only a suitable, but also a central instrument for enabling transactions of personal data [see 57, p. 43]. What sets the data market world's understanding of consent apart from the world of data protection rules is that the concepts of consent and contract do not differ but converge [52, p. 640].

In contrast to what its critics might assume, the data market world does not deny a certain imbalance between both parties [see 52, p. 639]. Yet, it would be a mistake to jump to "paternalistic" conclusions [see 52, p. 637]. Data protection should not protect users against themselves [53, p. 499]. The imbalance between data subjects and controllers is not ultimately harmful. Quite the contrary, most commercial data processing is harmless and, in fact, often beneficial to the data subject [see already 51, p. 18]. However, to be able to weigh the risks and benefits, the user needs to be informed about the modalities of the transaction. Most importantly, it must be made clear to the user that the service is not free to her but that she is, in fact, paying with her data [see 57, p. 41, 58, p. 159]. In short, the data market world highlights the problem of information asymmetries and the requirement of redressing them through the requirement of informed consent.

Yet, the data market world does not entirely dispense with the requirement of freely given consent and the related concept of linkage prohibition. In my analysis, I observed two ways how its proponents deal with the issue of freely given consent. The first one is to reinterpret what "freely given" means. Some authors propose to reserve the notion of freely given consent, and thus the linkage prohibition, for those situations where the data controller is a public authority, an employer [58, p. 158] or where there is a "coercive" dependency, as in the case of banking or insurance contracts [53, p. 504]. Information society services, in contrast, should not by default be subject to the linkage prohibition [see already 59, p. 399]. In most cases, freely given consent can be incorporated into the requirement for informed consent instead: "A person who is not informed cannot assess the implications of its decision and thus is not giving consent freely." [60, p. 156]. Yet, this positioning remains largely unexplained. The implicit assumption seems to be that a strict application of the linkage prohibition is "removed from reality", since the linkage prohibition forbids what is considered the "life blood" [52, p. 637] of the relationship between users and Internet platforms: the further processing of personal data in exchange for using a service. The second way in which the world of the data market deals with the issue of freely given consent is by omitting it, focusing on the informedness of consent instead. This development is evidenced by the introduction of the term "informed consent" into the German debate [see 55, 56, 61]. Along with it comes a burgeoning literature on how to improve informed consent, ensuring that data subjects read and understand privacy policies and decide in their best interest [see 24]. The concrete measures that are discussed concern the idea to simplify privacy policies into "one pagers" and privacy icons [55]. Another related discussion concerns the idea of improving young peoples' data protection literacy [62, p. 769]. Finally, technical means to support users' informed consent are discussed in this context [see already 51, p. 19].[23] While those two options of sidestepping the issue of freely given consent appear rather separate from each other, they have at least two things in common. First, they embody an evidence-based approach to data protection, drawing on insights into users' everyday reality. Second, although appearing grounded in facts rather than norms, both options reify the normative value of user choice and thus consent.

---

[23] The latter examples are not confined to the discussion on ensuring informed consent.

In sum, for the data market world, the question is not whether but *how* consent can be implemented within data protection. Presenting itself as a fact-based and pragmatic way of reasoning, the data market world does not give the impression of being ideologically charged. Its aims and rationale lead the data market world to a reformist problematization of consent. Speaking of reforms, the data market world is quite specific when it comes to improving the informedness of consent. However, its advocates remain rather vague on other important questions, such as what the concrete implications of a more contractual understanding of consent are.

5 Discussion and Conclusion: Data Protection as a Critique of Power

In this paper, I have set out to account for the *consent paradox*, that is, the prominent role ascribed to consent in data protection despite its numerous critiques. To elucidate the consent paradox, I first reviewed the scholarly critiques of consent. I showed that critiquing consent in terms of information asymmetries confirms rather than calls into question the prominent role of consent and thus reproduces the consent paradox. A problematization of consent based on power asymmetries, in contrast, provides a more substantive critique of consent, casting doubts on the centrality of consent in data protection. Yet, the literature review appeared too broad and too narrow at the same time. On the one hand, it did not tell us much about the legal technical consequences of the respective arguments. On the other hand, the literature review could not account for the fact that criticizing consent in terms of information asymmetries is more common than problematizing consent in the language of power asymmetries. To address these gaps, I supplemented the literature review by conducting a discourse analysis of the debate on consent among German data protection professionals, distinguishing two common ways of discussing consent. Problematizing consent in terms of power asymmetries is linked to the discourse of data protection rules, which stresses data subjects' dependence on digital platforms, and for that reason, calls into question *whether* data protection can continue to rely on consent. It, however, fails to provide a coherent narrative articulating why power asymmetries are problematic. The fact that consent, when given in situations of factual dependency, might result in non-compliance with data protection law, does not present a particularly powerful narrative. Highlighting information asymmetries, in contrast, is linked to the popular and intuitive narrative of the data market. The data market discourse is supported by an evidence-based approach of reasoning. On the data market, consumers exchange "their data" in order to benefit from the services provided by internet companies. As a last word of caution, the worlds of *data protection rules* and the *data market* represent ideal types: They are scientific constructs to make sense of a more complex reality. They neither explain all aspects of the consent debate, nor necessarily correspond to the intentions of the actors therein. For example, conducting a research project that improves the informedness of consent does not necessitate the researcher to be convinced or even aware of the data market discourse.[24]

Among scholars it is conventional wisdom that the meaning of data protection is far from settled [see 19, p. 272] and maybe even "impossible to define" [see 63, p. 330]. Yet, the search for data protection's meaning goes beyond the realm of data protection law. It is also influenced by wider societal discourses and conflicts. My discussion of the consent paradox speaks to an emerging strand of literature exploring how political, scientific and popular discourses shape the field of data protection [21, 64–67]. Quite a few of those works come to similar conclusions: They observe an increasing individualization and commodification of data protection [10, 21, 64, 65]. It is tempting to dismiss these studies as broad and undifferentiated attempts to explain developments in data protection as influenced by a neoliberal zeitgeist. In fact, these studies paint a more nuanced picture, attempting to show (1) how data protection oscillates between different aims and understandings, most notably the free flow of data and the protection of individuals [see 63, p. 336], (2) how these understandings translate into laws and instruments and vice versa [see 64], and (3) how the field and its perceptions change over time [see 7]. Yet, further research is needed on all three points.

Looking at the case of the consent paradox, future work needs to retrace in more detail how the world of data protection rules, the data market world, or varieties of those discourses shape the interpretation of freely given and informed consent in practice, especially under the new GDPR. The EU's new data protection rules leave room for interpretation on these points, especially in their take on the linkage prohibition in article 7(4) and recital 43. In this analysis, I have suggested that freely given consent could be incorporated into the requirement of informedness, thus redefining power asymmetries as information asymmetries. Another possibility that is more in line with the world of data protection rules is a strong take on the linkage prohibition. This, in turn, could reduce the omnipresence of consent in practice, leading data controllers to rely on other legal grounds, most importantly contracts. However, this might only shift the discussion over take-it-or-leave-it choices from the legal ground of consent to that of contracts [see 22, p. 7].[25] Another research gap left by my study concerns the development of the consent debate and its underlying discourses over time. Due to its research design, my paper does not account for this diachronic perspective in a representative manner. It only allows for the tentative hypothesis that the data market discourse has become more dominant in recent years.

What are the practical consequences of my findings? Asking this question implies that I consider the "consent paradox" not only an empirical phenomenon but also as a political problem. The consent paradox is problematic since it discourages more comprehensive critiques on the limits of consent and thus hinders more substantial reforms to consent. As others have proposed, meaningful reforms of consent should include reducing the burden on consent by regulating what kind of processing practices

---

[24] Matzner et al. make the same point in the context of the German "DIY data protection discourse" [21, p. 289].

[25] During the finalization phase of this article, the discussion on how to deal with the linkage prohibition and take-it-or-leave-it choices in the GDPR has just begun [68, 69].

can be subject to individual choice in the first place [see 70, p. 527]. The omnipresence of consent also limits our ability to think beyond consent, tying up resources needed to advance in other issue areas of data protection such as organizational and enforcement measures [see 5]. Finally, the consent paradox and its underlying market discourse risks omitting the collective values of data protection and privacy [see 65, p. 94]. My analysis suggests that a break with the consent paradox can only be achieved by reintroducing a more compelling critique of power into data protection than the rule-oriented and bureaucratic data protection discourse is able to articulate. As others have argued, the early justifications of data protection with their focus on holding the powerful accountable might be instructive for this purpose [7, 71]. Articulating data protection as a critique of power necessitates us to make clear how power and data processing relate to each other, what are the risks associated with it, and consequently, what should be the ends and means of data protection.

References

1. Bergemann, B.: Der "informed consent" im Datenschutz: Eine politikwissenschaftliche Analyse, Master thesis. Freie Universität Berlin (2017). https://www.econstor.eu/handle/10419/162861
2. Schermer, B.W., Custers, B., van der Hof, S.: The crisis of consent: how stronger legal protection may lead to weaker consent in data protection. Ethics Inf. Technol. 16, 171–182 (2014)
3. Boltanski, L., Chiapello, È.: The New Spirit of Capitalism. Verso, London (2007)
4. Austin, L.M.: Enough about me: why privacy is about power, not consent (or harm). In: Sarat, A. (ed.) A World Without Privacy: What Law Can and Should Do?, pp. 131–189. Cambride University Press, New York (2014)
5. Zanfir, G.: Forgetting about consent. why the focus should be on "suitable safeguards" in data protection law. In: Gutwirth, S., Leenes, R., De Hert, P. (eds.) Reloading Data Protection, pp. 237–257. Springer, Dordrecht (2014). https://doi.org/10.1007/978-94-007-7540-4_12
6. Koops, B.-J.: The trouble with European data protection law. Int. Data Priv. Law. 4, 250–261 (2014)
7. van der Sloot, B.: Do data protection rules protect the individual and should they? An assessment of the proposed general data protection regulation. Int. Data Priv. Law. 4, 307–325 (2014)
8. Barocas, S., Nissenbaum, H.: Big data's end run around anonymity and consent. In: Lane, J., Stodden, V., Bender, S., Nissenbaum, H. (eds.) Privacy, Big Data, and the Public Good: Frameworks for Engagement, pp. 44–75. Cambridge University Press, Cambridge (2014)
9. Rouvroy, A., Poullet, Y.: The right to informational self-determination and the value of self-development: reassessing the importance of privacy for democracy. In: Gutwirth, S., Poullet, Y., De Hert, P., de Terwangne, C., Nouwt, S. (eds.) Reinventing Data Protection?, pp. 45–76. Springer, Netherlands, Dordrecht (2009). https://doi.org/10.1007/978-1-4020-9498-9_2
10. Crain, M.: The limits of transparency: data brokers and commodification. New Media Soc. 20, 88–104 (2016)
11. McDermott, Y.: Conceptualising the right to data protection in an era of Big Data. Big Data Soc. 4, 1–7 (2017)

12. Manson, N.C., O'Neill, O.: Rethinking Informed Consent in Bioethics. Cambridge University Press, Cambridge (2007)
13. Laurie, G.T.: Genetic Privacy: A Challenge to Medico-Legal Norms. Cambridge University Press, Cambridge (2004)
14. Kosta, E.: Consent in European Data Protection Law. Martinus Nijhoff Publishers, Leiden (2013)
15. Bennett, C.J.: The Privacy Advocates: Resisting the Spread of Surveillance. MIT Press, Cambridge (2008)
16. Gutwirth, S.: Short statement about the role of consent in the European data protection directive. Vrije Universiteit Brussel, Brussels (2012)
17. De Hert, P., Papakonstantinou, V.: The new general data protection regulation: still a sound system for the protection of individuals? Comput. Law Secur. Rev. **32**, 179–194 (2016)
18. Quelle, C.: Not just user control in the general data protection regulation. In: Lehmann, A., Whitehouse, D., Fischer-Hübner, S., Fritsch, L., Raab, C. (eds.) Privacy and Identity 2016. IAICT, vol. 498, pp. 140–163. Springer, Cham (2016). https://doi.org/10.1007/978-3-319-55783-0_11
19. Lynskey, O.: The Foundations of EU Data Protection Law. Oxford University Press, Oxford (2015)
20. von Uckermann, E.F.: Einwilligung nach BDSG – ein Mißverständnis? Datenschutz Datensich. DuD. **3**, 163–168 (1979)
21. Matzner, T., Masur, P.K., Ochs, C., von Pape, T.: Do-it-yourself data protection—empowerment or burden? In: Gutwirth, S., Leenes, R., De Hert, P. (eds.) Data Protection on the Move, pp. 277–305. Springer, Netherlands, Dordrecht (2016). https://doi.org/10.1007/978-94-017-7376-8_11
22. Rhoen, M.: Beyond consent: improving data protection through consumer protection law. Internet Policy Rev. **5** (2016)
23. Solove, D.J.: Privacy self-management and the consent dilemma. Harv. Law Rev. **126**, 1880–1903 (2013)
24. Arnold, R., Hillebrand, A., Waldburger, M.: Personal data and privacy. Final report (Study for Ofcom). WIK-Consult, Bad Honnef (2015)
25. Acquisti, A., Sleeper, M., Wang, Y., Wilson, S., Adjerid, I., Balebako, R., Brandimarte, L., Cranor, L.F., Komanduri, S., Leon, P.G., Sadeh, N., Schaub, F.: Nudges for privacy and security: understanding and assisting users' choices online. ACM Comput. Surv. **50**, 1–41 (2017)
26. Calo, R.: Against notice skepticism in privacy (and elsewhere). Notre Dame Law Rev. **87**, 1027–1072 (2012)
27. Kauppi, N., Madsen, M.R. (eds.): Transnational Power Elites: The Social and Global Structuration of the EU. Routledge, London (2013)
28. Acquisti, A., Taylor, C.R., Wagman, L.: The Economics of Privacy. Social Science Research Network, Rochester (2016)
29. Simitis, S. (ed.): § 4a Einwilligung. In: Kommentar zum Bundesdatenschutzgesetz, pp. 432–466. Nomos, Baden-Baden (2011)
30. Rogosch, P.M.: Die Einwilligung im Datenschutzrecht. Nomos, Baden-Baden (2013)
31. Hermstrüwer, Y.: Informationelle Selbstgefährdung: zur rechtsfunktionalen, spieltheoretischen und empirischen Rationalität der datenschutzrechtlichen Einwilligung und des Rechts auf informationelle Selbstbestimmung. Mohr Siebeck, Tübingen (2016)
32. Hajer, M.: FAQ http://www.maartenhajer.nl/?page_id=14
33. Gottweis, H.: Argumentative policy analysis. In: Peters, G., Pierre, J. (eds.) Handbook of Public Policy, pp. 461–479. Sage, London (2006)

34. Bennett, C.J., Raab, C.D.: The Governance of Privacy: Policy Instruments in Global Perspective. Ashgate, Aldershot (2003)
35. Klein, B., Moss, G., Edwards, L.: Understanding Copyright: Intellectual Property in the Digital Age. SAGE, Los Angeles (2015)
36. Strauss, A.L., Corbin, J.M.: Basics of Qualitative Research: Techniques and Procedures for Developing Grounded Theory. Sage Publications, Thousand Oaks (1998)
37. Keller, R.: Analysing discourse. an approach from the sociology of knowledge. Forum Qual. Sozialforschung Forum Qual. Soc. Res. **6** (2005)
38. Haverland, M., Yanow, D.: A hitchhiker's guide to the public administration research universe: surviving conversations on methodologies and methods. Public Adm. Rev. **72**, 401–408 (2012)
39. Saldaña, J.: The Coding Manual for Qualitative Researchers. SAGE, Los Angeles (2009)
40. Schwartz-Shea, P., Yanow, D.: Interpretive Research Design: Concepts and Processes. Routledge, New York (2012)
41. Boltanski, L., Thévenot, L.: On Justification: Economies of Worth. Princeton University Press, Princeton (2006)
42. Fischer, F., Gottweis, H.: Introduction: the argumentative turn revisited. In: Fischer, F., Gottweis, H. (eds.) The Argumentative Turn Revisited: Public Policy as Communicative Practice, pp. 1–27. Duke University Press, Durham (2012)
43. Menzel, H.-J.: Datenschutzrechtliche Einwilligungen: Plädoyer für eine Rückkehr zur Selbstbestimmung. Datenschutz Datensicherheit DuD. **32**, 400–408 (2008)
44. Schaar, P.: Datenschutzrechtliche Einwilligung im Internet. Multimed. Recht MMR **2001**, 644–648 (2001)
45. Iraschko-Luscher, S.: Einwilligung – ein stumpfes Schwert des Datenschutzes? Datenschutz Datensicherheit DuD. **30**, 706–710 (2006)
46. Roßnagel, A., Pfitzmann, A., Garstka, H.: Modernisierung des Datenschutzrechts. Gutachten im Auftrag des Bundesministeriums des Innern. Bundesministerium des Innern, Berlin (2001)
47. Zscherpe, K.: Anforderungen an die datenschutzrechtliche Einwilligung im Internet. Multimed. Recht MMR **2004**, 723–727 (2004)
48. Kutscha, M.: Mehr Datenschutz — aber wie? Z. Für Rechtspolit. ZRP **43**, 112–114 (2010)
49. Kamp, M., Rost, M.: Kritik an der Einwilligung: Ein Zwischenruf zu einer fiktiven Rechtsgrundlage in asymmetrischen Machtverhältnissen. Datenschutz Datensicherheit DuD **37**, 80–84 (2013)
50. Körner, M.: Informierte Einwilligung als Schutzkonzept. In: Simon, D., Weiss, M. (eds.) Zur Autonomie des Individuums: Liber Amicorum für Spiros Simitis, pp. 131–150. Nomos, Baden-Baden (2000)
51. Ladeur, K.-H.: Datenschutz – vom Abwehrrecht zur planerischen Optimierung von Wissensnetzwerken. Zur "objektiv-rechtlichen Dimension" des Datenschutzes. Datenschutz Datensicherheit DuD **24**, 12–19 (2000)
52. Bräutigam, P.: Das Nutzungsverhältnis bei sozialen Netzwerken - Zivilrechtlicher Austausch von IT-Leistung gegen personenbezogene Daten. Multimed. Recht MMR **2012**, 635–641 (2012)
53. Schafft, T., Ruoff, A.: Nutzung personenbezogener Daten für Werbezwecke zwischen Einwilligung und Vertragserfüllung. Comput. Recht CR **22**, 499–504 (2006)
54. Bull, H.P.: Zweifelsfragen um die informationelle Selbstbestimmung – Datenschutz als Datenaskese? Neue Juristische Wochenschr. NJW **59**, 1617–1623 (2006)
55. Pollmann, M., Kipker, D.-K.: Informierte Einwilligung in der Online-Welt. Datenschutz Datensicherheit DuD **40**, 378–381 (2016)

56. Arnold, R., Hillebrand, A., Waldburger, M.: Informed Consent in Theorie und Praxis: Warum Lesen, Verstehen und Handeln auseinanderfallen. Datenschutz Datensicherheit DuD **39**, 730–734 (2015)
57. Buchner, B.: Die Einwilligung im Datenschutzrecht – vom Rechtfertigungsgrund zum Kommerzialisierungsinstrument. Datenschutz Datensicherheit DuD **34**, 39–43 (2010)
58. Buchner, B.: Grundsätze und Rechtmäßigkeit der Datenverarbeitung unter der DS-GVO. Datenschutz Datensicherheit DuD **40**, 155–161 (2016)
59. von Lewinski, K.: Privacy Policies: Unterrichtungen und Einwilligung im Internet. Datenschutz Datensicherheit DuD **26**, 395–400 (2002)
60. Petri, T.: Datenschutzrechtliche Einwilligung im Massengeschäftsverkehr. Recht Datenverarb. RdV **23**, 153–158 (2007)
61. Beisenherz, G., Tinnefeld, M.-T.: Aspekte der Einwilligung: Zivil- und strafrechtliche Bezüge der Einwilligung im Datenschutzrecht. Datenschutz Datensicherheit DuD **35**, 110–115 (2011)
62. Caspar, J.: Soziale Netzwerke – Endstation informationelle Selbstbestimmung?: Ein Bericht aus der Behördenpraxis. Datenschutz Datensicherheit DuD **37**, 767–771 (2013)
63. Bellanova, R.: Digital, politics, and algorithms: governing digital data through the lens of data protection. Eur. J. Soc. Theory **20**, 329–347 (2017)
64. Draper, N.A.: From privacy pragmatist to privacy resigned: challenging narratives of rational choice in digital privacy debates: challenging rational choice in digital privacy debates. Policy Internet **9**, 232–251 (2017)
65. Hull, G.: Successful failure: what Foucault can teach us about privacy self-management in a world of Facebook and big data. Ethics Inf. Technol. **17**, 89–101 (2015)
66. Bellanova, R.: Data protection, with love. Int. Polit. Sociol. **8**, 112–115 (2014)
67. van Dijk, N., Gellert, R., Rommetveit, K.: A risk to a right? Beyond data protection risk assessments. Comput. Law Secur. Rev. **32**, 286–306 (2016)
68. Borgesius, F.J.Z., Kruikemeier, S., Boerman, S.C., Helberger, N.: Tracking walls, take-it-or-leave-it choices, the GDPR, and the ePrivacy regulation. Eur. Data Prot. Law Rev. **3**, 353–368 (2017)
69. Article 29 Data Protection Working Party: Guidelines on Consent under Regulation 2016/679. WP 259 (2017)
70. Gellert, R., Gutwirth, S.: The legal construction of privacy and data protection. Comput. Law Secur. Rev. **29**, 522–530 (2013)
71. Rauhofer, J.: One step forward, two steps back? Critical observations on the proposed reform of the EU data protection framework. University of Edinburgh School of Law, Edinburgh (2013)

Life-Long Privacy in the IoT? Measuring Privacy Attitudes Throughout the Life-Cycle of IoT Devices

Alexandr Railean[1,2(✉)] [iD] and Delphine Reinhardt[2,3] [iD]

[1] Unabhängiges Landeszentrum für Datenschutz, Kiel, Germany
arailean@datenschutzzentrum.de
[2] University of Bonn, Bonn, Germany
delphine.reinhardt@cs.uni-bonn.de
[3] Fraunhofer FKIE Bonn, Bonn, Germany

Abstract. The novelty of the Internet of Things (IoT) as a trend has not given society sufficient time to establish a clear view of what IoT is and how it operates. As such, people are likely to be unaware of the privacy implications, thus creating a gap between the belief of what a device does and its actual behaviour. The responses collected in our online survey indicate that participants tend to see IoT as computer -like devices, rather than appliances, though there are some important misconceptions about the way these devices function. We also find that privacy is a primary concern when it comes to IoT adoption. Nevertheless, participants have a propensity to keep using IoT devices even after they find out that the device abuses their trust. Finally, we provide recommendations to IoT vendors, to make their products more transparent in terms of privacy.

Keywords: Internet of Things · IoT · Privacy · Usability

1 Introduction

The IoT is composed of *devices, sensors or actuators, that connect, communicate or transmit information with or between each other through the Internet* (adapted from [13]). It is rapidly growing, as the number of connected devices per person has increased from 1.84 to 3.3 between 2010 and 2016 [11,26]. Many IoT devices, such as light bulbs, power switches, air quality monitors, or fitness trackers, are widely available. There is also strong support in the "do it yourself" community: there are 21,714 hits on Github.com, and 49,000 hits on Instructables.com when searching for the term "IoT". Moreover, some appliance manufacturers aim at increasing the share of their connected products. For instance, Samsung's CEO stated that all their products will be part of the IoT by 2020 [24]. Governments have also expressed interest in the IoT. For example, the Federal Trade Commission (FTC) issued a privacy and security guide [6] for businesses involved in IoT

© IFIP International Federation for Information Processing 2018
Published by Springer International Publishing AG 2018. All Rights Reserved
M. Hansen et al. (Eds.): Privacy and Identity 2017, IFIP AICT 526, pp. 132–149, 2018.
https://doi.org/10.1007/978-3-319-92925-5_9

development, while the European Commission is working on regulations that have provisions for IoT communications [23]. This indicates that IoT is on the path of becoming an indispensable part of our daily lives, based on the current attention of all involved parties, i.e., enterprises, governments, and end users.

However, such products may expose end users and product owners to privacy risks that can occur at the interplay of factors like resource-constrained hardware, poor usability, ubiquitous deployment or the availability of many pools of data. These factors can make the implementation of well-established privacy and security mechanisms difficult. Additionally, users may get little or no feedback about the data collected while interacting with an environment that lacks an interface (e.g. when sensors are seamlessly embedded into walls or furniture). A ubiquitous deployment means that insights about the users can be gathered in locations where they are not expecting data collection. Moreover, linking different data pools having information about the users can facilitate their identification, and hence lead to their deanonymization. For example, studies show that information about a person can be derived by correlating data from disparate sources, such as smartphone sensors [8,16], social media [15] or online reviews [20]. At the same time, most people are not technically proficient [21], and even those who are often subvert their privacy [14]. This has been shown in the use of social media [5] or instant messengers [9].

This paper starts with a review of related work in Sect. 2. We then investigate whether the aforementioned patterns apply to IoT in Sect. 3, by means of an online questionnaire introduced in Sect. 4. The results, based on the answers of 110 participants, are shared in Sect. 5. The answers show that most participants are aware of privacy risks, though they are inclined to keep using a device that infringes on their privacy. Moreover, our results provide an understanding of the reasons behind the adoption of IoT devices by end users, and give a clearer picture of the attention our participants pay to privacy throughout the life-cycle of their IoT devices. We then test our hypotheses in Sect. 6. In Sect. 7 we discuss the results and limitations of our survey, as well as provide recommendations for IoT vendors. Section 8 concludes the paper and summarizes our findings. All the materials needed to replicate the survey are given in Appendix A.

2   Related Work

Naeini et al. explore people's preferences regarding IoT data collection and notifications of data collection in [19]. They found that the participants of their study were more open towards data collection in public settings, and less so when data collection occurs in a private environment, if it involves biometric data, or if the data will be stored for long periods of time. They also develop a model that can predict one's data-collection preferences based on three data-points. Other works examine IoT from a legal perspective, a definition of IoT privacy is given in [29], the paper identifies the possible privacy risks related to IoT. Peppet conducts another legal analysis in [22] and discusses how privacy is affected by the difficulty of sensor data de-identification, thus questioning the distinction between personal data and other data. Another raised concern is that some IoT device vendors conflate the notion of "notice" with that of "consent", assuming that informing users about what a technology does is sufficient to indicate that use of technology implies consent (S_0, please note that the *statements* marked with S_n will be referred to in Sect. 7.2). The analysis also includes a comparison of the packages of several IoT devices with respect to privacy-related information, as well as their privacy policies. An extensive literature review and summary of IoT privacy issues is provided in [4,7,17]. Other works are focused on location privacy [10,18], while [28] focuses on fitness trackers. Volkamer et al. discusses the importance of mental models formed by end-users and the role these models play in the trust and acceptance of new technologies in [27]. There are other papers that present IoT life-cycle models, however they take a data-centered approach, examining what happens to the personal data acquired and transmitted by IoT devices [18,29]. Our work, on the other hand, takes a user-centered approach, focusing on the different stages of the relationship between users and their IoT devices.

3   Research Goals

To examine the participants' *privacy attitudes* and *user experience* in the context of IoT device ownership, we focus on the following *Research Questions* (RQ):

- RQ_1: What motivates potential users to acquire IoT devices?
- RQ_2: Would they continue using a device that infringes on their privacy?
- RQ_3: Are users aware of the extent to which IoT devices can interact with other equipment they own?

We then map the answers to the corresponding phases of the IoT device life-cycle (defined in Sect. 4), and look for user interface friction points that can potentially affect the privacy of end-users. This, in turn, enables us to suggest usability improvements and creates new research questions for the future.

The answers to the research questions help us test the following hypotheses (referred to as H), which are formulated on the basis of autoethnographic observations:

- H_1: When dealing with IoT devices, most users treat them as *appliances*, rather than *computers*.
- H_2: Users are inclined to keep IoT devices that infringe on their privacy, if those devices have a high *monetary value*.
- H_3: Users are inclined to keep IoT devices that infringe on their privacy, if those devices were *a gift from a close person*.

4   Methodology

To answer the questions and test the hypotheses, we designed an online questionnaire, which covers the phases of the IoT device life-cycle we consider to have an impact on privacy: pre-acquisition, set-up, usage, maintenance, and decommissioning, as illustrated in Fig. 1. Note that we are not concerned with the factors that lead to decommissioning (e.g. resale, recycling, etc.), we only focus on the privacy implications due to removal of IoT devices from service, regardless of the cause. In our questionnaire, we take a human-centered perspective and focus on what a person does with the device, rather than on what the device does with the data, in contrast to [18,29]. We have especially phrased our questions in a way that should elicit what participants *think* about the device and what their *beliefs* about its behaviour are.

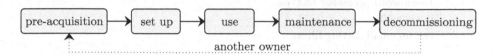

Fig. 1. IoT device lifecycle

4.1 Distribution and Audience

We have invited our participants via word of mouth, mailing lists, social media, and survey sharing platforms. Because it appeals to a wide audience, we have particularly taken care that non-experts could understand the goal of our questionnaire. To this end, we have defined and detailed the terminology used and given concrete examples. The introduction also provided key details about how the collected data would be handled, i.e., full anonymity and no disclosure of individual answers.

In total, 193 participants have answered our online questionnaire. Among them, 110 participants have fully filled it out. We have therefore discarded the incomplete ones for computing the following results. The majority of our participants are male (57%), 5% preferred not to disclose their gender. The most represented age category is between 21 and 30 (52%), followed by 31 and 40 (28%), then by 41 and 50 (8%). 45% of the participants have a bachelor degree, 33% have a master degree, 8% have a secondary school level of education, 5% preferred not to disclose information about their education, while 3% have earned a doctorate degree. Geographically, most of our participants are from Eastern Europe (45%), followed by 31% from Western Europe and 14% from North America.

4.2 Self-selection Bias

Since we have initiated the distribution of the survey ourselves, it is possible that the recruited participants fit a similar profile, thus biasing the sample. We have therefore asked the participants to indicate the different computer-related skills they have in question Q_{30} (see Appendix A). We then assign to each skill a number of points according to the distribution presented in Table 1. The total

Table 1. Distribution of points for each considered computer-related skill (Q_{30})

Points	Skills	Points	Skills
2	Play video games	5	Type complex documents in word processors (e.g. macros, automatic indexes, dynamic fields)
2	View photos and watch videos	10	Assemble computers or other electronics from components
2	Browse the Internet and send emails	15	I know at least one programming language
2	Use a word-processor to type documents		
5	Set up email sorting filters		

number of points obtained by a participant finally determines the category they belong to. We categorize participants with a total number of points below 8 as *novice*, between 8 and 20 as *medium*, and greater than 20 as *expert*. Our sample counts 55% rated as expert, 37% are medium and 7% are novice.

4.3 Priming Concerns

To avoid priming participants into a privacy-oriented mindset, the topic of the survey has been announced as "IoT usability". There was no mention of the term "privacy" in the call for participation, e.g. *"You're invited to participate in an IoT usability survey"*. Additionally, privacy-themed questions and answer choices were uniformly distributed among other topics.

5   Results

Our results are based on the responses of 110 participants and are mapped to phases of our IoT lifecycle model. The first set of questions is aimed at all the participants, whether they own an IoT device or not. We have found that 41% of them do not own IoT devices, whereas the others own smart TVs (38%), smart watches (23%), fitness bracelets (18%), thermostats (12%) and voice assistants (12%) (multiple choices possible). 39% of the participants are planning to purchase new IoT devices in the next 6 months (74% of them already own an IoT device), 30% have no such plans (33% of them own an IoT device), while 27% are not sure about it (47% of them own an IoT device).

5.1   Pre-acquisition

We have then asked the participants to indicate, in a non-prioritized way, the "reasons to buy Internet-connected appliances" (Q_{21}). They have indicated 86 reasons in a free-text field, which we have clustered as follows: automation of routine tasks (38%), better remote control (31%), and new capabilities (31%). Being socially connected (16%) and health improvements (12%) were selected by fewer participants. On the other hand, the participants have given 109 reasons why they would not buy such appliances. The most represented concerns are privacy (34%), security (30%) and cost (12%). Some of the arguments supporting the latter concern being (a) interaction with IoT devices will consume their data plan and inflate the bill, (b) an insecure IoT device that can make purchases can be taken over, allowing hackers to order items for free, (c) the cost of IoT devices is usually greater, due to their novelty, not due to their actual benefits, and (d) these devices become obsolete very fast.

Table 2 shows what participants would be looking for, if they were purchasing an IoT device. The responses indicate that *convenience* plays a key role. 72% look for ease of use, while 66% seek compatibility with existing devices. We have also seen that privacy is not of particular importance, it ranked 46%, close to "good brand reputation" (48%) and "low price" (47%). Another important highlight is that certifications from organizations like Technischer Überwachungsverein (TÜV) or Federal Communications Commission (FCC) play little role in the choice of IoT devices. Such an attitude may be explained by a greater level of trust in product reviews published on the Internet, or by the fact that brand reputation is sufficient to decide which device to purchase.

Table 2. Desired IoT features (Q_{20})

Feature	%	Feature	%
Ease of use	72	Recommendations from friends and others	39
Compatibility with my existing devices	66	Stylish design	35
Good brand reputation	48	Availability of technical documentation	35
Low price	47	Certifications by authorities (e.g. TÜV, FCC)	20
Clear privacy policy	46	Other (please specify)	8

Other features mentioned in a free-text field by participants were (a) guaranteed updates period (2 mentions), (b) open hardware/software and firmware access (2 mentions), (c) good security record (3 mentions), (d) wide functionality and customizability (3 mentions). One participant specifically indicated that the privacy policy should be "SHORT and clear" (S_1).

To learn the reasons why our participants chose to acquire their IoT devices, we have asked them to "[...] indicate the benefits of connected devices that appeal to [them] personally" (Q_{23}). Although this question is similar to Q_{21}, it enables us to differentiate between benefits participants have heard of in principle, and benefits that they themselves are looking for. The results in Table 3 show that the responses are similar, the most common and least common reasons follow the same distribution, with a difference in health improvements. 12% chose it as a reason to buy IoT devices, 30% indicated that it is what appealed to them

Table 3. IoT benefits that appeal to you personally (Q_{23})

Option	%	Option	%
Automation of routine tasks	59	Health improvements	30
Better remote control	55	Being connected to friends or family in a new way	26
New capabilities	52	Being connected to strangers or society in general	10
Energy saving	49	I don't know	10
Easier data management	34		

in particular. This observation leads us to the conclusion that in our sample, participants acquire IoT hardware for practical reasons, rather than because it is fashionable to do so.

5.2 Set up

In this and subsequent sections, we provide the results related to questions that involved participants who own IoT devices. Note that these questions were not displayed to those who indicated that they do not own an IoT device. Therefore the percentages shown are relative to a total of 65 participants. In Q_6, we have asked participants "how satisfied [they] are with the process of using the device 'brand'?", the answers are expressed on a 5-point Likert scale, ranging from "very dissatisfied" (1) to "very satisfied" (5), based on several criteria in Fig. 2.

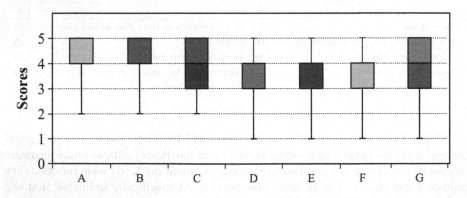

Fig. 2. Extrema and quartiles of the valid participants' answers to Q_6 based on the following criteria: plugging it in and connecting the cables (**A**, valid answers: 49), connecting it to [a] network or the Internet (**B**, 48), configuring the device settings (**C**, 50), accompanying documentation (**D**, 46), online materials (e.g. product site, support services) (**E**, 45), accompanying smartphone application (**F**, 43), resetting to default settings and wiping all data (**G**, 37). Invalid answers correspond to participants who skipped the questions or chose not to answer.

We have found that "satisfied" and "very satisfied" are the most common answers to all the questions, except when it comes to the level of satisfaction with the accompanying documentation, where 42% chose the "neutral" option. A possible explanation is that the manual was never consulted due to lack of need, preference, or lack of interest. Lack of need can be the result of a successful configuration based solely on the clarity of the interface, or the technical experience of the end user. It can also be explained by the fact that the majority of participants rated "online materials (e.g. site, support services)" as "satisfying", which could indicate that whatever questions they had were addressed online, as such materials are easier or faster to search.

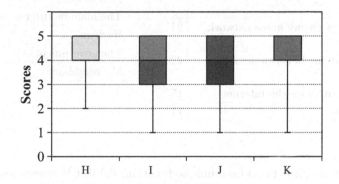

Fig. 3. Extrema and quartiles of the valid participants' answers to Q_9 based on the following criteria: configuring the device is easy (**H**, valid answers: 55), configuring it via a smartphone app is easy (**I**, 54), configuring it via a web-interface is easy (**J**, 54), set it up without reading the manual (**K**, 53).

We have further probed this matter by asking participants "when it comes to configuring [the IoT device], how much do [they] agree with the following statements" in Q_9, and find that 71% agreed and strongly agreed to being able to set up and configure their device without reading the manual (Fig. 3). This supports the assumption that *lack of need* is what leads to the documentation being neglected. Such a level of success can have an undesired effect: satisfied end-users can stop tinkering with the device as soon as they accomplish their primary goals, thus missing potentially critical security and privacy tips the documentation could offer. We conclude that important privacy-related controls should be incorporated into the initial setup procedure, to ensure that end-users make informed privacy-related decisions (S_2).

5.3 Usage

When asked about continued use of an IoT device that infringes on the owner's privacy (Q_{24}), two of the top three reasons are related to the monetary value of the product, "it was an expensive purchase" and "it is difficult to return it or get a refund" got a combined score of 53%. In contrast, options related to family values are the least convincing reasons to keep it (14%). Other mentioned

Table 4. Which of these resources you think are exposed to the IoT device? (Q_7)

Option	%
My smartphone	69
Other computers on my home network	40
Communications between other devices in my home and the Internet	31
Purpose-specific data (e.g. temp., humidity)	25
Other devices on my home network (e.g. printer)	24
Communications between devices in my home	22
Other computers on the Internet	15
I don't know	11

Table 5. Who can interact with the IoT device? (Q_8)

Option	%
Me	84
Others in my household (e.g. family)	65
The manufacturer	38
Hackers	35
The government	13
My neighbors	4

reasons were: (a) if it provides a unique function, (b) if it is crucial for daily use, or (c) if the infringement is negligible. *Convenience* is a major factor and its importance is often expressed throughout the collected answers. We have found that *entertainment* scores as high as health-related benefits (20%). This attitude resonates with the "dancing pigs" adage in computer security: *"The user's going to pick dancing pigs over security every time"* [25]. While studies [2] concluded that a better user interface helps people make wiser security-related decisions, those findings are not necessarily applicable in our context. Our question asks about a participant's choice *in principle*, which implies that this is a conscious decision they would make, no matter what the interface looked like.

When it comes to discarding an IoT device that infringes on the owner's privacy (Q_{25}), the reasons chosen by participants were: "ethical and moral convictions" (46%), "it is easy to get a refund" (45%), "installing custom firmware voids the warranty" (38%), and "it is easy to re-sell" (32%). Among the reasons indicated in the free-text field, 2 participants mentioned that the decision depends on the magnitude of the infringement.

To get a better understanding of what IoT device owners think about the capabilities of their hardware, we have asked them to indicate "the resources [they] think are exposed to the IoT device" in Q_7. The distribution of the answers is shown in Table 4. In 69% of the responses, it is expected that an IoT device can interact with a smartphone, presumably because that is how it is configured and controlled. Other options have been chosen by fewer than 40% of the participants.

We have asked participants "who, in [their] opinion, can use, or otherwise interact with IoT [devices] installed in your home?" in Q_8. The responses show that 35% of participants consider that hackers are capable of doing so, while 13% think the government can do that as well (Table 5). These numbers indicate that the efforts of IoT device vendors are insufficient to establish trust and convince the participants that their product is secure (S₃), as it has been argued in [27]. We have also found, by means of a Kruskal-Wallis test, that expert participants are more likely $(\chi^2 = 6.857, p = 0.032)^1$ to consider that the government can access their IoT hardware. Note that they do not hold the same opinion about hackers. This may be explained by an expert's confidence in their own ability to secure a system from typical attackers. On the other hand, their awareness of the fact that state-level actors have much more resources may justify the belief that governments could conduct successful attacks, if they choose so. We have finally asked our participants whether they have "examined the privacy policy" of their IoT device in Q_{12}, and find that 22% have done so. To understand whether IoT device adoption is a conscious decision, rather than a forced one (i.e. the IoT-enabled device was purchased because there was no "dumb" analog), we have asked our participants if they "own any appliances, the IoT capabilities of which are not used" (Q_{17}). 22% of the participants who own IoT devices always use the IoT features, 5% turn them off explicitly, 5% are aware of the features but are ignoring them, while 2% use various external means to disable them. Among the recorded means, we have found stickers over cameras (two mentions), positioning the device with the camera pointing down (one mention) and using a network router to limit the traffic of particular devices (one mention).

5.4 Maintenance

To understand the participants' attitudes towards software updates, we have asked them "do [they] think IoT devices require software updates?" (Q_4). 92% consider that IoT devices require software updates, 5% do not know if that is the case, while 3% believe that updates are not necessary. In Table 6, we present the answers to the question "who should be responsible for updating the IoT device, in your opinion?" (Q_5). Although 60% of the participants consider that the manufacturer should be responsible for pushing updates to IoT devices (S₄), two participants indicated that they want to be the ones who decide whether an update is installed or not. This could be the result of prior experience with unwanted updates, that disabled useful features or added undesired ones (S₅). This could explain why some are aware of the availability of newer versions, but are not installing them (Table 7).

The results indicate that our participants see IoT devices as computer-like systems that require software updates, rather than "plug in and forget" devices. We emphasize that the most common expectation is for the updates to be rolled out by the manufacturer. This is an important point to be considered by IoT device designers, because if this expectation will not be met, it is possible that the devices will run outdated firmware, potentially exposing owners to security and privacy risks. The data also reveal a gap between those who expect updates to be automatically installed by the manufacturer (60%) and those who are

---

^{1} When $p \leq 0.5$, it indicates that the results are not likely to be caused by chance, and that another set of participants would provide similar answers.

Table 6. Who should be responsible for updating IoT devices? (Q_5)

Option	%
The manufacturer	60
Me, as the device owner	44
The seller of the device	15
A government agency	1
I don't know	1

Table 7. Is your IoT device running fully up-to-date firmware/software? (Q_3)

Option	%
N/A, I do not own any IoT device	41
Yes, it updates itself automatically	27
Yes, I update it manually	11
I don't know	10
No, but newer firmware is available	5

aware that updates are automatic and are certain that their IoT device uses the latest version (27%). This difference could be explained in different ways, e.g. the IoT devices do not adequately reflect their update availability status (if at all) (S_6) or end users did not bother to check that. We measure that, using a 5-point Likert scale, by asking participants "How well does the device [...] express what it is currently doing?", listing several use cases, of which one is "installing an update" (Q_{10}). We have found that participants consider this to be expressed clearly (20%) to very clearly (35%), while another 20% have not experienced this use case. Sect. 5.5 discuses other implications related to update policies.

5.5   Decommissioning

To determine whether participants have gone through this procedure and measure their level of satisfaction with it, we have asked them "how satisfied are you with the process of [...] resetting [...] to default settings and wiping all data?" (Q_6) and "how well does the device express [...] that it is currently resetting itself to default settings and wiping the data?" (Q_{10}). We have found that many of our participants have not had the experience of wiping the data off their IoT device (31%) or have not had the chance to see how this process is reflected in the interface (45%). It should be noted that some of the participants could have chosen the "N/A" option because their IoT device does not provide such a feature or it is not relevant for its function, the survey does not distinguish between these possibilities. Since this use case has been less explored by end users, manufacturers have fewer opportunities to receive feedback about this procedure. Thus, any existing usability shortcomings can possibly remain in the product for a longer period of time. In contrast, use cases related to set up and usage are likely to attract far more attention. We conclude that IoT device manufacturers should not perceive the lack of customer complaints as an indicator of good usability of their product in the decommissioning phase. Instead, they ought to conduct tests targeting this particular scenario (S_7).

6   Testing the Hypotheses

In what follows, we successively test the hypotheses defined in Sect. 3, based on the answers given by participants.

H_1: **When dealing with IoT devices, most users treat them as** *appliances***, rather than** *computers***.** On one hand, the arguments detailed in Sect. 5.4 suggest that most of the participants consider IoT devices to be computers, rather than appliances, based on their awareness of the fact that such devices require regular updates and have to be secured. However, the analysis in Sect. 5.3 indicates that this awareness is limited. For example a smart TV that runs an operating system with network capabilities is exposed to all of the resources listed in Q_7, yet the participants' responses failed to reflect that. This could mean that some participants' level of confidence exceeds their actual understanding, which can lead to the false belief that the measures taken to protect their privacy are sufficient, when they are not. We cannot definitively support or refute H_1, because the premise appears to be wrong. It is possible that there exists another model in the spectrum between *computer* and *appliance*, which describes more accurately how IoT devices are perceived. For example, participants may be used to smartphones and tablets, which require updates, but are nevertheless not treated as computers.

H_2: **Users are inclined to keep IoT devices that infringe on their privacy, if those devices have a high** *monetary value***.** The sampled population perceives privacy as a major concern in IoT adoption, but the concern can be overridden if the purchased IoT hardware was expensive, if it has an entertainment or utility value. In these circumstances, a substantial number of participants would continue using an IoT device, even if they are certain that it infringes on their privacy (Q_{24}, Q_{25}). This can be partially explained by *loss aversion*, thus what matters is whether the owner can get reimbursed easily, regardless of the cost of the IoT device. When a refund is not possible, or if it is a tedious process, an inexpensive device is more likely to be discarded than an expensive one. Thus H_2 is supported, although we have to emphasize that other factors are at play.

H_3: **Users are inclined to keep IoT devices that infringe on their privacy, if those devices were** *a gift from a close person***.** We have also found, by means of a Mann-Whitney U test, that females are more likely to keep using a rogue IoT device ($U = 1066$, $n = 42$, $p = 0.012$)[2] if it was a gift from a close person, thus H_3 is partially supported. It is possible that such attitudes are caused by emotional attachment to a person, however there may be other conditions too, e.g. the device has a likeable design, or it stores valuable content, like photographs. These additional factors were not checked by the questionnaire, so they should be investigated separately.

---

[2] This indicates that the results are not likely to be caused by chance, and that if the same questions were given to other participants, the results would be similar.

7 Discussion

The answers to Q_7, "Which of these resources you think are exposed to the IoT device?" discussed in Sect. 5.3 could be a reason of concern. For example, in the case of a smart TV, a typical feature is to stream videos from remote sources, which requires some form of communication over networks, such as the Internet. This, in turn, implies that the device has to have an implementation of a network stack and software that leverages it. However, only two participants (rated at a medium skill level) indicated that their smart TV can access both, computers on their home network as well as other computers on the Internet. The same reasoning applies to voice-activated assistants (e.g. "Amazon Echo"). Only one participant correctly identified that their "Echo" can interact with local and remote hosts, which means that some participants are unaware of the fact that this device can transmit information via the Internet. While it is possible that some IoT devices are deliberately constrained by their owners (e.g. using firewalls), this should not be the case for assistants like "Echo", because they rely on an Internet connection for their basic features. Moreover, configuring Internet access is a required step in the setup phase, which the participants had to go through. This could be explained by the fact that they have an incomplete understanding of the capabilities of their device, or that someone else configured it for them (S_8). Product designers should consider this, because some of the user categories who could benefit from IoT, such as the elderly, may not be digitally literate, yet they must be aware of the implications of using the IoT device. Either the set-up procedure should be easy enough for anyone, or there should be a separate privacy summary that does not use technical or legal jargon and is easy to understand. We did not anticipate such results, therefore our survey was not crafted in a way that would enable us to determine whether this is a deliberate decision made by manufacturers, or an oversight, thus this matter has to be investigated separately.

Another important aspect is *obsolescence*, which we examine by analogy with smartphones. For example, the most common version of Android today has a market share of 31%, it was released two years ago [3]. The two latest versions, 8.0 and 7.1, have a combined market share of 3.3%. Thus, a substantial number of smartphones are running outdated software. This is one of the reasons why the American Civil Liberties Union (ACLU) filed an FTC complaint over Android security issues [1]. If the same pattern arises in IoT, end-users will be stuck with outdated devices which, at best, can only be secured by applying external technical means (e.g. firewalls) or custom firmware. Neither of these options is novice-friendly. A strategy consumers can adapt is to decommission the device before the support period ends. While this solves *their* problem, the obsolete device will become someone else's problem. This creates the premises for a "tragedy of the commons" [12], where the cost of security and privacy risks is distributed among all Internet users, instead of affecting IoT vendors or users specifically. Thus, the incentives to continue supporting and updating these devices is weak. This problem should be resolved in the future, otherwise it could hinder IoT adoption (S_9).

We have found some variation in attitudes, based on technical skills. Experts are more likely to indicate that they use a firewall, encrypted volumes and ad-blockers. They are also better-informed about IoT-related privacy and security news such as those about the Mirai botnet or the German steel factory incident. Note that we chose these topics because they were also covered by the international mainstream press, so non-experts could have heard about them. More surprisingly, the expert participants in our sample are also more likely to consider that manufacturers should be responsible for deploying IoT updates.

Note that our tests show that gender, age, and location do not have a significant impact on the participants' answers, unless otherwise stated.

7.1 Limitations

We encountered several limitations while running the survey. Firstly, people below the age of 18 were excluded, because of strict EU regulations concerning data collection from minors. However, this population segment could represent a significant portion of IoT technology consumers, thus their opinions should be accounted for. Secondly, we reached out to a technologically proficient audience (only 7% fell into the "novice" category), which is not representative of society in general. The modest number of participants finally gave us some hints about questions worth pursuing, but a study of a larger scale is required to make definitive claims about privacy attitudes.

7.2 Recommendations for IoT Vendors

Based on the different statements S_0 to S_9 we highlighted in the paper, we would like to make the following recommendations to IoT manufacturers, to improve their privacy practices:

- S_0 Do not conflate "notice" with "consent" (based on [22])
- S_1 Write concise privacy policies
- S_2 Make privacy-related settings a mandatory part of the set-up phase
- S_3 Find ways to address people's security and privacy concerns
- S_4 Provide an automatic update feature
- S_5 Make the list of version changes public
- S_6 Reflect the update availability status clearly
- S_7 Include decommissioning in usability tests
- S_8 Consider that someone other than the end-user can set up the IoT device
- S_9 Planned obsolescence should be more future-oriented.

8   Conclusions

We have organized an online survey with 110 participants, to explore their privacy attitudes towards IoT devices. The results reveal a generally positive opinion about IoT, despite the awareness of existing privacy and security risks. The challenge is to address these issues before the end-users' skepticism creates a barrier in IoT adoption.

We have found a potential void in the user experience related to the decommissioning of such devices. Most participants have not gone through such a use case and there is a possibility that they will run into issues when they do so. Device manufacturers should consider this before releasing their products to the market. We have also found that the expected norm is that IoT devices are updated automatically and that it is the responsibility of the manufacturer to ensure the smoothness of the process. IoT device designers should implement such a capability in their product and provide clear information to end users when automatic updates are not available, and it is the user's responsibility to keep the device up to date.

Acknowledgments. This project has received funding from the European Union's Horizon 2020 research and innovation programme under the Marie Skłodowska-Curie grant agreement No 675730. We would like to thank the survey participants, Harald Zwingelberg and the anonymous peer reviewers for their helpful comments.

Appendix A   Survey questions

The questions that featured in the survey are shown in Table 8. The list does not include the provided choices or other accompanying materials, they are available at https://www.datenschutzzentrum.de/projekte/privacy-us/. The site also provides the source code needed to replicate the survey and analyze the data.

Note that not all questions were shown to all participants (e.g. those who do not own IoT devices were not asked about their experience with such products). The label 'brand' was replaced with the IoT device name provided by participants in Q_2. The table also mentions the type of each question, FT: free-text, MS: questions that allowed *several* options to be selected at the same time, MC: questions for which participants had to choose *only one* option out of several, L: Likert scale questions.

Table 8. Survey questions

ID	Type	Question
Q_1	MS	Which of these IoT appliances do you own?
Q_2	FT	Focus on a specific device (note: here the participant is asked to name a specific device they own)
Q_3	MC	Is the selected device running fully up-to-date software/firmware?
Q_4	MC	Do you think IoT devices require software updates?
Q_5	MS	Who should be responsible for updating the device, in your opinion?
Q_6	L	How satisfied are you with the process of using the device 'brand'?
Q_7	MS	Which of these resources you think are exposed to the device 'brand'?
Q_8	MS	Who, in your opinion, can use, or otherwise interact with a 'brand' installed in your home?
Q_9	L	When it comes to configuring the device 'brand' how much do you agree with these statements?
Q_{10}	L	How well does the device 'brand' express what it is currently doing?
Q_{11}	L	How confident are you that the device 'brand' respects your privacy?
Q_{12}	MC	Have you examined the privacy policy of 'brand'?
Q_{13}	FT	What would make the device 'brand' more usable, in your opinion?
Q_{14}	FT	What are the most important things that you like in 'brand'?
Q_{15}	FT	What do you dislike the most about your experience with 'brand'?
Q_{16}	MC	Do you plan to buy any IoT devices in the next 6 months?
Q_{17}	MC	Do you own any appliances, the IoT capabilities of which are not used?
Q_{18}	FT	If you answered yes above, please list those appliances here. Optionally, indicate the feature
Q_{19}	MC	Do you think it is possible that some of your devices or appliances are connected to the Internet without your knowledge?
Q_{20}	MS	Which qualities would you be looking for if you were buying an IoT device?
Q_{21}	FT	What are the reasons to buy Internet-connected appliances, in your opinion?
Q_{22}	FT	What are reasons NOT to buy such appliances, in your opinion?
Q_{23}	MS	Please indicate the benefits of connected devices that appeal to you personally
Q_{24}	MS	You discover that an IoT device infringes on your privacy and you have no capability to change that. Which of these reasons will influence you to KEEP the device?
Q_{25}	MS	You discover that an IoT device infringes on your privacy and you have no capability to change that. Which of these reasons will influence you to DISCARD the device?
Q_{26}	MC	If you have a WiFi network at home, which of the options below best describes its security settings
Q_{27}	MS	Which of these security tools have you got on your computer?
Q_{28}	MC	What is your age?
Q_{29}	MC	What is your gender?
Q_{30}	MS	Please specify the computer-related skills you have
Q_{31}	L	Have you heard anything about these in the news?
Q_{32}	MC	What is the highest level of education that you successfully completed?
Q_{33}	MC	Which of these best describes your location?
Q_{34}	FT	If you have any remarks that you would like to make, please use the form below

References

1. ACLU Files FTC Complaint Over Android Smartphone Security. https://aclu. org/blog/national-security/aclu-files-ftc-complaint-over-android-smartphone-security. Accessed 14 Nov 2017
2. Akhawe, D., et al.: Alice in warningland: a large-scale field study of browser security warning effectiveness. In: Usenix Security (2013)
3. Android API Versions. https://developer.android.com/about/dashboards/index. html. Accessed 14 Nov 2017
4. Atzori, L., et al.: The Internet of Things: a survey. In: Computer Networks (2010)
5. Barnes, S.B.: A privacy paradox: social networking in the United States. First Monday **11**, 9 (2006)
6. Careful Connections: Building Security in the Internet of Things (2015). https:// ftc.gov/system/files/documents/plain-language/pdf0199-carefulconnections-buildingsecurityinternetofthings.pdf. Accessed 02 May 2017
7. Caron, X., et al.: The Internet of Things (IoT) and its impact on individual privacy: an australian perspective. Comput. Law Secur. Rev. **32**, 4–15 (2016)
8. Christin, D.: Privacy in mobile participatory sensing: current trends and future challenges. J. Syst. Softw. **116**, 57–68 (2016)
9. De Luca, A., et al.: Expert and non-expert attitudes towards (secure) instant messaging. In: Proceedings of the 12th Symposium on Usable Privacy and Security (SOUPS) (2016)
10. Elkhodr, M., et al.: A review of mobile location privacy in the Internet of Things. In: Proceedings of the 10th International Conference on ICT and Knowledge Engineering (2012)
11. Evans, D.: The Internet of Things - How the Next Evolution of the Internet is Changing Everything. Cisco (2011). http://www.cisco.com/c/dam/en_us/about/ ac79/docs/innov/IoT_IBSG_0411FINAL.pdf. Accessed 25 Apr 2017
12. Hardin, G.: The tragedy of the commons. J. Nat. Resour. Policy Res. **1**, 243–253 (2009)
13. Internet of Things: Privacy & Security in a Connected World. Stareport. FTC (2015). https://ftc.gov/system/files/documents/reports/federal-trade-commission -staff-report-november-2013-workshop-entitled-internet-things-privacy/150127iot rpt.pdf
14. Kang, R., et al.: "My data just goes everywhere" user mental models of the internet and implications for privacy and security. In: Proceedings of the 11th Symposium on Usable Privacy and Security (SOUPS) (2015)
15. Kosinski, M., et al.: Private traits and attributes are predictable from digital records of human behavior. In: Proceedings of the National Academy of Sciences (2013)
16. Lane, N.D., et al.: On the feasibility of user de-anonymization from shared mobile sensor data. In: Proceedings of the 3rd International Workshop on Sensing Applications on Mobile Phones (2012)
17. Mendez, D.M., et al.: Internet of Things: survey on security and privacy. arXiv:1707.01879 [cs] (2017)
18. Minch, R.P.: Location privacy in the era of the Internet of Things and big data analytics. In: Proceedings of 48th Hawaii International Conference on System Sciences (HICSS) (2015)
19. Naeini, P.E., et al.: Privacy expectations and preferences in an IoT World. In: Proceedings of the 13th Symposium on Usable Privacy and Security (SOUPS) (2017)

20. Narayanan, A., et al.: How to break anonymity of the netix prize dataset. arXiv preprint cs/0610105 (2006)
21. OECD: Skills Matter. OECD Skills Studies (2016). http://www.oecd-ilibrary.org/education/skills-matter_9789264258051-en. Accessed 15 Sept 2016
22. Peppet, S.R.: Regulating the Internet of Things: first steps toward managing discrimination, privacy, security and consent. Tex. L. Rev. **93**, 85 (2014)
23. Regulation of the European Parliament and of the Council Concerning the Respect for Private Life and the Protection of Personal Data in Electronic Communications and Repealing Directive 2002/58/EC (Regulation on Privacy and Electronic Communications) (2017)
24. Samsung: By 2020, All of Our Products Will Be Connected to the Web. http://mashable.com/2015/01/05/amsung-internet-of-things. Accessed 14 Nov 2017
25. Schneier, B.: Secrets and Lies: Digital Security in a Networked World (2008)
26. Trends 17: Globalwebindex (2016). http://insight.globalwebindex.net/hubfs/Reports/Trends-17.pdf. Accessed 25 Apr 2017
27. Volkamer, M., Renaud, K.: Mental models – general introduction and review of their application to human-centred security. In: Fischlin, M., Katzenbeisser, S. (eds.) Number Theory and Cryptography. LNCS, vol. 8260, pp. 255–280. Springer, Heidelberg (2013). https://doi.org/10.1007/978-3-642-42001-6_18
28. Zhou, W., et al.: Security/privacy of wearable fitness tracking IoT Devices. In: Proceedings of the 9th Iberian Conference on Information Systems and Technologies (CISTI) (2014)
29. Ziegeldorf, J.H., et al.: Privacy in the Internet of Things: threats and challenges. Secur. Commun. Netw. **7**, 2728–2742 (2014)

Improving Privacy and Security in the Ear of Smart Environments

Secure and Privacy-Friendly Storage and Data Processing in the Cloud

Pasquale Chiaro[1], Simone Fischer-Hübner[2], Thomas Groß[3],
Stephan Krenn[4(✉)], Thomas Lorünser[4], Ana Isabel Martínez Garcí[5],
Andrea Migliavacca[6], Kai Rannenberg[7], Daniel Slamanig[4],
Christoph Striecks[4], and Alberto Zanini[6]

[1] InfoCert, Milan, Italy
`pasquale.chiaro@infocert.it`
[2] Karlstad University, Karlstad, Sweden
`simone.fischer-huebner@kau.se`
[3] University of Newcastle upon Tyne, Newcastle upon Tyne, UK
`thomas.gross@newcastle.ac.uk`
[4] AIT Austrian Institute of Technology GmbH, Vienna, Austria
`{stephan.krenn,thomas.lorunser,daniel.slamanig,`
`christoph.striecks}@ait.ac.at`
[5] ETRA Investigacion y Desarrollo, S.A., Valencia, Spain
`amartinez.etraid@grupoetra.com`
[6] Lombardia Informatica S.p.A., Milan, Italy
`andrea.migliavacca@cnt.lispa.it, alberto.zanini@lispa.it`
[7] Goethe University Frankfurt, Frankfurt, Germany
`kai.rannenberg@m-chair.de`

Abstract. At the IFIP Summer School 2017, the two H2020 projects CREDENTIAL and PRISMACLOUD co-organized a workshop dedicated to introducing the necessary background knowledge and demonstrating prototypes of privacy-preserving solutions for storing, sharing, and processing potentially sensitive data in untrusted cloud environments. This paper summarizes the given presentations and presents the discussions and feedback given by the workshop attendees, including students and senior researchers from different domains as well as relevant non-academic stakeholders such as public data protection agencies.

Keywords: Privacy · Data protection · Demonstration

1 Introduction

Storing, sharing, and processing data in the cloud play vital roles in many everyday scenarios, ranging from private data vaults and company backups over identity and access management (IAM) to eHealth and eBusiness. However, besides

---

The projects contributing to this work have received funding from the European Union's Horizon 2020 research and innovation programme under grant agreement No 644962 (PRISMACLOUD) and 653454 (CREDENTIAL).

M. Hansen et al. (Eds.): Privacy and Identity 2017, IFIP AICT 526, pp. 153–169, 2018.
https://doi.org/10.1007/978-3-319-92925-5_10

the many benefits of the cloud setup such as cost-effectiveness and scalability, many of these applications pose very high security and privacy requirements to the solutions in use as data owners have no control over how their data is used once it is released to the cloud. Consequently, a large body of work on privacy-enhancing technologies has been proposed by the academic community, and many results have reached a high maturity level; however, as pointed out by Lorünser et al. [1], a large fraction of these results is purely academic and does not sufficiently address the needs of users and service providers, and thus does not get adopted in the real world.

The ambition of the two large-scale European Horizon 2020 (H2020) research and innovation actions PRISMACLOUD[1] and CREDENTIAL[2] is to close this gap for certain cryptographic primitives, by developing promising candidates for integration into commercial cloud offerings. This is achieved by involving all relevant stakeholders in the design process. Based on their inputs, a careful selection of cryptographic technologies was made, and efficient and secure first prototype implementations were developed. To showcase the usability and usefulness of these prototypes, they were then integrated into multiple pilot scenarios coming from the real world.

After already having held independent workshops at the IFIP Summer Schools 2015 [2] and 2016 [3], the two projects organized a joint workshop in 2017, in order to raise awareness of their solutions, and to receive feedback and inputs on the developed pilots. During the remaining runtime of the projects, this feedback will be used to further improve the developed tools in order to guarantee that they indeed serve the needs of real users and cloud service providers, and to adequately address any concerns, specific requirements, or ideas.

This paper summarizes the content of this workshop, and gives an overview of the discussions with students and senior researchers from different domains, legal experts, and other relevant non-academic stakeholders.

1.1 Outline

This document is structured as follows. After briefly explaining the challenges of identity management in the cloud in Sect. 2, Sect. 3 briefly summarizes the main ambitions of the two projects CREDENTIAL and PRISMACLOUD. Section 4 then gives detailed descriptions of five pilots executed in the two projects, two from CREDENTIAL and three from PRISMACLOUD. A summary of the feedback given by the workshop participants and the projects' advisory board members is then given in Sect. 5. Finally, we briefly conclude in Sect. 6.

2 Cloud Privacy and Identity Management

In the following, we give an introduction to privacy-friendly and trustworthy identity management. We discuss the privacy and security issues of typical

---

[1] https://prismacloud.eu/.
[2] https://credential.eu/.

federated identity management architectures, namely over-identification and the "Calling Home" problem, and present possible solutions to both of them.

Over-identification occurs, when users need to present credentials, that contain more information than needed to justify the respective access claim, e.g., when an ID card is presented to prove legal age often the precise birth date is presented, while a certified Boolean statement, that the person is of legal age, would be satisfactory and would avoid misuse of the birth date information.

The "Calling Home" problem is caused by credentials, that are always double-checked with the issuer, which causes a lot of information there, which user is using which credentials for which service at which point in time. It can also be caused by situations in which users need to ask for a credential on the spot, exactly when they need it.

Technical solutions for addressing these issues include the following: partial identities, attribute-based credentials (especially Privacy-ABCs) and redactable signatures for cloud identity management:

Partial identities and identities as such are defined in ISO/IEC 24760 [4] as a "set of attributes related to an entity". Partial identities support the building of identity management systems, that enable users to select the appropriate attributes for the respective situation and so help against over-identification.

Attribute-based credentials (especially Privacy-ABCs) enable the user to have the relevant attributes certified without having to recur to the original certifiers of the attributes: If a set of attributes is certified in a Privacy-ABC the certified users can choose their own subset of attributes as needed and derive the certificate themselves from the original one. More details on the nature and the trialling of Privacy-ABCs in real life scenarios can be found, e.g., in Rannenberg et al. [5].

Redactable signatures for cloud identity management as developed in the CREDENTIAL project enable the editing of encrypted credentials (e.g., to protect them when stored in a cloud-based identity management system). So redactable signatures enable the editing of Privacy-ABCs.

Further approaches for a more privacy-friendly Internet and respective cloud services are:

- Decentralisation;
- Minimum disclosure;
- Strong sovereign assurance tokens (e.g. smart cards, if appropriate mobile devices).

3   Project Overview

The following section briefly explains the approaches of CREDENTIAL and PRISMACLOUD to address them.

3.1   Privacy-Friendly IAM with CREDENTIAL

CREDENTIAL is an innovation action dedicated to the design and implementation of a privacy-preserving platform for sharing of authenticated data, including identity and access management scenarios, thereby directly addressing the problem of overidentification and partially addressing the "calling home" problem [6, 7].

The security and privacy of the developed platform, the so-called CREDENTIAL Wallet, is mainly based on two cryptographic building blocks, *redactable signatures* and *proxy re-encryption*. Redactable signatures [8] allow the signer to define parts of the message which can later be blanked out by any party knowing the message and the signature. That is, any party, not requiring access to the secret signing key, can later remove (subsets of the) redactable parts of the message and simultaneously adapt the signature such that the obtained signature still certifies the authenticity of the revealed information. On the other hand, proxy re-encryption [9] is an extension of traditional public key encryption schemes, where a dedicated third party (the *proxy*) can transform ciphertexts encrypted for a user A to ciphertexts encrypted for a user B, without itself every gaining access to the plain data. This is achieved by letting A use his secret key and (depending on the concrete scheme being used) B's public or secret key to compute a so-called re-encryption key, which is then sent to the proxy and can only be used for re-encryption but not decryption.

The overall approach of CREDENTIAL now is as follows. Users can obtain certificates on personal attributes from an issuer who signs them using a redactable signature scheme. The encrypted attributes together with the signature are then uploaded to the CREDENTIAL Wallet. Furthermore, when a user first wants to authenticate himself towards a specific service provider, the user computes a re-encryption key from his own public key to the service provider's public key, and stores this re-encryption key in his account at the CREDENTIAL Wallet. Now, for subsequent authentications, the Wallet re-encrypts only those attributes that the user does chooses to reveal to the service provider and redacts the remaining ones. By doing so, the service provider will still be convinced that the revealed attributes have not been altered, hereby solving the problem of over-identification similar to attribute-based credentials systems [10–12]. The approach is also illustrated in Fig. 1.

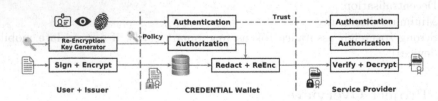

Fig. 1. The CREDENTIAL approach, adapted from Karegar et al. [3].

The CREDENTIAL approach is not directly susceptible to the "calling home" problem as the issuer is not contacted upon authentication. However, the CREDENTIAL Wallet as a central entity is contacted upon every authentication process, and therefore learns which service a user accesses at which time. A partial solution to this problem, where the Wallet only learns that a user is authenticating to *some* service but not to which one, was recently suggested by Krenn et al. [13].

The feature set and usability of the CREDENTIAL Wallet is demonstrated using use case scenarios from the domains of eGovernment, eBusiness, and eHealth, cf. also Sect. 4.

3.2 PRISMACLOUD **Overview and Applications**

PRISMACLOUD is a research and innovation action dedicated to enabling secure and trustworthy cloud-based services by improving and adopting novel tools from cryptographic research [14,15]. Cloud computing raised the need for application of cryptography to be more secure and privacy-friendly. However, the adoption of cryptography for modern information and communication (ICT) technologies is not hampered by the lack of technical feasibility, but more by accompanying factors like usability, missing knowledge in IT security community, and regulation.

The PRISMACLOUD approach is to propose a layered architecture of secure and trustworthy cloud-based services that utilizes strong and novel cryptographic primitives and tools to be adapted to several real-world applications. This layered approach is illustrated in Fig. 2.

Layer 1 (Primitives). PRISMACLOUD is focusing on a broad range of cryptographic primitives on the lowest layer, including attribute-based credential systems for privacy-preserving user authentication [10–12], secret sharing for secure distributed storage of data at rest [17,18], malleable signature schemes for controlled modifications of authenticated data [8,19–21], or graph signatures for topology certification [22]. Malleable signatures are a super set of redactable signatures, that allow for even advanced functionality besides the redaction of signed messages. Secret sharing on the other hand allows for secure distribution of sensitive data. Thereby, the message is split into shares and distributed to many cloud databases. Inherently, the system has redundancy in the sense that only a fraction of the cloud databases is needed to reconstruct the message. Graph signatures encode graph data structure into the underlying digital signature scheme in a way that for all components of a graph (i.e., edges, vertices, labels), proof-of-knowledge properties can be stated. Together with attribute-based credentials, malleable signatures tackle the over-identification and "Calling home" problems.

Layer 2 (Tools). On the next layer, the primitives from Layer 1 are included into more complex tools. For example, attribute-based credentials and malleable signatures are used as building blocks for Flexible Authentication with Selective Disclosure and Verifiable Data Processing, respectively. Further, the Topology Certification tool is presented in more detail in Sect. 4.5.

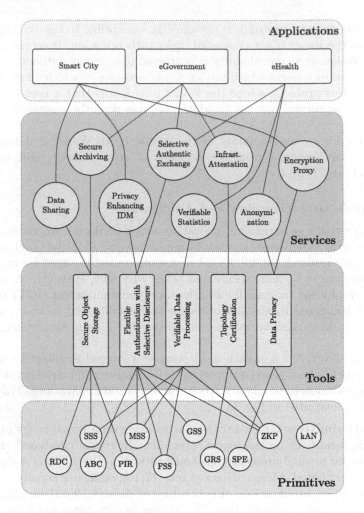

Fig. 2. The layer approach of PRISMACLOUD from Lorünser et al. [16].

Layer 3 (Services). On the service layer, the tools from the Layer 2 are the building blocks for more advanced functionalities. For example, Flexible Authentication with Selective Disclosure and Verifiable Data Processing are used as building blocks for Privacy Enhancing Identity Management (IDM) and Verifiable Statistics, respectively. Furthermore, Secure Archiving is derived from Secure Object Storage (cf. also Sect. 4.4) and directly serves as a example for the Decentralization approach mentioned in Sect. 2.

Layer 4 (Applications). The application layer deploy the services from Layer 3 in real-world scenarios such as Smart City, eGovernment, and eHealth, cf. also Sect. 4.3.

Note that in contrast to Layers 1 and 2, almost no cryptographic knowledge is needed any more on Layers 3 and 4, making them also accessible to software developers and product designers without requiring deep mathematical background.

PRISMACLOUD also has a strong focus on human computer interaction (HCI) design patterns, the implementation of modular and reusable software libraries, and the design of cloud services that can be seamlessly integrated into existing software applications via the layered approach. This holistic approach enables PRISMACLOUD to achieve its main ambition, namely to enable end-to-end security and privacy for cloud users without negatively impacting usability neither for users nor for service providers.

4   Pilots and Discussions

The following section introduces some of the pilots designed, implemented, and executed within PRISMACLOUD and CREDENTIAL. Furthermore, it summarizes the feedback, questions, suggestions, and concerns received from the workshop participants, who were able to get hands-on experience of the pilots during the IFIP Summer School 2017.

4.1   eGovernment Pilot (CREDENTIAL)

The CREDENTIAL eGovernment pilot focuses on identity management to authenticate citizens towards services provided by public authorities. Based on standardized protocols such as SAML or OpenID Connect, the service provider can request authentication and identity attributes from the CREDENTIAL Wallet. By requesting the user's consent for granting the service provider access to the requested data, the user is given full transparency and control over which data is requested and revealed; furthermore, because of the encryption technology being used, the CREDENTIAL Wallet never obtains access to the user's attributes in an unencrypted form. The pilot not only enables authentication via national eID solutions, but also cross-border authentication according to the eIDAS regulation, aims at high interoperability with existing authentication protocols, and minimizes the integration effort on the service provider's side.

A bit more precisely, the eGovernment pilot considers a user owning a CREDENTIAL account that already contains a set of authentic data items. The user wants to authenticate himself towards a service hosted by Lombardia Informatica S.p.A. (LISPA), a public-capital service company in northern Italy. Specifically, we assume that the user wants to authenticate himself towards SIAGE, a web portal used to request tax breaks and other types of fiscal advantages. When browsing to the login page, the user has the option to choose CREDENTIAL as an identity provider, and is then redirected to an URL published by the OpenAM component in charge of initiating the authentication flow according to the OAuth2 standard. The user then receives a notification on his mobile phone listing all the required and optional attributes SIAGE wants to access for

Fig. 3. eGovernment pilot.

authentication and the subsequent process, and can decide whether or not to disclose these values, cf. Fig. 3. In case the user gives his consent, the requested data is re-encrypted by the CREDENTIAL Wallet and sent to SIAGE, who can then decrypt the data and verify its authenticity.

4.2   eBusiness Pilot (CREDENTIAL)

Many business processes can nowadays be performed online. However, there is often a trade-off between security and usability: that is, systems that are easy to use often do not sufficiently protect security and privacy, while safer processes often partially sacrifice usability. The CREDENTIAL eBusiness pilot addresses some of the most often performed processes and provides privacy-friendly, secure, and usable solutions for authentication and Single Sign-On (SSO), purchase processes and online form subscription, and forwarding of encrypted communication. The first scenario is strongly related to the authentication use case in the eGovernment pilot presented in Sect. 4.1. The second scenario reliefs users from having to enter all their personal information like name, date of birth, or address everytime they subscribe to a service; rather, the user's information that is already stored in the CREDENTIAL Wallet can automatically be filled into the registration forms. In the following we will put our main focus on the third scenario on encrypted communication.

InfoCert is an Italian organization offering trust based business solutions for organisations and businesses to interact with customers and citizens. Among others, InfoCert offers Legalmail, an email service realizing legally binding mail exchange. The goal of CREDENTIAL is to add an end-to-end encryption layer to Legalmail. However, due to the legal properties of the communication it is important to support proper mail forwarding possibilities for such mails. This

Fig. 4. eBusiness pilot.

is because an email is legally considered delivered once it reaches the recipients
mailbox, independent of whether it was read or not; thus, in the case of a longer
absence, it might happen that the receiver otherwise misses important deadlines
or similar. However, using the standard forwarding capabilities of the mail server
is not sufficient for encrypted emails for obvious reasons: either, the delegatee
cannot decrypt the received message, or the original receiver would have to
share his secret keys with the substitute. Within CREDENTIAL, this problem is
addressed by using proxy re-encryption [9], where the receiver can deposit a
re-encryption key that allows the mail server to translate the cipher text into
an encryption under the delegatee's public key without itself learning the plain
message.

After explaining the scenario, interactive mockups were used to show how
Legalmail users can setup the encrypted mail forwarding within a slightly
extended Legalmail app. Figure 4 shows how a user first accesses into the setup
section, then selects "filter setting" and "add new filter", finally defines the forwarding rules.

Discussion and Feedback. Considering that Legalmail was new to all workshop participants, the received feedback was quite interesting: both technical
and not technical attendees agreed about the perceived value of a legally binding communication. They also founded coherent the need to enhance the security
in sharing some kind of sensitive information. Furthermore, several concrete suggestions on how to improve the user interfaces and experience were made by the
workshop participants.

4.3 Smart-City Pilots (PRISMACLOUD)

During the tutorial, demos of two PRISMACLOUD pilots applied within the smart-
city environment SIMON[3] were shown. Each of them integrates one secure cloud
service, developed inside the PRISMACLOUD project. SIMON is another European
project dedicated to remove and prevent barriers that cause problems for persons
with disabilities when using products, services and public infrastructure. One
goal of SIMON is to ensure that only disabled persons are able to park in reserved

---

[3] http://simon-project.eu/.

lots in a city. Instead of only putting the parking card into the car, the disabled person first uses the SIMON mobile application and the smart-parking card for marking the location in which he/she is parking. As parking cards are very easy to duplicate, SIMON help authorities and end users to fight fraud, because operators can check if the smart card is duplicated. In Fig. 5, screenshots of the end-user's mobile parking application are given.

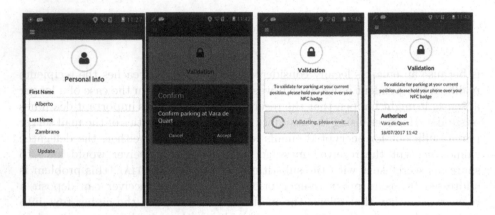

Fig. 5. SIMON application for end users.

The first demo showed the PRISMACLOUD Encryption Proxy (EP) service integrated in SIMON. Since SIMON is in the cloud, the first problem it deals with is the treatment of sensitive data. SIMON is managing sensitive data such as personal information, which do not have to be accessible to other people except for the dedicated end users. This EP service encrypts sensitive data on the fly, leaving non-sensitive data not encrypted. Therefore, the messages and the information stored on the database contain non-sensitive data in clear text and sensitive data in encrypted format.

The second demo showed the integration of Privacy Enhancing Identity Manager (PIDM) service in SIMON. Another problem of SIMON in the cloud is that the user's personal identifier is sent in clear for each operation, so users are identified. This is a big problem due to legal implications. In SIMON, city areas or neighborhood are defined and users have permissions to park in lots belonging to those areas that they belong to. The PIDM has been integrated in order to anonymize those operations. The user's identifier is replaced in messages by a proof of belonging to the area in which the lot is; thus, the system does not know which user is going to park. It only knows that a user which has permission for the area is going to park. The proof is generated by cryptographic mechanisms in the service, i.e., by means of suitable group signatures [23].

Discussion and Feedback. During the presentation, students were very interested in the two demos and some technical question were asked. The first point

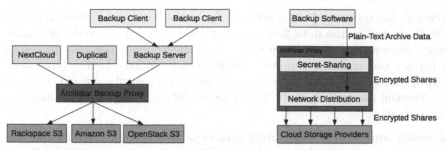

(a) High-level network system overview.   (b) Example data-flow from backup client.

Fig. 6. High-level network system overview and example data-flow from backup clients to the cloud storage servers.

of discussion was where personal data or private keys have to be stored and it was necessary to explain that the private keys belong to the end user, so they are generated and stored on the mobile memory, and the smart-card only has the firmed message in order to be checked by the parking operator. The second point was related to how to decide what is sensitive in any application. In the case of SIMON is mainly the user's personal information. Finally, students appreciated that all these cryptographic resources have use in an practical environment, due they usually deal with theoretical problems.

4.4   Distributed Storage Pilot (PRISMACLOUD)

During the tutorial the PRISMACLOUD solution for secure object storage in distributed multi-cloud settings [14] was shown. In order to protect data at rest in the cloud, the project builds on secure information dispersal, i.e., secret sharing techniques, which achieves security, integrity and availability at the same time in a very flexible and efficient way [24,25].

To give users easy access to the developed technologies, a secure archiving service (SA or SAaaS) specifically tailored to the needs of trustworthy backups was implemented [16]. Its functional key features were motivated from our eGovernment use case and it has been designed to support most commonly encountered cloud backup scenarios. The general idea of the secure archiving service is to provide an extremely reliable and secure storage back-end which can be easily hosted and used. The archiving use case focuses on data retention over long time periods and can even provide full quantum safe security when combined with adequate transport layer encryption, e.g., like in [26,27].

The prototype provides compatibility with multiple providers and legacy systems to support hybrid cloud storage scenarios which integrate local storage with public cloud offerings in a seamless way. Therefore, the Simple Storage System (S3) industry standard was chosen as main API and the service was made compatible with this standard on both sides, the back-end provider side as well as the front-end client side. Additionally, because we avoid the use of active components on the provider side, deployment can be very straight forward [28].

Overall, the service acts as a proxy [29] and the basic architecture is shown in Fig. 6a as well as the data flow model in Fig. 6b. It is part of the Archistar software framework [30] and supports the following main features: increased data privacy and availability, prevention from vendor lock-in, keyless (credential based) operation, reduced data remanence, long-term security support, support for multimodal encryption, support for remote auditing, plug-in replacement for legacy systems.

Discussion and Feedback. During prototype presentation the audience was particularly impressed by the ease of use and integration of the provided solution and saw a great potential for exploitation. Additionally, they recommended to think about a version where no single point of trust exist, if this is possible. They also liked the idea of making the software available as open source software, such that it can be reviewed by a larger audience. Furthermore, one participant mentioned that similar technology is already used in commercial high-end storage solutions for data centers, but no solutions for broad adoption or multi-cloud configurations exist, especially for small end medium enterprises, are known. Finally, the participants also recommended to look into the field of mix networks and the security modeling used there, which has many similarities that may be transferred to multi-cloud approaches.

Besides feedback on the technical integration, we were also interested in feedback on the perception of security in systems based on data splitting. In its very pure nature, the data security is solely based on non-collusion of cloud providers, which is a different security model from what we typically use today. During the discussions of the demo we therefore tried to find suitable configurations for such storage systems and also discussed the necessity of an additional cryptographic layer to protect from collusion attacks. The feedback was very valuable for us and will be included into the configurations guidelines we are currently preparing in PRISMACLOUD.

4.5   Infrastructure Certification Pilot (PRISMACLOUD)

The tutorial workshop offered an introduction to the Infrastructure Certification (IA) of PRISMACLOUD. The overall goal of the IA work is to enable the capacity to certify infrastructures, such as virtualized infrastructures in the Cloud in such a way that their security properties can be proven to others without disclosing sensitive data. Therein, this work follows the principles of *Confidentiality-Preserving Security Assurance*.

The core technical contributions presented in the workshop are the Topology Certification tool, called TOPOCERT, its underlying Graph Signature library and a demonstration functionality to prove the separation of machines by geo-separation, which we shall discuss in turn.

Confidentiality-preserving topology certification was first proposed in the work by Groß [22]. The core idea of this proposal is that an Auditor could issue a certificate on the topology on an infrastructure to the Provider, which is usable for subsequent zero-knowledge proofs of knowledge on a wide range of security properties. This work is founded on earlier research on topology-based security assurance [31–33], which analyzes the configuration of infrastructures to determine components, sub-systems and their inter-connectivity and derives a graph representation for a security analysis. Confidentiality-preserving security assurance takes this method one step further in signing the graph representation for further proof protocols.

The graph signing and corresponding zero-knowledge proofs of knowledge are facilitated by a dedicated graph signature library. It realizes the cryptographic protocols between a Signer and a Recipient of graph signatures as well as between a Prover and a Verifier of the corresponding proofs of knowledge. Graph signatures were proposed by Groß [34] as a means to encode graph data structures into an underlying digital signature scheme, such that the components of the graphs, the vertices, edges and labels are still accessible to proofs of knowledge. In a first construction, this is facilitated by employing the Camenisch-Lysyanskaya signature scheme [35] and using techniques first introduced for the efficient encoding of credential attributes [36,37]. The first construction for graph signatures [34] has still a number of short-comings, most notably requiring the signing of one certificate per proof. However, it shows intriguing properties in that the signatures are general in that they could be used to answer a wide range of questions not known at signing time and expressive in that they could encode arbitrary statements from NP languages.

The tutorial workshop included an example application for *geo-location separation* [38]. The idea for that is that the Auditor could certify the physical geo-location of the physical hosts. In this case, we might think of the Auditor as a tamper-proof appliance, which can obtain a secure fix on its current geo-location. In this case, the Auditor could, for instance, label the physical machines of an audited infrastructure with labels denoting the UN countries these machines are located in. The geo-location separation proof protocols executed by the Prover and the Verifier would then convince the Verifier that the machines are in at least k different countries, without disclosing which countries are involved.

5   Advisory Board Feedback

The tutorial workshop ended with a panel of Advisory Board members of the two projects that provided feedback and suggestions for future directions and topics to be addressed by the projects. While in general the panelists appreciated the work presented, they raised a few issues.

One issue mentioned was that a cloudified approach as provided by the CRE-DENTIAL project relies on one central server, which even if all data are encrypted, still needs to be trusted, as it can monitor all traffic data, is able to derive meta information from them (e.g., it can profile the users' usages of different services - see also [3]) and represents one single point of failure. For users it might not be clear whether this cloudified approach can be fully trusted and it remains a challenge to communicate the trust assumptions to the users. Further research should also address the questions what is meant by trust and distrust in the whole service solution. For this, the complete process of gaining, losing and re-establishing trust in the service needs to be considered.

Furthermore, it was discussed that Open Source (such as PRISMACLOUD's Archistar) would often be seen as a means for gaining user trust, as the code is openly published and can be reviewed by the users, and that it could be easier for the projects to put their solutions as open source into practice. However, it needs to be considered also that according to the EU General Data Protection Regulation (GDPR) it is not the software producer who is responsible for achieving Data Protection by Design. Pursuant Art. 25 GDPR, the responsibility for the implementation of appropriate technical and organisational measures, which are designed to implement data protection principles, rather lies with the controller. Art. 25 (3) mentions that approved certification mechanisms pursuant to Article 42 may be used as an element to demonstrate compliance of the controller with the Data Protection by Design requirements, and such privacy certification schemes could also be means for gaining or increasing user trust.

Another comment by the Advisory Board members concerned PRISMACLOUD's Smart City parking app. It was pointed out that restricting and framing it as an app for booking parking places for disabled users could mean that users that are installing and using the app could be easily associated as handicapped and thus be discriminated. Hence, the app should have a wider framing and should also provide features that would be useful also for non-disabled users.

Finally, it was discussed and emphasized that in practice "pretty good" usable cryptographic and privacy solutions can already be very helpful for end users. Hence, the projects' research should not only try to achieve provably secure solutions, but should also look at practical and usable solutions that provide good enough security for the majority of use cases.

6   Conclusion

Storing, sharing, and processing sensitive data in untrusted cloud environments is the central goal of the H2020 projects CREDENTIAL and PRISMACLOUD. This tutorial paper summarizes given presentations and demonstrations within a workshop at IFIP Summer School 2017 co-organized by both projects. In particular, the workshop aimed at introducing the necessary background knowledge and presenting prototype demonstrations of CREDENTIAL and PRISMACLOUD to a wider academic audience (e.g., students, senior researcher) as well as to participant from the non-academic field (e.g., public data protection agencies).

To this end, we briefly introduced the two projects and described the talks given within the workshop. Furthermore, all demonstration pilots were presented and findings discussed. Valuable feedback was gathered from the advisory-board members to enhance the further projects' development.

References

1. Lorünser, T., Krenn, S., Striecks, C., Länger, T.: Agile cryptographic solutions for the cloud. e&i Elektrotechnik und Informationstechnik **134**, 364–369 (2017)
2. Alaqra, A., Fischer-Hübner, S., Groß, T., Lorünser, T., Slamanig, D.: Signatures for privacy, trust and accountability in the cloud: applications and requirements. In: Aspinall, D., Camenisch, J., Hansen, M., Fischer-Hübner, S., Raab, C. (eds.) Privacy and Identity 2015. IAICT, vol. 476, pp. 79–96. Springer, Cham (2016). https://doi.org/10.1007/978-3-319-41763-9_6
3. Karegar, F., Striecks, C., Krenn, S., Hörandner, F., Lorünser, T., Fischer-Hübner, S.: Opportunities and challenges of CREDENTIAL - towards a metadata-privacy respecting identity provider. In: Lehmann, A., Whitehouse, D., Fischer-Hübner, S., Fritsch, L., Raab, C. (eds.) Privacy and Identity 2016. IAICT, vol. 498, pp. 76–91. Springer, Cham (2016). https://doi.org/10.1007/978-3-319-55783-0_7
4. ISO/IEC: ISO/IEC 24760: A Framework for Identity Management - Part 1: Terminology and Concepts, Part 2: Reference Framework and Requirements, Part 3: Practice (2011–2016). http://standards.iso.org/ittf/PubliclyAvailableStandards/index.html
5. Rannenberg, K., Camenisch, J., Sabouri, A. (eds.): Attribute-Based Credentials for Trust: Identity in the Information Society. Springer, Cham (2015). https://doi.org/10.1007/978-3-319-14439-9
6. Hörandner, F., Krenn, S., Migliavacca, A., Thiemer, F., Zwattendorfer, B.: CREDENTIAL: a framework for privacy-preserving cloud-based data sharing. In: ARES 2016, pp. 742–749. IEEE Computer Society (2016)
7. Kostopoulos, A., Sfakianakis, E., Chochliouros, I.P., Pettersson, J.S., Krenn, S., Tesfay, W., Migliavacca, A., Hörandner, F.: Towards the adoption of secure cloud identity services. In: ARES 2017, pp. 90:1–90:7. ACM (2017)
8. Johnson, R., Molnar, D., Song, D., Wagner, D.: Homomorphic signature schemes. In: Preneel, B. (ed.) CT-RSA 2002. LNCS, vol. 2271, pp. 244–262. Springer, Heidelberg (2002). https://doi.org/10.1007/3-540-45760-7_17
9. Blaze, M., Bleumer, G., Strauss, M.: Divertible protocols and atomic proxy cryptography. In: Nyberg, K. (ed.) EUROCRYPT 1998. LNCS, vol. 1403, pp. 127–144. Springer, Heidelberg (1998). https://doi.org/10.1007/BFb0054122
10. Chaum, D.: Untraceable electronic mail, return addresses, and digital pseudonyms. Commun. ACM **24**, 84–88 (1981)
11. Chaum, D.: Security without identification: transaction systems to make big brother obsolete. Commun. ACM **28**, 1030–1044 (1985)
12. Camenisch, J., Krenn, S., Lehmann, A., Mikkelsen, G.L., Neven, G., Pedersen, M.Ø.: Formal treatment of privacy-enhancing credential systems. In: Dunkelman, O., Keliher, L. (eds.) SAC 2015. LNCS, vol. 9566, pp. 3–24. Springer, Cham (2016). https://doi.org/10.1007/978-3-319-31301-6_1
13. Krenn, S., Lorünser, T., Salzer, A., Striecks, C.: Towards attribute-based credentials in the cloud. In: Chow, S.S., Capkun, S. (eds.) Cryptology and Network Security - CANS 2017 (2017, to be published)
14. Lorünser, T., et al.: Towards a new paradigm for privacy and security in cloud services. In: Cleary, F., Felici, M. (eds.) Cyber Security and Privacy. CCIS, vol. 530, pp. 14–25. Springer, Cham (2015). https://doi.org/10.1007/978-3-319-25360-2_2
15. Lorünser, T., Länger, T., Slamanig, D.: Cloud security and privacy by design. In: Katsikas, S.K., Sideridis, A.B. (eds.) e-Democracy 2015. CCIS, vol. 570, pp. 202–206. Springer, Cham (2015). https://doi.org/10.1007/978-3-319-27164-4_16

16. Lorünser, T., Slamanig, D., Länger, T., Pöhls, H.C.: PRISMACLOUD tools: a cryptographic toolbox for increasing security in cloud services. In: 11th International Conference on Availability, Reliability and Security, ARES 2016, Salzburg, Austria, 31 August–2 September 2016, pp. 733–741. IEEE Computer Society (2016)
17. Shamir, A.: How to share a secret. Commun. ACM **22**, 612–613 (1979)
18. Blakley, G.R.: Safeguarding cryptographic keys. In: AFIPS National Computer Conference (1979)
19. Ahn, J.H., Boneh, D., Camenisch, J., Hohenberger, S., Shelat, A., Waters, B.: Computing on authenticated data. In: Cramer, R. (ed.) TCC 2012. LNCS, vol. 7194, pp. 1–20. Springer, Heidelberg (2012). https://doi.org/10.1007/978-3-642-28914-9_1
20. Haber, S., Hatano, Y., Honda, Y., Horne, W.G., Miyazaki, K., Sander, T., Tezoku, S., Yao, D.: Efficient signature schemes supporting redaction, pseudonymization, and data deidentification. In: Abe, M., Gligor, V.D. (eds.) ASIACCS 2008, pp. 353–362. ACM, New York (2008)
21. Camenisch, J., Derler, D., Krenn, S., Pöhls, H.C., Samelin, K., Slamanig, D.: Chameleon-hashes with ephemeral trapdoors - and applications to invisible sanitizable signatures. In: Fehr, S. (ed.) PKC 2017. LNCS, vol. 10175, pp. 152–182. Springer, Heidelberg (2017). https://doi.org/10.1007/978-3-662-54388-7_6
22. Groß, T.: Efficient certification and zero-knowledge proofs of knowledge on infrastructure topology graphs. In: CCSW 2014, pp. 69–80. ACM (2014)
23. Derler, D., Slamanig, D.: Fully-anonymous short dynamic group signatures without encryption. IACR Cryptology ePrint Archive 2016/154 (2016)
24. Krenn, S., Lorünser, T., Striecks, C.: Batch-verifiable secret sharing with unconditional privacy. In: Proceedings of the 3rd International Conference on Information Systems Security and Privacy, ICISSP, INSTICC, vol. 1, pp. 303–311. ScitePress (2017)
25. Demirel, D., Krenn, S., Lorünser, T., Traverso, G.: Efficient and privacy preserving third party auditing for a distributed storage system. In: 11th International Conference on Availability, Reliability and Security, ARES 2016, Salzburg, Austria, 31 August–2 September 2016, pp. 88–97. IEEE Computer Society (2016)
26. Lorünser, T., Querasser, E., Matyus, T., Peev, M., Wolkerstorfer, J., Hutter, M., Szekely, A., Wimberger, I., Pfaffel-Janser, C., Neppach, A.: Security processor with quantum key distribution. In: 2008 International Conference on Application-Specific Systems, Architectures and Processors, ASAP 2008, pp. 37–42. IEEE (2008)
27. Neppach, A., Pfaffel-Janser, C., Wimberger, I., Lorünser, T., Meyenburg, M., Szekely, A., Wolkerstorfer, J.: Key management of quantum generated keys in IPsec. In: International Conference on Security and Cryptography SECRYPT, 26–29 July 2008, SECRYPT 2008, pp. 177–183. Institute for Systems and Technologies of Information, Control and Communication Press (2008)
28. Happe, A., Krenn, S., Lorünser, T.: Malicious clients in distributed secret sharing based storage networks. In: Anderson, J., Matyáš, V., Christianson, B., Stajano, F. (eds.) Security Protocols 2016. LNCS, vol. 10368, pp. 206–214. Springer, Cham (2017). https://doi.org/10.1007/978-3-319-62033-6_23
29. Happe, A., Wohner, F., Lorünser, T.: The archistar secret-sharing backup proxy. In: Proceedings of the 12th International Conference on Availability, Reliability and Security, ARES 2017, pp. 88:1–88:8. ACM, New York (2017)
30. Lorünser, T., Happe, A., Slamanig, D.: ARCHISTAR: towards secure and robust cloud based data sharing. In: 2015 IEEE 7th International Conference on Cloud Computing Technology and Science (CloudCom), pp. 371–378 (2015)

31. Bleikertz, S., Groß, T., Schunter, M., Eriksson, K.: Automated information flow analysis of virtualized infrastructures. In: Atluri, V., Diaz, C. (eds.) ESORICS 2011. LNCS, vol. 6879, pp. 392–415. Springer, Heidelberg (2011). https://doi.org/10.1007/978-3-642-23822-2_22

32. Bleikertz, S., Vogel, C., Groß, T.: Cloud radar: near real-time detection of security failures in dynamic virtualized infrastructures. In: ACSAC 2014, pp. 26–35. ACM (2014)

33. Bleikertz, S., Vogel, C., Groß, T., Mödersheim, S.: Proactive security analysis of changes in virtualized infrastructures. In: ACSAC 2015 (2015)

34. Groß, T.: Signatures and efficient proofs on committed graphs and NP-statements. In: Böhme, R., Okamoto, T. (eds.) FC 2015. LNCS, vol. 8975, pp. 293–314. Springer, Heidelberg (2015). https://doi.org/10.1007/978-3-662-47854-7_18

35. Camenisch, J., Lysyanskaya, A.: A signature scheme with efficient protocols. In: Cimato, S., Persiano, G., Galdi, C. (eds.) SCN 2002. LNCS, vol. 2576, pp. 268–289. Springer, Heidelberg (2003). https://doi.org/10.1007/3-540-36413-7_20

36. Camenisch, J., Groß, T.: Efficient attributes for anonymous credentials. In: ACM CCS 2008, pp. 345–356. ACM Press (2008)

37. Camenisch, J., Groß, T.: Efficient attributes for anonymous credentials. TISSEC 15, 4:1–4:30 (2012)

38. Groß, T.: Geo-location separation of virtualized systems. Technical report CS-TR, Newcastle University (2017)

On Anonymizing Streaming Crime Data: A Solution Approach for Resource Constrained Environments

Aderonke Busayo Sakpere[1(✉)] and Anne V. D. M. Kayem[2]

[1] Department of Computer Science,
University of Cape Town, Cape Town, South Africa
olfade001@myuct.ac.za
[2] Internet Technologies and Systems Group,
Hasso-Plattner-Institute, Potsdam, Germany
anne@mykayem.org

Abstract. A typical resource constrained environment is restrained in terms of availability of resources such as skilled personnel, equipments, power and Internet connectivity. Designing privacy-based service-oriented architectures therefore requires re-adapting existing solutions to cope with the constraints of the environment. In this paper, we consider the case of mobile crime-reporting systems that have emerged as an effective and efficient data collection method in developing countries. Analyzing the data, can be helpful in addressing crime but, law enforcement agencies in resource-constrained contexts typically do not have the expertise required to handle these tasks. A possible cost-effective strategy is thus to outsource the data analytics operations to third-party service providers. However, the sensitivity of the data makes privacy an important consideration. In this paper we propose a two-pronged approach to addressing the issue of privacy in outsourcing crime data in resource constrained contexts. We build on this in the second step to propose a streaming data anonymization algorithm to analyse reported data based on occurrence rate rather than at a preset time on a static repository. Results from our prototype implementation and usability tests indicate that having a usable and covet crime-reporting application encourages users to declare crime occurrences and anonymizing streaming data contributes to faster crime resolution times.

1 Introduction

While organizations generate data that can contribute to improving performance daily, many of these organizations do not have the in-house expertise required to analyse the data. The lack of expertise is prominent in resource constrained environments manifested in rural/remote developing world regions, for instance, where constraints on resources such as access to computational power, reliable electricity, and the Internet pose a further challenge. A cost-effective solution is to outsource the data to a professional third-party data analytics service provider.

© IFIP International Federation for Information Processing 2018
Published by Springer International Publishing AG 2018. All Rights Reserved
M. Hansen et al. (Eds.): Privacy and Identity 2017, IFIP AICT 526, pp. 170–186, 2018.
https://doi.org/10.1007/978-3-319-92925-5_11

A study [1] carried out in technologically resource-constrained environments has revealed that collected crime data are usually not studied or analysed to support crime resolution. A possible reason for this is the lack of the necessary in-house expertise, both in terms of human capital and computational processing power [5,15,24]. This deprives policy makers in these regions of the benefits that could have been derived through data analytics. A possible solution to this is to involve a third-party data analytics service provider [1,2]. However, because of the sensitive nature of crime data it makes sense to ensure that the outsourced data are protected from all unauthorized access including that of an honest-but-curious data mining service provider. Therefore, this paper focuses on developing a test bed framework to preserve privacy during real-time information sharing using the crime domain as an application scenario. However, it is important to stress that the ideas and approaches considered in this study are applicable to other areas or domains as well.

2   Related Work

A naive approach to preserve privacy or anonymity in data is to exclude explicit identifiers such as name and/or identification number. However linking attacks aimed at data deanonymisation, can be provoked successfully by combining non-explicit identifiers (such as date of birth, address and sex) with external or publicly available data [3,25,26]. To illustrate how a linking attack can be provoked, let us consider Fig. 1, which shows two compartments (or storage) that contains data. The upper compartment contains a portion of a publicly available table in which "name" is an explicit identifier attribute and the lower compartment shows a portion of a data stream that has been sanitized to exclude explicit identifiers (name) in order to disguise the identities of the individuals associated with the data. However, when a joining operation is performed on both compartments using attributes common to both compartments, the supposedly anonymized individual is re-identified successfully as Ade who lives at 10 Pope Street and also revealing her sensitive information that she has been a victim of rape.

According to Sweeney [18,19] 87% of the population in the United States were uniquely identified by the combination of non-explicit identifiers such as gender, zip code and date of birth from the 1990 census dataset using linking attack. Therefore, Sweeney et al. came up with a better approach named k-anonymity to anonymize data in a manner that linking attack is minimized.

K-anonymity ensures privacy is preserved by hiding each individual in a cluster which contains at least k individuals such that an adversary finds it difficult to get additional individual information, but rather information about a group of k individuals [18,20]. To understand how k-anonymity works, let us assume an attacker tries to identify a friend in a k-anonymized table, but the only information he has is her birth date and gender. K-anonymity ensures that the adversary finds it difficult to identify the individual by guaranteeing that at least k people have the same date of birth and gender. Thus minimizing the rate of linking

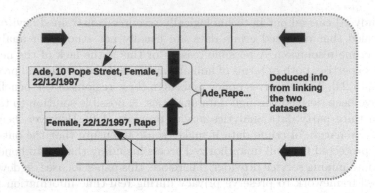

Fig. 1. Illustration of linking attack

attack to at least $1/k$. K-anonymity algorithms can generally be grouped into two categories, namely hierarchy-based generalization and hierarchy-free generalization [3]. In the hierarchy-based generalization, data anonymization requires a generalization tree as an input to aid in the anonymization process while in the hierarchy-free generalization, generalization tree is not required as an input rather the algorithm makes use of clustering concepts and some heuristics.

The evolution of k-anonymity has led to the birth of newer privacy models to address its inherent limitation. Some of the popular and newer privacy models that extend k-anonymity are ℓ-diversity and t-closeness [29,30]. The main essence of ℓ-diversity is to address homogeneity attack to which k-anonymity is vulnerable and it does this by requiring that each cluster in a k-anonymized table has at least ℓ distinct sensitive values [29]. T-closeness further complements ℓ-diversity by ensuring that distribution of sensitive values in a cluster is similar to that of the entire anonymized table [30].

An equally fast-growing data preservation technique is differential privacy. Differential privacy achieves anonymization by altering the data (i.e. unanonymized data) with the addition of mathematical "noise" [13]. In other words, differential privacy preserves privacy through the "difference" between the data supplied and the noise added to it. Interestingly, recent research [16,17] has shown that the use of t-closeness with k-anonymity can yield similar privacy result as those of differential privacy. In this research we focus on k-anonymity and its complementary techniques because of the simplicity [29], effectiveness [19] and high utility [31] offered, especially when compared to an evolving counterpart such as differential privacy. In addition, recent research [31,32] has shown that differential privacy is achieved as long as a dataset is anonymized using k-anonymity and t-closeness. Therefore this paper focuses on the use of k-anonymity, ℓ-diversity and t-closeness to achieve anonymization.

The adaptation of k-anonymity & its complementaries to data stream (real-time data) has led current research to integrate the concept of a buffering (or sliding window) mechanism and delay constraint into data stream anonymization [3,4,22,25–27]. The buffer is designed to hold a portion of the data stream at every instant of time, after which an anonymization algorithm can be applied to data in the buffer. Delay constraints is required to put a check on each tuple so that it does not stay in the buffer beyond a pre-defined deadline. Inspite of this, many of the existing algorithms adapted for anonymization of data streams face the following challenges:

- First, buffering according to delay constraints, can result in certain records being held in the buffer for long periods [3,8,10]. When such records are time-sensitive or need to be processed in real time, occurrence of delay usually results in high levels of information loss. Since a key requirement of a good anonymization scheme is high data utility, high levels of information loss due to expired tuples or dropped (or suppressed/unanonymizable) records are undesirable.
- Second, building on the first problem, we note that many of the existing data stream anonymization schemes based on k-anonymity and its derivatives do not take distribution of future data streams into consideration during anonymization [4]. An implication of this is that a record that is likely to offer better anonymization at a lower rate of information loss in a future sliding window or data stream can be anonymized with such a future sliding window rather than the current sliding window or data stream. Therefore, there is a need to have a model that can predict the best sliding window or stream with which a record should be anonymized.

Therefore, the focus in this paper is to present a data-stream anonymization framework that addresses the aforementioned challenges inherent in existing framework. More detailed literature review can be found in [14].

3 Data Stream Anonymization Framework

Figure 2 presents an overview of our Data Stream Anonymization Framework using the crime domain as an application scenario. Users make crime reports electronically and the reports are anonymized in real time at the anonymization layer. The results from the anonymization layer are transferred to third party for data mining process at the application layer.

3.1 Users Layer: Crime Reporting Layer

As noted in previous sections, this research considers the crime domain as an application scenario for achieving data stream anonymization. However, the ideas in this research extend to any other domain that requires real-time anonymization of sensitive data. Thus, to enable us to create an application that allow people to report crime in a secured and covert way, we converted the existing paper-based crime reporting system of a University Campus Setting in South Africa into a digitized Crime Reporting System. We chose to use mobile device as platform for crime reporting because the use of mobile devices provides a good security platform for crime report [11,23].

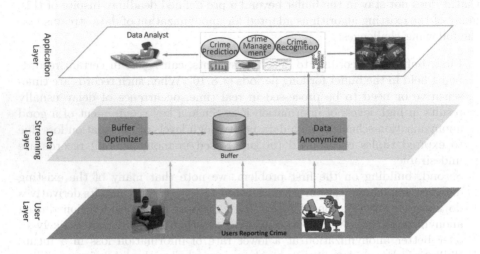

Fig. 2. System overview

In order to ensure that our mobile crime reporting system is acceptable and usable in real-life we applied an iterative user-centered design methodology. To this effect we interviewed different key stakeholders within law enforcement agencies and crime victims. We had different iterations in our design until we came up with a final prototype acceptable to all stakeholders. Figure 3 presents the screenshots of our final prototype. More details about the research on the development and deployment of the crime reporting application,CryHelp, can be found in [5].

3.2   Anonymization Layer: Data Stream Anonymization

In our proposed crime reporting application scenario, data arrives in form of streams and contains information that is analyzed for statistical or data mining predictions. These data are temporarily stored in a buffer in order for anonymization to take place. A buffer is used to hold portions of the continuous data stream based on delay constraints that specify the duration for which tuples can remain in the buffer just before anonymization takes place. As illustrated in Fig. 4, the buffer optimizer uses time-based sliding window and Poisson probability to monitor the data in the buffer, ensuring that tuples are anonymised before the expiry time threshold is reached while Fig. 5 illustrates the data anonymizer which uses k-anonymity, ℓ-diversity and t-closeness for data privacy preservation. We opted for Poisson distribution because it is concerned with the number of success that occurs within a given unit of measure. This property of the Poisson distribution makes viewing the arrival rate of the reported crime data as a series of events occurring within a fixed time interval at an average rate that is independent of

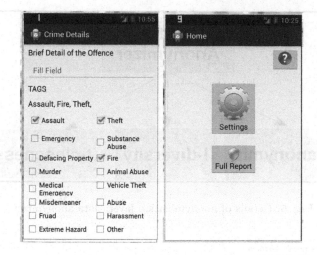

Fig. 3. Screenshot of our crime reporting application

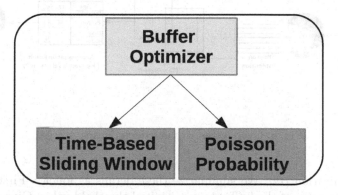

Fig. 4. Details of anonymization layer: buffer optimizer

occurrence of the time of the last event [6]. Only one parameter needs to be known, the rate at which the events occur which in our case is the rate at which crime reporting occurs.

4 Adaptive Buffer Re-sizing Scheme

As illustrated in Fig. 6, a "sliding window (buffer)", sw_i, is a subset of the data stream, DS, where DS = $\{sw_1, sw_2, sw_3, \ldots, sw_m\}$ implies that the data stream consists of m sliding windows. The sliding windows obey a total ordering such that for $i < j$, sw_i precedes sw_j. Each sliding window, sw_i only exists for a specific period of time T and consists of a finite and varying number of records, n, so that $sw_i = R_0, \ldots, R_{n-1}$.

Our adaptive buffer sizing scheme as illustrated in Fig. 7 is categorized into 6 phases and detailed explanation about how each of these phases work is in our

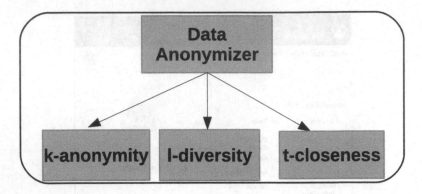

Fig. 5. Details of anonymization layer: data anonymizer

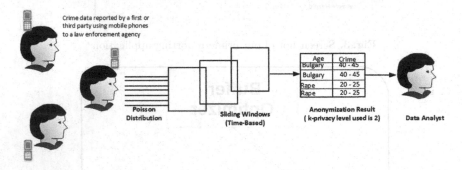

Fig. 6. Overview of dynamic buffer sizing process

earlier publication [12]. We summarize these details as follows. First we begin by setting the size of the buffer to some initial threshold value. Given the time-sensitivity of the data, we set the size of the sliding window, sw_i, to a value, T. T is a time value that is bounded by a lower bound value, t_l, and an upper bound value, t_u. The anonymization algorithm is applied to the data that was collected in the sliding window sw_i during the period T. So, essentially $sw_i = T$. All records that are not anonymizable from the data collected in sw_i are either included in a subsequent sliding window, say sw_{i+1} or incorporated into already anonymized clusters of data that are similar in content wise.

In order to determine whether or not an unanonymizable record can be included in a subsequent sliding window, say sw_{i+1}, we compute its expiry time T_E and compare its values to the bounds for acceptable sliding window sizes $[t_l, t_u]$. We compute T_E as follows:

$$T_E = sw_i - T_S - T_A \tag{1}$$

where T_E is the time to expiry of a record , T_S is the time for which the record was stored in sw_i, and T_A is the time required to anonymize the data in sw_i.

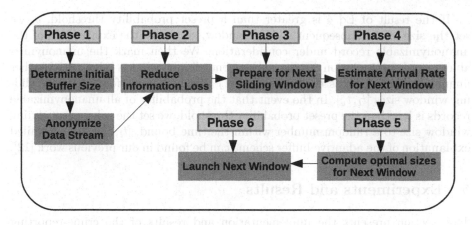

Fig. 7. Phases of adaptive buffer re-sizing scheme

Starting with the unanonymizable record, R_i, that has the lowest T_E and whose value falls within the acceptable bound, $[t_l, t_u]$, we check for other unanonymizable records, n, that belong to the same data anonymization group as R_i. We then proceed to find the rate of arrival, λ, of data in that anonymization group. We compute the arrival rate of records required to anonymize R_i within time T_E as follows:

$$\lambda = \frac{n}{sw_1} \times T_E \tag{2}$$

The expected arrival rate, λ, is used to determine the probability of arrival of at least the number of records needed to guarantee that delaying anonymizing the unanonymizable record, R_i, to the next sliding window sw_{i+1} will not adversely increase information loss. We next determine the minimum number of records, m, required to guarantee anonymization of R_i in the next sliding window, sw_{i+1}. When the decision is to include the R_i into the next sliding window sw_{i+1}, we need to then compute the optimal size for sw_{i+1} in order to minimize information loss from record expiry. We achieve this by finding the probability that m records will actually arrive in the data stream within time, T_E, in order to anonymize the unanonymizable record, R_i. We use Eq. 3 to compute the probability of having $i = 0 \ldots m$ records arrive in the stream within T_E

$$f(sw_{i+1}, \lambda) = \Pr(i = 0 \ldots n) = \frac{\lambda^i e^{-\lambda}}{i!} \tag{3}$$

where λ is the expected arrival rate, e is the base of the natural logarithm (i.e. $e = 2.71828$) and i is the number of records under observation.

Therefore the probability of having greater that m or more records arrive in the stream within time T_E is

$$1 - \sum_{i=0}^{m-1} pr \tag{4}$$

where pr is the probability outcome of Eq. 3.

If the result of Eq. 4 is greater than a preset probability threshold, δ, we set the size of the subsequent sliding window, sw_{i+1}, to the expiry time of the unanonymizable record under consideration. We then mark the unanonymizable record for inclusion in the subsequent sliding window along with other unanonymizable records that have their T_E within bounds for acceptable sliding window sizes $[t_l, t_u]$. In the event that the probability of all unanonymizable records is less than the preset probability threshold, we set the subsequent sliding window size to a random number within the time bound, $[t_l, t_u]$. More detailed explanation of the adaptive buffer scheme can be found in our previous work [12].

5   Experiments and Results

This section presents the implementation and results of the crime-reporting Application, CryApp, and the adaptive buffering scheme algorithm.

5.1   CryHelp Application Evaluation

In order to evaluate the usability of our mobile crime reporting application, CryHelp, we developed a questionnaire. The questionnaire was based on IBM CSUQ [23]. The advantage of the IBM CSUQ [23] is that it allows questionnaires to be divided into scores and specific categories. These categories are: System Overall, System Usefulness, Information Quality and Interface Quality. These categories allow evaluation of each individual component of the system to gauge which aspects perform well or poorly on average. These results directly address the issue of whether a mobile device can be used to effectively and securely send a crime report.

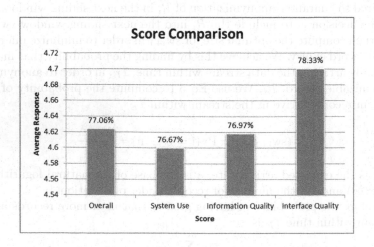

Fig. 8. The chart of the questionnaire score breakdown, with standard deviation 0.05

Figure 8 shows the result of each component of the system. From the figure, it can be seen that overall the system was well received with an overall system score of 77.06%, this suggests the users found the system very usable with a standard deviation of 0.05 for contributing scores System Use, Information Quality and Interface Quality. It is not surprising to find that the interface quality (78.33%), though marginally, is the most appreciated aspect of the system as the design process was centered on the users. These results bode very well for the feasibility of a mobile solution for crime reporting.

5.2   Experiments on Anonymization

Our feasibility study and experiment conducted on the prototype crime data collection application, CryHelp [5], informed the generation of more datasets for the second phase of experiment. The generation of more crime data was done using a random generator software[1] and pseudo-random algorithm based on a Gaussian distribution to populate the crime data-stream based on ground-truth provided by the users, UCT Campus Protection Service and the South African Police Service. Our data are in two sets, which contain 1000 and 10 000 records respectively, the first set contains 1000 records while the second set contains 10000 records, this is a reasonable bound for daily average crime report rates in South Africa [5].

Therefore, this section discusses the gains obtained using Poisson probability distribution to predict the time a sliding window should exist, while ensuring that records do not expire, the number of unanonymizable (or suppressed) records is minimal and privacy is maintained using k-anonymity, ℓ-diversity and t-closeness. The gains obtained are explained in the following sub-sections:

Recovered Unanonymizable Tuples: During anonymization there is usually a trade-off between the rate of IL, suppression and generalization. Usually if an equivalence class (cluster) is unable to satisfy the privacy requirement, such a class is either merged with another class or all its records are suppressed. A higher suppression rate implies that vital information is likely to be concealed from the recipient of the anonymized table, while merging of classes implies an increase in IL, which has the drawback of offering lower data utility. In order to curb this, Poisson probability distribution predicts the chances of such unanonymizable (suppressed) records undergoing anonymization in the next sliding window in a manner that preserves privacy and maximizes data utility with the goal of minimizing delay or expiration of records.

Figures 9 and 10 show the rate at which unanonymizable records were anonymized again, going by the predictions of Poisson probability distribution. It is evident from the figure that many unanonymizable records were recovered and allowed to go for anonymization again. It was also observed that the probability threshold influenced the number of unanonymizable records recovered. This leads to the conclusion that the higher the probability threshold, the lower

---

[1] http://www.mockaroo.com.

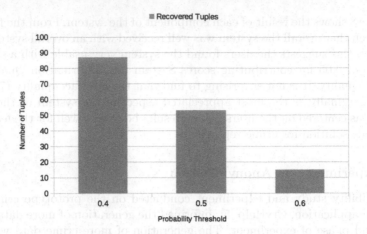

Fig. 9. Poisson probability threshold versus recovered tuples for dataset 1

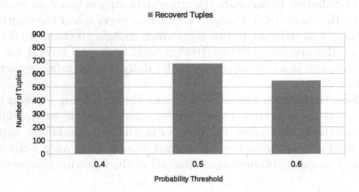

Fig. 10. Poisson probability threshold versus recovered tuples for dataset 2

the probability of unanonymizable records being given a chance for anonymization re-consideration in subsequent sliding window(s). The implication of this is that more records are likely not to be given the chance of another round of anonymization if higher threshold values are used. Another observation is that if a higher threshold value is used, then there are fewer changes or movements in records between sliding windows.

Privacy Value/Level Versus Recovered Unanonymizable Tuples: "Privacy level" simply means the degree of anonymity offered, while unanonymizable tuples are those tuples that belong to an equivalence class whose size is less than k. For the purpose of sliding windows that start with a small number of tuples, the minimum privacy level threshold was set as $k=2$ and the maximum at $k=15$; the ℓ-diversity value, ℓ, was varied between values 3 and 5 and finally the t-closeness value, t, was alternated between values 0.1 and 0.15 for the two datasets.

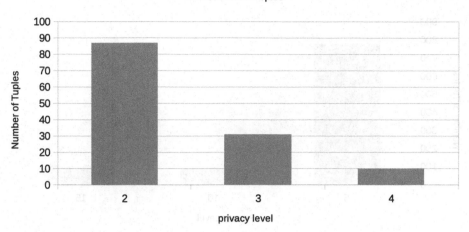

Fig. 11. Relationship between privacy level and recovered tuples for dataset 1

As illustrated in Figs. 11 and 12, it was observed that as the privacy value/level increases, the possible number of unanonymizable records that can be recovered using Poisson probability prediction is reduced. The main reason for this is that as the privacy level or degree increases, it is expected that the rate or possibility of achieving anonymization will become increasingly challenging. This definitely also influences the expectation of higher chances of anonymization rate for unanonymizable records. To understand the reason for the decline in the rate of recovered unanonymizable records better, let us assume the k privacy level is set to three and an equivalence class, EC_i, has two records; this implies that we are looking for at least one more record to make EC_i satisfy k-anonymity. In essence, using Poisson probability, the adaptive buffer resizing model attempts to predict the chance of at least one record in EC_i arrive within time, t, in the next sliding window. If k is set to four, this will mean the chance of at least two records arriving in the next sliding window. An implication of this is that the chances of having at least two records is more difficult or demanding compared to the chances of just one record. Thus, this explains why the model has a drop in recovered unanonymizable records as privacy level increases. Therefore, the conclusion is that the rate at which unanonymizable records in a current sliding window can be anonymized in a subsequent window is mainly dependent on the privacy value.

5.3   Benchmarking: Poisson Solution Comparison with Non-Poisson Solution

As a baseline case, for evaluating our proposed adaptive buffering scheme we implemented the proactive-FAANST and passive-FAANST. These algorithms are a good comparison benchmark because they are the current state-of-the-art

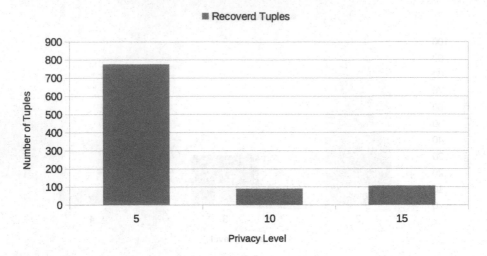

Fig. 12. Relationship between privacy level and recovered tuples for dataset 2

streaming data anonymization and reduce IL with minimum delay and expired tuples [3]. The proactive-FAANST decides if an unanonymizable record will expire if included in the next sliding window, while passive-FAANST searches for unanonymizable records that have expired. A major drawback of these two variants is that there is no way of deciding whether or not such unanonymizable records would be anonymizable during the next sliding window. This is necessary to avoid repeatedly cycling a tuple that has a low chance of anonymization in subsequent sliding window(s). Moreover, these algorithms do not consider the fact that the flow or speed of a data stream could change. These weaknesses of proactive-FAANST and passive-FAANST are what we attempt to address by using Poisson probability distribution to predict if such tuples would be anonymizable in subsequent sliding window(s) by taking into consideration the arrival rate of records, success rate of anonymization per sliding window, time a tuple can exist and rate of suppressed records.

Expired Tuples and Information Loss in Delay: A tuple expires when it remains in the system for longer than a pre-specified threshold called delay [3,10]. In order to decide whether a tuple has exceeded its time-delay constraint, additional attributes such as arrival time, expected waiting time and entry time were included. As a heuristic, the choice of delay values, $t_l = 2000$ ms and $t_u = 5000$ ms, is guided by values of delay that are used in published experimentation results [3].

In general, our approach shows that there are fewer expired tuples when compared to passive-FAANST and proactive-FAANST solutions. This is because before our Poisson prediction transfers suppressed records to another sliding window, it checks for the possibility of their anonymization. In other solutions, there is no mechanism in place to check the likelihood of the anonymizability of a suppressed record before allowing it to go to the next sliding window/round. As a result, such tuples are sent to the next sliding window and have high a tendency to expire eventually. Our solution also shows that the lower a k-value, the higher the number of expired tuples. This is because the outcome of Poisson prediction is lower for higher k-values. As a result, there are fewer changes of sliding windows as the k-value increases and this means there is a lower possibility of expired tuples.

One of the main goals of our solution is to reduce IL in delay (i.e. to lower the number of expired tuples). Figure 13 depicts that our solution is successful in achieving its main goal, and the IL (delay) in our solution is lower than in passive and proactive solutions. In order to determine the total number of records that expired, a simple count function was used to retrieve all records that had remain in the buffer longer than the upper limit threshold, t_u. To determine the average expired records, we sum up the expired records in all the experiments and divide the result by the total number of experiments.

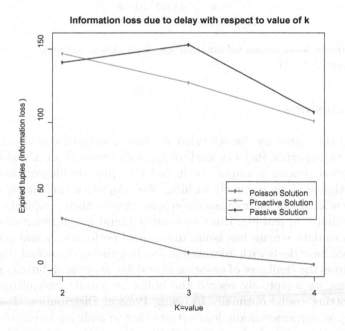

Fig. 13. Privacy level versus expired tuples for Poisson solution, passive-FAANST and proactive-FAANST

Data Utility and Information Loss in Record: An important factor that is considered in anonymization is the degree of usability of anonymized data for data analysis or data mining tasks [28]. Therefore, we compared the degree of IL in records of our solution with that of Passive-FAANST and proactive-FAANST. Our result, as illustrated in Fig. 14, shows that at the minimal level of privacy enforcement, the information loss of our solution is on par with the other two schemes, while at the maximal level our solution has better data utility.

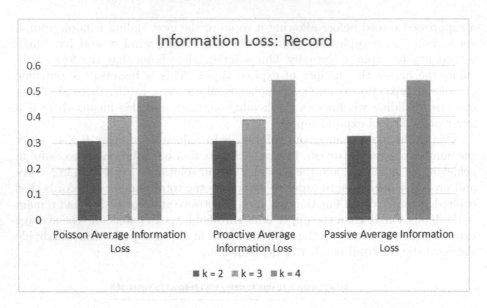

Fig. 14. Privacy level versus information loss for Poisson solution, passive-FAANST and proactive-FAANST

6   Conclusions

We started this paper on the note that resource constrained environments lack data analytic expertise that can analyze and mine crime data in real-time. This anonymization process is important in order to provide intervention that can carry out this analysis in timely fashion. We adopted k-anonymity, ℓ-diversity and t-closeness as our anonymization scheme due to their simplicity, efficiency and applicability in real-life. However current literature on integration of these techniques to data stream has issues in terms of performance and privacy. The performance issue deals with information loss in terms of delay and running cost.

To address the challenge of ensuring that delay is optimal during anonymization process, we adaptively resized the buffer to handle intermittent flows of crime reporting traffic optimally by using Poisson Distribution. Results from our prototype implementation demonstrate that in addition to ensuring privacy of the data, our proposed scheme outperforms other with an information loss rate of 1.95% in comparison to 12.7% on varying the privacy level of crime report data records.

References

1. Isafiade, O.E., Bagula, A.B.: Citisafe: adaptive spatial pattern knowledge using FP-growth algorithm for crime situation recognition. In: Ubiquitous Intelligence and Computing, IEEE 10th International Conference on Autonomic and Trusted Computing (UIC/ATC), pp. 551–556 (2013)
2. Qiu, L., Li, Y., Wu, X.: Protecting business intelligence and customer privacy while outsourcing data mining tasks. Knowl. Inf. Syst. 17(1), 99–120 (2008)
3. Zakerzadeh, H., Osborn, S.L.: Delay-sensitive approaches for anonymizing numerical streaming data. Int. J. Inf. Secur. 12, 1–15 (2013)
4. Guo, K., Zhang, Q.: Fast clustering-based anonymization approaches with time constraints for data streams. Knowl.-Based Syst. 46, 95–108 (2013)
5. Sakpere, A.B., Kayem, A.V.D.M., Ndlovu, T.: A usable and secure crime reporting system for technology resource constrained contexts. In: Proceedings of the 29th IEEE International Conference on Advanced Information Networking and Applications Workshops (WAINA 2015), Gwangju, Korea, 24–27 March 2015
6. Li, S.: Poisson process with fuzzy rates. Fuzzy Optim. Decis. Mak. 9(3), 289–305 (2006)
7. Sakpere, A.B., Kayem, A.V.D.M.: A state of the art review of data stream anonymisation schemes. IGI Global, PA, USA (2014)
8. Sakpere A.B., Kayem, A.V.D.M.: Adaptive buffer resizing for efficient anonymization of streaming data with minimal information loss. In: Proceedings of 1st International Conference on Information Systems Security and Privacy (ICISSP), pp. 191–201 (2015)
9. Sakpere, A.B.: User-defined privacy preferences for k-anonymization in electronic crime reporting systems for developing nations. In: proceedings of the 1st International Doctoral Symposium on Security and Privacy (2015)
10. Mohammadian, E., Noferesti, M., Jalili, R.: FAST: fast anonymization of big data streams. In: Proceedings of the 2014 International Conference on Big Data Science and Computing, p. 23. ACM (2014)
11. Lasley, J.R., Palombo, B.J.: When crime reporting goes high-tech: an experimental test of computerized citizen response to crime. J. Crim. Justice 23(6), 519–529 (1995)
12. Sakpere, A.B., Kayem, A.V.D.M.: Adaptive buffer resizing for efficient anonymization of streaming data with minimal information loss. In: Proceedings of the 1st International Conference on Information Systems Security and Privacy, pp. 191–201 (2015). https://doi.org/10.5220/0005288901910201. ISBN 978-989-758-081-9
13. Dwork, C.: Differential privacy. In: Bugliesi, M., Preneel, B., Sassone, V., Wegener, I. (eds.) ICALP 2006. LNCS, vol. 4052, pp. 1–12. Springer, Heidelberg (2006). https://doi.org/10.1007/11787006_1
14. Sakpere, A.B., Kayem, A.V.D.M.: A state of the art review of data stream anonymisation schemes. In: Information Security in Diverse Computing Environments. IGI Global, PA, USA (2014)
15. Jensen, K.L., Iipito, H.N., Onwordi, M.U., Mukumbira, S.: Toward an mPolicing solution for Namibia: leveraging emerging mobile platforms and crime mapping. In: Proceedings of the South African Institute for Computer Scientists and Information Technologists Conference, pp. 196–205. ACM (2012)
16. Domingo-Ferrer, J., Soria-Comas, J.: From t-closeness to differential privacy and vice versa in data anonymization. Knowl.-Based Syst. 74(151–158), 2015 (2015)

17. Soria-Comas, J., Domingo-Ferrer, J.: Differential privacy via t-closeness in data publishing. In: Proceedings of the 11th Annual Conference on Privacy, Security and Trust (PST), pp. 27–35. IEEE (2013)
18. Sweeney, L.: k-anonymity: a model for protecting privacy. Int. J. Uncertain. Fuzziness Knowl.-Based Syst. **10**(05), 557–570 (2002)
19. Sweeney, L.: Achieving k-anonymity privacy protection using generalization and suppression. Int. J. Uncertain. Fuzziness Knowl.-Based Syst. **10**(05), 571–588 (2002)
20. Sweeney, L.: Computational Disclosure Control: A Primer on Data Privacy Protection. Thesis (Ph.D.), Massachusetts Institute of Technology, Cambridge, MA (2001). http://www.swiss.ai.mit.edu/6805/articles/privacy/sweeney-thesis-draft.pdf
21. Iyengar, V.S.: Transforming data to satisfy privacy constraints. In: Proceedings of the Eighth ACM SIGKDD International Conference on Knowledge Discovery and Data Mining, pp. 279–288. ACM (2002)
22. Cao, J., Carminati, B., Ferrari, E., Tan, K.L.: Castle: continuously anonymizing data streams. IEEE Trans. Dependable Secur. Comput. **8**(3), 337–352 (2011)
23. Lewis, J.R.: IBM computer usability satisfaction questionnaires: psychometric evaluation and instructions for use. Int. J. Hum.-Comput. Interact. **7**(1), 57–78 (1995)
24. Burke, M.J.: Enabling anonymous crime reporting on mobile phones in the developing world. Masters Dissertation, University of Cape Town (2013)
25. Wang, W., Li, J., Ai, C., Li, Y.: Privacy protection on sliding window of data streams. In: Collaborative Computing: Networking, Applications and Worksharing. IEEE (2007)
26. Li, J., Ooi, B.C., Wang, W.: Anonymizing streaming data for privacy protection. In: IEEE 24th International Conference on Data Engineering, pp. 1367–1369. IEEE (2008)
27. Zhang, J., Yang, J., Zhang, J., Yuan, Y.: KIDS: K-anonymization data stream base on sliding window. In: 2nd International Conference on Future Computer and Communication (ICFCC), vol. 2, pp. V2–311. IEEE (2010)
28. Li, T., Li, N.: On the tradeoff between privacy and utility in data publishing. In: Proceedings of the 15th ACM SIGKDD International Conference on Knowledge Discovery and Data Mining, pp. 517–526. ACM (2009)
29. Machanavajjhala, A., Kifer, D., Johannes, G.: l-diversity: privacy beyond k-anonymity. ACM Trans. Knowl. Discov. Data (TKDD) **1**(1), 3 (2007)
30. Li, N., Li, T., Venkatasubramanian, S.: t-closeness: privacy beyond k-anonymity and l-diversity. In: International Conference on Data Engineering (ICDE), no. 3, pp. 106–115 (2007)
31. Soria-Comas, J., Domingo-Ferrer, J.: Differential privacy via t-closeness in data publishing. In: Proceedings of the 11th Annual Conference on Privacy, Security and Trust (PST). IEEE (2013)
32. Soria-Comas, J., Domingo-Ferrer, J.: Differential privacy via t-closeness in data publishing. Knowledge-Based Systems. Elsevier (2015)

Towards a Broadening of Privacy Decision-Making Models: The Use of Cognitive Architectures

Yefim Shulman(✉)

Tel Aviv University, Tel Aviv 6997801, Israel
efimshulman@mail.tau.ac.il

Abstract. Over the last decades, people's behaviour and attitudes towards privacy have been thoroughly studied by scholars, approaching the issue from different perspectives. To address privacy-related decisions, it is necessary to consider aspects of human cognition, employing, for instance, methods used in Human-Computer Interaction and Information Science research. This paper analyses findings and contributions of existing privacy decision-making research, and suggests filling gaps in current understanding by applying a cognitive architecture framework to model privacy decision-making. This may broaden the range of factors and their relationships that can be integrated into the models of privacy decisions, beyond those in existing decision models.

Keywords: Decision making · Privacy · Model · Cognitive architectures
ACT-R

1 Introduction

Privacy issues have been a matter of growing importance for individuals, as well as for business entities and regulators.

The key element in privacy-related interactions with technology is the end-user (i.e., data subject), who is entitled to make, supposedly well-informed, choices about how to deal with one's own personal information. For the most part, decisions concerning privacy are decisions of people giving or revoking their consent. These decisions are imposed on the users whenever they desire to interact with an information service, as well as with some more traditional services.

Other, more particular, decisions can result from the users' initiative (e.g., requesting deletion of their personal information, instituting changes in the data they have shared or in the way the system is allowed to process it, requesting a report on their privacy status, etc.). Such decisions are not usually forced upon the users, and they can be made by users without prior notifications and requests from systems or data holders. Therefore, to address these important issues, it is useful to be able to model human behaviour, when it comes to making decisions on privacy-related interactions.

This paper investigates the state-of-the-art in privacy decision-making literature and suggests the use of ACT-R (Adaptive Control of Thought – Rational) modelling

M. Hansen et al. (Eds.): Privacy and Identity 2017, IFIP AICT 526, pp. 187–204, 2018.
https://doi.org/10.1007/978-3-319-92925-5_12

framework to bridge the identified gaps and provide for a better understanding of people's information disclosure behaviour.

Section 2 introduces the current stage of research and outlines and compares main approaches in privacy decision-making. Section 3 introduces the field of cognitive architectures, discusses applicability and potential contributions of models constructed with ACT-R framework. Section 4 provides concluding remarks and challenges of proposed modelling paradigm.

2   Research on Privacy-Related Decision-Making Models

Section 2.1 provides an outline of the literature selection process. In Sect. 2.2 I discuss identified approaches and theories, traversing privacy decision-making research. Section 2.3 gives more attention to the literature on the privacy calculus, which prevails in the state-of-the-art literature on privacy decision-making. Section 2.3 contains further comparisons of the state-of-the-art research and discusses opportunities for improvement.

2.1   Literature Selection

As the first step, I identify the existing literature on privacy-related decision-making that should form the body of work, through which we parse in this paper (see Table 1). In my approach, I relied on the guidelines by Webster and Watson [58].

Table 1. The outline of the selection process

Selection criterion	Restriction properties
Main sources databases	Google Scholar, Scopus, Web of Science
Venue locations	Not restricted
Journals/conferences	Not restricted
Disciplines	Not restricted
Amount of citations	Not restricted
Status	Published or "to-appear-in" state
Versions priority	First: official publication Second: final edition from an author's website Third: proceedings version and pre-print
Date of publication	Not restricted
Search terms	"model", "privacy", "decision", "making"
Exclusion criteria	"mental models" Court decision-making and legal cases Papers written not in the English language Medical disclosure and other papers related to rules, procedures, regulations, instructions and orders
Additional sources	Lists of references in the relevant papers Lists of mentions of the relevant papers

For the review I used broad multi-disciplinary databases. I included papers that did not draw significant attention from other scholars over the years. It was important for the purposes of this paper to try and highlight all the ideas applied to study privacy decision-making that had been tested so far.

2.2   Approaches and Theories in Privacy-Related Decision-Making

Researchers have studied human decision-making from a psychological and economic standpoints, using a variety of models, based on classical economics (i.e., expected value and expected utility theory) and its generalized extensions, as well as behavioural economics (see Fig. 1).

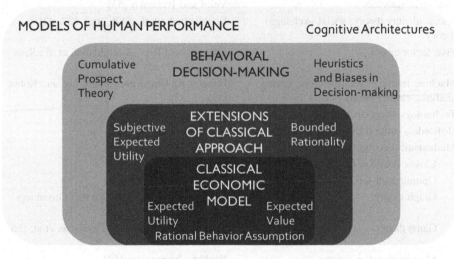

Fig. 1. The relations of approaches to modelling decision-making in economics

Acquisti et al. [1] discuss how privacy has been being regarded as an economic good and provide an explanation on how individuals' informed decisions about their privacy are being hindered, because of asymmetry of the information available to people, when they make privacy-related decisions.

Behavioural economics is a permeant theme in the more recent papers (e.g., Adjerid et al. [2]; Dinev et al. [10]; Dong et al. [12]; etc.). Arguably, it may be applicable for modelling human decisions in privacy-related interactions as an instance of decision-making under risk. Barberis [6] provides multiple examples of how it has been used to model decisions in areas spanning from finance and insurance to understanding betting markets, pricing, consumption-saving decisions, etc.

Overall, I identified 40 papers on user decisions on online privacy. Nine papers reported surveys, positions, system prototypes, case-studies or user-study experiments and did not deal with model development. They are still included in this paper, representing the current developments in the subject domain. The outline of the families of theories and frameworks used so far is presented in Table 2.

Table 2. Theories and frameworks in privacy decision-making literature

Theories and frameworks	Relying papers
Privacy Calculus, in conjunction with Theory of Reasoned Action (TRA) and Theory of Planned Behaviour (TPB)	Knijnenburg and Kobsa; Dinev et al.; Dong et al.; Kehr et al.; Zhu et al.; [10, 12, 23, 26, 60] etc. – Majority of papers is based on privacy calculus approach or its extensions, see Sect. 2.2 for more detailed discussion
TRA and (or) TPB, excluding Privacy Calculus	Kim et al.; Wang and Liu; Koohikamali et al. [25, 27, 57]
Bounded rationality and generalised expected utility	Pu and Grossklags; Kehr et al.; Zhu et al. [23, 42, 60]
Behavioural economics	Dinev et al.; Adjerid and Peer [2, 10]
Cognitive scarcities	Veltri and Ivchenko [53]
Social identity theory, social exchange theory	Koohikamali et al.; Shih et al. [27, 47]
Five factor model	Egelman and Peer; Koohikamali et al.; Ross et al. [13, 27, 45]
Machine learning (decision trees, cluster analysis, classification)	Dong et al.; Ghosh and Singh; Lee and Kobsa [12, 17, 32]
Technology acceptance model	Kim et al. [25]
Hofstede's cultural dimensions theory	Krasnova et al. [30]
Mathematical economics:	
Classic decision theory	Griffin et al. [20]
Optimization theory	Griffin et al. [20]
Graph theory	Mahmood and Desmedt; Pu and Grossklags [36, 42]
Game theory	Mahmood and Desmedt; Panaousis et al. [36, 40]
Markov decision process	Venkitasubramaniam [54]
Expectancy theory	Hann et al.; Keith et al. [21, 24]
Conjoint analysis	Hann et al. [21]
Fuzzy logic	Zhu et al. [60]
Stimulus-Organism-Response (S-O-R) Model	Li et al. [33]
Protection motivation theory	Li; Wang and Liu [34, 57]
Social contract theory	Malhotra et al. [37]
Elaboration likelihood model	Dinev et al. [10]
Valence framework	Dinev and Hart; Kim et al.; Eling et al. [8, 15, 25]
Experience sampling method	Lee and Kobsa [32]
Prototype willingness framework	Van Gool et al. [51]

Altman-Westin privacy, privacy concerns and attitudes constructs are the underlying theories in most of the reviewed papers. Since they are not directly related to model development, they are not mentioned in Table 2.

Looking at applied theories and frameworks, we can infer that, in general, research on privacy decision-making can be divided by subject areas into four major methodological groups: (1) most pronounced so far, an information science approach with the privacy calculus and its extensions; (2) a psychological, social and information science approach beyond the privacy calculus; (3) a mathematical-economic approach; and (4) a machine learning approach.

The overwhelming majority of research is based on the privacy calculus and its extensions. Hence, I deem appropriate to "detach" this bulk of research from subject-wise division and discuss this theory in more detail in the following Sect. 2.3. We return to the grand comparison and analysis of existing approaches in Sect. 2.4.

2.3 Privacy Calculus Modelling Approach

Multiple empirical and methodological studies on privacy decision-making draw from economic constructs such as expected utility theory, employing the privacy calculus (e.g., in Malhotra et al. [37]; Hann et al. [21]; Xu et al. [59]). Their results provide insights for understanding the "privacy paradox" and individuals' attitudes towards privacy-related preferences and decisions, and contribute to the assessment of privacy concerns.

Dinev and Hart [8] attempt to measure privacy concerns and estimate dependencies between factors and privacy constructs ("concerns of information finding" and "concerns of information abuse"). Later, Dinev and Hart [9] provide more ground for the use of an extended privacy calculus, showing that, at least for the example of e-commerce, Internet trust and personal interest can outweigh privacy concerns constructs. After employing common statistical methods of dimensionality reduction and supervised learning in the first work, structural equation modelling in the second, and joined by other researchers, a bigger collective of authors investigates privacy perceptions and develops a theoretical framework for understanding Internet privacy attitudes (Dinev et al. [11]), with an empirically developed structural model attesting to the validity of proposed constructs.

In a set of studies of privacy-related issues in social networking services, Krasnova et al. [28, 29] turn to the privacy calculus and produce structural models to investigate Internet users' privacy concerns and motivations regarding personal information disclosure. The former research develops and justifies categorisation of privacy concerns, and, then, tests it against self-disclosure dimensions to explore inter-relations between defined privacy concerns and postulated self-disclosure strategies. The latter paper commences in an attempt to build a model of self-disclosure in social networking services. Exploratory in nature, this paper identifies factors of self-disclosure, noting, however, that "(...) other factors beyond those investigated in our study can also have an impact on individual self-disclosure" (Krasnova et al. [29], p. 123).

Krasnova et al. [30] account for users' mental patterns and uncover cultural implications of privacy attitudes and behaviour. Here the authors address individualism and avoidance of uncertainty as two (out of commonly adopted five) cultural factors of self-disclosure that seem most relevant in terms of social networking services. The paper, as recognised by the authors, is limited in the scope of possible influencing effects. The model itself abstains from considering spatial and temporal factors, as well as cognitive effects and biases at the point of making a decision.

Keith et al. [24] apply the privacy calculus to show that consumer age is not a significant factor in decisions on online self-disclosure, and the relationship between decisions on personal information disclosure and the intention to disclose such information is weak, while still statistically significant. More practical conclusions reveal that privacy-concerned users do not necessarily properly understand the link between first- and second-order privacy risks of the same nature. Notwithstanding, authors admit that their research "does not account for a consumer's long-term intentions or disclosure behaviour" and "privacy calculus might be better modelled as a sub-theory within a larger framework aiming to elucidate how long term information disclosure relationships form." (Keith et al. [24], p. 1172). Moreover, the researchers name Kahneman and Tversky's Prospect Theory as a better way than the existing rational privacy calculus for accounting for bounded rationality and obtaining an insight on privacy-related decision-making. Lastly, another take-away from the paper is a seemingly valid point favouring exploration of possible non-linearity of relationship between perceived benefits and risks in self-disclosure decisions.

More and more attempts are made to extend the privacy calculus, apart from the aforementioned works (e.g., Li [34]). A paper by Wang et al. [56] is one successful example. The research probes extending the privacy calculus with more psychological factors and adds evidence of the importance of contextual factors in privacy decision-making. Relying on a structural model, the authors argue that users value benefits more than risks. The need for cognition effect has been studied, showing a significant relationship with risks and a non-significant relation with benefits.

The vast majority of decision-making models powered by the privacy calculus were built with expected utility or expected value in their core. To scrutinise decision-making behind disclosure in exchange for personalisation of services in e-commerce, Zhu et al. [60] introduce a rank-dependent generalised expected utility model. The authors run their mathematical model through a set of simulations for users with different levels of privacy concerns and companies with different reputation.

2.4   Comparison and Discussion

The existing theoretical body of research behind privacy decision-making draws from various subject areas. Let us look closer at the approaches scholars used to study privacy decision-making. Overall, achievements and limitations of the existing models, grouped by prevailing approaches, are represented in a comparative Table 3.

Li [34] designs a decision-making matrix, based on an elaborate overview of approaches and theories used in privacy research, and on the derived concept of a "dual-calculus model", which is defined as a combination of privacy- and risk-calculi for decision-making in privacy-related issues.

Table 3. Summary of approaches to studying privacy decision-making

Approaches		
Problems and measures	Motivations	Limitations
Information Science and (Extended) Privacy Calculus		
Problems addressed: users' personal information disclosure decisions in online environments: mobile applications, social networks, e-commerce, location tracking, personalisation and recommendations in online services; study of the "privacy paradox" **Methods:** linear regression; structural equation modelling (SEM); confirmatory factor analysis (CFA); exploratory factor analysis (EFA); systematic review and deduction; empirical studies; induction **Determinants (factors):** perceived risks, benefits, trust, and control; personal interest; privacy concerns; satisfaction; antecedents (experience; culture; context; personality, etc.); information sensitivity	**Achievements:** formulation and explanation of "Antecedents – Privacy Concerns – Outcomes" (APCO, Dinev et al. [10]) pathway of observable decision-making on practice **Advantages:** 1. Mature methodology 2. Findings are coherent between multiple studies 3. Empirically enabled research approach 4. Results easily tested and verified in practice 5. Uncovers relations between factors	1. Sample bias in surveys and experiments 2. External validity of the experiments can be challenged 3. Scope of factors is usually restricted 4. Perceptions are often studied in isolation from how they are being translated to behaviours 5. "Stimuli – Thought effort – Action" assumption, that is challenged by certain advancements in psychology and behavioural economics 6. Inter-temporal nature of privacy trade-offs is overlooked
Psychology, Social Science and Information Science beyond Privacy Calculus		
Problems addressed: users' personal information disclosure decisions in online environments: mobile applications, social networks, e-commerce, online services preferences; study of the "privacy paradox" **Methods:** multiple regression; principal components analysis; EFA; CFA; SEM; empirical studies **Determinants (factors):** personality traits; affect; familiarity; social identity; cognitive load; motivation;	**Achievements:** testing and explanation of effects of personality, cognitive load, environment, ethics and culture on intentions to disclose personal information **Advantages:** 1. Empirically enabled research approach. 2. Results easily tested and verified in practice 3. Uncovers relations between factors 4. Explains roles of social, cultural and psychological	1. Sample bias in surveys and experiments 2. External validity of the experiments can be challenged 3. Compromise between quantification capability of factors and practical applicability of models 4. Models do not usually possess predictive capability 5. Models are not particular: do not account for individual differences 6. Models explain intentions rather than behaviours

(*continued*)

Table 3. (*continued*)

Approaches		
Problems and measures	Motivations	Limitations
etc., sometimes in conjunction with privacy calculus	effects in privacy decision-making	
Mathematical Economics		
Problems addressed: (sub)optimal decision strategies; privacy-utility trade-offs; privacy-utility-profit trade-offs; decisions' payoffs; decision-making under budget restrictions **Methods:** SEM; game simulations; Markov process simulations; dynamic programming; ANOVA; cluster analysis **Determinants (factors):** valences; outcomes; risks; time; population	**Achievements:** mathematical formulations of privacy-constrained decision-making; utility calculation formulations; rational privacy decision-making formulation **Advantages:** 1. Outstanding theoretical rigour 2. Applicable for building macromodels	1. Models do not account for factors that cannot be expressed in terms of costs, benefits, risks, expected utility, probability of success, agent profit 2. Prone to quantification problem and reliability problem, when behaviouristic or cognitive extensions attempted 3. Real-world applicability may pose a challenge
Machine Learning		
Problems addressed: predicting users' behaviour; identifying influencing determinants **Methods:** decision trees; clustering; classification **Determinants (factors):** metadata; location; data holder properties; contextual factors, etc. Any quantifiable features	**Achievements:** privacy attitudes predictions; decisions on personal information sharing predictions **Advantages:** 1. Depending on data properties, models can always be constructed to have better-than-random level of predictive power 2. Predictions may be modelled for decisions with almost arbitrary set of determinants	1. Models are not descriptive 2. Models are not extendable factor-wise 3. Is not suitable for modelling human intelligence 4. Models are sample-bound and data-hungry 5. High level of abstraction from nature: factors lack explainability 6. Reasoning behind decisions cannot be inferred 7. Decision-making process is not modelled

Researchers try to probe privacy decision-making beyond privacy calculus as well. In that way, Van Gool et al. [51] base their research of disclosure behaviour in adolescents on a Prototype Willingness Model[1]. The authors study adolescents' relationship disclosure in online social networks, and they manage to show that said self-disclosure is a product of an analytical reasoned process, which can be more or less influenced by the situational context. Li et al. [33] adopt the S-O-R paradigm[2] in their attempt to model privacy-related decision-making. The authors find that decisions regarding personal information disclosure depend on impressions that users internalize during the first interaction with a website that prompts the users for said decisions to be made.

Mahmood and Desmedt [36] carry out an attempt to develop mathematical models of privacy, which results in devising a game theoretical model (stochastic almost combinatorial) and a graph theory model (attack and defence multigraphs with certain simplifications). The researchers argue that users cannot always be careful and thorough, due to bounded rationality and limitations of working memory.

Egelman and Peer [13] study privacy decision-making from a psychological standpoint. The authors consider the influence of such factors as personality dimensions on online privacy concerns and self-disclosure behaviour. As a result, they argue that individual differences are better predictors of decisions than the personality traits approach, testing their hypothesis against the Five Factor Model[3].

Koohikamali et al. [27] extend the modelling literature by addressing self-disclosure with the premises of Rest's ethical decision-making model[4]. In contrast with majority of research concerned with self-disclosure, the authors attempt to model decisions about disclosure of personal information about others. They show that disclosure about others is driven by the attitudes towards social network sites and concerns about others' privacy, and is not influenced by the social norms.

---

[1] Prototype Willingness Model (PWM) is a framework from the family of so called "dual processing models". It operates under the assumption that there are two paths of decision-making: a reasoned path (rational), and a social reaction path (heuristics-based). PWM was developed by M. Gerrard, F. X. Gibbons and their colleagues. It was aimed to be used for health studies, originating in Gibbons and Gerrard [18].

[2] Stimulus-organism-response (S-O-R) model postulates that environmental factors affect cognitive reactions in organisms, thusly affecting behaviour (Mehrabian and Russell [39]).

[3] Five Factor Model (FFM, also "Big Five Personality Traits") is a tool used to describe aspects of individual personality through five dimensions (or traits): Extraversion, Agreeableness, Conscientiousness, Neuroticism, and Openness to Experience. Modern version of FFM, mentioned by Egelman and Peer [13] and used by some other studies discussed in the current paper, refers to a work by Digman [7].

[4] Here the authors are referring to Rest's Four Component Model (Rest [44]). Determinants of ethical behaviour in that model include: ethical sensitivity, moral judgment, moral motivation and moral character.

Griffin et al. [20] formulate a mathematical model, acknowledging behavioural economics arguments and presumably able to predict privacy decisions. Through treating user behaviour as an optimization of comfort with sharing and perceived control, the model reconciles maximization of perceived user control and costs associated with providing that control by social networks. Validation and testing is needed to evaluate the quality of the model.

Eling et al. [15] take an inductive approach to build a decision-making model, linking trust in a service provider and intrusiveness of requested information to highlight the decisional calculus proposed in their paper. Although the authors manage to obtain (and corroborate with an experiment) a depiction of the cognitive process underlying the decisions about application acceptance, the paper does not proceed to construct a cognitive model behind situational decision-making. Overall, decisional calculus, unveiled in Eling et al. [15], is in line with the privacy calculus.

Ghosh and Singh [17] provide one of the use cases for applying machine learning to build a predictive model of privacy concerns. Feeding phone usage metadata, refined through classification algorithms, they manage to achieve enough accuracy (for their classification design) to predict users' privacy attitude category.

As particularly mentioned, most authors admit the limitations in their sets of influencing factors; unaccounted possible relations between factors, risks and benefits; and unexplored effects of cognition. Such usually unaddressed aspects may include the momentary awareness of privacy issues, the current level of fatigue and (or) mental workload, attention span and sense-making of privacy indications, and other mental effects (e.g., information overload, cognitive laziness, etc.).

Additionally, there is a discussion on the more convenient ways to convey privacy-related information to the individuals. As suggested by Wang et al. [55] regarding mobile applications, privacy notices requesting self-disclosure from users, inadequately reflect the scope of privacy intrusion or request unreasonable amounts of self-disclosure. In a survey comparing the effect of fine-grained privacy indications to the effect of coarse-grained ones Eling et al. [16] hypothesise that more concrete privacy indications may influence users' willingness to disclose information. In a controlled experiment Egelman et al. [14] demonstrate that the temporal aspect of privacy indications impacts the acceptable amount of costs that users are willing to bear to preserve their privacy.

The issue of defining a better way to communicate privacy-related information to assist users' decision-making is addressed in Bal et al. [4, 5]. Reflecting upon "privacy consequences" and echoing the problematic nature of "second-order privacy risks" with the aforementioned Keith et al. [24], the researchers argue that communicating privacy outcomes from privacy-related actions to mobile users should facilitate better decisions.

3 Opportunity for Future Research: Cognitive Architectures

In order to include various effects of internal and external factors influencing decision-making[5], as well as different interdependencies, we can try a broader model of cognition – one that simulates dynamic cognitive processes as functions in a system, consisting of input and data acquisition, memory, attention, decision-making, and output generation. The modelling of complex cognitive phenomena is widely and rigorously addressed in cognitive architectures. Most notable and well-established examples of cognitive architectures in use include ACT-R, SOAR, LIDA and EPIC.[6]

SOAR and LIDA focus on artificial general intelligence (Samsonovich [46]). SOAR specialises on task execution and problem-solving, providing software agents with spatial reasoning, anticipation and real-time strategy definition. LIDA has been applied to create software agents replacing human operators in certain tasks, but lacking visual and auditory input modalities and being limited in terms of learning capabilities (Ramamurthy et al. [43]). EPIC is poised as a framework for human-system interactions simulation, assisting in the development and validation of systems interfaces. Another example – 4CAPS – has been used to describe behavioural patterns in neuropsychology related to executive functions of cognitive control (Just and Varma [22]).

When it comes to privacy decision-making, the research model should be able to simulate dynamic cognitive processes as functions in complex systems, comprised of elements accounting for input and data acquisition, memory, attention, decision-making, and output generation. One of the most well-established cognitive architectures, which offers sufficient flexibility of application, is the ACT-R framework.

Section 3.1 introduces ACT-R in the field of human decision-making. Section 3.2 discusses possible contributions of ACT-R to privacy decision-making, and provides a comparison of ACT-R with the modelling approaches discussed in Chap. 2.

3.1 The ACT-R Modelling Framework

ACT-R is one of the most detailed frameworks for modelling perception, procedural cognition and decision processes (Anderson et al. [3]). As argued by Gonzalez and Lebiere [19], there are numerous benefits to the modelling of economic decision-making by using cognitive architectures, where ACT-R outcompetes its rivals, being in possession of a "more realistic characterization of the flexibility and adaptability of human behavior" (p. 26).

Attempts have been made to create a comprehensive integrated theory to approach modelling of the recognition heuristics and judgments (Marewski et al. [38]). Here the authors address issues of an "ecological model of decision-making", pointing out how scarce the research is on real-world decisions with utilizing "sense of prior encounter". Thomson et al. [50] argue that modelling paradigms (Taatgen et al. [48]) enabled in

---

[5] E.g., cognitive load, highlighted in Veltri and Ivchenko [53], or selective attention mechanisms, shown to be instrumental in reducing distraction effects (Lavie et al. [31]).

[6] See in more detail, for example, in Lieto et al. [35].

ACT-R, namely instance-based learning, can be applicable to modelling intuitive decision-making. Authors manage to show that by using this cognitive architecture it is possible to implement risk aversion in learned (not forced) strategy choice. Veksler et al. [52] demonstrate that the ACT-R framework can be used to implement human decision-making arising from "associative learning", not involving an a-priori notion of rewards and punishments.

Overall, the theoretical background and existing body of empirical research indicate that using ACT-R to model human decision-making can attain new value over the so far prevalent approaches. ACT-R is capable of modelling long-term (both declarative and procedural) and working memory functioning, perception and logic processes and, as shown by Peebles and Banks [41], it is suitable for dynamic decision-making, even though with certain limitations.

3.2   ACT-R: Applicability and Discussion

Aforementioned features may help to build a model that can accommodate the context, in which the decisions are made, including but not limited to, simulating momentary awareness, as well as the individual's attention and judgment processes, and other cognitive functions.[7] Additionally, incorporating the Cumulative Prospect Theory to model deviations from rational micro-economic decision-making with the ACT-R architecture seems as plausible as it may prove fruitful.

A summary of modelling opportunities enabled in ACT-R is outlined in Table 4.

It should be clearly stated, that, beyond any doubt, I am not denying the existing body of research all its achievements in formulation of the initial understanding of antecedents of privacy decision-making, and the inter-relations of various factors. As we have seen, though, with other approaches, their applicability can be limited by their theoretical background and, oftentimes, by the goal of each particular study. Additionally, each study usually does not allow for broader generalisations or – to the other extreme – particularisations (true for most of the mathematical economic models).

ACT-R may be capable of contributing to the field of human decision-making entailing privacy consequences in several ways. Consider a situation:

"A person X with a fatigue F in a situation S with environmental noise E, surrounded by the amount of people N, while exercising an activity A, is asked to disclose information M and receives a warning W with the properties T." What will be the X's response?

The comprehensiveness of the ACT-R modelling framework theoretically allows us to model the entire problem space of this situation. It makes it possible to come up with specific predictions about individual decisions of people, usually described by person-specific sets of features.

The extendibility of the ACT-R framework should help with building models in stages. Starting up with a certain simplistic basis of privacy-concerned decision-making,

---

[7] The importance of these factors is shown in numerous empirical studies – for example, see above Li et al. [33]; or Veltri and Ivchenko [53], who show that cognitive scarcity has a negative effect on the disclosure of personal information, raising the volume of disclosed information.

Table 4. Comparison of modelling capabilities of the identified approaches and the ACT-R functionalities (evaluations: *not applicable* (NA, feature is irrelevant in a given approach); *not provided* (feature is not enabled); *limited* (feature is enabled for each particular study; single use); *possible* (feature can be enabled with additional effort or study; should be specifically addressed); *provided* (feature is usually enabled "by design")).

Feature	Privacy calculus	Beyond privacy calculus	Mathematical economics	Machine learning	ACT-R
Behaviour predictive capability	Provided	Possible	Not provided	Provided	Possible
Behaviour descriptive capability	Possible	Provided	Provided	Not provided	Limited
Behaviour models based on human intelligence	Limited	Provided	Not provided	Not provided	Provided
Extendibility, scalability	Limited	Limited	Possible	Not provided	Possible
Individual decisions	Not provided	Possible	Not provided	Possible	Provided
Indication properties	Not provided	Possible	NA	Limited	Provided
Learning behaviour	NA	NA	NA	Provided	Provided
Personal traits	Possible	Provided	Limited	Possible	Provided
Cognitive effects	Limited	Possible	Limited	Possible	Provided
Environmental effects	Limited	Possible	Limited	Possible	Provided
Temporal outcomes	NA	NA	Provided	NA	Possible
Causal (exploratory) models	Provided	Provided	Not Provided	Provided	Limited
Executive functions	NA	NA	NA	NA	Provided
Practical application	Possible	Possible	Limited	Provided	Provided

new features can be gradually added to account for additional effects and factors of the situation, extending its complexity.

Scalability of the ACT-R framework may be used to "switch off" chosen features impacting decisions. That can shed light on some emergent effects and interactions between features, which might have been left obscured and unexplored otherwise.

Features like the learning process, larger sets of user characteristics, attention mechanism, fatigue dynamics and cognitive capacity, task-distraction conflict, environmental noise, and others are extremely cumbersome to address with other approaches. These features, including their inter-dependence, can be addressed with ACT-R in a more structured and explicit, less demanding fashion. With ACT-R we may tackle problems like:

- studying effects of factors in different combinations with each other;
- modelling non-linear relationships in people's perceptions of costs, benefits and risks of personal information disclosure;
- studying human privacy decisions in different mental states;
- modelling decisions made by users with different privacy attitudes according to various attitude taxonomies;
- accounting for intertemporal nature of privacy-related decisions;
- incorporating lower-level mental processes into the picture;
- comparing different models within ACT-R framework against each other.

Overall, at the current stage of developments in the field of privacy-concerned decision-making, we have obtained substantial knowledge about antecedents and factors of users' disclosure behaviour. Thus, based on what we have learnt so far, it may be possible, in principle, to build a decision-making model with the ACT-R framework, which should be able to contribute new knowledge and provide better understanding of situational privacy-concerned decision-making under various restrictions.

4   Conclusion

This paper provides an attempt to identify gaps in the current stage of research exploring users' decision-making with privacy considerations. The state-of-the-art models of decision-making under privacy restrictions show limitations attributed to their levels of flexibility, practical applicability, and comprehensiveness. A possible idea to overcome some limitations of existing models is proposed in the current paper. This idea of using cognitive architectures may also be a solution that can advance our understanding of human decision-making regarding such a "fuzzy" issue as privacy.

However, the mapping of the behavioural economics approach and (or) extended privacy calculus to decision-making onto the ACT-R cognitive architecture creates major challenges. Economic modelling does not provide a generalised method for defining the costs and benefits for every problem. Additional problems that should be resolved in order to apply, for instance, Cumulative Prospect Theory include: determining the reference point, from which gains and losses can be defined; quantifying the benefits and costs of personal information disclosure; and devising a justified probability weighting.

Simultaneously, ACT-R modelling can be a challenge in and of itself, as it is developed to be a comprehensive architecture, simulating human cognitive processes at large. To be successful in developing an ACT-R model, one needs to apply domain-specific knowledge to the architecture and conduct a proper scoping of the problem to be resolved. Of course, the biggest challenge "is that it takes a substantial intellectual commitment to learn to understand models of a particular architecture and to learn to construct models" (Taatgen and Anderson [49], p. 699).

Accompanied by empirical validation, the implementation of the ACT-R cognitive architecture in the field of privacy will be a major challenge that can help privacy research, as well as enrich the ACT-R modelling methods.

Acknowledgements. I gratefully acknowledge the suggestions from my Ph.D. advisor, Professor Joachim Meyer.

This paper is a part of the author's Ph.D. research on "Modelling Responses to Privacy-related Indications". The research is conducted under and supported by the Privacy & Us innovative training network (EU H2020 MSCA ITN, grant agreement №675730).

References

1. Acquisti, A., Taylor, C., Wagman, L.: The economics of privacy. J. Econ. Lit. **54**(2), 442–492 (2016). https://doi.org/10.1257/jel.54.2.442
2. Adjerid, I., Peer, E., Acquisti, A.: Beyond the privacy paradox: objective versus relative risk in privacy decision making (2016)
3. Anderson, J.R., Bothell, D., Byrne, M.D., et al.: An integrated theory of the mind. Psychol. Rev. **111**(4), 1036 (2004)
4. Bal, G., Rannenberg, K.: User control mechanisms for privacy protection should go hand in hand with privacy-consequence information: the case of smartphone apps (2014)
5. Bal, G., Rannenberg, K., Hong, J.I.: Styx: privacy risk communication for the Android smartphone platform based on apps' data-access behavior patterns. Comput. Secur. **53**, 187–202 (2015)
6. Barberis, N.C.: Thirty years of prospect theory in economics. J. Econ. Perspect. **27**(1), 173–195 (2013)
7. Digman, J.M.: Personality structure: emergence of the five-factor model. Annu. Rev. Psychol. **41**(1), 417–440 (1990)
8. Dinev, T., Hart, P.: Internet privacy concerns and their antecedents-measurement validity and a regression model. Behav. Inf. Technol. **23**(6), 413–422 (2004)
9. Dinev, T., Hart, P.: An extended privacy calculus model for e-commerce transactions. Inf. Syst. Res. **17**(1), 61–80 (2006)
10. Dinev, T., McConnell, A.R., Smith, H.J.: Research commentary—informing privacy research through information systems, psychology, and behavioral economics: thinking outside the "APCO" box. Inf. Syst. Res. **26**(4), 639–655 (2015)
11. Dinev, T., Xu, H., Smith, J.H., et al.: Information privacy and correlates: an empirical attempt to bridge and distinguish privacy-related concepts. Eur. J. Inf. Syst. **22**(3), 295–316 (2013)
12. Dong, C., Jin, H., Knijnenburg, B.P.: Predicting privacy behavior on online social networks. In: Anonymous ICWSM, pp. 91–100 (2015)
13. Egelman, S., Peer, E.: Predicting privacy and security attitudes. ACM SIGCAS Comput. Soc. **45**(1), 22–28 (2015)
14. Egelman, S., Tsai, J., Cranor, L.F., et al.: Timing is everything?: the effects of timing and placement of online privacy indicators. In: Anonymous Proceedings of the SIGCHI Conference on Human Factors in Computing Systems ACM, pp. 319–328 (2009)
15. Eling, N., Krasnova, H., Widjaja, T., et al.: Will you accept an app? Empirical investigation of the decisional calculus behind the adoption of applications on Facebook (2013)
16. Eling, N., Rasthofer, S., Kolhagen, M., et al.: Investigating users' reaction to fine-grained data requests: a market experiment. In: 2016 49th Hawaii International Conference on IEEE Anonymous System Sciences (HICSS), pp. 3666–3675 (2016)
17. Ghosh, I., Singh, V.K.: Predicting privacy attitudes using phone metadata. In: Xu, K., Reitter, D., Lee, D., Osgood, N. (eds.) Anonymous Social, Cultural, and Behavioral Modeling: 9th International Conference, SBP-BRiMS 2016, pp. 51–60. Springer, Cham (2016). https://doi.org/10.1007/978-3-319-39931-7_6

18. Gibbons, F.X., Gerrard, M.: Predicting young adults' health risk behavior. J. Pers. Soc. Psychol. **69**(3), 505 (1995)
19. Gonzalez, C., Lebiere, C.: Instance-based cognitive models of decision-making (2005)
20. Griffin, C., Rajtmajer, S., Squicciarini, A.: A model of paradoxical privacy behavior in online users. In: 2016 IEEE 2nd International Conference on IEEE Anonymous Collaboration and Internet Computing (CIC), pp. 206–211 (2016)
21. Hann, I., Hui, K., Lee, S.T., et al.: Overcoming online information privacy concerns: an information-processing theory approach. J. Manag. Inf. Syst. **24**(2), 13–42 (2007)
22. Just, M.A., Varma, S.: The organization of thinking: what functional brain imaging reveals about the neuroarchitecture of complex cognition. Cogn. Affect. Behav. Neurosci. **7**(3), 153–191 (2007)
23. Kehr, F., Kowatsch, T., Wentzel, D., et al.: Blissfully ignorant: the effects of general privacy concerns, general institutional trust, and affect in the privacy calculus. Inf. Syst. J. **25**(6), 607–635 (2015)
24. Keith, M.J., Thompson, S.C., Hale, J., et al.: Information disclosure on mobile devices: re-examining privacy calculus with actual user behavior. Int. J. Hum Comput Stud. **71**(12), 1163–1173 (2013)
25. Kim, D.J., Ferrin, D.L., Rao, H.R.: A trust-based consumer decision-making model in electronic commerce: the role of trust, perceived risk, and their antecedents. Decis. Support Syst. **44**(2), 544–564 (2008)
26. Knijnenburg, B.P., Kobsa, A.: Making decisions about privacy: information disclosure in context-aware recommender systems. ACM Trans. Interact. Intell. Syst. (TiiS) **3**(3), 20 (2013)
27. Koohikamali, M., Peak, D.A., Prybutok, V.R.: Beyond self-disclosure: disclosure of information about others in social network sites. Comput. Hum. Behav. **69**, 29–42 (2017)
28. Krasnova, H., Günther, O., Spiekermann, S., et al.: Privacy concerns and identity in online social networks. Identity Inf. Soc. **2**(1), 39–63 (2009)
29. Krasnova, H., Spiekermann, S., Koroleva, K., et al.: Online social networks: why we disclose. J. Inf. Technol. **25**(2), 109–125 (2010)
30. Krasnova, H., Veltri, N.F., Günther, O.: Self-disclosure and privacy calculus on social networking sites: the role of culture. Bus. Inf. Syst. Eng. **4**(3), 127–135 (2012)
31. Lavie, N., Hirst, A., De Fockert, J.W., et al.: Load theory of selective attention and cognitive control. J. Exp. Psychol. Gen. **133**(3), 339 (2004)
32. Lee, H., Kobsa, A.: Privacy preference modeling and prediction in a simulated campuswide IoT environment. In: 2017 IEEE International Conference on IEEE Anonymous Pervasive Computing and Communications (PerCom), pp. 276–285 (2017)
33. Li, H., Sarathy, R., Xu, H.: The role of affect and cognition on online consumers' decision to disclose personal information to unfamiliar online vendors. Decis. Support Syst. **51**(3), 434–445 (2011)
34. Li, Y.: Theories in online information privacy research: a critical review and an integrated framework. Decis. Support Syst. **54**(1), 471–481 (2012)
35. Lieto, A., Chella, A., Frixione, M.: Conceptual spaces for cognitive architectures: a lingua franca for different levels of representation. Biol. Inspired Cogn. Arch. **19**, 1–9 (2017)
36. Mahmood, S., Desmedt, Y.: Two new economic models for privacy. ACM SIGMETRICS Perform. Eval. Rev. **40**(4), 84–89 (2013)
37. Malhotra, N.K., Kim, S.S., Agarwal, J.: Internet users' information privacy concerns (IUIPC): the construct, the scale, and a causal model. Inf. Syst. Res. **15**(4), 336–355 (2004)
38. Marewski, J.N., Pohl, R.F., Vitouch, O.: Recognition-based judgments and decisions: what we have learned (so far). Judgm. Decis. Making **6**(5), 359–380 (2011)

39. Mehrabian, A., Russell, J.A.: An Approach to Environmental Psychology. The MIT Press, Cambridge (1974)
40. Panaousis, E., Laszka, A., Pohl, J., et al.: Game-theoretic model of incentivizing privacy-aware users to consent to location tracking. In: 2015 IEEE Anonymous Trustcom/BigDataSE/ISPA, vol. 1, pp. 1006–1013. IEEE (2015)
41. Peebles, D., Banks, A.: Modelling dynamic decision making with the ACT-R cognitive architecture. J. Artif. Gen. Intell. 2(2), 52–68 (2010). https://doi.org/10.2478/v10229-011-0009-1
42. Pu, Yu., Grossklags, J.: An economic model and simulation results of app adoption decisions on networks with interdependent privacy consequences. In: Poovendran, R., Saad, W. (eds.) GameSec 2014. LNCS, vol. 8840, pp. 246–265. Springer, Cham (2014). https://doi.org/10.1007/978-3-319-12601-2_14
43. Ramamurthy, U., Baars, B.J., D'Mello, S.K., et al.: LIDA: a working model of cognition (2006)
44. Rest, J.R.: Moral development: advances in research and theory (1986)
45. Ross, C., Orr, E.S., Sisic, M., et al.: Personality and motivations associated with Facebook use. Comput. Hum. Behav. 25(2), 578–586 (2009)
46. Samsonovich, A.: Comparative table of cognitive architectures. BICA Society (2012)
47. Shih, H., Lai, K., Cheng, T.: Constraint-based and dedication-based mechanisms for encouraging online self-disclosure: is personalization the only thing that matters? Eur. J. Inf. Syst. 26(4), 432–450 (2017)
48. Taatgen, N.A., Lebiere, C., Anderson, J.R.: Modeling paradigms in ACT-R. In: Cognition and Multi-Agent Interaction: From Cognitive Modeling to Social Simulation, pp. 29–52 (2006)
49. Taatgen, N., Anderson, J.R.: The past, present, and future of cognitive architectures. Top. Cogn. Sci. 2(4), 693–704 (2010)
50. Thomson, R., Lebiere, C., Anderson, J.R., et al.: A general instance-based learning framework for studying intuitive decision-making in a cognitive architecture. J. Appl. Res. Mem. Cogn. 4(3), 180–190 (2015)
51. Van Gool, E., Van Ouytsel, J., Ponnet, K., et al.: To share or not to share? Adolescents' self-disclosure about peer relationships on Facebook: an application of the prototype willingness model. Comput. Hum. Behav. 44, 230–239 (2015)
52. Veksler, V.D., Gray, W.D., Schoelles, M.J.: Goal-proximity decision-making. Cogn. Sci. 37(4), 757–774 (2013). https://doi.org/10.1111/cogs.12034
53. Veltri, G.A., Ivchenko, A.: The impact of different forms of cognitive scarcity on online privacy disclosure. Comput. Hum. Behav. 73, 238–246 (2017)
54. Venkitasubramaniam, P.: Decision making under privacy restrictions. In: 2013 IEEE 52nd Annual Conference on IEEE Anonymous Decision and Control (CDC), pp. 4693–4698 (2013)
55. Wang, N., Wisniewski, P., Xu, H., et al.: Designing the default privacy settings for Facebook applications. In: Anonymous Proceedings of the Companion Publication of the 17th ACM Conference on Computer Supported Cooperative Work & Social Computing ACM, pp. 249–252 (2014)
56. Wang, T., Duong, T.D., Chen, C.C.: Intention to disclose personal information via mobile applications: a privacy calculus perspective. Int. J. Inf. Manage. 36(4), 531–542 (2016)
57. Wang, Z., Liu, Y.: Identifying key factors affecting information disclosure intention in online shopping (2014)

58. Webster, J., Watson, R.T.: Analyzing the past to prepare for the future: writing a literature review. MIS Q. **26**(2), xiii–xxiii (2002)
59. Xu, H., Luo, X.R., Carroll, J.M., et al.: The personalization privacy paradox: an exploratory study of decision making process for location-aware marketing. Decis. Support Syst. **51**(1), 42–52 (2011)
60. Zhu, H., Ou, C.X., van den Heuvel, W., et al.: Privacy calculus and its utility for personalization services in e-commerce: an analysis of consumer decision-making. Inf. Manag. **54**(4), 427–437 (2017)

Safeguarding Personal Data and Mitigating Risks

Data Protection Impact Assessment:
A Hands-On Tour of the GDPR's Most
Practical Tool

Felix Bieker[1](✉), Nicholas Martin[2], Michael Friedewald[2],
and Marit Hansen[1]

[1] Unabhängiges Landeszentrum für Datenschutz (ULD, Independent Centre
for Privacy Protection), Kiel, Schleswig-Holstein, Germany
{fbieker,marit.hansen}@datenschutzzentrum.de
[2] Fraunhofer Institute for Systems and Innovation Research ISI,
Karlsruhe, Germany
{nicholas.martin,michael.friedewald}@isi.fraunhofer.de

Abstract. This workshop introduced participants to the process of Data Protection Impact Assessment. This new tool of the GDPR is highly relevant for any processing of personal data, as it helps to structure the process, be aware of data protection issues and the relevant legislation and implement proper safeguards to protect data subjects. For processing operations posing a high risk for data subjects, a DPIA is mandatory from May 2018. The interactive workshop provided a framework for DPIA and guidance on specific questions such as when a high risk is likely to occur or how specific risks can be evaluated, which was assessed by participants in an interactive session with two different scenarios.

Keywords: Data Protection Impact Assessment · Risk to rights and freedoms
General Data Protection Regulation · Data protection · EU law

1 Introduction

The General Data Protection Regulation (GDPR) will replace the Data Protection Directive on 25 May 2018. Among the regulatory and governance instruments it introduces is the Data Protection Impact Assessment (DPIA), which serves to mitigate risks to the rights and freedoms of natural persons and is a tool for controllers to conform to the GDPR's legal requirements. DPIA builds on Privacy Impact Assessments (PIAs), as they have been encouraged by academia [1], Data Protection Authorities (DPAs) [2, 3] and the European Commission (e.g. for RFID applications [4]). However, DPIA focuses on conformity to EU data protection law and thus has a more specific scope. It is a very useful tool for controllers to control their processing of personal data and ensure compliance.

When a high risk to the rights of individuals is likely, carrying out a DPIA is mandatory according to Article 35(1) GDPR. While non-compliance with this obligation may incur a penalty of up to 2% of the world-wide annual turnover of a business

© IFIP International Federation for Information Processing 2018
Published by Springer International Publishing AG 2018. All Rights Reserved
M. Hansen et al. (Eds.): Privacy and Identity 2017, IFIP AICT 526, pp. 207–220, 2018.
https://doi.org/10.1007/978-3-319-92925-5_13

according to Article 83(4)(a) GDPR, the notion of high risk is not defined in the Regulation. Rather, Article 35(3) GDPR lists a few examples of data processing operations, which could potentially pose a high risk. Similarly, the GDPR does not offer much advice about how to carry out a DPIA; much less a methodology. Article 35 (4) GDPR contains only minimal requirements, and provides no further guidance about how to implement these in practice. Furthermore, existing processes for Privacy Impact Assessments (PIA) may not take due account of the GDPR's legal requirements, such as data protection by design and by default, which is now enshrined in Article 25 GDPR, or the risk-based approach adopted in this new legislation.

Thus, the goal of the workshop was to acquaint participants with the DPIA framework, how it can best be carried out and which specific issues may arise. Participants were first introduced to the DPIA framework developed by the German research consortium *Privacy Forum* (Forum Privatheit) [5, 6] and focuses on the rights of individuals. This framework is based on the legal requirements of the upcoming GDPR, in particular Article 35, as well as the Standard Data Protection Model (SDM) methodology adopted by the German data protection authorities [7], which operationalises these legal requirements, and best practices. The framework takes account of the *Guidelines on Data Protection Impact Assessment* of the Article 29 Data Protection Working Party [8]. In order to raise the participants' awareness of the risks to the rights and freedoms of individuals two case studies were discussed with a view to identifying the relevant risks by applying the data protection goals systematised in the SDM.

2   Introduction to Data Protection Impact Assessments

A DPIA begins before any data are processed and continues throughout the life cycle of a project and its data processing operations. It is a useful tool for any controller to implement their obligations under the GDPR and allows them to document this, as they are obliged to under Article 5(2) GDPR. At the heart of this process is the analysis of risks to the rights and freedoms of individuals that may emanate from the processing of personal data and is the basis for mitigating these risks through technical and organisational measures. This can best be achieved in four phases, as detailed in Fig. 1 below.

In the preparation phase (1.), a team is assembled to carry out the assessment and relevant information about the envisaged processing collected. In the execution phase (2.) the sources of risk (i.e. attackers) are identified, the gravity of the interference is determined and the risks for the rights and freedoms of natural persons are evaluated. Furthermore, the controller identifies appropriate measures and documents the results of the evaluation in a DPIA report. On the basis of this evaluation, the controller then decides whether to carry out the envisaged processing operation or not. If the DPIA finds that the risks to the rights of individuals remain high even with the identified measures, the controller has to consult the supervisory authority according to Article 36 GDPR before the processing can start. The controller may also decide to abandon the processing operation.

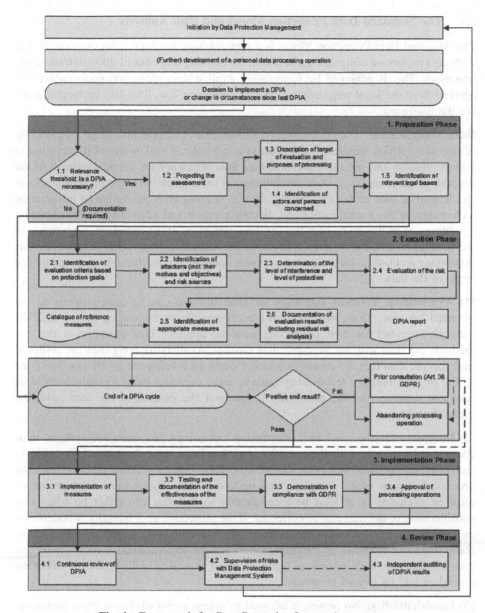

Fig. 1. Framework for Data Protection Impact Assessment

If adequate measures could be identified to address the risks and ensure the protection of the rights of individuals (or this is achieved during the consultation with the supervisory authority), the controller implements these measures, tests and documents their effectiveness and demonstrates compliance with the GDPR (3.), before approving the processing operation. In the review phase (4.) the controller monitors the risks for the rights and freedoms of natural persons and repeats (parts of) the assessment when necessary.

2.1   The Standard Data Protection Model and Risk Analysis

The Standard Data Protection Model is a methodology to ensure effective compliance with data protection obligations and allows for auditing and control through transparent processes. This is achieved by formulating explicit data protection goals, which are derived from the legal requirements of data protection law. The data protection goals are the following:

Data Minimisation. Data minimisation substantiates and operationalises the principle of necessity, which requires of any process as a whole as well as any of its steps not to collect, process and use more personal data than necessary for the achievement of the purpose of the processing. Data minimisation is to be taken into account proactively as an element of data protection-friendly design. Starting with the design of information technology by the manufacturer and its configuration and adaptation to the operating conditions, to its use in the core and auxiliary processes of the operation, for instance in the maintenance of the systems used; from the collection of personal data, through its processing and use, to its erasure or complete anonymization; throughout the entire life cycle of the data.

(1) Availability. Personal data must be available and can be used properly in the intended process. Thus, the data must be accessible to authorised parties and the methods intended for their processing must be applied. This presupposes that the methods can deal with the available data formats. Availability comprises the ability to find specific data (e.g. by means of address directories, reference or file numbers), the ability of the employed technical systems to make data accessible to individuals in an adequate manner, and the possibility to interpret the content of the data (semantic ascertainability).

(2) Integrity. On the one hand, information technology processes and systems must continuously comply with the specifications that have been determined for the execution of their intended functions. On the other hand, integrity means that the data to be processed remain intact, complete, and up-to-date. Deviations from these properties must be excluded or at least be ascertainable so that this can either be taken into consideration or the data can be corrected. If the protection goal integrity is understood as a form of accuracy within the meaning of Article 5(1)(d) GDPR, this leads to the claim that there is sufficient congruency between the legal-normative requirement and common practice, both in terms of technical detail as well as in the broad context of the procedure and its overall purpose.

(3) Confidentiality. No person is allowed to access personal data without authorisation. A person is not only unauthorised when it is a third party external to the controller, regardless of whether they act with or without a criminal intent, but also employees of technical service providers who do not need access to personal data for the provision of the service, or persons in organisational units who are unrelated to the respective procedure or data subject.

(4) Unlinkability. Data shall be processed and analysed only for the purpose for which they were collected. Data sets can in principle be processed for further purposes and can be combined with other, potentially publicly available data. Larger and more meaningful data sets also increase the potential for abuse, i.e. to use the data unlawfully, for purposes beyond the legal basis. Such further processing is lawful only in strictly defined circumstances. The GDPR only allows them to be used for archival purposes which are in the public interest, for scientific or historical research purposes or for statistical purposes, and explicitly calls for safeguards for the rights and freedoms of the data subjects. These safeguards are to be achieved through technical and organisational measures. In addition to measures of data minimisation and pseudonymisation, other measures that allow the further processing to be separated from the source processing are also suitable, ensuring separation both on the organisational and on the system side. The data base can, for example, be adapted to the new purpose by pseudonymisation or reduction of data volume.

(5) Transparency. The data subject as well as the system operators and the competent supervisory authorities must be able to understand, to a varying extent, which data are collected and processed for a particular purpose, which systems and processes are used for this purpose, where the data flow for which purpose, and who is legally responsible for the data and systems in the various phases of data processing. Transparency is necessary for the monitoring and control of data, processes, and systems from their origin to their erasure and is a prerequisite for lawful data processing. Informed consent, where it is necessary, can be given by data subjects only if these criteria are met. Transparency of the entire data processing operation and of the parties involved can help ensure that data subjects and supervisory authorities can identify deficiencies and, if necessary, demand appropriate procedural changes.

(6) Intervenability. Data subjects are effectively granted their rights to notification, information, rectification, blocking and erasure at any time, and that the controller is obliged to implement the appropriate measures. For this purpose, controllers must be able to intervene in the processing of data throughout the process; from the collection to the erasure of the data.

All of these protection goals can be linked to specific provisions in the GDPR, and all except availability, which is an implicit requirement throughout the GDPR, are mentioned in the principles relating to personal data processing in Article 5(1) [7].

Consequently, they can be used in the assessment of the risks to the rights and freedoms of natural persons in order to identify potential sources of risks and potential damages to these rights and freedoms. According to recital 76 the likelihood and severity of potential damages should be determined objectively and with reference to the nature, scope, context and purposes of the processing. However, as the phrasing of the risk already makes clear, recital 75 emphasises that this potential damage includes also non-material damage, such as discrimination, reputational damage, social disadvantages, the deprivation of data subjects' rights or preventing them from exercising control over their personal data. When read jointly with the second sentence of recital 94 it further becomes clear that besides such potential damages, interferences with fundamental rights, for instance the right to the protection of personal data under Article 8 CFR, the right to private life under Article 7 CFR, freedom of speech under

Article 11 CFR or the right to be protected against discrimination under Article 21 CFR, are also risks to be considered in this assessment [9].

When considering this fundamental rights dimension of risk in the GDPR it also becomes clear that mathematical formulas, such as the common $R = \sum_{k=1}^{n} I_k \times p(I_k)$, where R is the risk, which is the product of the impact multiplied by the probability of potential damage, are not applicable here. Instead, the evaluation should classify the effect of potential damages or interferences with fundamental rights as well as the likelihood of their realisation into certain categories, such as marginal, limited, serious and severe. By applying each data protection goal to a processing operation to identify potential risks and then evaluating these, controllers can ensure that they fulfil their obligations with regard to the rights and freedoms of natural persons.

2.2 Data Subject Participation

As data protection law is ultimately concerned with safeguarding the rights of individuals, scientific studies have been demanding for years that DPIAs (or PIAs) should not only include the views of (technical and legal) experts. Making use of the expertise of technical experts alone may lead to a very narrow perspective (e.g. limiting an assessment to legal aspects alone) and also to a technocratic-paternalistic approach that takes decisions without taking citizens' concerns duly into account. Rather, a comprehensive and broad consultation of stakeholders is necessary to increase the quality of the assessment results and their legitimacy. However, the questions of which actors are considered to be 'relevant' at all and who determines this [10, 11] should be kept in mind. This idea is reflected in Article 35(9) GDPR that stipulates that the views of data subjects or their representatives on the intended processing should be taken into account – if appropriate. The provision limits the controller's obligation to allow participation with reference to the effort needed or other conflicting interests (security, intellectual property rights, etc.).

Without prejudice to such limitations, the question arises as to how the different stakeholder groups and interests can be involved in the evaluation process of a DPIA. In terms of methodology, relatively simple and proven methods are available, with which companies already have experience in the areas of product design and marketing (e.g. focus groups), but of course more elaborate methods from participatory Technology Assessment (pTA) can also be used [12, 13]. However, an evaluation with data subject participation poses particular challenges in terms of timing and circumstances:

- The consultation should best start early in the process, so as to allow for an impact on the design of the processing operation.[1]
- The involvement of data subjects can be problematic, as careful and systematic assessment often requires expertise that lay people usually do not have. The key

---

[1] However, when a DPIA is conducted prior to market launch or in parallel with the development process the inclusion of external persons may be undesirable. Reasons might be the immaturity of the technology, the organisation's desire for confidentiality or fear of a bad public image.

question here is therefore how this expertise can be conveyed to enable discussions on equal footing between lay people and experts.

- The vocabulary used in the evaluation process has implications for the intensity and quality of the involvement of different groups of actors. For example, certain forms of wording are likely to favour particularly technophile actors or those with legal knowledge. It will therefore be crucial to organise a neutral translation process between the different groups.

Extensive participatory DPIAs involving external stakeholders are, however, likely to remain the exception, since this process is time-consuming and could lead to consultation fatigue among certain stakeholder groups. Under normal circumstances the data subjects' views should be taken into account by involving units from the organisation that are in close and regular contact with the data subjects, i.e. sales, service or the works or staff council [14].

3 Hands-On: Practical Assessment of the Risks for the Rights and Freedoms of Natural Persons

After the input statements, participants were divided into two groups to discuss the two following case studies and identify risks for the rights and freedoms of natural persons. These were then summarized by participants of each group and discussed with all participants.

3.1 Case Studies

Case Study 1: Smart Surveillance in Train Stations

After successful pilots, the national police force of an EU Member State has proposed setting up cameras with automated biometric recognition and behavioural analysis capabilities in all of the country's train stations. The system will have access to the images and biometric data from the national identity-card database, as well as police databases of terrorist and criminal suspects, political extremists and religious fanatics, and persons of interest or concern. It is supposed to be able to identify individuals with a very high degree of accuracy. The data will be stored for up to 1 year.

Besides identifying individuals, the system performs behavioural analysis to identify a range of suspicious behaviours (e.g., looking about a lot, avoiding security personnel, leaving luggage behind). It also identifies dangerous behaviour or behaviour indicating suicidal tendencies, especially of vulnerable individuals (e.g. drunken gait, straying close to platforms).

When the system picks up suspicious (or dangerous) behaviour or individuals, it sends automated messages to the station security personnel, city anti-terror units, and/or the station health and safety personnel (for drunks, etc.), whereupon these initiate enhanced monitoring or other interventions (e.g. arrest).

Case Study 2: Emotional Decoding for In-store Advertising

A supermarket chain operating in an EU Member State has revamped its in-store advertising system with a smart camera system operated by Echeloon, a company specialising in targeted advertising. Through a camera integrated into a screen displaying advertisements, the system recognises when and for how long a person looks at the screen, their sex (and what it presumes to be their gender), approximate age and worn attire. Furthermore, the system deduces the customer's presumed emotional state (anger, happiness, anxiety, etc.) from their facial expression. The data is then used to personalise advertisements to pre-defined groups of customers and their presumed interests and preferences. Additionally, the system can promote special offers to certain groups of customers or offer specific rebates to an individual customer.

Customers are informed about video surveillance at the entrance of the market where the terms and conditions are posted on signs. However, they contain no reference to the smart camera system. In a press release the chain stated that the system is operated exclusively by Echeloon and the supermarkets have no access to the data. It goes on to state that the system processes only encrypted data and any photos of customers are processed automatically and deleted once the data has been extracted, after approximately 150 ms. Thus, Echeloon assures, no personal data were collected and there was no obligation to inform customers specifically.[2]

3.2   Group Discussions: Applying the Data Protection Goals to the Case Studies

The group discussions as well as the legal background of the case studies will be discussed in the following. In order to determine whether there is a high risk, the controller, in a first step should refer to examples of high risk processing operations provided by the Article 35(3) GDPR, recitals 71, 75 and 91 as well as the Article 29 Working Party [8]. These include the innovative use of technology, data processing on a large scale as well as publicly accessible areas such as privately-owned shopping centres.

While the case study both fall within these examples and it is thus indicated that a high risk is likely and a DPIA should be carried out, the workshop aimed to enable participants to engage in the evaluation of the risks to the rights of individuals, as it is required in step 2.4 of the DPIA framework.

During the group discussions, the workshop participants sought to apply the Data Protection Goals to the case studies, to analyse the risks to the rights of individuals posed by the processing operations described in the cases. This section summarizes the results of these discussions. Due to the natural flow of the debate, not all protection goals were given equal attention.

The question of whether a processing operation is lawful is paramount in data processing. It is thus assessed as one of the first steps in a DPIA (see step 1.5 of the

----

[2] For further discussion on legal, regulatory and ethical issues surrounding 'smart' advertising of various kinds see [13].

DPIA framework). While the case studies pose serious questions as to their lawfulness,[3] this was not a focus of the workshop and was therefore not addressed in detail. As the workshop focused on the identification of risks to the rights of individuals, the case studies did not include specific information on legal bases. However, as will be seen below the protection goals are able to identify the risks to the rights of individuals caused by the processing operations lined out in the case studies, which also uncover risks concerning the lawfulness of the processing as the SDM operationalises the legal requirements of the GDPR.

Case Study 1: Smart Surveillance in Train Stations

Data Minimisation. The first group found that there are several issues concerning data minimisation, which are linked to the extremely broad purpose of the smart surveillance system. It is supposed to identify not only various kinds of offenders, suspects or persons of interests included in a police database, but also any individual in the train station that acts suspiciously and thus allows for the tracking of all passengers frequenting the train station. Furthermore, the system is supposed to alert authorities of dangerous behaviour to prevent harm to individuals. As participants pointed out, these sweeping purposes can already be seen as colliding with the principle of purpose limitation of Article 5(1)(b) GDPR.

Participants also found that the storage of the cameras' raw data in a centralised system for one year violated the principle of data minimisation, as it was not specified why the data would be needed retrospectively, if the person identified did not lead to a match with the police database or act suspiciously or dangerously. Essentially, storage of the raw data beyond the assessment of their identity/behaviour would entail mass-scale data retention on train passengers, the vast majority of whom are neither suspects nor persons of interest. Furthermore, it was questioned, whether the purposes of identifying suspects or persons or interest and dangerous behaviour could not be met through other, less data-invasive means than the proposed smart-camera system.

Availability. As to the availability of the data it was discussed that it had to be ensured that the automated algorithm that automatically notifies the pre-defined authorities is revisable and allows for review of its functionality by the controller, e.g. through a logging mechanism. However, the contents of these logs should, with regard to the

---

[3] Participants discussed that while the first case study would have to be based on an express legal basis of national law, the scope of the processing raised serious question of its proportionality. Regarding the second case study participants pointed out that Echeloon's claim that the data processed was not personal was not true, as the duration for which data are processed, and whether or not they are encrypted, is irrelevant to whether the data classify as personal data in the sense of Article 4(1) GDPR. Participants pointed out that the general information at the entrance of the store was not sufficient to obtain informed consent within the meaning of Article 7 GDPR, as it included only general information on video surveillance and not the specific processing operation of emotional decoding. It should be added that just as in the first case study, as the system identifies individuals by use of biometric data, it processes special categories of data according to Article 9 GDPR and thus explicit consent would be required. Beyond these issues, the case further raises issues of price discrimination based on age, gender, race or income (through the analysis of worn attire).

protection goal of data minimisation, only log data that are necessary to monitor the correct functioning of the system.

Integrity. Concerning the integrity of the data processing operation, the first group had general concerns about the properties of the system and the cameras and their safety and security. As the case study did not specify any of these issues an actual system would have to ensure that the entire surveillance system continuously complies with the specifications (including a definition of data flows, concerning access and sharing of the data) and the data processed in it would remain complete or any changes made by employees or external parties could be traced. In this regard the participants emphasised further that, given the amount of passengers frequenting a major train station, even a highly accurate algorithm would produce a significant amount of false positives and false negatives. Hence, it would have to be ensured that these are minimised and the persons operating the surveillance system would be able to adequately interpret these results in order to avoid the risk of false accusations against train passengers. However, the complicated nature of human-machine interactions – especially in the context of hierarchical organisations – exacerbates the risks that false positives or other analytical errors pose to data subjects. Given the complicated and 'inhuman' nature of machine 'thought' [15, 16], staff operating and responding to the system can be presumed not to have more than a rudimentary understanding of how the system reaches its conclusions. Given that they are by definition also likely to hold only low-ranking and possibly insecure positions in their organisation, they will likely be highly reluctant to question or go against the conclusions drawn by the system: even in the event of the system reaching very questionable conclusions, they will likely have organisational incentives to go along with the machine's conclusions, rather than go against the machine.

Confidentiality. The surveillance system entailed multiple risks with regard to the protection goal of confidentiality, the participants of the first group found. Given the broad database, access to the data would have to be defined restrictively and authorized access would have to be logged. This was needed in order to ensure that misuse of the collected data could be prevented or at least be detected and prosecuted. Persons with access to the system would be able to track the daily movements of a vast amount of people. This of course, was not only limited to the controller, who could also be tempted to expand the purposes of the processing even further, but also made the system a high-level target for third party attackers and hackers. A further point of concern was the interface of the system, such as when dangerous or suspicious behaviour is identified and interventions by the station police or security personnel are triggered. Participants stated that it would be a crucial question how much and which data about the individual concerned were made available to the security staff.

Further risks to the rights of the individuals could emanate from the storage location of the data. Participants argued that if, for example, the data were to be stored in a cloud rather than locally, the risk to the confidentiality of the data would be increased even further. Participants again pointed to the risks presented by false positives, false associations, and the potential for bias and subjectivity to infect the analysis. Given the very large number of individuals passing through major train stations, even error rates of less than 1% can quickly result in thousands of misidentifications with potentially very serious consequences for the individuals concerned and could subject them to discrimination.

Unlinkability. Due to the already overly broad purpose of the surveillance system, the participants focussed especially on unlinkability. The automated matching of individuals with the entire police database was seen as a heavy interference with the rights of individuals. Further, the possibility to identify any individual by matching their photo to the national ID card database was seen as yet another heavy interference with the rights of individuals on a mass-scale. The participants argued that the processed data could easily be used beyond their original purpose in order to discriminate certain groups of people. Due to the raw data of the camera footage being stored, this could also be done retroactively and the data could be combined with data from other sources to track the movements of individuals. Additionally, the data flows and the authorities that can access the data were not sufficiently clear. Lastly, the purpose of the collection could be expanded even further and the system could be linked to other state systems, for instance those of the welfare or health authorities, for instance to monitoring welfare recipients for signs of undeclared employment or other benefit fraud.

Transparency. Concerning the protection goal of transparency, it was argued that the train passengers were confronted with the risk of not knowing when, how or why their data was being processed. The individuals would have to be informed of the fact and the amount of surveillance as well as how the data is processed, including whether it is shared with other authorities or private parties, the participants found in their discussion. This had to include the monitoring and/or certification of the algorithm that carries out the biometric recognition and behavioural analysis.

Due to high numbers of individuals concerned they were already subject to a risk of being falsely identified as a suspicious person or as behaving dangerously, especially as these terms were not defined sufficiently. Furthermore, individuals could be identified merely because a person of interest for the police would ask them for the time, as one participant remarked, or the algorithm would identify their behaviour as dangerous. Thus, there was the additional risk of not being able to determine when an individual's behaviour would be registered by the system.

Intervenability. Similarly, the individuals faced risks concerning their possibilities of intervention with regard to the surveillance system. The participants argued that the lack of transparency led directly to a risk of the data subjects' not being able to exercise their rights. Furthermore, there was no second instance before the data was shared by the automated system. It was unclear how (and if at all) data subjects who have been identified as suspicious or engaged in dangerous behaviour may challenge a decision, and indeed how they would even find out about such decisions.

Case Study 2: Emotional Decoding for In-store Advertising

Data Minimisation. With regard to the purpose of targeted advertising to customers of a supermarket, the participants of the second group found it questionable whether all of the envisaged categories of data (sex and presumed gender, approximate age, worn attire and emotional state) where strictly necessary, as demanded by the principle of data minimisation. The data collected concern special categories of data according to

218   F. Bieker et al.

Article 9 GDPR, as the system uses the biometric data to identify individuals[4] and allows conclusions on categories such as race, ethnicity, religious beliefs (e.g. when wearing a hijab or kippah). Furthermore, the data on the emotional state of customers were derived from the biometric data, could arguably be seen as health data, as Article 9 GDPR includes data relating to mental health (cf. Article 4(15) GDPR). These broad categories of data, the participants argued, were not necessary to personalise product offers in a supermarket. While the automated deletion of the pictures taken by the system is a step to reduce the amount of data used, the sensitive biometric data is retained indefinitely and therefore the dataset is not reduced to the minimum required to achieve the intended purpose.

Availability. The availability of the data here is not an issue, as they are highly available.

Integrity. Much as in the first case study, the participants of the second group found that concerning the integrity of the data processing operation the properties of the system had to be further defined.

Confidentiality. As the data is processed by a processor, the risk of disclosures is higher. Thus, employees of both the controller and the processor could potentially use the biometric data stored in the system for an unspecified period and use them in other processes, such as biometric identification, for identity theft or fraud. Furthermore, other customers or employees could observe the targeted advertisements on the display, which could cause the individual distress, which could, depending on the promoted product, range from mild embarrassment to more serious consequences.

Unlinkability. With regard to the storage of the data that is derived from the pictures taken of customers, it was pointed out that the continued storage and further use for other purposes would pose risks to the data subjects, given the nature of the data, which relates to the private life of the individual. For example, if the further processing was aimed at assembling profiles of shopping behaviour – perhaps even drawing on data generated at other stores that use the same camera system – this would amount to tracking of individual preferences.

Transparency. In the group discussion transparency was the main issue. The participants argued that the system provided no transparency to data subjects as they were not at all informed about the system. This also extends to the analytical principles governing the system's algorithms: How and on what basis does the system identify certain kinds of behaviour as suspicious or dangerous (including to the individual him or herself)? How reliable is this identification?

The system could also be used to manipulate the emotions of data subjects (e.g., making them unhappy by denying them expected promotions or giving them the 'wrong' ones; making them happy by giving them particular discounts, etc.).

---

[4] Unlike the pictures itself, these data are also stored and further processed.

Intervenability. As data subjects are not informed of the processing, they would also have no means of intervention in the processing and thus be faced with a negation of their data subject rights.

4 Conclusion

The main objective of the workshop was to introduce participants to the DPIA methodology developed by Privacy Forum with a particular focus on the evaluation of risks based on the systematic approach of the SDM, which operationalises the legal requirements of EU data protection law. This was achieved by means of an introductory presentation, and a hands-on exercise in which the workshop participants analysed two data processing operations with regard to the risks they pose to the rights of individuals. As was to be expected both groups found that due to the numerous risks to the rights of individuals the envisaged processing operations of both case studies could not be carried out.

Beyond the details of the case studies and the particular methodology presented, the workshop discussions yielded insights that are of more general significance for DPIA processes. The discussions among participants confirmed that a multidisciplinary perspective is needed in order to identify and mitigate risks to the rights of individuals in a coherent and holistic manner. The workshop demonstrated that the SDM's data protection goals allow for a structured analysis of risks to the rights of individuals in accordance with the requirements of data protection law. Due to the manifold risks data processing entails such a structured analysis is crucial and at the heart of every DPIA. Nevertheless, the risk analysis in accordance with the GDPR needs further refinement and research. The discussions showed that it can be difficult to discuss risks for rights of individuals, if the legal basis for the processing and the potential risk sources, i.e. attackers, have not been identified beforehand, as stipulated in the DPIA framework. Furthermore, the fine-grained evaluation of the risks to the rights of individuals requires clarification. While recital 75 GDPR refers to the varying likelihood and severity of potential damages, which originated in information security, will have to be adapted in order to allow for the correct application within the fundamental rights framework of the GDPR and in conformity with the requirements of the EU Charter of Fundamental Rights. This future work can then also be integrated in the SDM in order to provide controllers, processors, manufacturers and supervisory authorities with guidelines on how to assess risks to the rights of individuals in practice.

Acknowledgement. This work is partially funded by the German Ministry of Education and Research within the project 'Forum Privacy and Self-determined Life in the Digital World', https://www.forum-privatheit.de/forum-privatheit-de/index.php.

References

1. Wright, D., De Hert, P.: Introduction to privacy impact assessment. In: Wright, D., De Hert, P. (eds.) Privacy Impact Assessment. Law, Governance and Technology Series, vol. 6. Springer, Dordrecht (2012). https://doi.org/10.1007/978-94-007-2543-0_1
2. CNIL (Commission Nationale de l'Informatique et des Libertés): Privacy Risk Assessment: Methodology (how to carry out a PIA). Paris (2015). http://www.cnil.fr/fileadmin/documents/en/CNIL-PIA-1-Methodology.pdf
3. ICO (Information Commissioner's Office): Conducting privacy impact assessments. Code of practice. UK Information Commissioner's Office, Wilmslow (2014). https://ico.org.uk/media/for-organisations/documents/1595/pia-code-of-practice.pdf
4. European Commission: Privacy and Data Protection Impact Assessment Framework for RFID Applications. Brussels (2011). http://cordis.europa.eu/fp7/ict/enet/documents/rfid-pia-framework-final.pdf
5. Friedewald, M., et al.: White Paper Datenschutz-Folgenabschätzung (2016). https://www.forum-privatheit.de/forum-privatheit-de/texte/veroeffentlichungen-des-forums/themenpapiere-white-paper/Forum_Privatheit_White_Paper_Datenschutz-Folgenabschaetzung_2016.pdf
6. Bieker, F., Friedewald, M., Hansen, M., Obersteller, H., Rost, M.: A process for data protection impact assessment under the european general data protection regulation. In: Schiffner, S., Serna, J., Ikonomou, D., Rannenberg, K. (eds.) APF 2016. LNCS, vol. 9857, pp. 21–37. Springer, Cham (2016). https://doi.org/10.1007/978-3-319-44760-5_2
7. The Standard Data Protection Model (SDM): V.1.0 EN1 (2017). https://www.datenschutz-mv.de/static/DS/Dateien/Datenschutzmodell/SDM-Methodology_V1_EN1.pdf
8. Article 29 Data Protection Working Party: Guidelines on Data Protection Impact Assessment (DPIA) and determining whether processing is "likely to result in a high risk" for the purposes of Regulation 2016/679. WP 248 (2017). http://ec.europa.eu/newsroom/document.cfm?doc_id=44137
9. Bieker, F.: Die Risikoanalyse nach dem neuen EU-Datenschutzrecht und dem Standard-Datenschutzmodell. Datenschutz Datensicherheit 42(1), 27–31 (2018)
10. Wright, D., Friedewald, M.: Integrating privacy and ethical impact assessment. Sci. Pub. Policy 40(6), 755–766 (2013)
11. Wright, D., Friedewald, M., Gellert, R.: Developing and testing a surveillance impact assessment methodology. Int. Data Priv. Law 5(1), 40–53 (2015)
12. Hennen, L.: Why do we still need participatory technology assessment? Poiesis Prax. 9(1–2), 27–41 (2012). https://doi.org/10.1007/s10202-012-0122-5
13. Slocum, N., Steyaert, S., Berloznik, R.: Participatory Methods Toolkit: A practitioner's manual. King Baudouin Foundation, Brussels (2006)
14. Kiesche, E.: So funktioniert die Folgenabschätzung. Comput. Arbeit 26(2), 31–36 (2017)
15. Burrell, J.: How the machine thinks: understanding opacity in machine learning algorithms. Big Data Soc. 3, 1–12 (2016)
16. Metz, C.: How Google's AI viewed the Move no Human could Understand. Wired, 14 March 2016. https://www.wired.com/2016/03/googles-ai-viewed-move-no-human-understand/

Designing a GDPR-Compliant
and Usable Privacy Dashboard

Philip Raschke[1]([✉]), Axel Küpper[1], Olha Drozd[2], and Sabrina Kirrane[2]

[1] Service-centric Networking, Telekom Innovation Laboratories,
Technical University Berlin, Berlin, Germany
[2] Vienna University of Economics and Business, Vienna, Austria
{philip.raschke,axel.kuepper}@tu-berlin.de,
{olha.drozd,sabrina.kirrane}@wu.ac.at

Abstract. The role of personal data gained significance across all business domains in past decades. Despite strict legal restrictions that processing personal data is subject to, users tend to respond to the extensive collection of data by service providers with distrust. Legal battles between data subjects and processors emphasized the need of adaptations by the current law to face today's challenges. The European Union has taken action by introducing the General Data Protection Regulation (GDPR), which was adopted in April 2016 and will inure in May 2018. The GDPR extends existing data privacy rights of EU citizens and simultaneously puts pressure on controllers and processors by defining high penalties in case of non-compliance. Uncertainties remain to which extent controllers and processors need to adjust their existing technologies in order to conform to the new law. This work designs, implements, and evaluates a privacy dashboard for data subjects intending to enable and ease the execution of data privacy rights granted by the GDPR.

Keywords: Data privacy · Privacy dashboard
General Data Protection Regulation
Usability · Transparency-enhancing tools · Privacy-enhancing tools

1 Introduction

In the age of digitalization, the data privacy of an individual can be severely violated by technology. Cases like Google Spain v AEPD and Mario Costeja González[1] highlight the extent of harm technology can do to an individual person by simply providing inaccurate (in this case outdated) information about the *data subject*. Its controversy had to be eventually decided by the European Court of Justice (ECJ), the highest court of the EU. While the case was solved with a verdict in favor of individuals' data privacy, doubts remained, which were

---

[1] ECLI:EU:C:2014:317. http://curia.europa.eu/juris/documents.jsf?num=c-131/12, last accessed: 07/04/2017.

© IFIP International Federation for Information Processing 2018
Published by Springer International Publishing AG 2018. All Rights Reserved
M. Hansen et al. (Eds.): Privacy and Identity 2017, IFIP AICT 526, pp. 221–236, 2018.
https://doi.org/10.1007/978-3-319-92925-5_14

fueled by the revelations of Edward Snowden in 2013, also called the *Snowden Effect*[2], and underlined by the invalidation of the *Safe Harbor Privacy Principles* by the ECJ[3] in 2015. The EU addresses these concerns with the General Data Protection Regulation (GDPR)[4], which comes into force in May 2018. The GDPR replaces the Data Protection Directive[5] of 1995 by extending the data privacy rights of data subjects in the EU with the goal to adapt to modern data privacy challenges.

A major change of the GDPR, among others, is the explicit requirement of *transparency* when processing personal information.[6] In the recitals of the GDPR the lawmakers explain that "[t]he principle of transparency requires that any information and communication relating to the processing of those personal data be easily accessible and easy to understand, and that clear and plain language be used".[7] Taking it literally, this would mean data subjects should be able to obtain *any information* they want, including the time a *controller* (i.e. a legal entity that processes personal information) accessed their personal data, from which source, to which *processors* (i.e. legal entities that process personal information on behalf of the controller) it has been forwarded, which data has been derived from it, and so on. However, in times of *Big Data* and *Cloud Computing*, providing this information can be very complex, considering the sheer amount of data a controller might process of a single data subject. Moreover, the processing often involves external third parties, since controllers might use the infrastructure of one or multiple service providers.

The personal data in question is mostly processed digitally, thus it is accessed and assessed by technical means. Granting the privacy rights of the GDPR should be realized by the same means. For this reason, we propose a privacy dashboard, which aims to offer and manage these data privacy rights. To tackle the complexity of the task and achieve a user-friendly result, a usability engineering methodology is applied.

The remainder of the paper is structured as follows. Section 2 discusses requirements for the privacy dashboard imposed by the GDPR. In Sect. 3, we give an overview of related work in the field of transparency-enhancing tools (TETs) as which privacy dashboards are classified. Section 4 presents the methodology, which is adapted to design the privacy dashboard. In Sect. 5, we analyze the potential users of the dashboard and the tasks they are supposed to fulfill with it. Based on the analysis, a design is derived that is presented and discussed

---

[2] What is Snowden effect? - Definition from WhatIs.com. http://whatis.techtarget.com/definition/Snowden-effect, last accessed: 07/17/2017.

[3] ECLI:EU:C:2015:650. http://curia.europa.eu/juris/documents.jsf?num=c-362/14, last accessed: 07/17/2017.

[4] Regulation (EU) 2016/679 of the European Parliament and of the Council of 27 April 2016 on the protection of natural persons with regard to the processing of personal data and on the free movement of such data, and repealing Directive 95/46/EC (General Data Protection Regulation), OJ L 119, 4.5.2016, p. 1–88 [hereinafter GDPR].

[5] Council Directive 95/46, 1995 O.J. (L 281) 31 (EC) [hereinafter Directive 95/46].

[6] GDPR art. 5(1)(a).

[7] GDPR Recital 39.

in Sect. 6. The development of a prototype and its evaluation are presented in Sects. 7 and 8 respectively. Finally, we conclude our work in Sect. 9.

2 GDPR

The GDPR will be law in 28 countries, but more will be affected by it due to its territorial scope. Controllers from abroad will be subject to it if they offer goods or services to European data subjects or monitor behavior, which happened in the Union.[8] The GDPR consists of 99 articles and 173 recitals. It is a comprehensive regulation covering multiple scenarios in which personal data is processed. This can be seen in Article 6 of the GDPR, which defines conditions for lawful processing of personal data. Given informed consent by the data subject[9] is only one out of a number of bases, including processing personal data to fulfill legal obligations[10] or for tasks carried out in the public interest[11]. To narrow the scope, we only focus on processing of personal data based on consent given by the data subject.

To access, review, and manage personal data in a digital format, technological means are necessary. Thus, compliance with the GDPR requires technology to adapt to it. Furthermore, new means must be introduced to grant and use the data privacy rights of the GDPR. Bier et al. [2] draw the same conclusion.

As stated above, the explicit requirement of transparency is one of the major changes of the GDPR compared to its predecessor, the Data Protection Directive of 1995. It required personal information to be "processed fairly and lawfully"[12], which is extended by the GDPR by adding the expression "*and in a transparent manner*"[13] to it. As mentioned in the previous section, the recitals attempt to narrow the transparency principle down, however, it remains debatable which information has to be provided to the data subject to meet the transparency requirement. The data subject can be provided with an overwhelming amount of meta information that is measured whenever personal data is processed. The meta data could give answers to the questions: When was the data collected? From which device was it obtained? To whom was it forwarded? What is the physical location of the processing servers? A first step towards transparency is to grant the *right of access*[14]. Siljee's [14] *Personal Data Table* fulfills all requirements to realize the execution of this right. The Personal Data Table should be extended by an element to depict data flows to involved processors.

Articles 16 and 17 of the GDPR grant data subjects the right to request rectification[15] and erasure[16] of data *without undue delay*. Moreover, the controller

---

[8] GDPR art. 3(2).
[9] GDPR art. 6(1)(a).
[10] GDPR art. 6(1)(c).
[11] GDPR art. 6(1)(e).
[12] Directive 95/46 art. 6(1)(a).
[13] GDPR art. 5(1)(a).
[14] GDPR art. 15(1).
[15] GDPR art. 16.
[16] GDPR art. 17(1).

is obliged to respond to these requests within one month. This time period is extendable by two additional months with regard to the complexity of the task and the number of requests.[17] For our design of the dashboard, this means the Personal Data Table must offer the possibility for each data item to request rectification or erasure of the corresponding information.

The Data Protection Directive required consent to be given *unambiguously*[18], while the GDPR now requires the informed consent to be given for *one or more specific purposes*[19]. The recitals advise that if data is used for multiple purposes, consent shall be given for each purpose separately.[20] Furthermore, the data subject shall have the right to withdraw consent at any time and as easy as it was to give consent.[21] The dashboard must include a possibility to review consents given, the purposes they were given for, and a functionality to withdraw them at any time.

The dashboard is supposed to work as interface between data subject and controller. Requests for rectification, erasure or withdrawal of consent cannot be expected to be responded to immediately. Thus, a message section to obtain status information about pending requests is reasonable. The controller may approach the data subject via the dashboard to ask for consent of processing personal data for additional purposes. This way the privacy dashboard may be extended by ex ante capabilities, while being mainly designed as ex post TET.

3 Related Work

Since decades there are numerous and manifold tools that address data privacy issues. Hedbom [5] provides a classification of TETs in 2008. The criteria to classify the tools include the possibilities of control and verification, the target audience and the scope of the tool, the information it presents, technologies it uses, and its trust and security requirements. Hedbom discusses his classification by applying it to examples. For this reason, the Transparent Accountable Data Mining (TAMI) system [16], the Privacy Bird[22], the PRIME project [4], the approach to obtain privacy evidence in case of privacy violations by Sackmann et al. [12], and Amazon's book recommendations service [17] are presented and explained.

Based on his work, Janic et al. [6] further develop the classification and extend its definitions of TETs by identifying and discussing 13 tools. According to them, tools like the Mozilla Privacy Icons[23] and Privacy Bird fall under tools that address the complexity of privacy policies of websites. The PrimeLife

---

[17] GDPR art. 12(3).
[18] Directive 95/46 art. 7(a).
[19] GDPR art. 6(1)(a).
[20] GDPR Recital 32.
[21] GDPR art. 7(3).
[22] Privacy Bird. http://www.privacybird.org, last accessed: 07/20/2017.
[23] Privacy Icons. https://disconnect.me/icons, last accessed: 07/20/2017.

Privacy Dashboard[24] and the Google Dashboard[25] are ex post TETs, which provide information on collected and stored data by service providers. Lightbeam[26] and Netograph[27] visualize user tracking that is realized via third party cookies. The tool Web of Trust[28] ranks websites according to their trustworthiness, which bases on a reputation system. Janic et al. classify Me & My Shadow[29], Firesheep[30], Panopticlick[31] and Creepy[32] as tools that aim to raise privacy awareness by informing the user about techniques commonly used to violate their data privacy. The tool Privacy Bucket[33] and the Online Interactive Privacy Feature Tool by Kani-Zabihi and Helmhout [8] have been released after the paper of Janic et al. was published, but fit in the previous described category.

To the best of our knowledge, the most recent privacy dashboards under development are GenomSynlig, which was merged into the Data Track project[34] by Angulo et al. [1] published in 2015, and the tool PrivacyInsight by Bier et al. [2] presented in 2016. While Data Track visualizes data disclosure in a so-called *trace view* and thus realizes the transparency principle of the GDPR, PrivacyInsight aims to address the GDPR as whole including the transparency principle, right to rectification and erasure, and the withdrawal of consent. Bier et al. identify legal and usability requirements for a privacy dashboard. In total they present 13 constraints, eight that are legal and five that are usability requirements. A brief summary of the legal prerequisites is given below, while the usability requirements are left out due to page limitations.

R1 The right to access must not be formally or technically constrained.

R2 A privacy dashboard must be accessible by every data subject.

R3 Access to all data must be provided.

R4 All data must be downloadable in machine-readable format.

R5 Data flows to all processors and internal data flows must be visualized.

R6 All sources of personal data must be named.

R7 For all processing steps a purpose must be given.

R8 Means to request rectification, erasure, or restriction must be provided.

---

[24] PrimeLife Dashboard. http://primelife.ercim.eu/results/opensource/76-dashboard, last accessed: 07/20/2017.

[25] Google Dashboard. https://myaccount.google.com/dashboard, last accessed: 07/20/2017.

[26] Lightbeam for Firefox - Mozilla. https://www.mozilla.org/en-US/lightbeam, last accessed: 07/20/2017.

[27] netograph. http://netograph.com, last accessed: 07/20/2017.

[28] WOT (Web of Trust). https://www.mywot.com, last accessed: 07/20/2017.

[29] Me and my Shadow. https://myshadow.org, last accessed: 07/20/2017.

[30] Firesheep - codebutler. http://codebutler.com/firesheep, last accessed: 07/20/2017.

[31] Panopticlick. https://panopticlick.eff.org, last accessed: 07/20/2017.

[32] Creepy by ilektrojohn. http://www.geocreepy.com, last accessed: 07/20/2017.

[33] mfredrik/Privacy-Bucket Wiki. https://github.com/mfredrik/Privacy-Bucket/wiki, last accessed: 07/20/2017.

[34] pylls/datatrack: A tool that visualizes your data disclosures. https://github.com/pylls/datatrack, last accessed: 07/20/2017.

The requirement R2 includes in particular design strategies that enable access for data subjects with disabilities like visually impaired people. The privacy dashboard must implement accessibility interfaces like the WAI-ARIA[35] standard by the World Wide Web Consortium. The requirements R3, R5, R6, R7, and R8 impose a usability challenge with respect to the sheer amount of data taken into consideration. Internal and external data flows, as demanded by R5, can be complex to be visualized depending on the number of internal entities and external processors. Designing these data flows as graph in a comprehensible manner can be challenging. However, the information it depicts is fundamental in order to enable transparency. To support the data subject and to improve the intelligibility of this graph, it is reasonable to categorize and label personal data. A data subject might not be able to review each data flow to all processors in detail, but is interested in certain data categories.

4   Methodology

For the design and implementation of the dashboard, we adapt Nielsen's *Usability Engineering Lifecycle* [11]. It is considered fundamental in the field of usability engineering. In addition, it suits the design of systems well which address inexperienced users that desire to solve complex tasks [15]. For the following summary of the Usability Engineering Lifecycle Möller's notation [10] is used.

The development process starts with the *Analysis* phase, which examines the users, the tasks to be solved with the system, and the context of use. In the *Design* phase, the system is designed iteratively, however there may be parallel design versions, which are tested separately. In the *Prototyping* phase, the system is partly implemented. In this phase a differentiation is made between *horizontal*, *vertical*, or *scenario-based* prototypes. Horizontal prototypes present all functional capabilities of the system to the user, but do not provide the actual functionality. Vertical prototypes implement a certain feature of the system in depth, but do not include and present all planed functionalities to the user. The presentation but not full implementation of a certain feature is called scenario-based prototype.

The resulting prototype is evaluated in the *Expert Evaluation* phase by so-called usability experts in contrast to the *Empirical Testing* phase, which involves real users of the system, who are invited to test the tool under laboratory conditions. In the context of software engineering, this means a specific environment is set up including a predefined and tested device, a certain network connection, specific input tools, and so on. Various user studies can be conducted in both phases to either measure the overall quality of the system, or to identify flaws in the design. One of them is the cognitive walkthrough, which was first introduced by Lewis et al. [9] in 1990. After this phase, the next iteration starts, beginning

---

[35] WAI-ARIA (Web Accessibility Initiative). https://www.w3.org/WAI/intro/aria.php, last accessed: 07/25/2017.

with the Design phase. If the system is eventually deployed, feedback from real users in real-life scenarios can be collected and evaluated to further improve the system.

5 Analysis

Users of the privacy dashboard are potentially all natural persons in the EU. According to the statistics provider Eurostat of the European Commission, over 500 million humans lived in the Union in 2016.[36] These millions of people live in 28 countries, speak 24 official languages and almost the same amount of migrant languages, while using three different writing systems.[37] In 2016, 15.6% of the European population were younger than 14 years, 11.1% of them were between the age of 15–24, 34.1% between 25 and 49, 20.1% between 50–64, 13.8% between 65–79, and 5.4% older than 80 years.[38] These numbers highlight the challenge a uniform interface for this user base will be, however, it is further reasonable to investigate the user base's affiliation with information and communication technology. In 2016, about 71% of all individuals in the EU and 92% between the age of 16 to 24 accessed the Internet on a daily basis.[39] Moreover, 8 out of 10 users use a mobile device to access the Internet.[40] In 2012, 80% of individuals between the age of 16 and 24 used the mobile Internet to participate in social networks.[41]

Consequently, it can be inferred that a technological mean like a privacy dashboard reaches the majority of the user base, since it is rather familiar with technology and with the Internet. Web applications, which are optimized for mobile devices, suit well as platform. The privacy dashboard is intended to be used to execute data privacy rights granted by the GDPR. These rights are identified as the following tasks the tool should be used for:

T1 Execute the right of access
T2 Obtain information about involved processors
T3 Request rectification or erasure of data
T4 Consent review and withdrawal.

---

[36] Eurostat - Population. http://ec.europa.eu/eurostat/tgm/table.do?tab=table& init=1&language=en&pcode=tps00001&plugin=1, last accessed: 07/18/2017.
[37] Europeans and their Languages. http://ec.europa.eu/commfrontoffice/publicopi nion/archives/ebs/ebs_386_en.pdf, last accessed: 07/25/2017.
[38] Eurostat - Population by age group. http://ec.europa.eu/eurostat/tgm/refreshTable Action.do?tab=table\&plugin=1\&pcode=tps00010\&language=en, last accessed: 07/25/2017.
[39] Eurostat - Internet use and activities. http://ec.europa.eu/eurostat/web/products-datasets/-/isoc_bde15cua, last accessed: 07/25/2017.
[40] Eurostat - Internet use by individuals. http://ec.europa.eu/eurostat/documents/ 2995521/7771139/9-20122016-BP-EN.pdf/f023d81a-dce2-4959-93e3-8cc7082b6edd, last accessed: 07/25/2017.
[41] Eurostat - Purpose of mobile internet use. http://ec.europa.eu/eurostat/web/ products-datasets/-/isoc_cimobi_purp, last accessed: 07/25/2017.

The Analysis phase also includes the investigation on how the identified tasks would be or are solved without the tool. To the best of our knowledge, there is no dedicated tool to exercise any of these data privacy rights. Consequently, the execution of these rights heavily depends on the context of the controller. If the controller processes personal information digitally and offers the data subject a user interface, then the right to access, rectify, and erase data can be expressed or realized via this user interface. However, to inform about involved processors or to review and withdraw previously given informed consent, data subjects have to revert to written correspondence with the controller or to long privacy policies that nobody reads [3], but may give all required information on how data is forwarded to external third parties or the formal procedure to withdraw consent. It often remains uncertain how and whether controllers respond to these written requests of data subjects. In cases of severe privacy violations with social or economic damage, legal actions need to be taken.[42]

6   Design

This section discusses two possible architectures to deploy and operate the privacy dashboard and presents a first design approach, which serves as a basis for the development of the prototype.

6.1   Architecture

We ideally envision one privacy dashboard to manage all privacy rights with regard to all controllers a data subject is concerned with. As Fig. 1 shows, Approach 1 requires each controller to deploy and operate their own instance of the tool, which the data subjects can access individually, while Approach 2 allows data subjects to access one instance of the dashboard to manage all controllers they deal with.

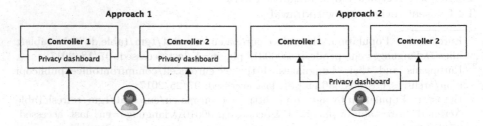

Fig. 1. Architectural alternatives for the deployment of the privacy dashboard. Either as single point to manage all controllers, or as data privacy management tool for every controller separately.

---

[42] ECLI:EU:C:2014:317   http://curia.europa.eu/juris/documents.jsf?num=c-131/12, last accessed: 07/25/2017.

A controller-operated instance of the privacy dashboard is easier to integrate into the data processing infrastructure of the controller. Consequently, no conversion of the personal data in question is necessary to adapt to an interface of an external third party. The controller would be able to modify and extend the privacy dashboard, for instance, to implement the visualization of customized or proprietary data formats. Security vulnerabilities are avoided, since the personal data in its entirety does not leave the boundaries of the controller, but queried chunks of it are transmitted to the data subject. The proximity of the privacy dashboard to the infrastructure of the controller eases the immediate and automated application of requests to rectify or erase inaccurate personal data. Requests made by the data subject could directly trigger internal processes providing all necessary parameters to take instant action. If the controller uses authentication mechanisms to authenticate data subjects in order to provide a service, the same technique can be used by the privacy dashboard to authenticate a data subject before delivering personal data.

While the data subject might benefit from a single end point to address all privacy concerns to, Approach 2 also implies a series of challenges. This approach is more challenging from an architectural perspective, since personal data from all controllers needs to be aggregated and served by a dedicated component. This would either require the standardization of a common data format or an agreement on an existing one. Interestingly, the right to data portability[43] granted by the GDPR may force controllers to develop or agree upon a common data format to exchange personal data. Still a transformation of the personal data is necessary, to adapt to the visualization logic of the external-operated privacy dashboard. A single machine that stores personal data of one or more individuals from multiple controllers is a security and privacy risk itself. Therefore, programmable interfaces should be defined by each controller to allow querying certain chunks of data. These interfaces require an authentication mechanism to ensure that personal data is transmitted to the right data subject. In this architecture distributed authentication techniques have to be used to solve the task. Consequently, the dashboard is ideally executed on the data subject's device, so no third party has to be involved, however, this comes along with hardware requirements that could violate Requirement R1 (*The right to access must not be formally or technically constrained.*) of Sect. 3.

In general, the adoption of the privacy dashboard by all controllers appears as a more likely approach, if it saves controllers the development of an individual privacy dashboard from scratch. Again, the assumption is made here that compliance with the GDPR implies the introduction of a privacy dashboard (see Bier et al. [2] R2).

6.2   Data Taxonomy

The GDPR's explicit requirement of personal data to be processed transparently highlights the significance of the right to access. In order to execute T1 (as

---

[43] GDPR art. 20.

defined in Sect. 5), all personal data has to be presented to the user. This data is displayed ex post like Siljee's [14] Personal Data Table. This enables answering the question: Which data collected the controller in question about me? The most challenging aspect of this task is to realize the visualization of huge amounts of diverse data. Consequently, the first approach to reduce the complexity of the data is to drill down the amount by limiting the presented data based on a time criteria such as data of the last month, week, or day. Simultaneously, by introducing this limit the dashboard needs to offer a functionality to select a time range the data subject wants to consider and review. This way, the data subject is able to ask more precisely the above mentioned question for a specific time range.

Despite this limitation, it might be that the sheer amount of data still overwhelms the data subject. Thus, it is reasonable to categorize the data and display the different categories. Since the context of use is data privacy, it is consequent to categorize the data according to a data taxonomy that addresses data privacy. Fortunately, Schneier [13] developed such a data taxonomy for social networks. A brief description of the categories is given below:

Service data is any kind of data that is required in order to provide the service in question (name, address, payment information).

Disclosed data is any data that the data subject intentionally provides on the own profile page or in their posts.

Entrusted data is any data that the data subject intentionally provides on other users' profile pages or in their posts.

Incidental data is any kind of data provided by other users of the service about the data subject (a photo showing the data subject posted by a friend).

Behavioral data is any kind of data the service provider observes about the data subject while he or she uses the service (browsing behavior).

Derived data is any kind of data derived from any other category or data source (profiles for marketing, location tracks, possible preferences).

To apply the data taxonomy to all kinds of controllers and not just to online social networks, we propose a generalization of Schneier's taxonomy. For this reason, we categorize disclosed and entrusted data into the category *Intentional data*, since both types of data are provided by the data subject intentionally. Furthermore, comprehensible labels for the categories are defined below:

Service data - Service data
Intentional data - Data I provided
Incidental data - Data of me provided by others
Behavioral data - Data of my behavior
Derived data - Inferred data about me.

These categories can be applied to all kinds of controllers, although not each controller processes all categories of data. In our design for each category a view is offered with an individual Personal Data Table and the time limitation functionalities described above. In case that one or more categories are not applicable to the domain of the controller, a simple information can be given that no data for this category is available. This might also confirm expectations of the data subject with regard to data collection practices of certain controllers. By applying the data taxonomy and offering separated views for each data category, the dashboard allows the data subject to easily find out whether a controller collects behavioral data of him or her or whether another user disclosed information about him or her.

7   Prototype

A prototype was developed with the JavaScript framework *React*[44] and the library *Material-UI*[45] to comply with Google's design standard *Material Design*[46]. The prototype has been made publicly available online[47]. With respect to the chosen methodology, a horizontal prototype has been developed that implements and presents all features to the user, however, provides reduced or no actual functionality. In practice, this means the scenario of our prototype is completely artificial.

We therefore define an online social network provider as our made-up controller that processes personal data of its users similar to popular services like *Facebook* or *Twitter*. All data presented in the dashboard is fake and does not belong to a natural person. However, to simulate a person's personal profile as accurate as possible with regard to the amount of data, we adapt an existing model from a study of the advertising agency Jung von Matt[48]. Furthermore, requests to rectification, erasure, or withdrawal of consent are not processed by a controller's backend. The filtering of data according to its processing context, data type, or time of its processing is implemented.

As it can be seen in Fig. 2, we designed a three-column layout for the dashboard. We define general functionalities like reviewing given consent, displaying the privacy policy, and obtaining information about involved third parties, which are presented in the left column. Also in the left column and under the general functionalities, filter options are provided allowing the user to display personal data processed in a specific context, of a certain data type, and in a defined time range. The meaning of each processing category and each data type is visually supported by an icon, which is used in other components of the dashboard as well. In the center of the layout, the queried personal data is listed vertically in chronological order beginning with oldest entry. Each entry is furnished with an

---

[44] React - A JavaScript library for building user interfaces. https://reactjs.org/, last accessed: 11/13/2017.

[45] Material-UI. http://www.material-ui.com/, last accessed: 11/13/2017.

[46] Material Design. https://material.io/, last accessed: 11/13/2017.

[47] Privacy dashboard — IFIP Summer School 2017. http://philip-raschke.github.io/GDPR-privacy-dashboard, last accessed: 01/19/2018.

[48] Jung von Matt study on typical German Facebook profile. https://de.linkedin.com/pulse/das-h%C3%A4ufigste-facebook-profil-deutschlands-raphael-brinkert, last accessed: 11/13/2017.

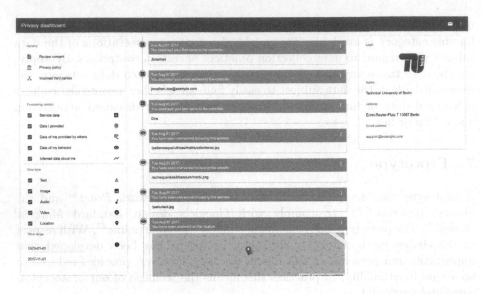

Fig. 2. The layout of the developed prototype. General functionalities and filter options are presented on the left-hand side. The queried data is in the center sorted chronologically beginning with the oldest entry. General information about the controller are presented on the right-hand side.

icon that gives information on its processing context. Under the actual date of when the processing took place, a short descriptive text about it is presented in the header of an entry, which is displayed above the actual personal data. On the right-hand side, general information about the controller are given, such as name, physical address, and email address to directly contact the controller.

In order to use the dashboard to execute task T2, a graph is displayed that shows the user data flows between controllers and involved processors (see Fig. 3). In real-life scenarios often many processors are involved in the processing of personal data. There can be multiple controllers as well (so-called joint controllers[49]). Depending on the number of involved processors in the processing of the data subject's personal data, the complete graph can be shown as whole or processors can be clustered into groups according to their business domain for instance. Edges are annotated with data categories giving information on which data is exchanged. The arrows denote the direction of the data flow to clarify whether parties are just provided with data or if parties are actively exchanging data with each other. For the implementation of this graph the JavaScript library *vis.js*[50] has been used. Angulo et al. [1] propose a similar but more detailed approach with the trace view. To reduce complexity, data categories instead of specific data items are used in our approach.

---

[49] GDPR art. 26.

[50] vis.js - A dynamic, browser based visualization library. http://visjs.org/, last accessed: 11/13/2017.

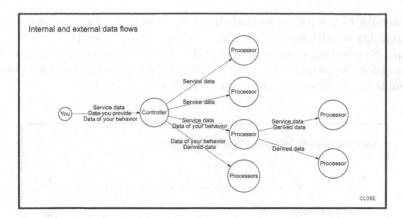

Fig. 3. A graph visualizing internal and external data flows between controller and processors. Edges are labeled with data categories indicating which data is exchanged with whom.

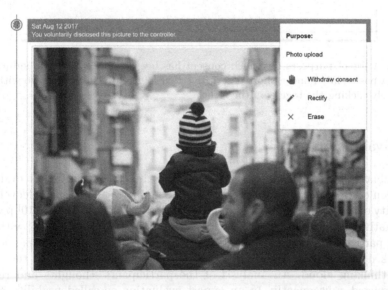

Fig. 4. For each specific data item the user is given information on the purpose of its processing, where applicable the possibility to withdraw consent, and the possibility to request rectification or erasure of the data.

Task T3 requires the privacy dashboard to offer a possibility to request rectification or erasure of the data item in question (see Fig. 4). Additionally, for each data item information on the purpose of its collection and processing is given (see Fig. 4). Multiple purposes can be listed here, if data is processed for more than one purpose. With the help of this component the data subject can answer the question: For what reason does the controller collect and process this data?

A redirection to a separate section allows the user to review given consent and the possibility to withdraw it (see Fig. 5). Since consent is supposed to be bound to a specific purpose, there is a label and a short description text to give more details about the purpose in question. With a simple interaction, like a click, it is possible to withdraw consent as easily as it was to give it.[51]

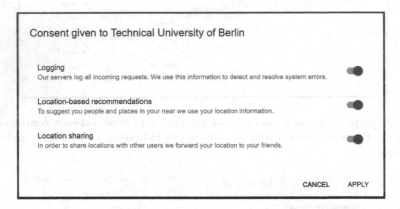

Fig. 5. A list of purposes for which consent has been given by the data subject. For each purpose a label and a short descriptive text is given. Consent can be withdrawn by simply clicking the toggle on the right.

8   Evaluation

To evaluate the design approach presented in this paper, an expert evaluation has been carried out according to Nielsen's Usability Engineering Lifecycle. The usability of the data categories is in focus of this evaluation. Möller [10] proposes a formative analysis consisting of a so-called *Thinking Aloud* test [7] with three to five participants to identify design flaws in a system. In the test, participants are asked to solve one or more specific tasks by interacting with the system while thinking aloud. An analysis of the participants' thoughts and remarks is conducted subsequently. In an expert evaluation so-called usability experts instead of real users are used, since the system might be in a too early stage to present it to external users. For this reason, three fellow researchers were given the following task consisting of multiple questions that have definitive answers.

"European law gives you the right to request from any entity that processes your personal data access to it. Imagine you requested access to your personal data from a company and you're confronted with the tool in front of you. Please answer the following questions:"

- *Which data did you have to provide when creating an account for this service?*
- *Did you provide any voice recordings to the service?*

---

[51] GDPR art. 7(3).

- *Have you disclosed your location voluntarily?*
- *Has anyone provided the controller with photos of you?*
- *Does this service provider track your location?*
- *Has the service provider knowledge about your gender?*
- *Does the service provider know your income?*
- *Does the service provider know which websites you visit?*

All participants struggled to answer the questions at the beginning, but managed to improve quickly answering the last questions rather fast and confidently. All participants answered the first question using the chronological order instead of using the respective data category assuming the data provided first is the data required for the registration. This is a clear indicator that the data category *Service data* is redundant and can be categorized as intentional data ("Data I provided"). The so-called *AppBar* at the top also contributed to confusion. The participants understood the privacy dashboard as a service itself, therefore tried to answer the first question with regard to required information in order to use the privacy dashboard itself. The participants found that the filter options were not visible enough and should be placed more prominent, considering that they are an essential part in the task solving process. Another concern of the participants is the technical feasibility of the data categories. This applies to incidental data ("Data of me provided by others") and derived data ("Inferred data about me") in particular. Generally, the scenario of the privacy dashboard is important. The participants were interested whether the system is operated by the controller or as a separate service, and if it can be used offline or if an Internet connection is required. The evaluation reveals that refining the data categories is necessary in order to improve the usability of the dashboard. However, it also shows that the developed prototype can be used by data subjects to answer questions relating to their data privacy.

9 Conclusion

This work presents the design and implementation of a privacy dashboard, which addresses the requirements of the GDPR and enables the data subject to execute data privacy rights with the tool. To substantiate the dashboard's design, its potential users and the tasks they are supposed to fulfill with it were analyzed and discussed. A prototype has been developed and evaluated. The results of the evaluation indicate that our design approach is worth pursuing and reasonable, yet needs further improvements and user tests. The redefinition of the data categories and their technical feasibility will be researched in future work. Furthermore, architectures for the deployment of the privacy dashboard need more investigation. Comprehensive user studies are necessary to refine the current design of the dashboard and to develop alternative approaches.

Acknowledgments. Supported by the European Union's Horizon 2020 research and innovation programme under grant 731601. The authors would like to thank Dirk Thatmann, Iwailo Denisow, and Sebastian Zickau for their valuable feedback to the prototype.

References

1. Angulo, J., Fischer-Hübner, S., Pulls, T., Wästlund, E.: Usable transparency with the data track - a tool for visualizing data disclosures. In: Proceedings of the 33rd Annual ACM Conference Extended Abstracts on Human Factors in Computing Systems - CHI EA 2015, pp. 1803–1808 (2015)
2. Bier, C., Kühne, K., Beyerer, J.: PrivacyInsight: the next generation privacy dashboard. In: Schiffner, S., Serna, J., Ikonomou, D., Rannenberg, K. (eds.) APF 2016. LNCS, vol. 9857, pp. 135–152. Springer, Cham (2016). https://doi.org/10.1007/978-3-319-44760-5_9
3. Borgesius, F.Z.: Informed consent: we can do better to defend privacy. IEEE Secur. Priv. 13, 103–107 (2015)
4. Hansen, M., Borcea-Pfitzmann, K., Pfitzmann, A.: PRIME - a European project for privacy-enhancing identity management. IT - Inf. Technol. 47, 352–359 (2005)
5. Hedbom, H.: A survey on transparency tools for enhancing privacy. In: Matyáš, V., Fischer-Hübner, S., Cvrček, D., Švenda, P. (eds.) Privacy and Identity 2008. IAICT, vol. 298, pp. 67–82. Springer, Heidelberg (2009). https://doi.org/10.1007/978-3-642-03315-5_5
6. Janic, M., Wijbenga, J.P., Veugen, T.: Transparency enhancing tools (TETs): an overview. In: Workshop on Socio-Technical Aspects in Security and Trust, STAST, pp. 18–25 (2013)
7. Jaspers, M.W.M., Steen, T., Van Den Bos, C., Geenen, M.: The think aloud method: a guide to user interface design. Int. J. Med. Inform. 73, 781–795 (2004)
8. Kani-Zabihi, E., Helmhout, M.: Increasing service users' privacy awareness by introducing on-line interactive privacy features. In: Laud, P. (ed.) NordSec 2011. LNCS, vol. 7161, pp. 131–148. Springer, Heidelberg (2012). https://doi.org/10.1007/978-3-642-29615-4_10
9. Lewis, C., Polson, P.G., Wharton, C., Rieman, J.: Testing a walkthrough methodology for theory-based design of walk-up-and-use interfaces. In: Proceedings of the SIGCHI Conference on Human Factors in Computing Systems Empowering People - CHI 1990, pp. 235–242. ACM Press, New York (1990)
10. Möller, S.: Quality Engineering. Springer, Heidelberg (2003). https://doi.org/10.1007/978-3-642-11548-6
11. Nielsen, J.: Usability Engineering. Elsevier, New York (1994)
12. Sackmann, S., Strüker, J., Accorsi, R.: Personalization in privacy-aware highly dynamic systems. Commun. ACM 49, 32 (2006)
13. Schneier, B.: A taxonomy of social networking data. IEEE Secur. Priv. Mag. 8, 88 (2010)
14. Siljee, J.: Privacy transparency patterns. In: Proceedings of the 20th European Conference on Pattern Languages of Programs - EuroPLoP 2015, pp. 1–11. ACM Press, New York (2015)
15. Thatmann, D., Raschke, P., Küpper, A.: "Please, No More GUIs": a user study, prototype development and evaluation on the integration of attribute-based encryption in a hospital environment. In: Proceedings - International Computer Software and Applications Conference, pp. 496–502. IEEE (2016)
16. Weitzner, D.J., Abelson, H., Hanson, C., Hendler, J., Mcguinness, D.L., Jay, G., Waterman, K.K., Berners-lee, T., Kagal, L., Sussman, G.J.: Transparent accountable data mining: new strategies for privacy protection, pp. 1–12 (2006)
17. Zwick, D., Dholakia, N.: Whose identity is it anyway? Consumer representation in the age of database marketing. J. Macromarketing 24, 31–43 (2004)

Blockchain-based Identity Management and Data Usage Control (Extended Abstract)

Ricardo Neisse[✉], Gary Steri, and Igor Nai Fovino

European Commission Joint Research Centre (JRC),
Via E. Fermi 2749, 21027 Ispra, VA, Italy
{ricardo.neisse,gary.steri,igor.nai-fovino}@ec.europa.eu

The General Data Protection Regulation (GDPR) [1], which will be enforceable from May 2018, introduces significant changes on the obligations of data controllers and processors in the context of the data protection legistlation of the European Union (EU). These obligations are defined by a single set of rules that should be adopted by all EU Member States including, among others, the need for explicit consent with the possibility of withdrawal and the right to erasure. The GDPR applies to data controllers (organizations) that access data of a data subject (persons) and data processors (organizations) that process data on behalf of the controller.

The focus of our work is on a blockchain-based solution using smart contracts, in the scope of the GDPR, to support data accountability and provenance tracking when subject's data is accessed by controllers and possibly forwarded to data processors. The main goal is to empower subjects with a trusted and transparent solution allowing the tracking of who has accessed their data or identity attributes, to verify if the access and usage of the data did not violate their consent encoded in privacy preferences, and to give the possibility of withdrawing or modify their preferences in case they change their mind. Furthermore, such a solution also benefits controllers and processors with a way to prove they have rightfully obtained consent and are processing data without violating the data protection obligations. The main advantage of using blockchain technologies is the transparency, auditability, and immutability features that potentially enable trust and trasparency on the proposed solution.

In our analysis [2] we identified three possible models for the solution, which are depitect in Fig. 1. In the first model data subjects express their privacy preferences by means of usage control policies that are embedded in specific smart contracts deployed in the blockchain for each controller or processor receiving their data. In the second model, subjects create smart contracts for each data item that is possibly shared with multiple data controllers. In the third model, each controller expresses their privacy conditions in a smart contract with an interface allowing users to join or leave the contract, meaning they are giving or withdrawing their consent for each data controller or processor. These policies, which can be selected before hand or on request from a library of policy templates, express the conditions for data access, usage, and transfer to data

M. Hansen et al. (Eds.): Privacy and Identity 2017, IFIP AICT 526, pp. 237–239, 2018.
https://doi.org/10.1007/978-3-319-92925-5_15

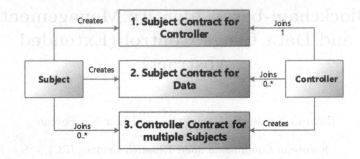

Fig. 1. Provenance and accountability tracking models using blockchain.

processors. Our contribution is the analysis of design choices, implementation, and performance/scalability analysis of these blockchain-based data accountability and provenance tracking solutions.

With respect to user privacy, data accountability, and data tracking granularity each model provides different properties. In the first model there is one contract per pair Subject/Controller, the contract tracks data provenance, events, and encodes specific policies for each controller. Since subjects can use a different pseudonym for each controller, contracts are unlinkable among controllers. In the second model there is one contract per pair Subject/DataInstance, the contract tracks data provenance, events, and a shared policy for all controllers accessing the respective data. Controllers may be able to uniquely identify a subject in case a unique identifier is shared (e.g. name, e-mail, etc.). In the third model there is one contract per controller that is shared for multiple subjects, the contract includes only the general privacy conditions of each controller without the possibility of customization for each data subject. Thee evaluation/tracking of events is done off-blockchain and subjects are also able to benefit from the use of pseudonyms for each controller.

From the three analyzed models we provided two concrete implementations for the first and third model described above, with an extensive analysis with respect to data accountability features, provenance tracking granularity, privacy, anonymity, performance, and scalability. The second model was excluded since it allows linkability of subjects across different controllers. For the first and third model contracts were implemented using a shared secret nonce to prevent linkability across multiple smart contracts of a subject, and to obfuscate the privacy preferences, data, and identity provenance information using a one-way hash function. We show that for more sensitive data with less frequent exchanges, such as medical data, a more fine-grained solution where subjects create contracts with each controller and processors is more adequate (first model). On the other hand, for more dynamic data with more frequent exchanges and strict scalability and performance requirements, controllers or processors should manage a contract that registers all subjects accepting all or part of the data usage conditions (third model).

A possible solution for scalability issues we are currently investigating is the use of sharding, where the blockchain is divided into separate chains that are responsible for contracts of a subset of all controllers and processors. These separate private chains then synchronize with the public chain on regular intervals, for example every N blocks, in order to allow for public verifiability [5]. In case the separated chains are managed privately, data protection supervisory authorities can then join all chains just as observers in order to prevent censorship and guarantee that transactions of data subjects are not indiscriminately refused. As future work we also plan to investigate the possibility of using business blockchain approaches such as the Hyperledger solution, which uses a different algorithm for reaching consensus and also has a more ambitious scalability and performance goal with thousands of transactions per second [3,4].

References

1. Regulation (EU) 2016/679 of the European Parliament and of the Council of 27 April 2016 on the protection of natural persons with regard to the processing of personal data and on the free movement of such data. Official Journal of the European Union L119/59, May 2016. http://eur-lex.europa.eu/legal-content/EN/TXT/?uri=OJ:L:2016:119:TOC
2. Neisse, R., Steri, G., Fovino, I.N.: A blockchain-based approach for data accountability and provenance tracking. In: Proceedings of the 12th International Conference on Availability, Reliability and Security, Reggio Calabria, Italy, 29 August–01 September 2017, pp. 14:1–14:10. ACM (2017). https://doi.org/10.1145/3098954.3098958
3. Vukolić, M.: The quest for scalable blockchain fabric: proof-of-work vs. BFT replication. In: Camenisch, J., Kesdoğan, D. (eds.) iNetSec 2015. LNCS, vol. 9591, pp. 112–125. Springer, Cham (2016). https://doi.org/10.1007/978-3-319-39028-4_9
4. Vukolić, M.: Rethinking permissioned blockchains. In: ACM Workshop on Blockchain, Cryptocurrencies and Contracts (BCC 2017), April 2017. http://vukolic.com/rethinking-permissioned-blockchains-BCC2017.pdf
5. Ethereum Wiki: Sharding FAQ - on sharding blockchains. https://github.com/ethereum/wiki/wiki/Sharding-FAQ (2017). Accessed 06 Apr 2017

Identification Services for Online Social Networks (OSNs) Extended Abstract

Elena Ferrari(✉)

Department of Theoretical and Applied Sciences,
University of Insubria, Via Mazzini 5, Varese, Italy
elena.ferrari@uninsubria.it

Abstract. On-line Social Networks (OSNs) have dramatically changed
how users connect, communicate, share content, and exchange goods and
services. However, despite all the benefits and the flexibility that OSNs
provide, their users become more reliant on online identities with often
no means to know who really is behind an online profile. Indeed, to facilitate their adoption and encourage people to join, identities in OSNs
are very loose, in that not much more than an email address is required
to create an account and related profile. Therefore, the problem of fake
accounts and identity related attacks in OSNs has attracted considerable
interest from the research community, and resulted in several proposals
that mainly aim at detecting malicious nodes that follow identified and
formalized attack trends. Without denying the importance of formal-
izing Sybil attacks and suggesting solutions for their detection, in this
extended abstract we also consider the issue of identity validation from
a user perspective, by briefly discussing the research proposals aiming at
empowering users with tools helping them to identify the validity of the
online accounts they interact with.

An OSN is an online service that provides a virtual socializing platform through
which people can connect to each other and share information. OSNs allow
users to create personal profiles by which they present themselves to the rest of
the network, share knowledge and different types of information, and connect
with a large network of users (either friends or strangers). To facilitate their
adoption, OSNs use very loose identity validation mechanisms: usually, only a
valid email address is required for a new user to join an OSN. This way of
managing identities has the advantage of encouraging users to join, however, it
poses the problem of fake identities that can result in several threats to OSN
users security and privacy. One of the most notable identity-related attack is
represented by Sybils, a set of bogus accounts that represent multiple different
identities, while in reality they are created, manipulated, and owned by one single
entity (e.g., a user or a bot). Sybils can be created for different malicious aims,
such as spreading malware, spying on users activity and personal information,
or polluting the environment with fake content or fake support for a given cause,
such as increasing the reputation of a politician or of a brand [6].

© IFIP International Federation for Information Processing 2018
Published by Springer International Publishing AG 2018. All Rights Reserved
M. Hansen et al. (Eds.): Privacy and Identity 2017, IFIP AICT 526, pp. 240–242, 2018.
https://doi.org/10.1007/978-3-319-92925-5_16

Given their large impact, Sybil attacks have been widely studied in the literature from different perspectives [3], leading to the definition of both automated and human-assisted techniques [1]. Although these approaches use a variety of techniques to discriminate between Sybil and non Sybil node, they can be classified into three main groups: *Sybil prevention*, *Sybil detection*, and *Sybil tolerance* approaches. Sybil prevention aims at preventing Sybil creation. This can be mainly achieved by strengthening the identity validation process, a solution which is rarely adopted in practice due to the possible user resistance and privacy implications. The most crowded class of approaches is represented by Sybil detection techniques, which do not prevent Sybil to be created. Rather they try to identify Sybil accounts as soon as possible. Detection techniques can be further classified into *topology-based*, *activity-based*, or a mix between the two. Under the topology-based approaches, the topological structure of the underlying OSN graph is studied to discriminate between honest and malicious users. These approaches work under the assumption that the regions of honest and Sybil nodes are two separate parts in an OSN graph, where connections between them exist through attack links. However, some studies conducted on real OSN datasets have shown that this assumption does not always hold [6]. Therefore, activity-based approaches have also been explored, where the idea is to find behavioral features (e.g., frequency of sending friend requests, frequency of making new friends, ratio of outgoing to incoming activities) that could be used to reliably differentiate between fake and real accounts, using automated classifiers. Other proposals have developed a hybrid approach, combining both topological and behavioral features (e.g., [4,5]). Finally, Sybil tolerance approaches do not prevent Sybil creation nor they explicitly try to identify Sybils. Rather, they try to avoid that Sybil accounts can be used to perform malicious activities (e.g., by limiting spam in messaging systems).

All the above techniques provide good results when Sybils match known patterns of misbehavior, however they are vulnerable to some extent against adaptive attackers and their infiltration into honest communities (which is always the case in today OSNs). Therefore, to mitigate this risk, researchers have started to explore complementary services wrt the Sybil detection ones, with the aim to provide honest users with indications on the validity of other strangers profiles they plan to interact with. This would help them to take better decisions in establishing new friendship relationships, and, therefore, they mitigate the risk of fake account infiltration into honest communities. An example in this direction is represented by [2]. In this paper, starting from the observation that undetected Sybils by automated tools are the ones that succeed in emulating real profiles features and/or in getting enough connections within specific honest user communities [3], the authors study how information on a profile could be exploited to evaluate its trustworthiness within OSN communities. The developed system exploits community effort to collaboratively estimate the validity of OSN users' identities based on the coherence of some of the information they provide on their profiles.

However, since OSNs continue to grow, both in terms of their user base and the heaviness by which they are used, attackers are showing an increasing degree of sophistication in emulating real accounts. As such, we believe that identity management will continue to be an ever challenging problem, also because of the interplay with privacy and efficiency issues, that will require more efforts from both the research and industrial communities.

References

1. Al-Quirishi, et al.: Sybil defence techniques in online social networks: a survey. IEEE Access **5**, 1200–1219 (2017)
2. Bahri, L., Carminati, B., Ferrari, E.: COIP - continuous, operable, impartial, and privacy-aware identity validity estimation for OSN profiles. ACM Trans. Web **10**(4), 23:1–23:41 (2016)
3. Kansara, K.B., Shekokar, N.M.: At a glance of sybil detection in OSN. In: Proceedings of IEEE International Symposium on Nanoelectronic and Information Systems (2015)
4. Laleh, N., Carminati, B., Ferrari, E.: Risk assessment in social networks based on user anomalous behaviour. IEEE Trans. Dependable Secur. Comput. **15**, 295–308 (2016)
5. Li, Y., Martinez, O., Chen, X., Li, Y., Hopcroft, J.E.: In a world that counts: clustering and detecting fake social engagement at scale. In: Proceedings of the 25th International Conference on World Wide Web (2016)
6. Yang, Z., Wilson, C., Wang, X., Gao, T., Zhao, B.Y., Dai, Y.: Uncovering social network sybils in the wild. ACM Trans. Knowl. Discov. Data (TKDD) **8**(1), 2 (2014)

Cyber Security and Privacy Experiments: A Design and Reporting Toolkit

Kovila P. L. Coopamootoo[✉] and Thomas Groß

Newcastle University, Newcastle upon Tyne, UK
{kovila.coopamootoo,thomas.gross}@newcastle.ac.uk

Abstract. With cyber security increasingly flourishing into a scientific discipline, there has been a number of proposals to advance evidence-based research, ranging from introductions of evidence-based methodology [8], proposals to make experiments dependable [30], guidance for experiment design [8,38], to overviews of pitfalls to avoid when writing about experiments [42]. However, one is still given to wonder: What are the best practices in reporting research that act as tell-tale signs of reliable research.

We aim at developing a set of indicators for complete reporting that can drive the quality of experimental research as well as support the reviewing process.

As method, we review literature on key ingredients for sound experiment and studied fallacies and shortcomings in other fields. We draw on lessons learned and infuse them into indicators. We provide definition, reporting examples, importance and impact and guiding steps to be taken for each indicator.

As results, we offer a toolkit with nine systematic indictors for designing and reporting experiments. We report on lessons and challenges from an initial sharing of this toolkit with the community.

The toolkit is a valuable companion for researchers. It incites the consideration of scientific foundations at experiment design and reporting phases. It also supports program committees and reviewers in quality decisions, thereby impacting the state of our field.

1 Introduction

Cyber security and privacy are both exciting fields that weave together methodologies, theories and perspectives from various disciplines: mathematics, engineering, law, psychology and social sciences. As consequence, it gains a collective tapestry, a definite strength that exemplifies inter-disciplinary fields. However, the sharing of expertise and drawing on best practices of each discipline is a challenge. For example, the research area of human factors of cyber security and privacy is inter-disciplinary research area. It clearly benefits from the systematic design and reporting standards characteristic of the rigorous methodology of experimental psychology at its best.

© IFIP International Federation for Information Processing 2018
Published by Springer International Publishing AG 2018. All Rights Reserved
M. Hansen et al. (Eds.): Privacy and Identity 2017, IFIP AICT 526, pp. 243–262, 2018.
https://doi.org/10.1007/978-3-319-92925-5_17

Without guidelines, we rely on researchers to assess the quality of their designs and reporting. We ask program committees and reviewers to make best decisions on submissions to their best judgment. At the same time, these submissions impact the future of the field, may sow uncertainty in the research community and among policy makers alike, especially when they intend to transfer research findings into practice.

Workshop at IFIP Privacy and Identity Management Summerschool 2017. Our workshop on Evidence-Based Methods was intended as a first evaluation of a set of indicators we originally developed for a systematic literature review in the Research Institute in Science of Security (RISCS). We offered a presentation of each of the indicators and their specifications and offered participants a codebook and a marking sheet [9] as well as publications reporting experimental privacy studies.

Contribution. This paper aims to offer support for experimental cyber security and privacy research as scientific discipline. It provides nine clear guidelines to support the design and reporting of experiments and discusses challenges to dissemination from a first encounter with the community.

Outline. In the rest of the paper, we discuss our choice for the set of indicators before detailing each of the nine completeness indicators. For each indicator we proceed with theoretical background, benefits for fulfilling the indicators, outcome of not achieving them, practical steps to take in design and reporting, together with best practice examples. We then provide the lessons learnt from a first connection with the community before providing the discussion and conclusion.

2   Choice of Completeness Indicators

We chose indicators that contribute and build-up towards sound statistical inference. As a consequence, we addressed reproducibility, internal validity, correct statistical reporting and parameter estimation. We deliberately excluded criteria on external validity and ethics, but may consider them in future versions of the toolkit.

Benefits of this First Toolkit. The indicators are designed as a toolkit mainly for researchers, providing both a theoretical and a practical component. *First,* it acts as support for the design phase of a user study/experiment and aims to be one-stop resource. We provide a theoretical background with each indicator, substantiated with reasoning in the form of benefits for having the indicators and the outcome of not catering for them. *Second,* it acts as a companion for reporting via the practical steps to take, typical locations in articles and examples of good practice. Further, an additional benefit, is a clear list that can enable program committees to evaluate the reporting of research studies.

3   CI1: Upstream Replication

3.1   Theoretical Background

Similar to Coopamootoo and Groß [8], we call *replication* the attempt to recreate the conditions sufficient to obtaining a previously observed finding, a definition adapted from the Open Science Collaboration [7]. We refer to *upstream replication* when a study replicates existing studies or previously validated methods/instruments.

We note that replication of studies is an important research practice that provides confidence in the findings, where Cumming and Calin-Jageman [12] point out that rarely, if ever can a single finding give definitive answer to a research question, while the *Open Science Collaboration* notes the alarming discovery that a number of widely known and accepted research findings cannot be replicated [12].

We ask: *'Is the study reporting existing studies or methods?'*

Benefits of Fulfilling CI1. Researchers engaging in upstream replication are gaining sound foundations for their studies in employing methods whose exact properties are known and well-tested. For instance, for a measurement instrument we expect it to be known, which parameters of the population are measured. We expect of the instrument itself internal validity, repeatability and reproducibility. In the logic of the statistical inference of the given experiment we are then entitled to assume that the properties of the instrument are a given and will be the same for other researchers in the future. As a completeness indicator, CI1 thereby yields evidence whether the foundations of the given reported study are sound.

Outcome for Not Fulfilling CI1. Should evidence towards CI1 be missing, we would need to assume that the study did not pay attention to its sound foundations. This, in turn, means that the study is on uncertain footing. For the manipulation instruments, it is not assured that they cause the intended change in the participants reliably. For the measurement instruments, it is not assured that they measure the intended property. Consequently, instruments without evidence of sound *a priori* validation yield sources of errors that can well confound the main experiment and thereby put the overall inference in question.

3.2   Steps to Take

How to Achieve CI1. The key principle towards gaining evidence for CI1 is the use of validated tools. We recommend to select manipulation and measurement instruments that come with strong evidence of their validation and properties.

In the experiment design and execution, researchers will employ instruments *exactly* as validated, for example, using the defined scale and scoring sheet as provided. If adaptations are made to the instrument instructions, these will be documented.

In the reporting of the study, researcher will then document the evidence for their exact replication, for instance, by including the exact materials used and by citing the validation study they rely upon.

We note that documentation of instruments also apply to those employed for manipulation checks.

Typical Location in Articles. CI is reported in the methods section with subsections on measurement apparatus and manipulation apparatus or experimental conditions.

Reporting Example.

Example 1 (CI1 - Manipulation Apparatus, with amendments from Nwadike et al. [37]).
We induce a happy and sad affect via video stimulus, a mood induction protocol recommended by Westermann's critical review of different methods [47]. For happiness affect we used the restaurant scene from the movie *When Harry meets Sally* [clip length 155 seconds] while for sadness affect we used the dying scene from the movie *The Champ* [clip length 171 seconds]. We refer to Rottenberg et al. [40] to start and end the clips at the exact frames as previously validated.

Example 2 (CI1 - Manipulation Check, with amendments from [37]).
We used the 60-item full PANAS- X questionnaire [46] as manipulation check on the induced affect state. We focus on *sadness* and *joviality* as equivalent of happiness. The PANAS-X is scale is based on 5-point Likert-items anchored on 1 - very slightly or not at all, 2 - a little, 3 - moderately, 4 - quite a bit, and 5 - extremely. We anchored PANAS-X for affect "at the present moment."

Example 3 (CI1- Validated Measurement Apparatus).
"The State-Trait Anxiety Inventory for Adults (STAI-AD) [43] is a 40-question self-report questionnaire. We use the temporary construct of state anxiety, that is, "how you feel right now." It employs 4-point Likert items anchored on 1 – Not At All, 2 – Somewhat, 3 – Moderately So, and 4 – Very Much So."

3.3 Further Sources

Across sciences, a replication crisis has been observed. Prominently in psychology, a large scale replication endeavor by the Open Science Collaboration [7] of $N = 100$ studies across 3 psychology journals found that only 47% of the original effect sizes were in the 95% confidence interval of the replication effect size.

The Open Science Collaboration makes a case that research claims gain credibility when the supporting evidence undergoes sound replication [7]. We note that the replication needs to be done deliberately to increase the overall Positive Predictive Value of the results [25,34].

In security literature, Maxion [30] postulates that repeatability, reproducibility and validity are the main criteria differentiating a well designed experiment from those that are not.

4 CI2: Reproducibility

4.1 Theoretical Background

CI2 considers the enablement of *downstream replication*. While downstream replication includes *repeatability*, that is, whether a study can be replicated by the same researchers, CI2 considers especially, whether the study is sufficiently reported to be *reproducible* by *other* researchers. We refer to Maxion [30] for further discussion on repeatability and reproducibility.

CI2 establishes whether the reporting supports reproducibility, defined as the closeness of results obtained on the same test material under "changes of [...] conditions, technicians, apparatus, laboratories and so on" [13]. A key requirement of replicating existing studies is the availability of clear documentation, which ideally would entail a detailed step-by-step experimental protocol, which makes provisions for reproducibility.

The principle for reproducibility is diligent documentation of all variables of the study's lifecycle. We ask *'Is there correct reporting of manipulation apparatus, measurement apparatus, detailed procedure, sample size, demographics, sampling and recruitment method, contributing towards reproducibility?'*

Benefits of Fulfilling CI2. Offering sound reporting for reproducibility allows for downstream replication and contributes to the enablement of research synthesis in a field. This is crucial to enable falsification and hence empirical progress. Having a reproducible study at hand means that other researchers can test the theories evaluated in the given study and establish independent evidence on the theories, possibly falsifying the earlier result. Furthermore, replication studies inform the overall positive predictive value for the considered relations and allow for a meta analysis on the effect sizes and their confidence intervals.

Hence, as completeness indicator, CI2 checks whether evaluates whether the theories named in the given study can be empirically scrutinized in subsequent experimentation from the given reporting, and thereby whether the given study makes a sound contribution to empirical sciences.

Outcome for Not Fulfilling CI2. Should the evaluation for CI2 not offer evidence towards reproducibility, we need to assume that the given study cannot be replicated downstream. First, the lack of reproducibility leaves other researchers with a great ambiguity what was actually done. Second, following Poppers discussion on falsifiability [39], a study that cannot be reproduced does not actually yield strong empirical evidence because other researchers cannot execute the offered experiment to falsify the reported theory, which in turn casts doubt on the study advancing empirical knowledge.

4.2 Steps to Take

How to Achieve CI2. Researchers will provide detailed description of experiment design, including the all choices made, possibly supplemented by an experiment diagram, as well as the procedure executed in the experiment itself.

We note that documentation towards reproducibility will often also include planned analyses, which we consider under other CIs. A recommended practice in this case is to pre-commit the experiment and analysis plan at organizations such as the Open Science Framework[1] or AsPredicted[2]. As example, committed analysis plan and analysis report [22] published for password research [17].

Typical Location in Articles. C2 covers the whole method section including a detailed procedure, sample recruitment and demographics, manipulation and measurement instruments. Planned analysis will be in the analysis or the results section.

Reporting Example.

Example 4 (CI2- Demographics).
We refer to Table 3 of Kluever and Zanibbi [27] for a detailed demographics report that is relevant to the context of the study reported.

Example 5 (CI2 - Measurement Apparatus precisely referencing sources).
"We administered the NASA Task Load Index in an online form. The form exactly replicated the full NASA TLX questionnaire as specified on in *NASA Task Load Index* (TLX), v. 1.0, Appendix, pp. 13. [24]"

Example 6 (CI2- Procedure).
"The procedure consisted of (i) pre-task questionnaires for demographics and personality traits, (ii) a manipulation to induce cognitive depletion, (iii) a manipulation check on the level of depletion, (iv) a password entry for a mock-up GMail registration, and (v) a debriefing and memorability check one week after the task with a GMail login mockup. " This was followed with a details of each section.

4.3 Further Sources

First, for reproducibility of the experiment design, which is what this CI mainly focuses on, we refer to experiment design methodology [16,31,33].

Second, for reproducibility of the planned analyses, which involves the documentation of the plan as well as the recording of all the analyses done, we suggest inspiration from reproducibility principles from general computing science

---

[1] https://osf.io.
[2] https://aspredicted.org.

research [41] or more specific sources with focus on computation-supported scientific practice [45]. To render all computations, statistical analyses and graphs reproducible, we suggest the R framework knitr [48] as demonstrated within the analysis report [22].

5   CI3: Internal Validity

5.1   Theoretical Background

CI3 addresses internal validity of the experiment, which refers to the truth that can be ascribed to cause-effect relationships between independent variables (IV) and dependent variables (DV) [3], where the IV is a variable that is induced/manipulated and the DV is the variable that is observed/measured [32].

This CI asks for research questions and hypotheses that provide the foundations for null hypothesis significance testing (NHST) [36]. Operationalization enables systematic and explicit clarification of the predictors or independent variables, and hence the cause and manipulation, while the target variable or dependent variables clarify the effect, hence the measurements. Subject assignment points to whether and how participants were randomly assigned and balanced across experimental conditions.

Manipulation check refers to verification that the manipulation has actually taken effect, hence assuring systematic effects.

We ask *'Is there an explicit and operational specification of the RQs, null and alternative hypotheses, IVs, DVs, subject assignment method and manipulation checks?'*

Benefits of Fulfilling CI3. CI3 ensures internal validity and a solid statement of intention for Null Hypothesis Significance Testing (NHST) [36].

Outcome for Not Fulfilling CI3. Should evidence for CI3 be missing, we would need to assume other possible explanations for the cause-effect relationship investigated, that is that the reported design could involve variables contributing unsystematic effects. This in turn would mean that other researchers could not rely on the results reported.

5.2   Steps to Take

How to Achieve CI3. We propose in the first instance that following the step by step exercise we previously detailed [8] on 'An Exercise in Experiment Design' to be beneficial for internal validity. In particular, developing research questions, defining testable hypotheses, operationalizing hypotheses into IVs and DVs. For IVs, reseachers will answer 'What factor is being manipulated and influences the outcome?' For DVs, 'What is being measured?' and how can we measure the outcome of manipulation reliably.

Typical Location in Articles. The aims section can detail the research questions and hypotheses where as the method to include sub-sections on operationalizing the variables into measures and experimental conditions. The method section will also include subject assignment information.

Reporting Example.

Example 7 (CI3 - Research Question, from Cherapau et al. [5]).
"How availability of Touch ID sensor impacts users' selection of unlocking authentication secrets?".

Example 8 (CI3 - Hypotheses, from Cherapau et al. [5]).
For null hypotheses H_0: *"Use of Touch ID has no effect on the entropy of passcodes used for iPhone locking."* or *"Availability of Touch ID has no effect on ratio of users who lock their iPhones."*
For corresponding alternative hypotheses H_1: *"Use of Touch ID affects the entropy of passcodes used for iPhone locking."* or *"Availability of Touch ID increases the ratio of users who lock their iPhones"* [5].

Example 9 (CI3 - Subject Assignment, amended from Bursztein et al. [4]).
"Our task scheduler presented the CAPTCHAs to Turkers in the following way . . . Random Order - fully random, where any captcha from any scheme could follow any other."

We also refer to Example 2 for manipulation checks.

6 CI4: Limitations

6.1 Theoretical Background

CI4 establishes what other factors could affect the cause and effect relationship under investigation and hence limit validity including both internal and external validity. This CI is related to the requirement of controlled variables for experiment design, that is the assurance that an observed change in the dependent variable is a result of a systematic change in the independent variable [32].

We ask *'Was there a discussion on the limitations, possible confounders, biases and assumptions made?'*

Benefits of Fulfilling CI4. CI4 provides transparency of validity and assurance that other possible explanations for the stated causal relations, have been considered. This in turn provides confidence in the reported results.

Outcome for Not Fulfilling CI4. Should the limitations not have been discussed in the experiment report, we would need to assume that the researchers might have failed to control variables that impact the internal validity of the experiment. This puts the reported effects into question.

6.2   Steps to Take

How to Achieve CI4. Researchers are (1) to evaluate experimental designs for alternative explanations that could influence the observed effects, such as identifying confounding and controlling for variables, (2) to make explicit the boundaries and of the design, such as whether a convenient sample was used, and (3) acknowledge the limits in interpretations that can be inferred from the findings, such as whether the results are a correct reflection of estimates for the general population.

A discussion of the limits and boundaries of the study, identification of possible confounding variables whose presence affect the relationship under study, and possible assumptions made in setup, are all valuable inputs that strengthen the validity of the experiment.

Typical Location in Articles. While researchers may report and discuss limitations throughout the article, it is preferred to define a dedicated limitations section, that shows clarity and researcher awareness of the limits of their design.

Reporting Example.

> *Example 10 (CI4 - Sampling bias, from Akhawe & Felt [1]).*
> *"The participants in our field study are not a random population sample. Our study only represents users who opt in to browser telemetry programs. This might present a bias. The users who volunteered might be more likely to click through dialogs and less concerned about privacy. Thus, the clickthrough rates we measure could be higher than population-wide rates."*

7   CI5: Reporting Standard

7.1   Theoretical Background

Statistical reporting guidelines helps the reader, reviewer, policy maker to gain confidence in the reported statistical analysis and results. As example, we propose reporting recommendations of the American Psychology Association (APA) [2] as quality standard.

We ask *'Was the result reported in the APA style?'*

Benefits of Fulfilling CI5. Reporting standards provide a degree of comprehensiveness in the information that is reported for empirical investigations. Uniform reporting standards make it easier to generalize within and across fields, to understand implications of individual studies and supports research synthesis. Comprehensive reporting also supports decision makers in policy and practice towards understanding how the research was conducted [2].

Outcome for Not Fulfilling CI5. The impact of not fulfilling CI5 opens gaps and lead to questioning research quality, reuse and reproducibility.

7.2   Steps to Take

How to Achieve CI5. Researchers are to closely adhere to statistical reporting standards such as the APA [2] and reporting statistical inference as recommended whether in paragraphs, tables or figures. This include reporting actual p-values, that is not only whether the p-value is less that α, and effect sizes and confidence intervals.

Typical Location in Articles. Reporting standards usually focus on the specification of the results section, yet can also indicate the format of a structured abstract or the structure of the overall publication.

Reporting Example.

Example 11 (CI5 - with amendments from Coopamootoo et al. [10]).
We computed a one-way ANOVA. "There was a statistically significant effect of the experiment condition on the password strength score, $F(2, 63) = 6.716$, $p = .002 < .05$. We measure the effect size ... $\eta^2 = .176, 95\%$ CI $[0.043, 0.296]$ [...]."

---

8   CI6: Test Statistic

8.1   Theoretical Background

The reporting on the test statistic offers a precise interface on the result of the computed statistical analysis. This data allows for a future analysis of *a posteriori* likelihoods, such as in a Positive Predictive Value (PPV) [25]. Simply put, this data helps other researchers to ascertain whether the result could be a false positive or not.

We consider the precise documentation of the outcome of the statistical test. For instance, for a t-test we would expect to learn the t-value as well as the degrees of freedom, along with the exact p-value computed for this t.

We ask *'Did the result statement include test statistic and p-value?'*

Benefits of Fulfilling CI6. If the test statistic is fully specified, we gain important data for the subsequent analysis of the result. From the consistency of the reported test statistic and the p-value, we gain confidence in the correct reporting. In addition, the data includes sufficient redundancy that others can validate the presented p-values or use the reporting of the test statistic to compute standardized effect sizes for subsequent meta-analysis.

Outcome for Not Fulfilling CI6. Should the test static or the p-values not be reported, e.g., by just stating that the result "is statistically significant, $p < .05$, we lose a lot of information. We could neither ascertain the confidence level of the significance nor the internal consistency of the reported test. Hence, the reported result will lack internal credibility and not be particularly trustworthy.

8.2 Steps to Take

How to Achieve CI6. The key principle is to report sufficient data, such that others can cross-check the reported values and use them in further research synthesis. Usually, this involves reporting the test statistic itself, the degrees of freedom vis-à-vis of the sample size, and the exact p-value. When comparisons between conditions are made, then the descriptive statistics for the relevant conditions should be provided (e.g., mean and standard deviation for conditions of a t-test).

Typical Location in Articles. The test statistics will be specified in the results section of the paper. As a rule of thumb, for each result we claim as being statistically significant, we will provide the test statistic supporting that claim as suffix.

Reporting Example. We refer to the Example 11 for test statists and p-value reporting.

9   CI7: Assumptions

9.1   Theoretical Background

Statistical tests can easily lead us astray if their assumptions are not fulfilled: they may produce spurious results. Even though some tests have been shown to be somewhat robust against borderline violations of their underlying assumptions, the burden of proof that the assumptions were sufficiently fulfilled is on the researchers who conducted the test.

In general, the exact type of test in a family needs to be specified to inform which assumptions come to bear. For instance, the assumptions of an *independent-samples* t-test will be different from a *dependent-samples* t-test. Similarly, it needs to specified whether the test is "one-tailed" or "two-tailed" to put the reported p-values into perspective.

To ascertain whether the statistical analyses were correctly employed on the data, statistical assumptions need to be made explicit in reporting. For example, the assumptions for parametric tests, in general, are normally distributed data, homogeneity of variance, interval data and independence [15]. Parametric statistical tests often require a systematic treatment of outliers.

We ask '*Were significance level α and test statistics properties and assumptions appropriately stated?*'

Benefits of Fulfilling CI7. A precise specification of the test used and explicit documentation of the assumptions checked gives the reader confidence that the statistical tools were appropriately chosen and employed diligently.

Outcome for Not Fulfilling CI7. Should test properties and assumptions not be documented, we need to assume that researchers did not establish that they could reliably employ the statistical test. Consequently, the reported test statistics and p-values could be off and not be relied upon.

9.2   Steps to Take

How to Achieve CI7. One would choose the designated significance level *a priori* and state it explicitly. Similarly, the researchers need to establish whether the test will be one- or two-tailed in advance. Researchers check whether the data meets the assumptions of the planned statistical test and explicitly report whether and how the data met the test assumptions. Decisions on how the data was treated (e.g., outlier management) need to be reported explicitly.

We emphasize that complex statistical models (such as regressions) usually require comprehensive post-hoc model diagnostics to evaluate whether the model is sound.

Typical Location in Articles. The treatment of assumptions is documented in the results section, either close to the report of the statistical test or in a separate subsection. Often it will support the confidence in the reported results, if a comprehensive analysis report is published alongside the research paper that documents all checks of assumptions and diagnostics, transformations of the data, and decisions made.

Reporting Example.

Example 12 (CI7 - Significance level α & test statistics properties, from Groß et al. [23]).
"All inferential statistics are computed with two-tailed tests and at an α level of .05"

Example 13 (CI7 - Test statistics assumptions, from Groß et al. [23]).
"The distribution of the Passwordmeter password strength score is measured on interval level and is not significantly different from a normal distribution, Saphiro-Wilk, $D(100) = .99$, $p = .652 > .05$" [a].
"We computed Levene's test for the homogeneity of variances. For the password meter scores, the variances were not significantly unequal."

---

[a] We note here that numerical normality tests, such as Saphiro-Wilk may have too little sensitivity for small sample sizes and too much sensitivity for large sample sizes. [44]

10   CI8: Confidence Intervals on Effects

10.1   Theoretical Background

An effect size estimates the magnitude of an effect, an unknown parameter of the population, given the observed data of an experiment. Confidence interval procedures on the effect estimate the range of plausible values for the population parameter, if the experiment were repeated independently infinitely many times. We note that this is a frequentist view, in which the confidence level applies to the procedure. For instance, a series of 95% confidence intervals will tend to contain the population parameter on average 95% of the intervals.

Effect sizes and their confidence interval offer an informative view on an experiment's observed effect magnitudes. Consequently, the APA guidelines [2] state that "estimates of appropriate effect sizes and confidence intervals are the minimum expectations." QI8 includes that the effect sizes are reported in a easily human-interpretable form.

We ask 'Were the appropriate the effect sizes and confidence intervals (CI) reported?'

An effect that is statistically significant is not necessarily scientifically significant or important. To draw conclusions on an effect's importance or practical implications, we consult the magnitude of the effect, its effect size [6].

In estimation theory, the effect size (ES) provides a point estimate of effect in the population, while the confidence interval (CI) provides the interval estimate. While we endorse the use of estimation theory [12,19], we note that interpreting confidence intervals correctly requires diligence [35]. Notably, it is a fallacy to interpret a post-data X% confidence interval to have a X% probability to include the true population parameter.

Benefits of Fulfilling CI8. CI8 evaluates the robust reporting of effect magnitudes through parameter and interval estimation, which yields, in turn, the foundation for future meta-analysis and research synthesis.

Outcome for Not Fulfilling CI8. Without effect size estimate, we only have the significance of the results and p—values to go on. However, we will miss out on information on the magnitude of the claimed effects. For example a significant p-value does not say how important the observed effect is: it could well be trivial, and neither contribute much to research nor vouch for changes to practice.

10.2   Steps to Take

How to Achieve CI8. To compute effect sizes in experiments together with their confidence intervals and to report these in publications. Literature already provides a number of manuals and research articles on computing the different families of effect sizes [18,29] To also refer to the *New Statistics* [12] for the estimation approach, effect-size and confidence intervals.

Typical Location in Articles. Effect sizes and their confidence intervals are documented in the results section, either stated as a suffix after the p-value of the corresponding statistical inference or provided in dedicated tables.

Reporting Example. We refer to the Example 11 for effect size and confidence interval reporting.

10.3   Further Sources

Kirk [26] and Cumming [11] debated that the current research practice of exclusive focusing on a dichotomous reject-nonreject decision strategy of null hypothesis testing that can impeded scientific progress. Rather, they posit, the focus should be on the magnitude of effects, that is the practical significance of effects and the steady accumulation of knowledge. They advise to switch from the much disputed NHST to effect sizes, estimation and cumulation of evidence.

11   CI9: Statistical Inference

11.1   Theoretical Background

CI9 evaluates the overall correctness of the statistical inference, that is, how statements on statistical significance are expressed and what conclusions are drawn from the statement. As such, CI9 relies to some extent on observations made with respect to preceding completeness indicators.

We ask *'Was the significance and hypothesis testing decision interpreted correctly and put in context of effect size and sample size/power?'*

Nickerson [36] offers a comprehensive overview of the controversies around *Null Hypothesis Significance Testing (NHST)*, while Maxwell and Delaney [31, p.48] and Goodman [21] point to p-Value misconceptions, Morey et al. [35] analyze confidence interval fallacies and Ioannidis [25] argues "why most published research findings are false."

The evaluation in our work is founded on Nickerson's review [36] on misconceptions around NHST, which include:

- p misperceived as the probability that the hypothesis be true and $1 - p$ misperceived as the probability that the alternative hypothesis be true,
- a small p considered as evidence that the results be replicable,
- a small value of p misinterpreted as a treatment effect of large magnitude,
- statistical significance considered as theoretical or practical significance,
- significance level α misinterpreted as the probability that a Type I error will be made,
- Type II error rate β considered to mean the probability that the null hypothesis be false,
- failing to reject the null hypothesis misrepresented as equivalent to demonstrating it to be true,
- failure to reject the null hypothesis misinterpreted as evidence of a failed experiment.

While Nickerson's observations are concerned with the correct interpretation of NHST, for us CI9 also includes preparing the ground with population and sampling as well as *a priori* hypothesis specification, and post-hoc concerns such as multiple-comparison corrections.

Benefits of Fulfilling CI9. Evidence towards CI9 convinces us of the robustness and diligence of the statistical inference made, because common pitfalls and fallacies have been avoided. The result statement will offer a sound starting point for the interpretation of the findings.

Outcome for Not Fulfilling CI9. Should there be evidence of incorrect statistical inference or the presence of fallacies, we would need to assume that the researchers interpretation of said results be tainted by the misinterpretations and misrepresentations made. Hence, the overall conclusion of the study would be put into question. We perceive reviews on misconceptions and fallacies as important guard rails [21, 31, 35, 36].

11.2   Steps to Take

How to Achieve CI9. To achieve CI9, we recommend to investigate how p-values and confidence intervals can and cannot be interpreted. The key principle here is diligence: The devil is in the details.

Typical Location in Articles. The correctness of the statistical inference is prepared by the documentation of the *a priori* elements of a study in the methods section, supported by the correct reporting of statistical tests in the results and finally completed by the interpretation of the outcomes in the discussion.

Reporting Example.

> **Example 14 (CI9 - Type I error correction).**
> *"Given the number of comparative t-tests computed on the data set, we compute a multiple comparisons correction, where differences marked with a dagger † in Table 1 are statistically significant under Bonferroni-Holm correction for all comparisons made."*

12   Lessons Learnt from the Workshop

12.1   Aim

To assess whether and how the set of nine indicators could be applied in practice.

12.2   Method

Procedure. We gave a small presentation of the hallmarks of experiment design (following our 2016 workshop at the same venue) and then presented the nine indicators as a set of 'Quality Indicators', where quality assessment is a stage employed within Systematic Literature Review procedures [14]. These nine indicators were developed as a checklist of factors to be evaluated within experimental studies, as part of a UK Research Institute in Science of Cyber Security (RISCS) funded project, which had the overall aim to evaluate the state of the art in evidence-based methods in cyber security and privacy.

Prior to the workshop we developed a first version of a codebook which specified each of the indicators in terms of sub-criteria and examples and a codesheet providing a marking scheme.

Next, we facilitated open coding with the aim to *extract concepts* from the free-form text. We provided participants with (1) two example research articles reporting user experiments in the context of privacy [20, 28], (2) the CI specification as a codebook [9] and (3) the marking as a codesheet [9].

Participants. Participants worked in two groups to review the two articles. $N = 9$ participants attended the workshop, 6 female, 3 male. The 7 participants who provided their age had mean age 31.86 years ($SD = 8.28$). 5 participants were from a usable privacy and security background, while others were from other areas of privacy and security. Participants' first language varied (4 German, 2 English and 1 Tamil, 2 did not answer). With the sole aim to gauge participants' expertise, we offered participants three Likert questions to rate their frequency of use of evidence-based methods (from 1 – 'Never' to 5 – 'A great deal'), their skills (from 1 – 'Poor' to 5 – 'Excellent') and their familiarity (from 1 – 'Not at all familiar' to 5 – 'Extremely familiar') in designing experiments. Participants reported using evidence-based methods such as experiments with a median value of 3, to have a median skill level of 2 and median familiarity in designing experiments of 2.

12.3 Results

We provide results in the form of participant feedback and recommendations.

Practical Requirement. Participants recommended shaping of the indicators as a toolkit that can readily be employed by the community. This involves designing clear sections in the tool set that researchers and committee members can pick up. As a result, following the workshop, we have revised the indicators to match these requirements, as presented through sections CI1 to CI9. In this paper we provided the theoretical underpinnings for each CI together with 'Steps to Take' and 'Examples'.

Design Requirement. Participants noted the time commitment required if one does not know what to look for when applying the toolkit in a reviewing exercise. To address this, we provide clear examples for each CI together with typical sections in research papers that provide support for criteria fulfilling each CI.

Ethical Considerations. Participants suggested to factor in ethical considerations, as aspect of experimental reporting we omitted but foresee its benefits for completeness of reporting.

13 Discussion

Community Progress. A toolkit, such as the one we provide here, contributes to a standard to aspire to. It supports the community in developing the skills to design, run and report rigorous experiments in cyber security. At the same time, while the lack of defined best practices requires individual researchers to determine what the standards they adhere to, our toolkit offers a common ground.

It also supports the reviewing process and program committee decisions, by offering syntactic criteria to check for the completeness of scientific reporting. In addition, it contributes to a culture of well designed and reported experiments that can serve as notable examples to follow in the field.

Added Value for Researchers. We believe this toolkit can be a valuable ingredient for inter-disciplinary security and privacy research. It combines theoretical background and practical guidelines to support foundations in experiment design and reporting. By following the requirements of participants as voiced during the workshop, we provided clear sections that can be picked up by researchers and committee members. It supports both novice and experienced usable security and privacy researchers. While learning a methodology takes time for any novice, we believe that this toolkit may support the learning the nitty-gritty of experimental methodology by being designed as a one-stop resource. For more advanced researchers, it presents itself as a checklist and offers some good practices to follow.

Not Exhaustive. We observe that our current toolkit is not exhaustive and foresee that it will grow as discussions advance within the community. In line with this, we plan to facilitate further discussion exercises within the community and to seek ways for engagement.

14 Conclusion

This paper provides a first toolkit for experimental research in cyber security and privacy with a sampler of theoretical foundations and practical guidelines. I can support a study's lifecycle from conception, design, analysis and reporting to replication. It provides a companion for novice researchers as well as reviewers needing a structured checklist. Although the toolkit is certainly not exhaustive, it may still grow with discussions and evidence-based projects within the community. We believe that already in the current form, it can support a culture of robustly designed and reported experiments, thereby contributing to empirical research in the field.

Acknowledgment. We are indebted to the participants of the "Workshop on Evidence-Based Methods" at the 2017 IFIP Summerschool on Privacy and Identity Management for their generous feedback. This work was supported by the UK Research Institute in Science of Cyber Security (RISCS II) project "Scientific Methods in Cyber Security: Systematic Evaluation and Community Knowledge Base for Evidence-Based Methods in Cyber Security." It was in parts funded by the ERC Starting Grant CAS-CAde (GA n°716980).

References

1. Akhawe, D., Felt, A.P.: Alice in warningland: a large-scale field study of browser security warning effectiveness. In: USENIX Security Symposium, vol. 13 (2013)
2. American Psychological Association (APA): Publication manual. American Psychological Association, 6th revised edn (2009)
3. Brewer, M.B.: Research design and issues of validity. In: Handbook of Research Methods in Social and Personality Psychology, pp. 3–16 (2000)
4. Bursztein, E., Bethard, S., Fabry, C., Mitchell, J.C., Jurafsky, D.: How good are humans at solving captchas? A large scale evaluation. In: 2010 IEEE Symposium on Security and Privacy (SP), pp. 399–413. IEEE (2010)
5. Cherapau, I., Muslukhov, I., Asanka, N., Beznosov, K.: On the impact of touch id on iphone passcodes. In: SOUPS, pp. 257–276 (2015)
6. Cohen, J.: A power primer. Psychol. Bull. **112**(1), 155 (1992)
7. Open Science Collaboration, et al.: Estimating the reproducibility of psychological science. Science **349**(6251), aac4716 (2015)
8. Coopamootoo, K.P.L., Groß, T.: Evidence-based methods for privacy and identity management. In: Lehmann, A., Whitehouse, D., Fischer-Hübner, S., Fritsch, L., Raab, C. (eds.) Privacy and Identity 2016. IAICT, vol. 498, pp. 105–121. Springer, Cham (2016). https://doi.org/10.1007/978-3-319-55783-0_9
9. Coopamootoo, K.P., Groß, T.: A codebook for experimental research: the nifty nine indicators v1.0. Technical report 1514, Newcastle University, November 2017

10. Coopamootoo, K.P., Groß, T.: An empirical investigation of security fatigue- the case of password choice after solving a captcha. In: The LASER Workshop: Learning from Authoritative Security Experiment Results, LASER 2017. USENIX Association (2017)
11. Cumming, G.: The new statistics: why and how. Psychol. Sci. **25**(1), 7–29 (2014)
12. Cumming, G., Calin-Jageman, R.: Introduction to the New Statistics: Estimation, Open Science, and Beyond. Routledge, Abingdon (2016)
13. Everitt, B.: Cambridge Dictionary of Statistics. Cambridge University Press, Cambridge (1998)
14. Evidence-Based Software Engineering (EBSE): Guidelines for performing systematic literature reviews in software engineering. EBSE Technical report EBSE-2007-01, Keele University and University of Durham, July 2007
15. Field, A.: Discovering Statistics Using IBM SPSS Statistics. Sage, Thousand Oaks (2013)
16. Field, A., Hole, G.: How to Design and Report Experiments. Sage, Thousand Oaks (2003)
17. Fordyce, T., Green, S., Groß, T.: Investigation of the effect of fear and stress on password choice. In: Proceedings of the 7th ACM Workshop on Socio-Technical Aspects in Security and Trust (STAST 2017) (2017)
18. Fritz, C.O., Morris, P.E., Richler, J.J.: Effect size estimates: current use, calculations, and interpretation. J. Exp. Psychol.: Gen. **141**(1), 2 (2012)
19. Gardner, M.J., Altman, D.G.: Confidence intervals rather than P values: estimation rather than hypothesis testing. Br. Med. J. (Clin. Res. Ed.) **292**(6522), 746–750 (1986)
20. Gideon, J., Cranor, L., Egelman, S., Acquisti, A.: Power strips, prophylactics, and privacy, oh my! In: Proceedings of the Second Symposium on Usable Privacy and Security, pp. 133–144. ACM (2006)
21. Goodman, S.: A dirty dozen: twelve p-value misconceptions. In: Seminars in hematology, vol. 45, pp. 135–140. Elsevier (2008)
22. Groß, T.: Analysis report - investigation of the effect of fear and stress on password choice. OSF Report, Open Science Framework (2017). https://osf.io/3cd9h/
23. Groß, T., Coopamootoo, K., Al-Jabri, A.: Effect of cognitive depletion on password choice. In: The LASER Workshop: Learning from Authoritative Security Experiment Results (LASER 2016), pp. 55–66. USENIX Association (2016)
24. Hart, S.G., Staveland, L.E.: Development of NASA-TLX (task load index): results of empirical and theoretical research. Adv. Psychol. **52**, 139–183 (1988)
25. Ioannidis, J.P.: Why most published research findings are false. PLoS Med. **2**(8), e124 (2005)
26. Kirk, R.E.: The importance of effect magnitude. In: Handbook of Research Methods in Experimental Psychology, pp. 83–105 (2003)
27. Kluever, K.A., Zanibbi, R.: Balancing usability and security in a video captcha. In: Proceedings of the 5th Symposium on Usable Privacy and Security, p. 14. ACM (2009)
28. Korff , S., Böhme, R.: Too much choice: end-user privacy decisions in the context of choice proliferation. In: Symposium on Usable Privacy and Security (SOUPS), pp. 69–87 (2014)
29. Lakens, D.: Calculating and reporting effect sizes to facilitate cumulative science: a practical primer for t-tests and ANOVAs. Front. Psychol. **4** (2013)
30. Maxion, R.: Making experiments dependable. In: Jones, C.B., Lloyd, J.L. (eds.) Dependable and Historic Computing. LNCS, vol. 6875, pp. 344–357. Springer, Heidelberg (2011). https://doi.org/10.1007/978-3-642-24541-1_26

31. Maxwell, S.E., Delaney, H.D.: Designing experiments and analyzing data: a model comparison perspective, vol. 1, 2nd edn. Psychology Press (2004)
32. Miller, S.: Experimental Design and Statistics. Routledge, Abingdon (2005)
33. Montgomery, D.C.: Design and Analysis of Experiments, 8th edn. Wiley, Hoboken (2012)
34. Moonesinghe, R., Khoury, M.J., Janssens, A.C.J.: Most published research findings are false–but a little replication goes a long way. PLoS Med. 4(2), e28 (2007)
35. Morey, R.D., Hoekstra, R., Rouder, J.N., Lee, M.D., Wagenmakers, E.-J.: The fallacy of placing confidence in confidence intervals. Psychon. Bull. Rev. 23(1), 103–123 (2016)
36. Nickerson, R.S.: Null hypothesis significance testing: a review of an old and continuing controversy. Psychol. Methods 5(2), 241 (2000)
37. Nwadike, U., Groß, T., Coopamootoo, K.P.L.: Evaluating users' affect states: towards a study on privacy concerns. In: Lehmann, A., Whitehouse, D., Fischer-Hübner, S., Fritsch, L., Raab, C. (eds.) Privacy and Identity 2016. IAICT, vol. 498, pp. 248–262. Springer, Cham (2016). https://doi.org/10.1007/978-3-319-55783-0_17
38. Peisert, S., Bishop, M.: How to design computer security experiments. In: Futcher, L., Dodge, R. (eds.) WISE 2007. IIFIP, vol. 237, pp. 141–148. Springer, Boston, MA (2007). https://doi.org/10.1007/978-0-387-73269-5_19
39. Popper, K.: The Logic of Scientific Discovery. Routledge, Abingdon (2005)
40. Rottenberg, J., Ray, R., Gross, J.: Emotion elicitation using films. In: Coan, J.A., Allen, J.J.B. (eds.) Handbook of Emotion Elicitation and Assessment (2007)
41. Sandve, G.K., Nekrutenko, A., Taylor, J., Hovig, E.: Ten simple rules for reproducible computational research. PLoS Comput. Biol. 9(10), e1003285 (2013)
42. Schechter, S.: Common pitfalls in writing about security and privacy human subjects experiments, and how to avoid them. Microsoft (2013)
43. Spielberger, C.D., Gorsuch, R.L., Lushene, R.E.: Manual for the state-trait anxiety inventory (1970)
44. Laerd Statistics: Testing for normality. https://statistics.laerd.com. Accessed 20 Jan 2018
45. Stodden, V., Leisch, F., Peng, R.D.: Implementing Reproducible Research. CRC Press, Boca Raton (2014)
46. Watson, D., Clark, L.A.: The PANAS-X: manual for the positive and negative affect schedule-expanded form (1999)
47. Westermann, R., Stahl, G., Hesse, F.: Relative effectiveness and validity of mood induction procedures: analysis. Eur. J. Soc. Psychol. 26, 557–580 (1996)
48. Xie, Y.: knitr: a comprehensive tool for reproducible research in R. Implement. Reprod. Res. 1, 20 (2014)

Assistive Robots

Privacy and Socially Assistive Robots - A Meta Study

Tanja Heuer, Ina Schiering$^{(\boxtimes)}$, and Reinhard Gerndt

Ostfalia University of Applied Sciences, Wolfenbüttel, Germany
{ta.heuer,i.schiering,r.gerndt}@ostfalia.de

Abstract. This paper investigates studies about socially assistive robotics with focus on privacy and ethical concerns. Therefore, the privacy aspects are considered and the concerns expressed by users with regard to privacy are examined additionally. It becomes clear, there are still a lot of concerns regarding the use of robots, that's why robots are not well accepted so far. To get a more transparent view on that, two models are introduced which might improve the understanding towards important privacy aspects.

Keywords: Socially assistive robot · Robot ethics · HRI
Human-robot interaction · Human-robot friendship · Machine ethics
Privacy

1   Introduction

Some years ago robots were exclusively present in research laboratories and industrial facilities. Because of a miniaturization of components and the decline in price, robots are increasingly used for personal applications as e.g. smart home applications and social interaction now. According to the International Federation of Robotics (IFR) "about 5.4 million service robots for personal and domestic use were sold [in 2015], 16% more than in 2014." [24]. Two thirds of those "are robots for domestic tasks, including vacuum cleaning, lawn-mowing, window cleaning and other types" [24] and it is estimated that these numbers will rise up to 30 million until 2019. "Sales of robots for elderly and handicap assistance will be about 37,500 units in the period of 2016–2019. This market is expected to increase substantially within the next 20 years" [24].

Tasks of domestic robots (for elder care) are mainly categorized into three areas [46]: "(1) to assist the elder[s], and/or their carers in daily tasks; (2) to help monitor their behavior and health; and (3) to provide companionship". The aim of social robots is a (semi-) autonomously interaction with humans in a respectful way [35]. Several of the intended domestic tasks require sensors as e.g. cameras or microphones to allow individualized user interactions. Users of domestic robots expect a conversation in a "natural human-like manner" [19]. Because of these user expectations, robots are often considered as living beings

M. Hansen et al. (Eds.): Privacy and Identity 2017, IFIP AICT 526, pp. 265–281, 2018.
https://doi.org/10.1007/978-3-319-92925-5_18

like humans or animals and are treated as friends that accompany humans in their private environment [21]. Robots will be dangerously ubiquitous, but, as for other smart devices as e.g. smart phones, wearables, etc. that accompany users in their daily life, the privacy risks are not obvious. Hence, privacy should be an important aspect in robotics, but is not taken into consideration in a satisfactory way yet. At the moment robots are designed from an engineering perspective with a main focus on functionality. Privacy and other ethical aspects of robotics are investigated in general, but not adequately integrated in the engineering process of robotics.

In this paper the role of privacy in "Robotic Ethics" is investigated in the context of user studies with assistive robots. There the perception concerning privacy of different user groups is investigated and the effect of the type of robot on the perception of privacy is examined. Approaches to make privacy risks more transparent are discussed as a first step to foster the consideration of privacy in robot design processes.

The considered so called Socially Assistive Robots (SAR) together with an approach for categorization are described in Sect. 3. An overview of ethical concerns towards robotic is presented in Sect. 4. The role of privacy in this ethical context is emphasized. In Sect. 5 an overview about Socially Assistive Robots is given and privacy concerns of users are stated and evaluated in Sect. 6 followed by discussion and conclusion.

2   Methodology

The basis of the meta study is a literature survey. The retrieval was based on queries in databases and search engines for scientific publications, i.e Google Scholar and ScienceDirect. In addition, the following relevant conferences were considered ISCR (International Conference on Social Robotics), ISRR (International Symposium on Robotics Research) and RO-MAN (Robot and Human Interactive Communication). Main key words as "social robot", "robot/robotic and privacy", "robot/robotic study" and "robot/robotic and ethical aspects" were used. In addition, other surveys as Leite et al. [36] who already gave an overview of social robots for long-term interactions, are considered. Because of an increasing use of robots for home and health care the collection of papers has been limited to the last ~10 years.

Investigated robots are sorted into categories explained in Sect. 3. The categorization which is adopted by Fong et al. [18] points out the different types of robots and their appearances. Based on this categorization, it should be examined whether the perception of privacy depends on the appearance or on specific functionalities. Further we want to investigate, how participants and users perceive privacy issues and how users express their concerns in the context of the studies.

For each paper the duration, target group and the number of participants is described and summarized in Fig. 5. Duration gives an overview of the length of the studies. If a study for example just lasts one hour, the user may not think about privacy risks of the investigated robot. Also the target group is important for the assessment of human-robot interaction (HRI), since children might interact in a different way with robots than older people. The number of participants is also important. Studies with a larger number of participants could achieve more significant results about the perception of a robot.

The main focus in this meta study is on the ethical, especially privacy concerns, which are mentioned by the users during the HRI studies. With the introduction of individualized conversation between robots and users, the utilization of sensors, e.g. cameras and microphones in addition to standard sensors for autonomous behavior as ultrasonic sensors or laser range scanners, increases. But even though sensors use is increasing, it is not transparent to the user which data is recorded, stored and transmitted. In the studies users express skepticism, interest and curiosity. It is interesting to investigate, which of these attitudes prevails.

3   Socially Assistive Robots

In the context of this study social robots are in the focus. A robot is called social, when it is able to react to human actions in a (semi-) autonomously way either by speech or movements. Movement in this sense includes moving only the head or another part of the robot as an arm or a leg. The area of socially assistive robots (SAR) is defined as "a class of robots that is the intersection of assistive robotics [...] and socially interactive robotics [...]" [14]. Hence, socially assistive robots are able to substantially support human beings in many areas of their daily life: companionship, entertainment, security, transportation, education, customer service, personal assistance, sales and tourist guidance [46]. A huge variety of robots are developed to realize one or more of these tasks. Robots in this sense are divided into four categories defined by Fong et al. [18] as described in the following.

Functional. The focus of this category is the practical benefit of the robots. These robots are designed with the focus on the intended use. For instance, requirements in health care like a storage space or a removable tray need to be taken into account for the construction [39]. As an example the robot *Pillo* serves as a reminder of medication (see Fig. 1). It is able to store medicine and to dispense the medicine depending on the needs of the user [1]. Therefore it has a closed compartment for the medicine with restricted access and a special place is designated for a glass of water. Although it is designed in an abstract functional way, it shows eyes on its screen to look sympathetic.

Caricatured. Cartoons and caricatures are the background of this category. In cartoons, for example, characteristic features of a creature are particularly emphasized. By highlighting these features, other elements are neglected. The attention of the user should be focused on the emphasized part. Scheeff et al.

Fig. 1. Pillo (https:// assets.entrepreneur. com/content/3x2/1300/ 20160630152708-pillo. jpeg.)

Fig. 2. Care-O-bot 4 (http://www.care-o-bot- 4.de/.)

Fig. 3. Paro (https:// www.thestar.com/life/ breakingthrough/2014/ 06/09/robot_gets_seal_of_ approval.html.)

used cartooning techniques to design the robot *Sparky* [43]. This robot looks like a small turtle with focus on the face and the facial expressions. Another example is the *Care-O-bot 4* (see Fig. 2). It is equipped with arms for fetch-and-carry tasks and wheels instead of legs for moving. The head is a touch screen and it represents a face by showing abstract eyes as the *Pillo*.

Zoomorphic. A third design of robots is the imitation of zoomorphic creatures. There the robot design is either based on realistic or fantasy animals. In the context of children and elder care animal-like creatures are often used, eg. *Paro* and *Aibo* for entertainment. Fong et al. [18] suggest that for humans it is easier to build relationships to animals and interactions are possible on a lower level. These robots often do not have a wide range of functionalities but mainly act as a companion. *Paro*, a seal robot is able to move its head, tail and the eyes when it is touched (see Fig. 3). Additionally it is able to express a sense of well-being by sounds.

Anthropomorphic. Anthropomorphism signifies the attribution of human appearances, behaviors and other characteristics to non-human-objects. The aim of anthropomorphic robots is to make human like actions of a robot easier to understand for human beings [13]. A meaningful human-robot interaction in a social way is supposedly easier when the robot has a physical and a mental personification [6,42]. DiSalvo et al. [11] suggest "that interaction through speech and movement will greatly effect the perception of humanness in robots". With the humanness of a robot, other deficits can be covered up.

4   Ethical Concerns in SAR and the Role of Privacy

In this section different concepts of ethical concerns in SAR are introduced. In 1942 Isaac Asimov created the first general three laws of robotics stating that a robot must obey a human being and is not allowed to hurt human beings. With increasing interest in the use of robots in various application areas, these

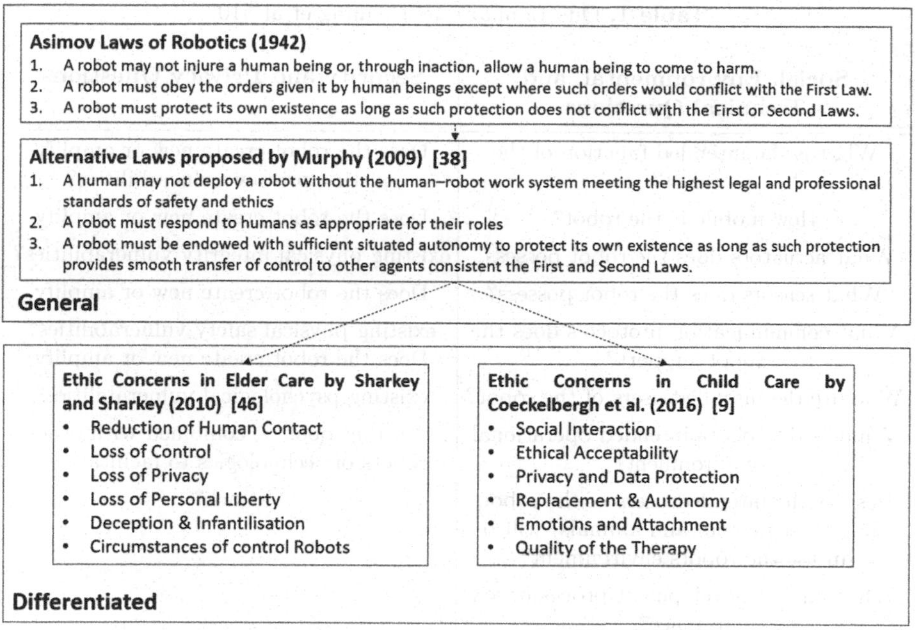

Asimov Laws of Robotics (1942)
1. A robot may not injure a human being or, through inaction, allow a human being to come to harm.
2. A robot must obey the orders given it by human beings except where such orders would conflict with the First Law.
3. A robot must protect its own existence as long as such protection does not conflict with the First or Second Laws.

Alternative Laws proposed by Murphy (2009) [38]
1. A human may not deploy a robot without the human–robot work system meeting the highest legal and professional standards of safety and ethics
2. A robot must respond to humans as appropriate for their roles
3. A robot must be endowed with sufficient situated autonomy to protect its own existence as long as such protection provides smooth transfer of control to other agents consistent the First and Second Laws.

General

Ethic Concerns in Elder Care by Sharkey and Sharkey (2010) [46]
- Reduction of Human Contact
- Loss of Control
- Loss of Privacy
- Loss of Personal Liberty
- Deception & Infantilisation
- Circumstances of control Robots

Ethic Concerns in Child Care by Coeckelbergh et al. (2016) [9]
- Social Interaction
- Ethical Acceptability
- Privacy and Data Protection
- Replacement & Autonomy
- Emotions and Attachment
- Quality of the Therapy

Differentiated

Fig. 4. Overview of general robotic laws and ethical concerns

rules were further specified in 2009 [38]. These two approaches comprise mainly a professional standard for a safe human-robot interaction but specific ethical aspects of this safe interaction are not considered. A detailed overview of ethical concerns is proposed by Sharkey and Sharkey [46] and Coeckelbergh et al. [9] focused on specific topics in health care. Whereas Sharkey and Sharkey [46] discuss concerns of using robots in elder care, Coeckelbergh et al. [9] investigate ethical concerns of using robots in therapeutic childcare (see Fig. 4).

These detailed approaches show in general a broad consensus. Aspects like loss of privacy and data protection are mentioned. Also the ethical acceptability towards robots is introduced [9]. Several of these ethical concerns comprise also privacy aspects. For example, the personal liberty and the self-control of personal thinking and acting needs to be guaranteed. If the robot is regarded as a friend, emotions and attachment play a role. A friend is more entrusted than a machine. Therefore this needs to be investigated in a more detailed way.

Denning et al. [10] developed a questionnaire of considerable fundamental secure and privacy-respecting issues for the development of household robots. They focused on network security and possible attacks, e.g. spying on homes, acquisition of login credentials. The questions are divided into *Social, Environmental, Technical Questions* and *Security and Privacy Questions* (see Table 1).

Table 1. Questionnaire by Denning et al. [10]

Social, Environmental, and Technical Questions	Security and Privacy Questions
What is the intended function of the robot?	Does the robot create new or amplify existing privacy vulnerabilities?
How mobile is the robot?	Does the robot create new or amplify
What actuators does the robot possess?	existing physical integrity vulnerabilities?
What sensors does the robot possess?	Does the robot create new or amplify
What communication protocols does the robot support?	existing physical safety vulnerabilities?
Who are the intended users of the robot?	Does the robot create new or amplify existing psychological vulnerabilities?
What is the robots intended operational environment?	Can the robot be combined with other robots or technologies to facilitate an
Besides the intended users of the robot, what other people (and animals) will be in the the robots environment?	attack?
What kind of development processes are in place?	

5   Studies About (Socially) Assistive Robots

This section describes studies about assistive robots of the last decade with a focus on ethical concerns and privacy aspects mentioned by the participants. To answer the questions about user groups, the overview of the studies is divided into categories shown in Fig. 5 on the x-axis. Participants are divided into children, families, older people and mixed participant groups. The y-axis lists the different types of robots investigated. The duration and the number of participants of the studies is represented by icons. If a robot is used for a longer time by the participants, more interaction is possible and the user is able to build up a personal attitude towards the robot. The number of participants is an important indication of the significance of the study.

5.1   Functional

Families: Studies with the vacuum cleaner **Roomba** are all carried out in family environments. Families comprise in this context single households, households with children or couples. These studies were conducted in 2007 [4], 2009 [48], 2011 [16] and 2013 [15] and evaluated the change of cleaning routines and activities over time. Ethical concerns are mentioned by Fink et al. [15] stating "When people did not trust/rely on the robot, they did not want to leave the room/home when the robot was switched on". Even if the robot has no camera or microphone "[...] the Roomba changed people's cleaning activities [...]" [4].

Older People: Beer and Takayama [3] conducted a study on older people using the **MRP** (mobile remote telepresence system). Twelve older adults took part in this study which consisted of two sessions. The goal was the improvement of social communication with other people. The robot **Cafero** is used in a residential home by residents and staff for about 30 min [7]. It provides medication management based on web services and uses a camera for face recognition. There are no concerns mentioned and the researchers ensured the confidentiality of the data and employed anonymization techniques. In 2016 the **PeopleBot** was used and contrasted to Care-o-Bot in a study at the University of Hertfordshire on older people [49]. The robot e.g. offers functionalities as video telephony and the participants were allowed to use the robots for whatever they want to and whenever they like.

Mixed: Other studies also at the University of Hertfordshire [30,31,50] explored the habituation effects of different participant groups working with the **People-Bot**. Within the five weeks the preferences of the participants changed because they got used to the robot. Another important aspect is the fear of the loss of control mentioned by participants because of the autonomous behavior of PeopleBot [30]. In a further investigation the researchers focused on attitudes towards privacy. The participants attended a session where the concerns of using personal robots were in the focus. As main issues the storage of personal information and which data is stored are mentioned. Other concerns regarding usability and applicability are stated [50]. Kidd and Breazeal [28] introduced a robot called **Autom** for helping people to reduce their weight. A camera is included for face recognition and the conversation between robot and the human is personalized based on prior usage. The **ACE (Autonomous City Explorer)** [55] was driving through Munich, Germany for one day asking persons for the right way. Equipped with a stereo vision camera, a touch monitor and a loudspeaker it interacted with passers-by. No ethical aspects were mentioned. A study with **Spunik** [32] evaluated the differences of HRI with an avatar (i.e. virtual representation of a robot on a screen) or a physical robot. Participants expressed privacy as one of their main ethical concerns during that study. To work effectively as assistant, the robot needs a lot of knowledge about the user. Another important aspect is the "damage of the privacy space", when the robot is able to move on its own.

5.2   Caricatured

Children: **RoboVie** is used in different studies of Kanda et al. [26,27]. RoboVie acts for example as teacher for children in Japan [27] or as friend in Washington [26], but no concerns are brought up by the users. Kanda et al. [26] attribute the ability of friendship to the robot. But already in an earlier study [27] it is shown, that children lost their interest in the robot after a certain amount of time.

Older People: **Scitos** [12] interacted with people older than 60. The study investigates the idea of a robot as companion. The only hint towards ethical concerns

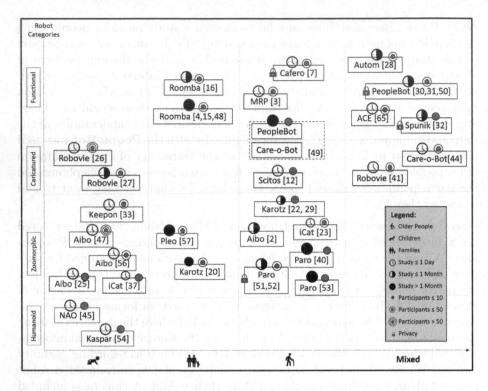

Fig. 5. Overview of robot studies

is mentioned as an idea for future work: *"Will there be effects of habituation in long-term-use– positive (e.g. increasing safety and trust) or negative (e.g. decreasing interest in interaction)"*. The study of PeopleBot and **Care-o-Bot** [49] is also part of this category.

Mixed: **RoboVie** was investigated in the context of shopping mall by Kanda [41]. There it could be used as a shopping assistant for everyone in Japan for three years. As an interesting result most of the adults only tried to interact with the robot when their children wanted to make use of RoboVie. Also **Care-o-Bot** assisted in an electronic market where it should show customers the way to products they asked for [44].

5.3 Zoomorphic

Children: **Aibo** is used in different studies on children. Kahn et al. [25] tested the impact on children in preschool, Weiss et al. [56] evaluated *"first time reactions in HRI"* in a shopping mall and Stanton et al. [47] tried to support autistic children. All the interventions last less than one hour per interaction and no privacy aspects are stated. Weiss et al. [56] point out the goal of "create[ing] an awareness for robots in general". **iCat** [37] interacts with children during a chess game. The robot is able the show facial expressions and has a camera in its nose. Although it is a study investigating children no ethical aspects are mentioned. Kozima et al. introduced a robot called **Keepon** [33]. Equipped with a camera and a microphone it is able to react on childrens behavior in a non-verbal way.

Families: Another toy robot is **Pleo** [57], a dinosaur. It has a camera and two microphones. Six families lived with Pleo from two up to ten month. Important statements of users were *"no long-term interest"* to use the robot and *"with another kind of toy, it may not have been a problem to claim that it sees, but several parents in this study seemed to take such information more literally as technical features."*. Parents expressed concerns about the cameras, instead of just accepting them as eyes of the robot. Another study employed the rabbit robot Karotz [20]. Karotz has a camera, a microphone and is able to connect to the internet although the internet connection is not really used.

Older People: **Paro** is a small seal robot with tactile and noise sensors. Wada et al. [51,52] investigate how older people with dementia react on that robot. Even though Paro has limited functionalities, one old lady prefers playing with Paro rather than with other habitants of the retirement house. Additionally, the psychological effects [40] and the general effects in care with older people of using Paro were investigated without significant results [53]. In 2010 a series of studies with the **Karotz** started in the Netherlands. Two studies are conducted with people older than fifty [22,29] to get an overview of how older people use robots. Ethical aspects are not mentioned, but users did not like to interact with the robot, because of the lack of functionality. A study with **Aibo** investigated the differences in the interaction with a robot and a real dog [2]. The robot **iCat** was used to investigate the acceptance of robots as companions with 30 participants (22 female, 8 male) [23].

5.4   Anthropomorphic

Children: **Kaspar**, a robot with cameras in the form of eyes, played a game with six children under ten years with *"low-level socially communicative behaviors"* [54]. The session lasts less than one hour. Again no ethical aspects are discussed. Another study with one autistic child was made with a **NAO** robot [45] for a session of 14 min. The robot has four directional microphones, loudspeakers, two cameras and can connect to the Internet autonomously. Concerning ethical aspects it is said that *"[...] proven reliability and safety need to be gained in advance"* and *"safeguarding the wellbeing [...] is crucial to ensure that their rights are always protected"*, but without any further explanation.

6   Privacy and Robotics

In this section the perception of privacy in studies about social robots is discussed and contextualized in the categories of types of robots and user groups.

Robot Groups *Functional:* A lot of studies are conducted in a public space. Users have typically not much time to interact with a robot. Mainly during studies in a home context, ethical concerns are identified. People are changing their habits, even though the robot being in their home has no sensors as cameras or microphones. The reason may be the robots functional appearance. Roomba is considered as a device that can move independently and users do not have control over it [15].

Caricatured: RoboVie and Care-o-Bot were used during several studies in different areas. But for the variety of functionalities there are only very limited examples of real use. Many of the available functionalities are not used or problematic [44]. The Care-o-Bot was e.g. of limited use in an electronic market and because of interfering noise. Additionally, a laboratory study was conducted. Users described the robot as interesting, but not very useful. Cafero was designed explicitly for the requirements of users but the study does not give any hints about the user perception. Instead the researchers list general issues of robotic studies as risks, quality of life (QoL), acceptance or confidentiality [7].

Zoomorphic: A lot of robots are already developed in this area. In the study with Pleo [57] the participants treated it as a real animal and were disappointed of restricted functionalities. Despite the fact, that Karotz has a microphone and a camera, its functionalities are very limited. However, Paro is an already accepted, commercially available robot in elder care. Regardless of the minimal set of functionalities, it is able to react and react to peoples actions in a satisfying way. Apart from Paro, there are not many zoomorphic robots that are accepted or can be used satisfactorily, independent of the user group.

Anthropomorphic: This category of robots is recently developed. Because of limited availability and the costs user interaction in studies is very restricted and it is not possible to investigate this area.

User Groups In several studies, users point out their concerns of using robots. Either they do not want to use a robot at all because of privacy concerns regarding data collection and the loss of private space. Or the users are afraid of using a robot because of a lack of technical expertise. Some users accept the robot in their household but change their behavior because of the fear of surveillance. Robot engineers often state that privacy is an important aspect in robotics but there is no typically further information how concerns should be addressed and how privacy might be achieved. Koay et al. [31] state that participants were glad, that the robot learns helpful information for improving functionality, but in a related study participants expressed their concerns about sensitive information [50].

Children: Interestingly, in studies on children ethical concerns are rarely considered. It is pointed out that privacy is important and respected, but concerns expressed by parents are not described. Children do not have the same perspective as adults and they have a more intuitive way of interacting with technology.

Additionally, it is stated that children loose interest in robots after a certain time.

Families: Until now, not many studies were conducted in family homes, because robots are not sufficiently robust, as stated by Graaf et al. [20]. The Roomba studies also incorporate families. In the case of Pleo, parents had concerns about accepting cameras as eyes [57].

Older People: Since elder care is one of the two main areas in social robotics, many studies are available. Although the studies do not directly focus on privacy, many users express concerns about various aspects of the area. Especially older people seem to be more sensitive with respect to robots. In the study of Graaf et al. [22] users were able to decide by clicking a button whether they agree to be filmed but it was not transparent if the robot is recording or not.

7 Discussion

Pillohealth[1] realizes personalized medication with the help of Pillo via face recognition. It promotes a secure storage of the medication and an additional mobile application is provided. But what happens in case of errors of the face recognition procedure? What happens, if attackers can manipulate Pillo which is connected to the internet? These questions should not only be raised for Pillo, but for all robots in a social context.

Currently, there are not a lot of robots commercially available [8]. Paro, Roomba and lawnmowers are mainly the only robots on the market. An important result of the studies is that a lot of users are not convinced and satisfied of using robots so far. Researchers still have to face a lot of problems as speech and image recognition and restricted functionalities. Additionally, participants stated a lot of concerns regarding sensors like cameras or microphones, storage of personal data or autonomous behavior. In most of the cases, clearly defined ethical principles are missing. Even though some robot features are not as sensitive as medication, the ethical consequences of every single feature need to be investigated. It is important for users, to be aware of the privacy risks of robots.

Therefore more transparency and a thorough consideration of privacy issues is essential to raise user acceptance. To figure out which aspects need to be dealt with, the features of robots need to be investigated. As already proposed in the questionnaire 1, sensors and actors should be considered because of the inherent risk. By using such a questionnaire, users might be able to understand the risks and possible countermeasures. Because the questionnaire has a focus on network security, it is important to address privacy aspects in addition. The model of seven types of privacy is a general approach, to investigate ethical aspects with a focus on privacy [17]. The following Table 2 gives an overview based on typical sensors employed in robotics. Depending on sensors and accompanying functionalities, different types of privacy are violated, e.g. with a camera, a robot is able to track people and their environment. This may influence users in their

---

[1] http://pillohealth.com/.

Table 2. Types of privacy and the impact of technical conditions

Privacy of ...	Camera	GPS	Loud-speaker	Micro-phones	Tactile Sensors	WiFi
the Person						
Behavior and Action	X	X	X	X	X	
Communi-cation			X	X	X	X
Data and Image	X			X		X
Thought and Feeling			X		X	
Location and Space	X	X				
Association	X			X		X

behavior [15]. Especially in the care area, this must be clearly transparent [22]. Concerning these aspects further correlation to other smart devices need to be investigated.

Another important privacy issue is the fact of *Thoughts and Feelings*. Robots are described as a friend or companion in many of the studies. That implies blind trust and an absolutely openness towards them [21]. Through the humanization of human-robot interaction, the topic of privacy gains even more importance. Breazeal introduced the relationship between emotional engagement and functional utility [5,23]. The more functionality a robot has, the more intimate is the emotional binding. The more functional it looks like, the more it is seen as a machine and not as a companion. Nevertheless, appearance of a robot is not the main characteristic for being skeptical.

In general, robots should not be too complex but more useful and helpful for daily routines. To address privacy concerns, transparency is needed concerning collection of personal data and it is important that the user is able to intervene, e.g. by switching off certain features. A lot of participants criticized the available features and missed some helpful ones. A robot e.g. does not need a camera when the functionalities using the camera are not perceived beneficial. Therefore it is of utter importance to involve potential users in robot design [7,34]. Users should be asked about preferences and aversions. This would ensure whether a specific sensor is really needed or not and thereupon a more specific analysis is possible.

8 Conclusion

Summarized, only a few ethical aspects have been investigated in robot studies so far. There are already some doubts mentioned regarding reduction of human contact, loss of control and loss of privacy related to recordings. The concern of emotions & attachments is not seen as problem so far.

Privacy should be a broad and important topic in robotic research. Zoomorphic robots, preferably used in health care are mostly simplistic but on the other hand very successful. With increasing demands, the complexity of robots will increase. Cameras, microphones and internet access will be a standard for robots. This allows an enlargement of robot functionalities, especially concerning social conversation and interaction between user and robot. Therefore the parallels to already available intrusive technical devices like mobile phones and their mobile applications are important to investigate. But for robots to be successful on the market, it must be helpful. If the robots have sensors it must be clear, why and for what reasons and scenarios they are needed. The two main target groups for social robots children and older people (with physical/psychological deficits) might have difficulties to be aware of the risks using them and the high complexity. Therefore risks and requirements need to be investigated during the whole development process to get a more transparent view.

Acknowledgment. This work was supported by the Ministry for Science and Culture of Lower Saxony as part of the program "Gendered Configurations of Humans and Machines (KoMMa.G)".

References

1. Amirfar, V.A.: A little robot with big promise may be future of personalized health care. Pharm. Today **22**(9), 38 (2016)
2. Banks, M.R., Willoughby, L.M., Banks, W.A.: Animal-assisted therapy and loneliness in nursing homes: use of robotic versus living dogs. J. Am. Med. Directors Assoc. **9**(3), 173–177 (2008)
3. Beer, J.M., Takayama, L.: Mobile remote presence systems for older adults: acceptance, benefits, and concerns. In: Proceedings of the 6th International Conference on Human-Robot Interaction, pp. 19–26. ACM (2011)
4. Breazeal, C.: How robotic products become social products: an ethnographic study of cleaning in the house. ACM, New York (2007). http://dl.acm.org/citation.cfm?id=1228716
5. Breazeal, C.: A Social Robot in Every Home. MIT Media Lab, Cambridge (2015)
6. Breazeal, C.L.: Designing Sociable Robots (Intelligent Robotics and Autonomous Agents). MIT Press, Cambridge (2002)
7. Broadbent, E., Jayawardena, C., Kerse, N., et al.: Human-robot interaction research to improve quality of life in elder care - an approach and issues. In: AAAI Workshop Conference on Artificial Intelligence (2011)
8. Broadbent, E., Stafford, R., MacDonald, B.: Acceptance of healthcare robots for the older population: review and future directions. Int. J. Soc. Robot. **1**(4), 319–330 (2009)

9. Coeckelbergh, M., Pop, C., Simut, R., Peca, A., Pintea, S., David, D., Vander-borght, B.: A survey of expectations about the role of robots in robot-assisted therapy for children with ASD: ethical acceptability, trust, sociability, appearance, and attachment. Sci. Eng. Ethics **22**(1), 47–65 (2016)
10. Denning, T., Matuszek, C., Koscher, K., Smith, J.R., Kohno, T.: A spotlight on security and privacy risks with future household robots: attacks and lessons. In: Proceedings of the 11th International Conference on Ubiquitous Computing, pp. 105–114. ACM (2009)
11. DiSalvo, C.F., Gemperle, F., Forlizzi, J., Kiesler, S.: All robots are not created equal: the design and perception of humanoid robot heads. In: Proceedings of the 4th Conference on Designing Interactive Systems: Processes, Practices, Methods, and Techniques, pp. 321–326. ACM (2002)
12. Döring, N., Richter, K., Gross, H.M., Schröter, C., Mueller, S., Volkhardt, M., Scheidig, A., Debes, K.: Robotic companions for older people: a case study in the wild. Stud. Health Technol. Inform. **219**, 147–152 (2016)
13. Duffy, B.R.: Anthropomorphism and the social robot. Robot. Auton. Syst. **42**(3), 177–190 (2003)
14. Feil-Seifer, D., Mataric, M.: Socially assistive robotics. IEEE Robot. Autom. Mag. **18**(1), 24–31 (2011)
15. Fink, J., Bauwens, V., Kaplan, F., Dillenbourg, P.: Living with a vacuum cleaning robot. Int. J. Soc. Robot. **5**(3), 389–408 (2013)
16. Fink, J., Bauwens, V., Mubin, O., Kaplan, F., Dillenbourg, P.: People's perception of domestic service robots: same household, same opinion? In: Mutlu, B., Bartneck, C., Ham, J., Evers, V., Kanda, T. (eds.) ICSR 2011. LNCS (LNAI), vol. 7072, pp. 204–213. Springer, Heidelberg (2011). https://doi.org/10.1007/978-3-642-25504-5_21
17. Finn, R.L., Wright, D., Friedewald, M.: Seven types of privacy. In: Gutwirth, S., Leenes, R., de Hert, P., Poullet, Y. (eds.) European Data Protection: Coming of Age, pp. 3–32. Springer, Heidelberg (2013). https://doi.org/10.1007/978-94-007-5170-5_1
18. Fong, T., Nourbakhsh, I., Dautenhahn, K.: A survey of socially interactive robots. Robot. Auton. Syst. **42**(3), 143–166 (2003)
19. de Graaf, M.M.A., Ben Allouch, S., van Dijk, J.A.G.M.: What makes robots social?: A user's perspective on characteristics for social human-robot interaction. In: Tapus, A., André, E., Martin, J.C., Ferland, F., Ammi, M. (eds.) ICSR 2015. LNCS (LNAI), vol. 9388, pp. 184–193. Springer, Cham (2015). https://doi.org/10.1007/978-3-319-25554-5_19
20. de Graaf, M., Ben Allouch, S., van Dijk, J.: Why do they refuse to use my robot? In: Mutlu, B., Tscheligi, M., Weiss, A., Young, J.E. (eds.) Proceedings of the 2017 ACM/IEEE International Conference on Human-Robot Interaction - HRI 2017, pp. 224–233. ACM Press, New York (2017)
21. de Graaf, M.M.: An ethical evaluation of human-robot relationships. Int. J. Soc. Robot. **8**(4), 589–598 (2016)
22. de Graaf, M.M., Allouch, S.B., Klamer, T.: Sharing a life with harvey: exploring the acceptance of and relationship-building with a social robot. Comput. Hum. Behav. **43**, 1–14 (2015)
23. Heerink, M., Kröse, B., Evers, V., Wielinga, B., et al.: The influence of social presence on acceptance of a companion robot by older people. J. Phys. Agents **2**(2), 33–40 (2008)

24. International Federation of Robotics: Executive summary world robotics 2016 service robots. https://ifr.org/downloads/press/02_2016/Executive_Summary_Service_Robots_2016.pdf
25. Kahn, P.H., Friedman, B., Perez-Granados, D.R., Freier, N.G.: Robotic pets in the lives of preschool children. Interact. Stud. **7**(3), 405–436 (2006)
26. Kahn Jr., P.H., Kanda, T., Ishiguro, H., Freier, N.G., Severson, R.L., Gill, B.T., Ruckert, J.H., Shen, S.: "Robovie, you'll have to go into the closet now": children's social and moral relationships with a humanoid robot. Dev. Psychol. **48**(2), 303 (2012)
27. Kanda, T., Hirano, T., Eaton, D., Ishiguro, H.: Interactive robots as social partners and peer tutors for children: a field trial. Hum.-Comput. Interact. **19**(1), 61–84 (2004)
28. Kidd, C.D., Breazeal, C.: Robots at home: understanding long-term human-robot interaction. In: IEEE/RSJ International Conference on Intelligent Robots and Systems, IROS 2008, pp. 3230–3235. IEEE (2008)
29. Klamer, T., Ben Allouch, S., Heylen, D.: "Adventures of harvey" – use, acceptance of and relationship building with a social robot in a domestic environment. In: Lamers, M.H., Verbeek, F.J. (eds.) HRPR 2010. LNICST, vol. 59, pp. 74–82. Springer, Heidelberg (2011). https://doi.org/10.1007/978-3-642-19385-9_10
30. Koay, K.L., Syrdal, D.S., Walters, M.L., Dautenhahn, K.: Living with robots: investigating the habituation effect in participants' preferences during a longitudinal human-robot interaction study. In: The 16th IEEE International Symposium on Robot and Human Interactive Communication, RO-MAN 2007, pp. 564–569. IEEE (2007)
31. Koay, K.L., Syrdal, D.S., Walters, M.L., Dautenhahn, K.: Five weeks in the robot house-exploratory human-robot interaction trials in a domestic setting. In: Second International Conferences on Advances in Computer-Human Interactions, ACHI 2009, pp. 219–226. IEEE (2009)
32. Koay, K., Syrdal, D., Dautenhahn, K., Arent, K., Małek, Ł., Kreczmer, B.: Companion migration-initial participants' feedback from a video-based prototyping study. In: Wang, X. (ed.) Mixed Reality and Human-Robot Interaction. Intelligent Systems, Control and Automation: Science and Engineering, vol. 1010, pp. 133–151. Springer, Heidelberg (2011)
33. Kozima, H., Michalowski, M.P., Nakagawa, C.: Keepon. Int. J. Soc. Robot. **1**(1), 3–18 (2009)
34. Lee, H.R., Šabanović, S., Chang, W.L., Nagata, S., Piatt, J., Bennett, C., Hakken, D.: Steps toward participatory design of social robots: mutual learning with older adults with depression. In: Proceedings of the 2017 ACM/IEEE International Conference on Human-Robot Interaction, pp. 244–253. ACM (2017)
35. Lee, K.M., Peng, W., Jin, S.A., Yan, C.: Can robots manifest personality? An empirical test of personality recognition, social responses, and social presence in human-robot interaction. J. Commun. **56**(4), 754–772 (2006)
36. Leite, I., Martinho, C., Paiva, A.: Social robots for long-term interaction: a survey. Int. J. Soc. Robot. **5**(2), 291–308 (2013)
37. Leite, I., Martinho, C., Pereira, A., Paiva, A.: As time goes by: long-term evaluation of social presence in robotic companions. In: The 18th IEEE International Symposium on Robot and Human Interactive Communication, RO-MAN 2009, pp. 669–674. IEEE (2009)
38. Murphy, R., Woods, D.D.: Beyond Asimov: the three laws of responsible robotics. IEEE Intell. Syst. **24**(4) (2009)

39. Pineau, J., Montemerlo, M., Pollack, M., Roy, N., Thrun, S.: Towards robotic assistants in nursing homes: challenges and results. Robot. Auton. Syst. **42**(3), 271–281 (2003)
40. Robinson, H., MacDonald, B., Kerse, N., Broadbent, E.: The psychosocial effects of a companion robot: a randomized controlled trial. J. Am. Med. Directors Assoc. **14**(9), 661–667 (2013)
41. Sabelli, A.M., Kanda, T.: Robovie as a mascot: a qualitative study for long-term presence of robots in a shopping mall. IJ Soc. Robot. **8**(2), 211–221 (2016)
42. Scassellati, B.M.: Foundations for a theory of mind for a humanoid robot. Ph.D. thesis, Massachusetts Institute of Technology (2001)
43. Scheeff, M., Pinto, J., Rahardja, K., Snibbe, S., Tow, R.: Experiences with sparky, a social robot. In: Dautenhahn, K., Bond, A., Cañamero, L., Edmonds, B. (eds.) Socially Intelligent Agents. Multiagent Systems, Artificial Societies, and Simulated Organizations, vol. 3, pp. 173–180. Springer, Heidelberg (2002). https://doi.org/10.1007/0-306-47373-9_21
44. Schmitt, C., Schäfer, J., Burmester, M.: Wie wirkt der care-o-bot 4 im verkaufs-raum? In: Mensch und Computer 2017-Usability Professionals (2017)
45. Shamsuddin, S., Yussof, H., Ismail, L.I., Mohamed, S., Hanapiah, F.A., Zahari, N.I.: Initial response in HRI- a case study on evaluation of child with autism spectrum disorders interacting with a humanoid robot NAO. Procedia Eng. **41**, 1448–1455 (2012)
46. Sharkey, A., Sharkey, N.: Granny and the robots: ethical issues in robot care for the elderly. Ethics Inf. Technol. **14**(1), 27–40 (2010)
47. Stanton, C.M., Kahn, P.H., Severson, R.L., Ruckert, J.H., Gill, B.T.: Robotic animals might aid in the social development of children with autism. In: 2008 3rd ACM/IEEE International Conference on Human-Robot Interaction (HRI), pp. 271–278. IEEE (2008)
48. Sung, J., Christensen, H.I., Grinter, R.E.: Robots in the wild: understanding long-term use. In: Proceedings of the 4th ACM/IEEE International Conference on Human Robot Interaction, pp. 45–52. ACM (2009)
49. Syrdal, D.S., Dautenhahn, K., Koay, K.L., Ho, W.C.: Views from within a narrative: evaluating long-term human-robot interaction in a naturalistic environment using open-ended scenarios. Cogn. Comput. **6**(4), 741–759 (2014)
50. Syrdal, D.S., Walters, M.L., Otero, N., Koay, K.L., Dautenhahn, K.: He knows when you are sleeping-privacy and the personal robot companion. In: Proceedings of Workshop Human Implications of Human-Robot Interaction, Association for the Advancement of Artificial Intelligence (AAAI 2007), pp. 28–33 (2007)
51. Wada, K., Shibata, T.: Living with seal robots-its sociopsychological and physiological influences on the elderly at a care house. IEEE Trans. Robot. **23**(5), 972–980 (2007)
52. Wada, K., Shibata, T., Kawaguchi, Y.: Long-term robot therapy in a health service facility for the aged-a case study for 5 years. In: IEEE International Conference on Rehabilitation Robotics, ICORR 2009, pp. 930–933. IEEE (2009)
53. Wagemaker, E., Dekkers, T.J., Agelink van Rentergem, J.A., Volkers, K.M., Huizenga, H.M.: Advances in mental health care: five n= 1 studies on the effects of the robot seal paro in adults with severe intellectual disabilities. J. Mental Health Res. Intellect. Disabil. **10**(4), 1–12 (2017)
54. Wainer, J., Dautenhahn, K., Robins, B., Amirabdollahian, F.: A pilot study with a novel setup for collaborative play of the humanoid robot kaspar with children with autism. Int. J. Soc. Robot. **6**(1), 45–65 (2014)

55. Weiss, A., Igelsböck, J., Tscheligi, M., Bauer, A., Kühnlenz, K., Wollherr, D., Buss, M.: Robots asking for directions: the willingness of passers-by to support robots. In: Proceedings of the 5th ACM/IEEE International Conference on Human-Robot Interaction, pp. 23–30. IEEE Press (2010)
56. Weiss, A., Wurhofer, D., Tscheligi, M.: "I love this dog"-children's emotional attachment to the robotic dog AIBO. Int. J. Soc. Robot. 1(3), 243–248 (2009)
57. Fernaeus, Y., Håkansson, M., Jacobsson, M., Ljungblad, S.: How do you play with a robotic toy animal? A long-term study of pleo. ACM, New York (2010). http://dl.acm.org/citation.cfm?id=1810543

From the Glass House to the Hive: The Private Sphere in the Era of Intelligent Home Assistant Robots

Silvia De Conca[✉] [iD]

Tilburg Institute for Law, Technology, and Society (TILT),
5000LE Tilburg, The Netherlands
s.deconca@tilburguniversity.edu

Abstract. This paper introduces a re-conceptualization of the private sphere, following the presence inside the house of intelligent personal assistant robots that observe and act through sensors and actuators, and aggregate the data collected in the Cloud. This processing inserts the personal sphere of individuals into a complex and multi-layered informational structure, a "hive" of private spheres. An abstract model, named Aggregated Privateness Model, is presented herein to explain the dynamics of the "hive". It sheds new light on a more collective dimension of 'private', a dimension which represents a context by itself, with normative mathematical rules and in which the expectations of privacy of individuals can be infringed based on the uses made of aggregated data. The Model also highlights how the behaviour of the individuals can influence the other private spheres in the cluster, as well as the Aggregation itself, due to a network effect, and how Diffused Network Liability could help compensating for such influences without incurring into practical impossibility.

Keywords: Privacy · Robotics · Artificial intelligence · Big data

1 Introduction

Small, sleek, minimal speakers, designed to be put on a desk or on the living room table. Bigger gadgets, with monitors showing a simple smiling face that follows with its 'eyes' the human while it moves around the room. Or else, little apparatuses with wheels and small arm-like tools, that can stroll with the human around the house while answering their requests. All around them, a multitude of connected 'smart' devices: thermostats, video/photo cameras, televisions, refrigerators, light switches, door locks, ear plugs, even wardrobe assistants. The products described above form a new family, identified in the rest of this paper as intelligent personal assistant robots, and are designed to help consumers during their daily lives by organising and coordinating tasks around the house controlling the smart devices connected to them. In this paper, I will argue how these small devices bring with them an important effect for our private spheres. The potential for surveillance and hacking of these devices has already caught the attention of the public and scholars. The focus of this paper will, however, be on how the presence of such intelligent devices (virtually) moves the house within a dense

M. Hansen et al. (Eds.): Privacy and Identity 2017, IFIP AICT 526, pp. 282–298, 2018.
https://doi.org/10.1007/978-3-319-92925-5_19

structure made of the information harvested from the private spheres of individuals, aggregated and combined to create patterns and profiles. Their unique combination of sensors, actuators, the central brain of the devices and their use of Internet and Cloud computing creates a fundamental change *inside* the most sacred space of protection of the private sphere: the house. and combined to create patterns and profiles. Their unique combination of sensors, actuators, the central brain of the devices and their use of Internet and Cloud computing creates a fundamental change inside the most sacred space of protection of the private sphere: the house.

It is this concurrence of elements (the intelligent personal assistant robots, their features, their contribution to Big Data, their presence inside the house) that makes this analysis meaningful and necessary. This paper contributes to the general discussion concerning privacy by proposing a Model to visualise and analyse the modalities with which the presence of such a new and permeating technology provokes changes in the relationship between the private sphere and the house. The Aggregated Privateness Model, as explained below, highlights new features for the private sphere, showing a shift from the individual to a more collective dimension of "privateness".

The scope of the analysis and the Model proposed is, however, far-reaching and goes beyond the specific case of intelligent personal assistant robots.

These robots stand at the crossroad of different industries, whose technologies build on each other: Internet of Things, Ambient Intelligence, Artificial Intelligence, and Big Data are only some of the elements combining into them and, as a consequence, into our houses. For this reason, while the starting point of this paper are intelligent personal assistant robots, the story it tells stretches to other domains too. While the starting point of the analysis was given by intelligent personal assistant robots, the Model has a broader scope, and can help analyse the effects on the private sphere of other technologies and industries too. It should be seen as a framework within which different stories can find their places, based on the technology, or technologies, it is applied to.

The first part of the paper sets the stage for the analysis, presenting the changes undergone by the house due to the introduction of new technologies. The features of intelligent personal assistant robots are also discussed, with a focus on their influences on the traditional construction of the private sphere. The first part is completed by an overview of what aggregation means based on how the data collected inside the house by the intelligent personal assistant robots are mined and processed with machine learning. The second part of the paper introduces a change of perspective. Tracing a line between the aggregation of data and the subsequent aggregation of the private spheres of the individuals to which those data belong, it culminates with the introduction and explanation of the Aggregated Privateness Model. This latter, inspired by the structure of snowflakes, provides for a conceptual framework to explain the main changes occurring in the private sphere: the introduction of a new context for individual perception of "privateness"[1], at aggregated level, and the capability for the individuals associated with a profile to influence, changing also how it will be applied to others.

---

[1] The use of the word privateness is here preferred over the word privacy. While, in fact, this latter retains a meaning strictly connected to the legal protection of the private sphere, the word privateness is meant to embed the idea of the very essence of the private dimension of individuals, regardless of its content, protection or of the legal status connected to it.

Finally, in the Conclusions the Aggregated Privateness Model is inserted into a broader context, with a brief explanation of its potential applications to privacy and personal data protection, for possible future developments of the analysis.

1.1   The Haunted House

In the last decades, we have witnessed a significant change in the way houses are equipped. Electronic and digital devices are becoming ordinary appliances, and the tendency shown by producers and designers is to integrate more and more a wide range of digital apparatuses into the domestic environment. So far, most of such devices were controlled one by one by the owners directly, through their mobile phones or computers. With the entrance in the market of intelligent personal assistant robots however, the coordination among the different sensors and devices can be carried out not directly by the owners, but by their assistant robots, whose main purpose is to organize and simplify the lives of those living inside the household environment.

Two prominent examples of intelligent personal assistant robots are Amazon Echo [1] and the newly presented Google Home [2]. Both Echo and Home do not possess kinetic capabilities. They consist of minimal design speakers, which can be activated via a trigger word or buttons. Rosie, the Jetsons' humanoid robot with wheels and arms carrying out chores around the house is replaced by decorative desk units run by software that interact with the owners through voice command ("Alexa, play the playlist named …", or "OK Google, increase the room temperature to…") [1, 2]. They do not present arms or other actuators, and the number of sensors directly embedded on the devices is very limited. To complete tasks they deploy other devices connected to them, such as a speaker or thermostat, in order to both collect the information necessary to elaborate a strategy, and then act following it.

Another significant feature of most intelligent personal assistant robots is given by the fact that while their functions necessitate huge amounts of data, they are not equipped with proportional storage hardware. Intelligent assistant robots transfer all the information they collect on Cloud, where they are stored for future use. In the Cloud, the information is also elaborated, in order to carry out the tasks requested by the owners. In the case of Echo, for example, logs of the voice commands are stored in the Cloud and processed to, among others, improve the robot's natural language recognition skills, in order to minimize errors for future requests by the owners. For this reason, the deletion of part or all the logs can give as a result a less efficient performance of the Echo.

Intelligent personal assistant robots coordinate the sensors and actuators, functioning as a central brain, with a certain degree of autonomy that builds upon machine learning and the deepening of the knowledge of their owners. Those are also the features distinguishing home-located personal assistant robots from simple smart phones, from which individuals can activate devices inside the household environment by means of special apps that, however, do not coordinate and do not operate in autonomy, serving as mere 'remote controls'.

Google Home, Amazon Echo, and other similar devices stand on the verge of several different technologies: Internet of Things, Ambient Intelligence, Artificial Intelligence, Robotics, Computing. Intelligent personal assistant robots present an additional element differentiating them from other similar technologies, such as Internet of Things or Ambient Intelligence: their proactivity, which also represents an important component of their intelligence. While acting as the central brain that coordinates all the other smart devices, intelligent personal assistant robots adapt their internal parameters thanks to their own self-learning algorithms. Even though they (mostly) follow the vocal commands of their owners, the decisions about how to accomplish their tasks are taken autonomously, based on what the robots have learned from the data collected around the house. In certain cases, the robots might prove even too much proactive, unexpectedly accomplishing tasks or providing for information unsolicited[2]. For these reasons, these devices are identified in this paper as robots, and not as mere "smart" speakers [3].

The embedding of connected devices and intelligent assistant robots inside the house, with the constant scanning for information and their subsequent transfer and elaboration, represents a powerful moment of evolution for the role traditionally assigned to the home in the protection of the private sphere.

The boundaries between the public and private sphere have been moving around the threshold of the house during the centuries [4, 5], sometimes pushed towards the inside of the household environment, sometimes lingering around the doorstep, and other times pulling towards the outside of the house. In the Western tradition, the house is considered the fulcrum of the private life: the place where individuals and families can hide from the sight of the community or the State, fully expressing their inner selves while carrying out their personal and intimate activities. In other words, the house is considered as the physical place where the private sphere could be protected from undesired interferences, and therefore find its full expression and expansion [6]. The private sphere, however, has not been unanimously and neatly defined. Its definition changes based on the time and culture, as well as on the tension between its conceptual opposite, the public sphere. For this reason, this paper uses as a starting point a functional definition of private sphere, consisting of the range of behaviors and knowledge, whose disclosure individuals desire to avoid (or at least limit) regardless of the addressee (other individuals, public or private entities). The increased availability and interconnectivity of smart consumer products destined to be placed inside the house, however, is often seen as a threat to the functions of seclusion and isolation provided by the house, whose (political) role is influenced by the economy-dictated values of home appliances, in what has been defined as a "democracy of the microwave" [7] (or, in our case, of the smart microwave).

Literary images such as Bentham's Panopticon, Orwell's Telescreens, or Zamyatin's glass houses are often evoked to describe the new vulnerability of the private sphere caused by the digitalization of home appliances. Cases like the one happened in Arkansas, in the United Stated contribute fueling those concerns. In a murder trial, in fact, an Amazon Echo sat on the witness bench, and its logs have been requested with

---

[2] As occurred with thousands Google Home Mini distributed during their launching even in the October 2016. In the following weeks, it was discovered that a fault in the products had made them activate up to over a thousand times a day, recording almost entire days of their users. The fault appeared to be an overly sensitive sensor that activated following the vibrations generated by a wide range of random sounds.

an affidavit by the public prosecutor as evidences against the Echo's owner. In such cases it is, however, possible to also have a glimpse of other mechanisms and aspects connected to the introduction of intelligent robotic devices inside the house. In the abovementioned murder trial case, for instance, Amazon's lawyers in a first moment challenged the request for the device's logs, claiming that both the recordings of the user/defendant's voice and the replies of Alexa (the software managing the device) fell within the protection of Freedom of Expression. While the recordings of the voice of the subjects were indeed directly protected under the First Amendment, Amazon's position is that the replies and tasks of Alexa, being tailored on the personality of the owner based on the data collected over time by the device, were also, indirectly, representing his forms of expression, as well as the forms of expression of the company's software and databases, Amazon Inc. [8]. It is in these, apparently minor, arguments that the issues connected to surveillance leave the stage to the issues deriving from the processing of the information made by the intelligent assistant robot starting from the private sphere of the individual, to how the processing affects the individual regardless of State intrusions.

While the first concerns are indeed justified and important, the focus of this paper will not be on surveillance, but on the complexity of the circulation of data within and around the house, switching the perspective from the eyes glazing from the outside, to the relationship between those complex interactions and the 'interior' of individuals' private spheres.

The issues raised by intelligent robotics in the home offer us the chance to change the perspective. While, in fact, anonymization and encryption techniques still contribute to the protection of the private sphere and to maintain the threshold (even if with some blurring sections) between public and private, the fluxes of data exiting and entering the house can shed a light on the structure in which the private sphere is inserted, a structure that highly depends on machine learning technology and fuels the hunger for data which characterises the Information Society. The protection of the private dimension of individuals must, therefore, not only consider the risks posed by invasive technologies, but also individual's behaviours and preferences in terms of consumer products and services, as well as the environment in which personal data are inserted.

While, in fact, new and updated provisions of law try to keep up with the technological progress, their concrete application might still rely heavily on judicial decisions. Ambiguous, industry-neutral provisions require years before a consolidated line of action is formed. For this reason, the paper proposes an approach that, notwithstanding its abstract nature, can provide for a much-needed uniform, conceptual basis, to avoid distortions and damages to individuals to occur while the law consolidates the lines of its implementation.

Before proceeding with the analysis, however, it is necessary to understand what do machine learning techniques and the Big Data phenomenon imply for the life cycle of personal data collected by intelligent personal assistant robots and for their elaboration. For this reason, the following paragraph will explain the fluxes in which information exit and enter the house, and will introduce the basis of the Model proposed in this paper: aggregated data. and enter the house, and will introduce the basis of the Model proposed in this paper: aggregated data.

1.2 Aggregated Data

Intelligent assistant robots collect information and data from the environment surrounding them via several sets of sensors: audio, video, movement, temperature, humidity, and so on.

Once in the virtual 'prairies' of the Internet the information collected from the private spheres of individuals are the object of different kinds of machine learning operations, aiming at creating categories of subjects, preferences, or behaviors.

Using mathematical rules (such as association, probabilistic, regressive rules), machine learning is capable of analyzing values, weighing them based on the data available, identifying direct or indirect influences among the quantitative or qualitative elements available. In this way recurring elements, or patterns, are highlighted that allow for categorizations and mapping of the behaviors of the subjects presenting similar characteristics.

The results of the processing of the information and data collected inside the private sphere are multiple. The most evident one is indeed the creation of profiles or models, either containing a projected description of a specific subject or, on the opposite, hypothetical and statistical representations. Both kinds of profiles are divided by Vedder [9] between distributive and non-distributive, meaning that the features of the profile respectively all apply to all the individuals or, on the contrary, do not all apply to each and every individual falling within such profile [10]. Since every profile relates to a specific purpose (marketing for different products or services, rating for financial institutions, medical services, criminal activities, etc.), individual information is elaborated to harvest a wide range of results, which translate into a wide range of profiles all being added, layer after layer, on top of the same subject.

Models/profiles also bring with them less obvious results. The main one is that flexibility and uncertainty are an intrinsic part of the elaboration. The models consist of correlations that go beyond the causal connection. The concrete accuracy of such predictions is, however not guaranteed, due to the many variables involved, and to approximation. Uncertainty is an intrinsic feature of profiling. A certain degree of flexibility is also often included in the system. Flexibility derives from the relationship between the descriptive assumptions (such as: "women age 18–40 are prone to online clothing shopping") and the numbers capable of statistically support such description (the percentages of online clothing shopping performed by women in that age range).

The profiles added on the subjects are not, therefore, immutable, but change based on the variations of the variables processed. The creation of models containing new and additional derived information, their juxtaposition over the individuals, and the uncertainty and flexibility embedded in them, as well as the introduction of information derived from background knowledge or from other sources, all contribute to the creation of additional layers on top of the individual [11]. Aggregated data are the product of the interdependency of information coming from the private sphere of different individuals. The final result of such clusters of data is eventually re-inserted among the data of the single subjects in an operation that might, or might not, correspond to the will and desires of the person profiled. single subjects in an operation that might, or might not, correspond to the will and desires of the person profiled.

Aggregated data can be found distributed in the multi layered structure of profiles that is juxtaposed to the individual sphere; they do not match the original data harvested around the individual, but they can, in part or in full, create an image that matches the one of the subject while, at the same time, connecting this latter to the images of the others included in the same profile.

To better exemplify the creation of the additional layers of profiles on the individual, consider the previous example of online purchases of women between 18 and 40. A first layer added on the individual is the one concerning the preference for online clothing shopping. In addition to that, another layer is given by the preferences for yoga attire over, for instance, volleyball clothes, based on the proximity or not to the address of a subject of a yoga center and on the information deriving from the credit card with which the subscription to the yoga classes was paid. Further processing might reveal additional patterns, such as the preference for neutral colors based on age ranges and professions. Other profiles and, therefore, further layers are added. The data concerning the thermostat and temperature preferences, as well as the geographical location of the subject, can also imply preferences in terms of entertainment, leading to the inclusion of the subject within the group of people that, for instance, prefers to stay in and purchase on demand movies or subscription to services such as Netflix. This additional layer, in turn, can provide insight over snack and alcohol consumption, and so on.

2   Proposing a New Approach

From the Aggregated Data to the Aggregated Private Spheres. The aggregation of data creates a 'hive', an informational structure composed of profiles and categories, the result of data mining and processing of information coming from different subjects. Once individuals are associated with certain profiles based on -and as a consequence of -the information harvested from them, their private sphere can be seen as annexed to the informational structure.

Figures 1 and 2 below show how profiles overlap on top of an individual. Figure 1 shows the result of mapping the musical preferences of an individual A. Based on the songs listened to by A on Spotify, crossed with the information concerning the classification of songs into different genres, and on the genres preferred by other individuals on Spotify belonging to the same age group and geographical location of A, a certain musical profile of A is created. Such profile is then used to suggest A new songs and bands. The processing and mining of A's data, as well as of the data of other subjects, led to the aggregation of their private spheres (consisting of the behaviors and tastes concerning music) into clusters based on age, gender, geographical location, and other features.

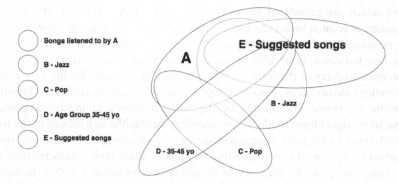

Fig. 1. The model created based on the data concerning musical tastes of A, the genres associated to songs, the Age Group A belongs to, and other songs listened to by subjects with similar age.

In Fig. 2, the aggregation leads to the insertion of the private sphere of A into another cluster: based on A's preference for jazz and on the age-group A belongs to, A's profile is associated with higher wine consumption (over liquors like vodka or tequila). Also in this case, A's private sphere is intertwined with the private spheres of all the other subjects whose data are used to identify the models, forming an information structure with them.

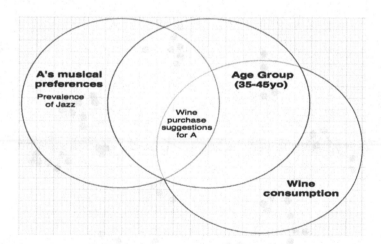

Fig. 2. The model created based on the data concerning musical tastes of A, the Age Group A belongs to, and habits of alcohol consumption of subjects with similar musical tastes and age.

As illustrated by Figs. 1 and 2 above, the circumstance that the profiles are created based on multiple individuals' preferences embeds the private spheres of those individuals, creating links among them. In this way, clusters or aggregations are created, some of which are connected or overlapping with others. This set of clusters and aggregations is what is here indicated, in abstract terms, as an informational structure. which are connected or overlapping with others. This set of clusters and aggregations is what is here indicated, in abstract terms, as an informational structure.

The main features of the informational structure are dictated by the very nature of the technology involved, as described above: machine learning collecting information from within the house, coordinated by the assistant robot's central brain, processing them based on algorithmic models, and returning them to the individuals in the form of tasks performed inside (and sometimes outside) the private sphere. Based on how the aggregation of data works, it is possible to identify three main characteristics of the informational structure: the presence of flexibility and uncertainty within the structure, influences deriving from network mechanisms within the structure, and a dichotomy between transparency and opacity. Such elements can have significant consequences on the way intelligent assistant robots in the house affect the private sphere.

In order to analyze the features and effects of the insertion of the private sphere inside the informational structure a conceptual model, defined by the author 'Aggregated Privateness Model', is now introduced.

2.1   The Aggregated Privateness Model

The Aggregated Privateness Model is represented by multiple clusters of private spheres, organized together to form complex structures, different among them, sometimes partially overlapping (see Fig. 3).

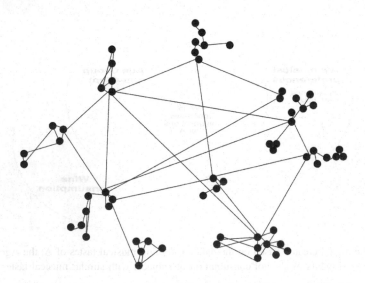

Fig. 3. A visual representation of the Aggregated Privateness Model.

The visual representation of the Aggregated Privateness Model has been inspired by the molecular composition of snowflakes. Each dot in the figure represents a private sphere. The different models and profiles in which the private sphere is intertwined are represented by the clusters in the model (for example the musical preferences cluster of Fig. 1 above), the 'edges' of a snowflake. They can be isolated, or connected to other clusters based on common features (in the example above, the model concerning musical preferences and the model concerning alcohol consumption preferences are connected). When the number of features shared by models increases, they are represented by the clusters in the model (for example the musical preferences cluster of Fig. 1 above), the 'edges' of a snowflake. They can be isolated, or connected to other clusters based on common features (in the example above, the model concerning musical preferences and the model concerning alcohol consumption preferences are connected). When the number of features shared by models increases, they are represented as partially overlapping, although still not completely identical due to the different purposes associated with each profile (for example marketing purposes versus healthcare ones). The connecting links among spheres and profiles represent the connecting features and elements shared within (and among) profiles. Their different length does not represent a property of the model, and is dictated only by reasons of composition. As explained above the Model is inspired by the molecular structure of snowflakes. It does, however, differ from it under certain perspectives. While a snowflake would present a symmetrical structure, the Model does not. This is because the informational structure and the clusters composing it do not originate all from a common element, but develop in a fashion that recalls that of distributed networks [12] with which, as will be explained below, it also shares certain dynamics. Just like the edges of a snowflake, individual private spheres are connected based on probabilistic predictions and models, and cooperate to create different forms and patterns. Such forms and patterns are influenced by how the molecules composing them combine, that is, by the information harvested in the private sphere and the way they are aggregated by machine learning, and by external factors, such as background knowledge or the crossing of data with other databases.

In addition to that, new models can build on previous models, just like snowflake and ice can keep growing. However, a snowflake leaves no trace once it melts. On the opposite, aggregated data structures are not so volatile, and their traces can last for long.

The uncertainty and flexibility also reflect on the informational structure. The snowflake Model, in fact, changes shapes constantly, and the patterns connecting its edges evolve. The models are expressly created to incorporate variables and weights, in order to be dynamic and respond to the new data collected within the house by the robots, or coming from other sources, such as the private spheres of other subjects. The reason for such dynamism is simple: a stiffening in the model would create unreliable profiles, not capable of reflecting the real preferences of the individuals, and therefore not useful or, worse, even prejudicial.

Furthermore, as briefly mentioned above, the Model has a structure similar to that of a distributed network. Similarly, within the Aggregated Privateness Model network mechanisms can occur. As highlighted by Actor Network Theory, within a network the communications among the nodes constituting it can affect the overall structure of the network itself, as well as the nodes and the connections between them [13]. The nodes of a network can, therefore, influence other nodes, the network (directly or indirectly) and the communication links among the nodes. These influences can be seen within the Aggregated Privateness Model as well, were the individuals, and their private spheres, can be influenced by the profiles they are associated with. In turns, however, individual preferences and behaviors can also modify the profiles and the models, which will, therefore, reflect differently on the other individuals also associated to the same profile. Such effect appears already at first, intuitive, sight and is also confirmed by the issues, recently very popular among experts, concerning discrimination and bias in profiling [14]. In the case of the music preferences of individual A above, for instance, the songs listened to by A contribute to enrich the profile A belongs to, introducing different genres that are weighed by the mathematical rules used to create the model and used to adjust or change it. The changed model will be applied to other subjects, possibly new ones, that might in this way also be included in the structure, and so forth. However, these influences might also affect negatively the other subjects included in the profile, as will be better explained below.

Finally, just like ice, the Model can be at the same time opaque and transparent. The opacity is given not only by the presence of encryption and anonymization mechanisms before or after the processing that happens in the Cloud. It is also given by the fact that many profiles, being probabilistic, are non-distributive, and therefore might not disclose information concretely belonging to a subject. It implies that while certain characteristics of individuals are disclosed once the profile is associated with them, others might not be. In addition to that, each profile usually focuses on certain aspects, based on marketing interests, and do not necessarily represent, each, a complete picture of the individuals involved. This dichotomy between transparency, given by the many and detailed information available, and the opacity embedded in the probabilistic system tends, naturally, to dissolve. The more accurate the profiles are, the more distributive profiles are associated to individuals, and the more the individuals become identifiable through de-anonymization procedures.

Thanks to the Aggregated Privateness Model, and based on its three main features briefly explained above, two main consequences of the insertion of intelligent assistant robots within the house can be highlighted.

De-contextualizing vs Re-contextualizing. The first consequence concerns the positioning, at abstract level, of the house with regard to the private sphere of individuals. As seen in the previous paragraphs, historically the house was considered the physical locus of protection of the private sphere. After the insertion within the informational structure, the house becomes a node of the aggregation.

It is not the first time that the introduction of digital technologies is identified as causing a shift of the role and conceptualization of the house vis-á-vis the private sphere. Tracking and surveillance, in fact, have been deemed to cause a re-positioning of the house: decontextualized, it has become a point in the flow of movements which is the object of surveillance [15].

In parallel with the surveillance shift, the Aggregated Privateness Model shows how the house turns from the precinct of protection of private sphere to a node within a structure. According to the Aggregated Privateness Model, however, the presence of intelligent personal assistant robots, while potentially contributing to decontextualizing the house, also introduces a new context. Intelligent personal assistant robots, therefore, do not solely contribute to subtracting features from the house, as it occurs in the case of surveillance, but also add a new level, in which the value of the house intended as place of protection of the private sphere still plays a role. Following the path created by Prof. Nissenbaum's contextual privacy theory [16], the hive, the informational structure, becomes a context on its own[3]. Within the aggregated context, rules are represented by the algorithms creating the different models and aggregating the data that compose the structure. Unlike within the private or public spaces normativity is, therefore, retained by mathematical rules more than social or legal norms. The mathematical rules employed by the algorithms revolve around processing, that is aggregating data and identifying patterns. Origin of the raw data and the subsequent use of the aggregated data resulting from the processing are not, at the state of the art, contemplated by the rules existing within the Aggregated Privateness context.

At the same time, however, the information and data are still collected within the house, where individuals do have a certain expectation of protection offered by the location. In a subsequent moment, the additional information derived from those originally collected are deployed for multiple uses which the individuals are not aware of. There is, therefore, a dissonance between the expectations existing at the moment and place of collection (within the house) and the uses made of the information within and without the Aggregated dimension. Building upon Nissenbaum's theory, such dissonance creates an issue in terms of protection of the private sphere, a privacy issue.

Practical effects of this circumstance can be seen in the cases that more and more frequently find space in the discourse surrounding the use of profiling and automated decisions [17]. Nowadays many banks and financial institutions utilize software that analyze between six and eight thousand data points in order to grant or reject loan applications. Decisions can be influenced by, for example, purchase patterns, the time elapsed before accepting the terms and conditions of a website, musical preferences, alcohol consumption, healthcare data, and so on [18]. This circumstance shows how data collected within the context of the private sphere of the individual are used outside of the aggregated context, infringing the expectations of the subjects connected to the original collection. It is that infringement that creates, then, the ethical and moral disconcert surrounding such decisions. Another example can be found in the Alexa's stand in the murder trial, described above. In that case, in fact, the public prosecutor required the use of data collected within the house by the device. The collection of said data, however, is consented to by an individual based on the expectation that they

---

[3] The author acknowledges that several critiques have been moved to Prof. Nissenbaum's Contextual Integrity Theory. The theory has been often considered more focused on the common law system and therefore less relevant for the European context, especially with regard to data protection, or it has been seen as a complementary element of a bigger, general conceptualization of privacy and not a comprehensive, self-standing theory (see, among others, Michael Birnhack's review of Helen Nissenbaum's theory in Jurimetrics: Journal of Law, Science, & Technology, 52(4), 2011). While these limitations of the Contextual Integrity Theory are indeed valid, its relevance for this paper still stands. Since the paper presents an abstract conceptualization of the private sphere with regard to the use of intelligent robotics inside a certain context (the home), Contextual Integrity (whether alone or as part of a bigger theorization) provides a general framework of reference that highlights the connections among the private sphere, the physical and virtual environments with which it relates and, consequently, privacy and its protection.

would be necessary for Amazon's intelligent assistant robot to satisfy the user's requests. The use outside of said consent represents an infringement of the expectation, and creates a dissonance within the informational structure.

The practical consequences of the dissonance acquire importance once the Aggregated Privateness Model is used to test the solidity of the existing legislation concerning the protection of the private sphere, such as the European e-Privacy Directive[4] [19] and the incoming General Data Protection Regulation [20]. Such test is, however, outside the scope of this paper, and should be the object of further research.

A Collective Dimension of Liability. In addition to the issues connected to the contextualization of the aggregated dimension, the Model also provides conceptual clarity on a more collective dimension of the protection of the private sphere. Having acknowledged the abovementioned network mechanisms within the cluster, in fact, the Model helps shedding light on their consequences, the main one being that the behavior of the individuals composing the cluster affects this latter and the other 'nodes'. Readers consider this example: if the above mentioned individual A (with the relating musical preferences, age range, occupation, geographical location, etc.) asks for a loan and then fails to re-pay it, this might influence the entire profile A belongs to. As a consequence, individuals B and C, belonging to the same profile of A, might see their possibilities to obtain a loan decrease, or might face an increase in their interest rates.

The underlying idea is, indeed, not new. Since ancient times in small communities individual behaviors were deemed to influence the other members, as well as the 'good name' of the community itself. What is introduced by the Model is the application of an idea of indirect responsibility deriving from their behavior to individuals vis-à-vis other, unknown, individuals due to a connection based solely on the belonging to the same model or profile. Such responsibility, while it appears difficult to solve in terms of practical application, can be seen as a new form of Network Diffused Liability [21], a liability deriving from distortions cause not by a single dot in a network, but by the combination of the dots and their interactions with the environments they operate in; in other words, a liability of the network itself. It can serve as a basis to justify regulatory intervention to attempt redistributing such responsibility within the entire system, even if not pinning it to any individual in particular. In this way the Model, while acknowledging and conceptually framing a collective dimension of protection of the private sphere, a collective dimension of privacy [22], also acknowledges its practical limits. Such acknowledgement, however, does not lead to ignoring the issues deriving therefrom in day to day life, focusing on providing a comprehensive basis that can guarantee, in the practice, a uniform application of concepts that, otherwise, would make judges and authorities navigate at sight, grasping intuitive ideas to adjust the existing regulation.

In this regard, it is worth noticing that in the abovementioned Alexa case, the replies provided by the machine and for which the authorities sought mandate are not only tailored on the owner. Alexa's replies are also adjusted based on the profiles and

---

[4] Or the Regulation that will most likely take its place and whose text is currently being negotiated in the European Commission and with the member States, after being approved in the October 2017 by the Justice Committee of the European Parliament and the European Parliament itself.

models the owner is associated with, which means that the device's replies not only contain traits of the personality of the individual that Amazon's lawyers tried to protect invoking the First Amendment. They also contain influences from the other individuals included in the same profiles, whose data have also been used. This is where the positions of both the public prosecutor and Amazon, although both indeed solid, fall short of considering the implications of a more collective dimension of the private sphere, and its protection. Possible distortions, as highlighted by the examples before, can translate in severe consequences for individuals and their fundamental rights.

The Aggregated Privateness Model, although maintaining a conceptual and abstract dimension, can offer a uniform basis to limit possible distortions and damages to individuals in the subsequent practical application of provisions created to protect the very private spheres that compose the Model itself.

3 Conclusions

This paper introduced an abstract model to understand the concept and role of the private sphere, in relation to the introduction within the house of machine learning powered intelligent assistant robots. The model, called 'Aggregated Privateness', is elaborated with the purpose of offering a conceptualization that can serve as a basis for an analysis of the existing tools protecting the private sphere, Privacy and Data Protection in particular.

While the Model maintains its validity also in relation to different technologies, such as Ambient Intelligence and the Internet of Things in general, the starting point for its elaboration is the insertion inside the house of intelligent personal assistant robots. The presence of intelligent personal assistant robots in the house implies, in fact, the insertion of the robots inside the private sphere of the inhabitants. The Model shows how intelligent robots collecting data within the house insert the private sphere into an informational structure, at an abstract level.

A combination of multiple anonymous probabilistic profiles created with machine learning bundles on the individual additional layers of information. The aggregation of data for the creation of the different profiles corresponds to the aggregation of the private spheres of the individuals associated with the profiles.

As highlighted in the paper, the Aggregated Privateness Model sheds light on three main consequences of the interaction of the private sphere with intelligent robotics. The model explains how, within the cluster, the juxtaposition of distributive and non-distributive profiles creates a dichotomy between transparency (given by the information about individuals contained in the profiles), and opacity (due to the fact that not necessarily all that information concretely corresponds to individuals' preferences and behaviors). This seems to walk away from the general idea of the exposure of the life occurring inside the household environment. With regard to the collection of data for commercial purposes, the walls of the house, while not necessarily made of glass, present a high level of permeability to the fluxes of information, and consequently to the statistical profiles built upon such information.

The model also helps explaining a flip in the role of the house. While this latter is decontextualized, the aggregation becomes a context by itself, with distinct rules. Due to the predominant role of machine learning, in the new context normativeness is given to the algorithm and its mathematical rules. Acknowledging the Aggregated Privateness as a context by itself can, therefore, help providing a conceptual basis for correcting some of the distortions such normativeness has created: discrimination and over/under inclusiveness. Once, in fact, the context is recognized, the deriving reasonable expectations of individuals can also be identified, offering support for the concrete application of provisions of law that still appear abstract, such as Article 22 of the GDPR on automated decisions. As explained by Nissenbaum's theory, the use of the information collected within a certain context outside of it breaches the rules and expectations connected to it. Similarly, the use of the information collected within the private sphere for a certain purpose and contained in the profiles for other circumstances, gives life to a mismatch between the expectations of the individuals providing the information and their effects.

Finally, the Aggregated Privateness Model helps grasping the weight and importance of the collective dimension of privacy and data protection. Once the individual is inserted in a cluster composed of anonymous profiles, the aggregation assumes a role in the protection of the private sphere of such individual.

Inside the cluster, each private sphere has the capability of influencing -and being influenced by -the other spheres, as well as the aggregation itself. The model highlights how, in turn, this translates into the circumstance that the behaviors of individuals inside their private spheres can affect other individuals, even without any relationships existing. This consequence of the use of probabilistic profiles which, as explained above, can also be interpreted in the light of ANT, opens the way to more collective dimensions of responsibility for the individuals inserted into a cluster. The paper has shown how the Aggregated Privateness Model works as a conceptual basis for the application of a form of Network Diffused Liability in the context of the protection of the personal sphere.

The combination of the dichotomy between opaqueness and transparency, the contextual use of the information contained in the aggregation, and the Network Diffused Liability within the clusters, can be used as conceptual bases to support the implementation of the existing legislation, such as the GDPR and the e-Privacy Directive in Europe, and avoid the distortions that have already been highlighted by experts and scholars. As shown by the Alexa role in the murder trial in the US, at stake are fundamental values and the protection of individuals, and while solutions can be developed in the span of a decade based on case law, the lack of a proper, uniform conceptual basis might amplify the discrepancies in the judicial and administrative decisions during such 'trial' period, penalizing and discriminating individuals. The Aggregated Privateness Model can provide such uniform basis with regard to the protection of the private sphere in the age of intelligent robotics entering our houses, to help directing technological development on a desirable, responsible path. the age of intelligent robotics entering our houses, to help directing technological development on a desirable, responsible path.

References

1. Amazon Echo Homepage. www.amazon.com/Amazon-Echo-Bluetooth-Speaker-withWiFi-Alexa/dp/B00X4WHP5E. Accessed 30 Mar 2017
2. Google Home Homepage. https://madeby.google.com/home/. Accessed 30 Mar 2017
3. D6.2 Guidelines on Regulating Robotics, RoboLaw Project: Regulating Emerging Robotic Technologies in Europe: Robotics facing Law and Ethics (2014)
4. Hansson, M.G.: The Private Sphere: An Emotional Territory and Its Agents, 1st edn. Springer, Dordrecht (2008). https://doi.org/10.1007/978-1-4020-6652-8
5. Smith, R.E.: Ben Franklin's Web Site: Privacy and Curiosity from Plymouth Rock to the Internet, 1st edn. Sheridan, California (2000)
6. Shapiro, S.: Places and spaces: the historical interaction of technology, home, and privacy. Inf. Soc. **14**(4), 275–284 (1998)
7. Kumar, K.: Home: the promise and predicament of private life at the end of the twentieth century. In: Weintraub, J., Kumar, K. (eds.) Public and Private in Thought and Practice, pp. 204–236, Chicago (1997)
8. Case No. CR-2016-370-2, Circuit Court of Benton County, State of Arkansas (USA)
9. Vedder, A.: KDD: the challenge to individualism. Ethics Inf. Technol. **1**, 275 (1999)
10. Hildebrandt, M.: Defining Profiling: A New Type of Knowledge?, 1st edn. Springer, Dordrecht (2008). https://doi.org/10.1007/978-1-4020-6914-7_2
11. Costa, L.: Virtuality and Capabilities in a World of Ambient Intelligence: New Challenges to Privacy and Data Protection, 1st edn. Springer, Dordrecht (2016). https://doi.org/10.1007/978-3-319-39198-4
12. Sassen, S.: Digital Networks and the State: Some Governance Questions. Theor. Culture Soc. **17**(4), 19–33 (2000)
13. Latour, B.: On actor network theory: a few clarifications plus more than a few complications. Soziale Welt **47**, 369–381 (1996)
14. Barocas, S., Selbst, A.D.: Big Data's Disparate Impact. Calif. Law Rev. **104**, 671732 (2016)
15. Bennett, C.J., Regan, P.M.: Editorial: surveillance and mobilities. Surveill. Soc. **1**(4), 449–455 (2004)
16. Nissenbaum, H.: Privacy in Context: Technology, Policy, and the Integrity of Social Life, 1st edn. Stanford University Press, Redwood City (2010)
17. Mendoza, I., Bygrave, L.A.: The right not to be subject to automated decisions based on profiling. In: Synodinou, T., Jougleux, P., Markou, C., Prastitou, T. (eds.) EU Internet Law: Regulation and Enforcement. Springer, Cham (2017). https://doi.org/10.1007/978 3 319 64955-9_4. University of Oslo, Faculty of Law Research, Paper No. 201720
18. Goodman, B., Flaxman, S.: European union regulations on algorithmic decision-making and a "right to explanation". In: Presented at 2016 ICML Workshop on Human Interpretability in Machine Learning (WHI 2016), New York (2016)
19. Directive 2002/58/EC of the European Parliament and of the Council of 12 July 2002 concerning the processing of personal data and the protection of privacy in the electronic communications sector (Directive on privacy and electronic communications), OJ L 201 (2002)
20. Regulation (EU) 2016/679 on the protection of natural persons with regard to the processing of personal data and on the free movement of such data, and repealing Directive 95/46/EC (General Data Protection Regulation), OJ L119/1 (2016)

21. Teubner, G.: Hybrid laws: constitutionalizing private governance networks. In: Kagan, R., Winston, K. (eds.) Legality and Community: on the Intellectual Legacy of Philip Selznick. Berkeley Public Policy Press, Berkeley (2002)
22. Taylor, L., Floridi, L., van der Sloot, B. (eds.): Group Privacy: New Challenges of Data Technologies, 1st edn. Springer, Dordrecht (2017). https://doi.org/10.1007/978-3-319-46608-8

Mobility and Privacy

A Comparative Study of Android and iOS Mobile Applications' Data Handling Practices Versus Compliance to Privacy Policy

Sophia Kununka[(✉)], Nikolay Mehandjiev, and Pedro Sampaio

Alliance Manchester Business School, The University of Manchester,
Manchester, UK
sophia.Kununka@postgrad.mbs.ac.uk,
{n.mehandjiev, p.sampaio}@manchester.ac.uk

Abstract. The prevalent use of mobile applications (apps) involves the dissemination of personally identifiable user data by apps in ways that could have adverse privacy implications for the apps' users. More so, even when privacy policies are provided as a safeguard to user privacy, apps' data handling practices may not comply with the apps' privacy commitments as stated in their privacy policies. We conducted an assessment of the extent to which apps' data practices matched their privacy policies. This study provides an exploratory comparison of Android and iOS apps' privacy compliance. Our findings show potential sensitive user data flows from apps in ways that do not match the apps' privacy policies and further, that neither Android nor iOS app data handling practices fully comply with their privacy policies.

Keywords: Mobile applications · Privacy policy · Compliance

1 Introduction

Mobile applications (apps) handle unprecedented quantities of user data. App users offer or entrust diverse personal data to organizations and traders. The data provided by users may be sensitive such as personally identifiable information (personal data) which is data that can be linked back to the owner or source for example; user name, email, telephone number, gender, age, social security number, card number etc. [1]. In contrast, non-personal data is deemed unidentifiable data and can be aggregated for various purposes. User data is provided with the confidence that users' data privacy (information privacy) will be maintained by limiting data utility to the specified purposes. Notwithstanding, gaps have been observed in privacy practices as research shows the fact that apps can communicate users' personal data to third parties without users' knowledge or consent [2].

While a range of approaches have been used in an endeavour to address non-consented use of users' data, a key focus has been on the provision of privacy policies. A privacy policy is a set of rules, or statements that specify which processing and sharing practices are permitted for different types of data collectable from the end user [3]. According the General Data Protection Regulation [4], privacy policies are a

© IFIP International Federation for Information Processing 2018
Published by Springer International Publishing AG 2018. All Rights Reserved
M. Hansen et al. (Eds.): Privacy and Identity 2017, IFIP AICT 526, pp. 301–313, 2018.
https://doi.org/10.1007/978-3-319-92925-5_20

means for data controllers to inform data subjects (end users of the app) about what personal data will be collected and for what purpose and as such are a key element in ensuring informed consent. As such, they help to dispel users' anxieties about the revelation of personal data [5]. Further, privacy policies build user trust and enable app to achieve regulatory compliance. However, several studies [6–8] indicate that privacy policies have been found to be inadequate in their attempt to preserve user privacy. For instance, privacy policies have been critiqued for being "far too long and complex" [9]. Similarly, while provision of privacy policies are an important step in reinforcing user data privacy, the extent to which this endeavour is successful is largely dependent on an app's adherence or compliance to its own privacy policy.

Moreover, privacy related challenges have been identified in apps that run on both Android and iOS app platforms even while they rank top in popularity [10]. Android apps present users with a permission list, during installation, on a take-it-or-leave-it basis with no specific reason for its requirement unless if user consults the provided privacy policy. This could facilitates possible privacy abuse as apps seek to access as much user data as possible irrespective of whether or not it's required for the apps' functionality [11]. A study [12] found that in spite of a user's call history having no direct influence on the ads a user might want, there were Ad libraries that collected and conveyed this information to the internet. Further, Ad libraries have been observed to engage in permissions usage that could introduce privacy risks [13]. Efforts to address privacy abuse led to the development of Android's Marshmallow version [14] which operates on a similar principle to iOS. In both cases, requests for specific permissions are made as and when they are needed using a pop up message that allows users to either accept or deny the permissions [15].

Comparing how easy it is to understand the way permissions are on both platforms, it is observed that while Android is more informative in terms of detail, it uses more technical terminology than iOS which could impact on extent of user understanding [14]. Nonetheless, [16] argues that privacy risks arise because users often lack the full picture of information that could be collected and the possibilities of using it in ways that are unknown to them. Security-wise, the android apps present more risk while the iOS apps tend to be safer [17]. However, [16] stresses that there is reduced privacy awareness and fear among iOS users. Notwithstanding, iOS apps have been found to be vulnerable in some instances [18, 19] and the vetting process implemented by Apple to ensure that iOS apps are aligned with Apple's privacy critiqued for its lack of transparency [20].

Companies that do not take user privacy concerns into consideration for instance when using personal data developing profiles that facilitate tailoring of Ads, are likely to counter public backlash [21]. Moreover, whereas regulation requires apps to provide privacy policies, the extent to which these policies are contractual is debatable as they change as and when the firm decides. However, increased privacy confidence increases online success. Users want government involvement through means such as enacting laws that protect the privacy of personal information collected through apps. Regulatory bodies such as the Federal Trade Commission (FTC) in the US and the European Data Protection Regulation [4] demand that users are informed of the data gathered by apps, why it is collected and that opt out provisions are made for users [22]. Notwithstanding, the existence of government regulation does not imply that companies comply with the requirement. This is underpinned by a recent study by several authors [23] in which a critical analysis of Facebook's revised policies and terms was conducted based on the EU Data Directive. The findings of the study indicate that Facebook engages in questionable privacy practices. As such, there is need to ascertain the extent of apps compliance to their privacy as a pointer to the extent to which users would have confidence in using the apps' service.

A study that examined the personal, behavioural and location data from 110 apps indicates that Android and iOS apps generally transmit sensitive data to 3.1 and 2.6 third party domains respectively [24]. Our work seeks to extend that study by exploring the apps data handling practices verses compliance of apps to their privacy policy. As such, our study conducts an investigation into whether the user data collected and disseminated by apps to third party domains is matches their privacy policies. The analysis was conducted based on a privacy compliance comparison between Android and iOS apps as these are the dominant app platforms, by exploring the extent to which apps adhere to their stated privacy policies and, the resulting effects of apps' data handling practices.

Our study seeks to answer the research question: Do mobile application privacy policies match their practices? To answer this question we consider mobile applications from the two dominant mobile application platforms i.e. Android and iOS. The remainder of the paper is organized as follows: related work is presented in Sect. 2, followed by the research method in Sect. 3, after which the findings of the study are presented in Sect. 4. In Sect. 5, a discussion on the findings is presented and Sect. 6 sums up the paper with conclusions and subsequent work.

2   Related Work

Related research conducted [25] has focused on availability, scope and transparency of mobile app privacy policy. That study found that two-thirds of the apps' contained content that was not directly related to the app. Further, information privacy practices were not clear. However, the study was limited to health. In another health privacy policy related study, [26] analysed website related vulnerabilities based on 23 website policies using goal mining techniques for the extraction of pre-requirements goals from post-requirements text artefacts from which a taxonomy was developed. Research [27] argue that the permissions system should be more fine grained and develop an sought to enhance user understanding by providing a mechanism of equipping users with information required before application downloads. Further work [1] explored the practicability of combining permissions and app requests in advising using on whether the risk of installing an app outweighs the expected benefits.

More so, another study presented by [24], used 110 widely used Android and iOS apps to explore the different user data that apps conveyed to third parties. Using an iPhone 5 and a Samsung Galaxy S3, HTTP and HTTPS traffic from the apps was captured using a proxy and examined for personally identifiable data. As a control, push notifications were blocked so as not to allow apps to transmit data in background when not being used. However, by limiting the analysis to text matches within the HTTP and HTTPS traffic, potentially sensitive user data may have missed being observed in instances in which other protocols are used by the apps or, in cases where user data was hashed so as to obscure it.

3   Research Method

Our study is based on the findings presented by [24] discussed in related work above. As such, our study inherited the measurement errors made in [24], as mentioned above.

First, in our study, the selection of the apps was done on the basis of the number of third party domains that the apps conveyed sensitive data to. We found that in the Zang et al. database, the number of third party domains associated with the apps ranged from none to 17. As such, we selected apps that conveyed sensitive data to two or more third party domains. This was based on the rationale that the greater the number of third party domains an app is linked to the higher the potential of user data dissemination. As a result, the selection yielded two non-identical sets of 15 apps on each platform (see Tables 1 and 2). The limited sample size facilitated a detailed analysis of the apps. The analysis of this sample size was feasible taking into consideration the effort and time required for an in depth analysis. The apps were from a cross range of categories such as; social, navigation, medical, business, games, health and fitness, lifestyle etc. Hence while the sample size was relatively small, the scope of representation was relatively spread. Due to a sample size limited because it was based on a predetermined database and the selection criteria, the results are not statistically significant. However, the significance of our findings are in that they serve as a preliminary indication of trends on how the Android and iOS apps data handling practices and compliance compare. This provides indicators of further research.

Table 1. Android apps and number of associated third parties

App	Third parties
American Well	4
Drugs.com	7
Expedia	4
Kayak	3
MapQuest	5
Priceline	4
Glide	8
Jobsearch	4
Snagajob	3
Monster Lengend	5
Myfitnesspal	4
Runkeeper	3
Pinger Text Free	11
Tango	4
Pinrest	4

Table 2. iOS apps and number of associated third parties

App	Third parties
Fruit Ninja	4
Piano Tiles	3
Instagram	2
Instasize	2
Leafly	3
Ovia Fertility	2
Urgent Care	4
MapMyRun	4
Nike	4
TimeShop	3
Walgreens	5
Groupon	3
Inrix	2
Local Scope	17
Phone Tracker	2

Second, after determining the apps to be used in the study, we planned to analyse the apps through the following steps; (a) establishing the practical data handling practices for each of the thirty apps, (b) determining the apps' privacy commitments to users on data handling as stated in their privacy policies and, (c) establishing the extent of compliance by apps to their own privacy policies.

To establish the practical data handling practices for each of the thirty apps, we analysed the types of user data they convey to third parties in practice based on the finding of [24]. In particular, 14 types of user data were found: address, birthday, email, gender, name, password, phone number, zip code, employment, friends, medical info, search, username and location.

Next, we sought to establish the apps' privacy commitments to users on data handling as stated in their privacy policies. The apps' privacy policies were sourced online using the privacy policy' link provided through each app. The privacy policies were source between September to December 2015 and as such should substantially correspond to the specific version of apps that were used in [24]'s study to extract the traces of sensitive data dissemination from apps. These privacy policies were uploaded into Nvivo software [28] to facilitate a qualitative analysis of their content. The process of content coding involved the review of privacy policies in order to establish a fundamental understanding of the policies. This was followed by coding using thematic analysis to identify content on data collection, use and dissemination to third parties etc., that were of particular interest to our study. The mechanism of coding and data interpretation was validated by two researchers so as to ensure substantial agreement on data interpretation and results. A study found that when six senior researchers individually coded a focus group, the results of their coding while showing major similarities in findings, also had elements of disagreement [29].

In the final stage, we determine the extent of compliance by apps to their own privacy policies. We systematically assessed the results from the apps' privacy commitments as stated in their policies, against their practical data handling practices involving the 14 user data types that were earlier identified. The analysis was restricted to the collected and transmitted data from the app and does not include what happens on the receiving entities. The results are presented in the next section.

4 Findings

Our results indicated that Android apps handle 64% of the types of the users' data examined while iOS handles 50%. Moreover, out of the types of user data gathered and disseminated by Android, 32% did not match the app privacy policies. Similarly, of the user data handled by iOS, 26% did not comply with their policies. Interestingly 14% of the iOS user data were found to be gathered and disseminated with no privacy policy available as shown in Fig. 1.

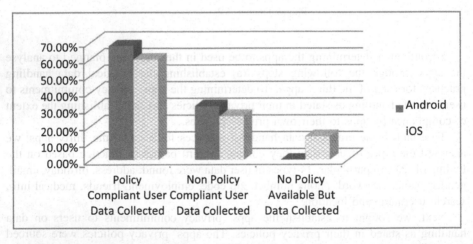

Fig. 1. A comparison of Android and iOS apps data practice verses privacy policy.

Most Collected User Data. Considering the overall figures of user data handled by the Android and iOS apps, the data attributes most collected and disseminated by Android were; address (15), email (15) and name (15) i.e. these three user data attribute were collected by all the Android apps in our study since the study involved fifteen Android apps. On the other hand, iOS' highest were; location (14), email (12) and name (12) i.e. none of iOS highest user attributes were collected by all the fifteen iOS attributes in the study.

Extent of Compliance Between Policy and Data Dissemination. Compliance was considered as per data type. Taking into account the extent to which the apps' policies match their data handling practices,

Android's most compliant users' data were; email (12), name (12) and location (10); whereas iOS had email (9), location (9) and, name and friends both (6). It appears that apart from iOS collecting friends, the other compliant user data attributes were the same for both platforms.

In contrast, considering non-compliance between the apps' policies and their data handling practices, Android's most non-compliant user data were; username (6), gender (5) and address (5) while for iOS the list comprised of; password (5), address (4), username and name both at (3) as shown Figs. 2 and 3. In both iOS and Android, the similarities in non-compliance was that the *username* and *address* user data was collected and disseminated outside the privacy policy agreement, while the differences in the data handled outside the policy was that Android collected *gender* user data attribute while iOS collected the *name* user data attribute.

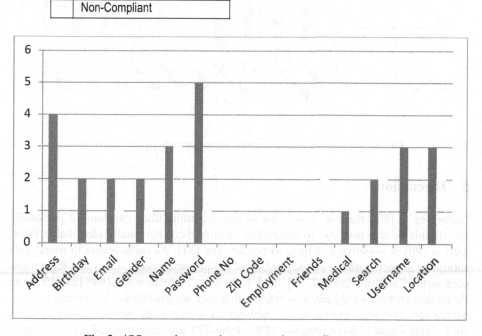

Fig. 2. iOS apps data practice versus privacy policy statements

Further, iOS apps were found to handle users' data without privacy policies. The affected user data included; name (3), friend (2) and search (2) as shown in Fig. 1.

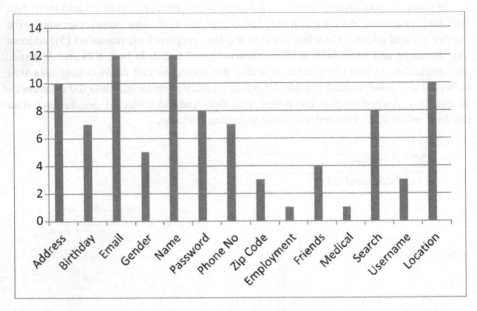

Fig. 3. Android apps data practice versus privacy policy statements

5 Discussion

According to [30], there is an increase in fear regarding illicit exposure of personally identifiable information due to increasing identity theft. Personally identifiable information (PII) is sensitive and focal to privacy law [31]. As such, access to users' data should be aligned with the privacy policy of online social media. Laws and regulations such as the California law [32, 33]; the UK the Data Protection Act 1998 [34], EU Data Protection Directive [35] etc. also require that user are provided with privacy policies before app download. However, our findings show that while the Android apps in the study were found to have policies, 14% of the iOS user data handled was from apps without policies. Similarly, [35] study of health apps found that iOS had a 61.7% likelihood of not having privacy policies as compared to Android at 77.3%. Differences in our results may arise from the fact that we considered fewer apps (30) with more categories while [35] considered 600 app limited to health apps. These findings highlight the fact that while the law demands for the provision of policies, major app platform are not fully complying. This is also an indicator that even when laws are enacted to protect user privacy, there is need for more effective mechanisms of enforcing these laws.

However, specifically considering compliance of apps' data handling practices their privacy policies, Android had an 18% likelihood of sharing personally identifiable information outside the limits of its policy whereas iOS' ranked slightly lower at 17%. While our study investigated the extent of compliance between the Android and iOS apps' data dissemination against their privacy policies, a related study by [24], compared Android and iOS likelihood to disseminate users' personally identifiable information in a manner not reflected by the permissions request at the apps' download, they found that Android was more likely to disseminate personal data in a way a way that breached the requested permissions.

However, taking into account the iOS apps found without privacy policies in our study, the probability of iOS sharing personally identifiable information in a non-policy compliant manner further increase from 17% to 23%, making it higher than Android (18%). Users' ability protect their personal data necessitates that they are aware of such leakages [30]. Moreover, our findings also contradict a general user perception that apps with user textual reviews are safer [16]. This is evidenced by the fact that the apps in our study had user reviews yet our findings show that some had no privacy policies.

Specifically in both Android and iOS apps studied, mismatches between the policies and the data handled were most observed involving the *username* and *address* user data which are both classified as personally identified information. Further, our findings indicated that the similarities in the most collected user data in both Android and iOS was that both collected *name* and *email* user data which are both personally identified information. Nonetheless our results also showed that these two types of user data were also among the leading policy compliant user data. Our results show that in both cases of compliance and non-compliance with the apps' policies, the user data involved is personally identified information. These trends indicate the immense interest that apps have in personally identifiable information data and hence the necessity of ensuring adequate and effective user privacy preservation measures.

Our results ascertained that neither Android nor iOS apps' data handling practices fully comply with the apps' privacy policy statements. These results are restricted to the observation of data collection and transmission at app level. They do not include whatever happens on the receiving servers. In addition, the measurement errors made in [24] were inherited, as mentioned above. Overall, taking into account both personal and non-personal user data analysed in the study, Android data handling practices are more compliant to policy than that of iOS with compliance figures of 68% and 40% respectively. Policies claim to limit the user data conveyed to third parties to non-personal data [30]. However, [36] state that metadata has the potential danger of re-identification of users or sources, stressing that it is still possible to expose specific users even from non-personal data. This is underpinned [30], asserting that certain third party servers have the ability to trace and combine different pieces of user data from which a user profile can be formed. According to a study [37], a combination of the zip code, gender and birthday is able to facilitate the identification of up to 87% of Americans.

Based on the finding of this study, which in tandem built on the results from [24], we argue that in the preservation and protection of app user privacy a number of aspects must be considered i.e. regulation, permissions requested at apps' download, privacy policies provided and, the dissemination of user data by the apps to other apps or third parties. The relevant regulations determine the privacy requirements or best practices that must be taken into consideration by apps in order to safe guard user privacy. As such, the apps permissions, policy and dissemination of user data should be aligned to regulation. This study established that there are instances in which user data was disseminated with no policy to guide the process. For cases in which no policy is provided, users could opt not to download such apps. However, this may be unlikely [38] and may depend on a users' level of privacy awareness, keenness and the personal reasons for which they require the apps service.

Further, this study shows that the dissemination of data by apps through their data handling practices does not always comply with their stated privacy policies, even in cases where potentially sensitive user data is involved. This is of concern since a study by [39] found that 72% of the participants assume that the provision of a policy implies that app providers comply with the policy and necessary regulation to safeguard their privacy. We further argue that one of the criticisms of current practice is that an app may request a user to grant access to personal data which is not required for its app's functionality. This excess data may have been stated in the privacy policies, in which case it would appear as acceptable. However, it may violate the minimize principle in some regulatory frameworks [4] but not necessarily the privacy policy. There is a user expectation that regulators will protect their privacy [39]. As such, this emphasizes the need for more effective mechanism of validation of apps' data handling practices against their policies.

Validation could be effected through more rigorous regulatory enforcement to monitor that apps comply to their policy. Another form of validation could take shape in form of automation of the validation process. An automated solution could function at platform level i.e. Android and iOS. At platform level, the solution could be developed first to check that and app indeed has a privacy policy before its acceptance onto the platform. Second, the automation could be used to validate compliance between apps policies and against their data dissemination practices. In a way, it would be similar to the Apple vetting process that validates that app comply with the license agreement before digital signing and uptake onto the iTunes store.

In addition to ensuring the provision of privacy policies and the validation of apps data handling practices against their policies either by regulators or through automation, several other solutions may be considered. These efforts have been geared improving policy representations in a bid to encourage or facilitate greater policy readability and user comprehension in order to encourage user reading of privacy policies so as to support informed decisions [40–42].

6   Conclusion and Future Work

Our results show that neither Android nor iOS apps' data handling practices meet the full requirements of their privacy policies even in cases of potentially sensitive user data. Further, instances in which iOS apps continue to disseminate user data in the absence of privacy policies were found. This is further complicated by the fact that there is no facility through which the users can confirm that the way their data is disseminated by apps matches the permissions requested by apps at download and their privacy policies. Drawing from our findings, we recommend the necessity of enhancing app platforms such that data collection is not merely checked against the app's request to use data, but that this process is enhanced by cross checking apps' data handling practices against the apps' privacy commitments to app users as stipulated within their privacy policies. As such, future research could explore ways of automating enforcement of privacy policies by drawing on privacy policy specification languages such as the Platform for Privacy Preferences (P3P) and the Enterprise Privacy Authorization Language (EPAL). This would also eliminate the transfer of data from apps that do not have privacy policies. In hindsight, a technological solution could prove the most feasible solution to this challenge through the development of a real-time graphical visual aid that depicts apps' compliance to their policies and, as well as provide automated opt-out options for users in cases of non-compliance. Taking into account considerations of the privacy requirements stipulated by regulatory frameworks such as the European General Data Protection Regulation would assist in enhancing and protecting users' privacy. In addition to building user confidence in apps' commitment to preserve user data privacy, it would also be of value to privacy regulatory bodies by automating compliance to stated privacy policies.

References

1. Sarma, B., Li, N., Gates, C., Potharaju, R., Nita-Rotaru, C., Molloy, I.: Android permissions: a perspective combining risks and benefits. In: 17th ACM Symposium on Access Control Models and Technologies, pp. 13–22 (2012)
2. Thurm, S., Kane, Y.: Your Apps Are Watching You. Wall Street Journal. http://online.wsj.com/news/articles/SB10001424052748704694004576020083703574602?mg=reno64-wsj&url=http%3A%2F%2Fonline.wsj.com%2Farticle%2FSB10001424052748704694004576020083703574602.html. Accessed 2010
3. Papanikolaou, N., Creese, S., Goldsmith, M.: Refinement checking for privacy policies. Sci. Comput. Program. **77**, 1198–1209 (2012)
4. European Union Directive: EUR-Lex. Access to European Union Law. http://eur-lex.europa.eu/search.html?qid=1516438784094&text=GDPR&scope=EURLEX&type=quick&lang=en. Accessed 2017
5. Westin, A.: Privacy and Freedom. Atheneum Publishers, New York (1967)
6. Anton, A.I., Reese, A.: Analyzing web site privacy requirements using a privacy goal taxonomy. In: IEEE Joint Requirements Engineering Conference, vol. 9, pp. 23–31, Essen (2001)
7. Jensen, C., Potts, C., Jensen, C.: Privacy practices of internet users: self-report versus observed behavior. Int. J. Hum Comput Stud. **63**(1–2), 203–227 (2005)
8. Sadeh, N., Hong, J., Cranor, L., Fette, I., Kelley, P., Prabaker, M., Rao, J.: Understanding and capturing people's privacy policies in a mobile social networking application. Pers. Ubiquit. Comput. **13**, 401–412 (2009)
9. Cellan-Jones, R.: BBC. http://www.bbc.co.uk/news/technology-30234789. Accessed 2014
10. Liu, R., Cao, J., Yang, L.: Smartphone privacy in mobile computing: Issues, methods and systems. Inf. Media Technol. **10**(2), 281–293 (2015)
11. Wei, X., Gomez, L., Neamtiu, I., Faloutsos, M.: Permission evolution in the Android ecosystem. In: ACSAC 2012 Proceedings of the 28th Annual Computer Security Applications Conference, Florida, pp. 31–40 (2012)

12. Grace, M., Zhou, W., Jiang, X., Sadeghi, A.: Unsafe exposure analysis of mobile in-app advertisements. ACM, Arizona (2012)
13. Book, T., Pridgen, A., Wallach, D.: Longitudinal Analysis of Android Ad Library (2013)
14. Ashnis: noeticforce. http://noeticforce.com/app-permissions-android-vs-ios. Accessed 2016
15. Hoffman, C.: How -To Geek. https://www.howtogeek.com/177711/ios-has-app-permissions-too-and-theyre-arguably-better-than-androids/. Accessed 2013
16. Benenson, Z., Gassmann, F., Reinfelder, L.: Android and iOS users' differences concerning security and privacy. In: Human Factors in Computing Systems, pp. 817–822 (2013)
17. Felt, A.P., Finifter, M., Chin, E., Hanna, S., Wagner, D.: A survey of mobile malware in the wild. In: SPSM (2011)
18. Seriot, N.: iPhone Privacy. Black Hat, USA (2010)
19. Bonnington, C.: First Instance of iOS App Store Malware Detected. http://www.wired.com. Accessed 2012
20. Egele, M., Kruegel, C., Kirda, E., Vigna, G.: PiOS: detecting privacy leaks in iOS applications. In: NDSS, pp. 177–183 (2011)
21. Liu, C., Arnett, K.P.: An examination of privacy policies in Fortune 500 web sites. Am. J. Bus. 17(1), 13–22 (2002)
22. Wetherall, D., Choffnes, D., Greenstein, B., Han, S., Hornyack, P., Jung, J., Schechter, S., Wang, X.: Privacy revelations for web and mobile apps. In: HotOS, vol. XIII (2011)
23. Van-Alsenoy, B., Verdoodt, V., Heyman, R., Wauters, E., Ausloos, J., Acar, G.: https://www.law.kuleuven.be/citip/en/news/item/facebooks-revised-policies-and-terms-v1-2.pdf. Accessed 2015
24. Zang, J., Dummit, K., Graves, J., Lisker, P., Sweeney, L.: Who knows what about me? A survey of behind the scenes personal data sharing to third parties by mobile apps. In: Technology Science (2015)
25. Sunyaev, A., Dehling, T., Taylor, P., Mandl, K.: Availability and quality of mobile health app privacy policies. J. Am. Med. Inf. Assoc. 22(e1), e28–e33 (2015)
26. Antón, A.I., Earp, J.B.: A requirements taxonomy for reducing Web site privacy vulnerabilities. Requirements Eng. 9(3), 169–185 (2004)
27. Rosen, S., Qian, Z., Mao, Z.M.: Approfiler: a flexible method of exposing privacy-related behavior in android applications to end users. In: 32 Annual ACM Conference on Human factors in Computing Systems, pp. 2347–2356 (2014)
28. QSR: What is NVivo?. http://www.qsrinternational.com/what-is-nvivo. Accessed 2017
29. Armstrong, D., Gosling, A., Weinman, J., Marteau, T.: The place of inter-rater reliability in qualitative research: an empirical study. Sociology 31, 597–606 (1997)
30. Krishnamurthy, B., Wills, C.E.: On the leakage of personally identifiable information via online social networks. In: 2nd ACM Workshop on Online Social Networks, pp. 7–12 (2009)
31. Schwartz, P., Solove, D.: PII problem: privacy and a new concept of personally identifiable information. NYUL Rev 86, 1814 (2011)
32. Harris, K.: Privacy on the go, FTC (2013)
33. CalOPPA: California Online Privacy Protection Act (CalOPPA). http://consumercal.org. http://consumercal.org/about-cfc/cfc-education-foundation-2014/what-should-i-know-about-privacy-policies/california-online-privacy-protection-act-caloppa/. Accessed 2015
34. TermsFeed: Privacy Policies are Mandatory by Law. https://termsfeed.com/blog/privacy-policy-mandatory-law/. Accessed 2017
35. European Union Directive.: EUR-Lex. Access to European Union Law. http://eur-lex.europa.eu/legal-content/EN/TXT/?uri=CELEX:31995L0046. Accessed 2017
36. Montjoye, Y., Radaelli, L., Singh, V.K.: Unique in the shopping mall on the reidentifiability of credit card metadata. Science 347(6221), 536–539 (2015)

37. Malin, B.: Betrayed by my shadow: learning data identify via trail matching. J. Priv. Technol. (2005)
38. Janger, E.J., Schwartz, P.M.: The Gramm-Leach-Bliley Act, Information privacy and the limits of default rules. Minnesota Law Rev. **86**, 1219–1230 (2002)
39. Yue, L.: User control of personal information concerning mobile-app: Notice and consent? Comput. Law Secur. Rev. **30**(5), 521–529 (2014)
40. Earp, J.B., Vail, M., Anton, A.I.: Privacy policy representation in web-based healthcare. In: 40th Annual Hawaii International Conference, p. 138 (2007)
41. Cranor, L., Kelley, P.G., Cesca, L., Bresee, J.: Standardizing privacy notices: an online study of the nutrition label approach. In: SIGCHI Conference, pp. 1573–1582 (2010)
42. Kununka, S., Mehandjiev, N., Sampaio, P., Vassilopoulou, K.: End user comprehension of privacy policy. In: International Symposium on End User Development, pp. 135–149, Eindhoven (2017)
43. Wei, T.E., Jeng, A.B., Lee, H.M., Chen, C.H., Tien, C.W.: Android privacy. In: Machine Learning and Cybernetics (ICMLC), pp. 1830–1837 (2012)
44. Van-Alsenoy, B.: Accessed 2015
45. Schwartz, P.M., Solove, D.: Notice and choice. In: The Second NPLAN/BMSG Meeting on Digital Media and Marketing to Children (2009)
46. Sunyaev, A., Dehling, T., Taylor, P., Mandl, K.: Availability and quality of mobile health app privacy policies. J. Am. Med. Inf. Assoc. **22**(1), 22–33 (2014)

Privacy Concerns and Behavior
of Pokémon Go Players in Germany

David Harborth[(✉)][iD] and Sebastian Pape[iD]

Chair of Mobile Business and Multilateral Security,
Goethe University Frankfurt am Main, Frankfurt, Germany
{david.harborth,sebastian.pape}@m-chair.de

Abstract. We investigate privacy concerns and the privacy behavior of
users of the AR smartphone game Pokémon Go. Pokémon Go accesses
several functionalities of the smartphone and, in turn, collects a plethora
of data of its users. For assessing the privacy concerns, we conduct an
online study in Germany with 683 users of the game. The results indicate that the majority of the active players are concerned about the
privacy practices of companies. This result hints towards the existence
of a cognitive dissonance, i.e. the privacy paradox. Since this result is
common in the privacy literature, we complement the first study with
a second one with 199 users, which aims to assess the behavior of users
with regard to which measures they undertake for protecting their privacy. The results are highly mixed and dependent on the measure, i.e.
relatively many participants use privacy-preserving measures when interacting with their smartphone. This implies that many users know about
risks and might take actions to protect their privacy, but deliberately
trade-off their information privacy for the utility generated by playing
the game.

Keywords: Privacy concerns · Augmented reality · Pokémon Go
Concerns for Information Privacy (CFIP) · Privacy calculus
Privacy behavior

1 Introduction

The location-based augmented reality (AR) smartphone game Pokémon Go (cf.
Fig. 1) is amongst the most successful smartphone applications of all time and led
to a major increase in public awareness about AR [26,32]. The game has broken
several records [44] and it was shown that its users develop a strong attachment
to the game [30]. Pokémon Go poses relatively strong privacy threats compared
to other smartphone applications, due to the AR functionalities and the location-
based nature. There is almost no research on privacy issues with regard to AR
technologies [21]. Thus, we investigate privacy concerns about organizational
information privacy practices and privacy-related behaviors of active Pokémon

© IFIP International Federation for Information Processing 2018
Published by Springer International Publishing AG 2018. All Rights Reserved
M. Hansen et al. (Eds.): Privacy and Identity 2017, IFIP AICT 526, pp. 314–329, 2018.
https://doi.org/10.1007/978-3-319-92925-5_21

Fig. 1. Pokémon Go on iOS [5]

Go players in Germany. Three research questions arise: First, are privacy concerns a relevant issue for Pokémon Go players and do they differ in magnitude between different groups of players? Second, is there a relationship between the different dimensions of privacy concerns and the actual use behavior? Third, what are active players doing to protect their privacy on their smartphone?

The success of Pokémon Go [50] allows it to address these questions for an AR technology based on a large scale user study for the first time. Understanding the heterogeneous perceptions on privacy is necessary since many experts predict that AR will become one of the next big technological innovations with a massive market potential [8,25]. Privacy aspects are especially important for AR because of its pervasiveness associated the advancements of wearable AR technologies (e.g. head-mounted displays). This leads to a situation where the user is continuously provided with context-sensitive information about her or his environment [19]. This, in turn, makes it necessary to continuously gather and process all kinds of data. Privacy violations can happen to actual users of a system – due to the increasing collection of several different data types [25] – or to the users' direct environment. The case of the social environment could be observed in the past for Google Glasses with several reports about angry civilians who had the feeling of being filmed by the wearer and bars which prohibited entry when wearing the glasses. This partly led to the failure of the device in the consumer market [49]. This case emphasizes the need to understand privacy concerns and behaviors of users in respect to AR technology even more. We investigate the privacy concerns based on a sample of 683 active players of Pokémon Go in Germany. The results indicate that privacy concerns are relatively strong throughout different demographic groups (cf. Table 1). This is a surprising result, considering that the participants are all active players of the game. Thus, in the second stage of the research, a second online survey with 199 participants is conducted to figure out specific measures how players protect their privacy.

The remainder of the paper is structured as follows. A brief background on Pokémon Go, AR and related work on privacy is given in Sect. 2. The methodology is described in Sect. 3 and the results are presented in Sect. 4. In Sect. 5 results and their limitations are discussed. Section 6 concludes this work.

2   Theoretical Background

In the following part, we provide theoretical background on Pokémon Go, augmented reality and the current literature on privacy.

2.1   Pokémon Go and Augmented Reality

Pokémon Go [3] is a location-based augmented reality (AR) smartphone game developed by Niantic, a former Google owned company [3,31]. Many people see Pokémon Go as the unofficial successor of Ingress [2], another location-based smartphone game, also developed by Niantic. Up to now, no homogeneous opinion, of whether Pokémon Go matches all criteria of AR is formed. However, there is broad agreement that it is a first important step towards AR [17,20,27,28]. Thus, we approach Pokémon Go as an AR application for the course of our research.

AR is defined in multiple ways, whereas the definition by Azuma et al. [4, p. 34] provides a comprehensive understanding of the technology. They define AR in a way that "[...] an AR system [...] combines real and virtual objects in a real environment; runs interactively, and in real time; and registers (aligns) real and virtual objects with each other". The differentiation towards virtual reality (VR) is currently not always done in the public discussion. Milgram et al. [29] illustrate the dimensions of mixed reality (MR) based on a x-axis (cf. Fig. 2). Based on this, it is important to distinguish whether the environment is real (AR) or virtual (VR). Up to now, research on AR mainly focused on technical aspects and not on the user behavior [21,43]. Since AR is expected to be one of the upcoming technologies [8], it is important to investigate user behavior and privacy issues.

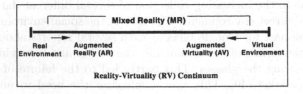

Fig. 2. The Reality-Virtuality Continuum [29]

2.2   Privacy and the Privacy Paradox

The definition of privacy in the literature consists of a variety of different perspectives [6,39]. An often cited definition is given by Warren and Brandeis in 1890. They say that privacy is "the right to be left alone" [48]. In the context of this paper, the privacy definition provided by Culnan [10, p. 344] is used, where "privacy is the ability of an individual to control the access others have to personal information". The notion of control plays a crucial role in the privacy literature [7] and for the concerns about organizational practices. Thus, we choose this definition for our research context. Previous literature shows that privacy concerns play an important role for the usage of internet services. For example, Tang et al. [45] argue that retailers can improve privacy and trust if they send clear signals that they will protect the privacy of the customers. Culnan and Armstrong [11, p. 107] provide a framework where users provide their personal data willingly, if they perceive the firm's information processes as "fair". Fair means in this context that these processes "provide individuals with control over the disclosure and subsequent use of their personal information". Differences in privacy behavior with regard to demographics [10,11,38,46] and cultural differences [14] are investigated in previous literature as well. But it is shown that the majority of literature focuses on student samples based in the United States [6]. In summary, it can be stated that privacy plays an important role for the usage of online services. However, it is important to mention that "privacy concern is only one of a number of factors affecting Internet and e-services use" [16, p. 51].

Closely related to the discussion on privacy concerns and behavior is the so called "privacy paradox". This phenomenon describes the divergence of the actual behavior of users compared to the stated attitudes when dealing with privacy issues [1,9,33,41]. The privacy paradox is a well-known topic in information systems research. Spiekermann et al. [41] experimentally show that participants reveal a multitude of information, which enables providers to construct a detailed profile during an online-shopping tour, although they stated to be concerned about their privacy before the experiment. The paper by Berendt et al. [9] is built on the previously mentioned paper and shows the existence of the privacy paradox by using an e-commerce experiment, too. Acquisti and Grossklags present another point of view on the privacy paradox. They show that while people have high standards regarding their privacy attitudes, their decision process is influenced by psychological factors like "incomplete information, bounded rationality and systematic psychological deviations from rationality" [1, p. 29]. These limitations lead to a trade-off of "long-term privacy for short-term benefits" [1, p. 24]. Norberg et al. [33] investigate why this divergence of actual behavior and attitudes towards privacy exists. The results support the hypothesis that risk perceptions of users when disclosing personal information influence the intentions to provide personal information. However, the second hypothesis about the effect of trust on the disclosure behavior could not be confirmed.

In summary, it is important to recognize that people do not always behave in the way they state that they would do. Therefore, all results that deal with attitudes of users, in particular regarding to privacy, have to be treated with caution if the goal of the research is to make valid statements for decision choices. Thus, we include the second survey on the actual privacy measures in this work.

3 Methodology

The methodology presents the design and data collection of the first and the second survey. The second survey on actual privacy related behavior was conducted after we conducted the first one on privacy concerns.

3.1 Questionnaire

Survey I We conducted the study with a German panel, thus all items had to be translated into German. As we wanted to ensure content validity of the translation, we followed a rigorous translation process [47]. First, the English questionnaire was translated into German with by a certified translator (translators are standardized following the DIN EN 15038 norm). Afterwards, the German version was given to a second independent certified translator who re translated the questionnaire to English. This step was done to ensure the equivalence of the translation. Third, a group of five academic colleagues checked the two English versions with regard to this equivalence. All items were found to be equivalent. In a last step, the German version of the questionnaire was administered to students of a Master's course to check preliminary reliability and validity.

Privacy concerns with regard to organizational information privacy practices are represented by the variables collection, errors, unauthorized secondary use and improper access. As these variables cannot be measured directly (latent variables), they have to be operationalized in order to quantify the concerns via a user study. We choose the privacy constructs by Smith et al. [40], as they are widely tested with regard to validity and reliability (cf. Stewart and Segars [42]). The constructs are built by calculating mean sum scores of the single items belonging to the respective construct (cf. Appendix A). *Collection* is defined as the concern of people that too much data about them is collected over time. *Errors* represent users' concerns about inaccurate or false personal data in databases. *Unauthorized secondary use* measures the concern that personal data is used for another purpose than initially disclosed without the user's authorization. *Improper access* captures concerns about unauthorized people having access to the user's personal data [40, p. 172].

Survey II The questionnaire of the second survey covers questions about actual privacy protecting measures, which active Pokémon Go players undertake. The questionnaire contains the same demographic questions about age, gender, education and smartphone experience, as well as actual use behavior of Pokémon Go as the first survey. The steps are derived from internet search [18], as well as valuable feedback from colleagues. Measure 1 (M1) asks about whether users turn off services that potentially collect location data. Measure 2 (M2) deals with the use of a separate e-mail address used only for games. Measure 3 (M3) specifies this furthermore and asks about the use of different e-mail addresses for games and social network sites (sns). Measure 4 (M4) asks the participants whether they review which applications can access other accounts (e.g. Facebook). Measure 5 (M5) asks whether users reset the advertising ID on their phone and measure 6

(M6) deals the camera access rights of Pokémon Go. All measures are formulated as statements and could be answered with "yes", "no", "sometimes" or "I don't know". The specific questions can be found in Appendix B.

3.2   Data Collection

Survey I In order to ensure high quality of the sample, a certified sample provider (certified with ISO 26362 norm) was employed to get access to their online panel for Germany. By focusing on German users of the game, we could address two potential problems. First, country-specific differences in privacy concerns are eliminated and controlled. Second, by focusing on one country, we could gather a relatively large data set. The survey itself was administered with LimeSurvey (version 2.63.1) [37]. The panel provider distributed the survey's link to 9338 participants until the aimed sample size of active players was reached. Of 9338 approached participants, 683 active Pokémon Go players remained, excluding participants who dropped out due to wrong answers to test questions and age restrictions (data was only collected for at least 18 year old participants). Table 1 presents summary statistics for this data set. Further information with regard to the demographics can be found in the paper by Harborth and Pape [22].

Survey II Since of the constructs in Survey I only provide information about attitudes and stated concerns, we wanted to consider actual use behavior with regard to privacy protecting measures. Because of anonymized answers in Survey I, we could not ask the same participants. In addition, we could not employ a panel provider as in Survey I due to limited resources. Thus, we created a very brief questionnaire (see Sect. 3.1) and administered it with LimeSurvey (version 2.63.1) [37]. We distributed the link of the online survey in three Pokémon Go Facebook groups (Germany, Frankfurt and Munich). All groups are closed groups with approximately 30,000 members altogether. The questionnaire was online for 4 days and 238 users started it, whereas only 200 participants finished it. One participant's answers were deleted, because he or she stated his/her age to be younger than 18 years. Table 2 presents the summary statistics for this data set.

3.3   Demographics

Survey I Table 1 shows that the median age is 32 years and that there is a larger share of women than men in the sample. Furthermore, the secondary school leaving certificate[1] and the A levels certificate[2] are the most common educational qualifications. With regard to these demographics, it can be argued that this data set represents the German population to an acceptable degree. The smartphone experience has a median of 6 years. The privacy constructs have all at least a median value of 5.5, implying that most players agree to the statements made in the constructs' items. The actual use frequency has a

---

[1] German: "Realschulabschluss".
[2] German: "Abitur".

Table 1. Descriptive statistics survey I (N = 683)

	Mean	Median	Std. Dev.	Min.	Max.
Age	34.539	32	(11.531)	18	66
Gender	0.572	1	(0.495)	0	1
Educational qualification	3.977	4	(1.207)	1	7
Smartphone experience	5.958	6	(2.359)	0	10
Collection	5.349	5.5	(1.172)	1	7
Errors	5.355	5.5	(1.198)	1	7
Unauthorized secondary use	6.015	6.5	(1.071)	1	7
Improper access	5.971	6.333	(1.090)	1	7
Frequency of actual use	5.517	5	(1.619)	1	10

median of 5 which stands for playing "several times a week". Improper access has a median of 6.333[3].

Survey II The demographics of the second survey are slightly different to the first survey with regard to age, gender and smartphone experience (cf. Table 2). The participants of the second survey are 6 years younger with regard to the median age and there are slightly more men than women in Survey II. The users in Survey II have one year more smartphone experience. Although the users in both surveys say that they are active Pokémon Go players, the participants in Survey II state that they play Pokémon Go several times a day (median of 7) and players of Survey I state that they play it only several times a week.

Apparently, the participants acquired through Facebook groups are rather heavy users compared to the ones acquired with the help of a sample provider. A

Table 2. Descriptive statistics survey II (N = 199)

	Mean	Median	Std. Dev.	Min.	Max.
Age	28.884	26	(8.695)	18	58
Gender	0.477	0	(0.501)	0	1
Educational qualification	4.261	4	(1.142)	1	7
Smartphone experience	7.156	7	(2.279)	2	11
M1	2.050	2	(0.827)	1	4
M2	1.658	2	(0.654)	1	3
M3	1.668	2	(0.689)	1	3
M4	1.563	1	(0.838)	1	3
M5	2.221	2	(0.652)	1	4
M6	1.492	1	(0.658)	1	3
Frequency of actual use	6.729	7	(1.783)	1	10

---

[3] This is possible because of the construct is calculated based on the mean sum score of three items (the other three concern constructs each consist of four items).

self-selection mechanism could explain this difference. In these Facebook groups, players exchange information about new offers, versions and places to hunt for special Pokémons. This is especially interesting for highly attached players, which would indicate that those are rather heavy users.

4   Results

We present the results of Survey I and Survey II in the following sections.

4.1   Survey I - Privacy Concerns

The variables collection, errors, unauthorized secondary use and improper access are not normally distributed while actual use is normally distributed according to the Shapiro-Wilk test for normality. In the first part of the empirical assessment, it is investigated whether users' privacy concerns and the actual use behavior (i.e. frequency of playing Pokémon Go) differ with regard to age, gender, education and smartphone experience. Therefore, categorical variables for group comparisons are created by dividing the scale of continuous variables into two meaningful groups. Categorical variables for group comparisons are created based on the variables age, smartphone experience and educational qualification. This is necessary because they are not binaries like gender. For creating a categorical variable, a threshold is needed that divides the scale into two meaningful groups.

The threshold for age is not clearly determinable because there are two rationales for dividing the data which are highly interesting to investigate in the context of privacy. The first approach is a median split, a commonly used technique for forming categorical variables in statistics [24]. This has the advantage of comparing two groups, similar in size, based on the actual median of the used data set. This results in the groups of participants aged 31 and younger and participants aged 32 and older. A categorical variable is created where 0 stands for participants aged 31 and younger and 1 for participants aged 32 and older. One group contains 341 participants and the second one 342. The second approach deals with the notion of "digital natives" (DN) versus "digital immigrants" (DI) [35]. Since there is a vivid discussion on whether the notion of DN is substantial [23], it is interesting in the context of privacy concerns to apply this threshold and investigate, whether it is true that DI are rather privacy sensitive and more concerned than the younger generation. A commonly named threshold for the oldest year of birth of a DN is 1980 [34]. The resulting two groups contain 446 entries for DN (37 years old and younger) and 237 entries for DI. The median split approach is applied for experience since this is the most meaningful approach, with groups with smartphone experience less than or equal to 5 years and greater than or equal to 6 years. Education is divided into a group with participants without university degree (NU), comprising all participants whose highest educational qualification is the German Abitur (N = 487) and a group with 196 participants holding at least a Bachelor's degree (U). Table 3 summarizes the

Table 3. Two-sample Wilcoxon rank-sum and two-sample t test (for actual use)

| Variables | Group Variables | | | | |
	Age_{Median}	Age_{DN}	Gender	Education	Smartphone exp
Collection	$z=-3.217**$	$z=-3.288**$	n.s.	n.s.	n.s.
Errors	$z=-6.644***$	$z=-5.852***$	n.s.	$z=2.766**$	n.s.
Un. sec. use	n.s.	$z=-3.020**$	$z=-4.019***$	n.s.	n.s.
Imp. access	$z=-2.516**$	$z=-3.870***$	$z=-2.589***$	n.s.	n.s.
Actual use	n.s.	n.s.	n.s.	n.s.	$t=-4.335***$

t statistic for t test and z statistics for Wilcoxon rank-sum test
* $p < 0.05$, ** $p < 0.01$, *** $p < 0.001$

results for the statistical assessment of whether the group differences in mean values are statistically significant or not.

Table 4. Regression analysis of privacy concern variables and use behavior (N = 683)

	(1)	(2)	(3)	(4)	(5)
	Dependent variable: actual use behavior				
Collection	0.0518				-0.00691
	(1.00)				(-0.11)
Errors		-0.0480			$-0.170**$
		(-0.91)			(-2.76)
Un. Sec. Use			0.124*		0.00368
			(2.05)		(0.03)
Imp. Access				0.149*	0.251*
				(2.53)	(2.19)
_cons	5.240***	5.774***	4.772***	4.630***	4.943***
	(18.70)	(20.00)	(12.85)	(13.01)	(12.78)

t statistics in parentheses
* $p < 0.05$, ** $p < 0.01$, *** $p < 0.001$

For collection there are only significant differences for the two different age groups. Users' perceptions of the errors construct differs between younger and older participants as well as between participants without and with university degree. Interestingly, the group comparison of unauthorized secondary use is different for the age groups. For the median split, there is no statistically significant difference in the evaluation between younger and older players, whereas there is one for the case of DN versus DI. The evaluation for this construct differs significantly between women and men. For the improper access construct, statistically significant differences are prevalent for age and gender. The variable actual use is homogeneous across the different characteristics of Pokémon Go players except for smartphone experience. The question of whether privacy concerns influence the use behavior is addressed in the second part of the empirical analysis. Due to the breakdown into four variables, it is possible to assess which kind of privacy concern exerts what kind of influence on use behavior. This question is addressed with a two-stage process (cf. Table 4). First, each privacy concern variable is treated as the independent variable in a simple linear regression model, with actual use behavior as the dependent variable. Second, a multiple regression model, containing all independent variables, is calculated in order to assess the effect of the different dimensions of privacy concerns on use behavior simultaneously.

The results of the regression analysis indicate that privacy concerns have no significant impact on the actual use behavior. Although there are statistically significant relationships, the effect sizes are rather small and therefore not relevant.

In summary, the results about privacy concerns indicate that there are significant differences in the different dimensions of concerns between younger and older players. Furthermore, gender matters for two of the four dimensions. An additional regression analysis with the actual use frequency revealed no clear impact of privacy concerns, indicating that players might well be aware of privacy dangers and are concerned about it, but are still playing the game. Thus, although privacy is perceived as important, it does not affect the use of Pokémon Go. The game requires several more types of data compared to other smartphone applications due to its location-based and AR nature. This contrary result could be a case of the privacy paradox [33], where people state that privacy is important for them, but act in the opposite way.

4.2 Survey II - Privacy Behavior

The distribution of the answers on the privacy protecting measures are illustrated in Fig. 3. The number of participants who turn off services that collect location data is approximately the same as those who do not and those who sometimes do it. 45% of the players use a separate e-mail address only for games and roughly the same number of players do not. The remaining users (10%) do it sometimes. The distribution for M3 (different e-mail addresses for games and sns) is almost the same as for M2. Interestingly, more than 65% of the Pokémon Go players review the access of applications to other accounts and only 10% do not. The remaining users undertake this measure sometimes. More than 80% of the users do not reset the advertising ID and only 10% do know about it at all. The majority of the players forbid Pokémon Go the camera access (60%) and 10% do it sometimes. The remaining participants do not forbid it.

5   Discussion

After we discussed the results of the two surveys independently of each other, we combine and interpret our results in the following part. After that, we discuss the limitations of our work.

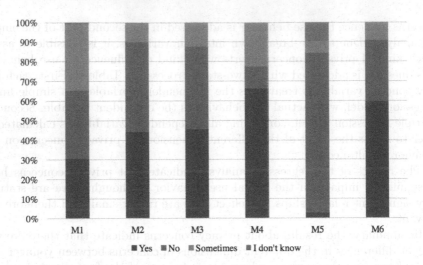

Fig. 3. Relative frequency of the measures taken by Pokémon Go players

5.1 Interpretation and Implications of the Results

As mentioned previously, there are significant differences in the different dimensions of the concerns between younger and older players. Furthermore, gender matters for two of the four dimensions. Gender differences in privacy concerns were also shown to be prevalent in past literature (e.g. [38,46]). For the age differences, the results indicate that relatively older players of Pokémon Go are more concerned. This is in line with the dominant notion of less concerned younger internet users compared to older users with a higher awareness. The regression analyses do not show any impact of the privacy concern dimensions on the actual use behavior of Pokémon Go. Based on this, it can be said that concerns about the privacy practices of organizations exist amongst players of the game and that they are heterogeneous with regard to the certain demographic characteristics. However, these users still play a game, which has access to several data types and processes them. This behavior is in line with the notion of the privacy paradox. However, this explanation becomes inconclusive, when looking at the actual privacy preserving measures of the players. It can be seen that, depending on the measure, approximately half of the participants of the second survey engage regularly or sometimes in doing these measures. A combination of these results imply that the majority of Pokémon Go players are aware about the risks (since they actively try to preserve their privacy with the measures tested) and almost all players are concerned. However, it seems that playing the game provides so much utility that they willingly agree to the implicit trade-off between playing the game and loosing a certain degree of control over their privacy. This explanation for an opposing behavior with regard to information privacy is known as the privacy calculus [12,13,15]. The privacy calculus is often mentioned in the literature as an explanation for the privacy paradox.

5.2   Limitations

The main limitations concern the sample characteristics. Both samples contain relatively more younger Pokémon Go players. With respect to this, the sample is not representative for the German population. This skewness might also be caused by the fact that digital games are played rather by younger users than older ones. In addition, our survey is only conducted with German players. Thus, the results could possibly differ from surveys conducted in other countries or cultural regions. But, this focus brings along advantages for this research (cf. Sect. 3.2), which can outweigh the limitations. Another limitation relates to the German translation of the English constructs. The constructs might have been understood differently by the participants than originally intended. This is always a possible threat when adapting original constructs from a language to another. The last limitation emerges due to the fact of analyzing two different samples. As described in Sect. 3.2, we could not ask the same participants from the first survey about their privacy preserving measures. Therefore, we are not able to compare the relationship between concerns and actual privacy behavior on an individual level. In addition, it is possible that people lie about their actual behavior in surveys. Thus, asking people what they actually do is also prone to errors that can hardly be controlled for in an online survey.

6   Conclusion and Future Work

We contributed to the literature on privacy and augmented reality in several ways. First, we contributed to the body of literature on information privacy by doing an empirical, not a normative work, that is based on a non-student sample with participants, who are not located in the United States [6,39]. Second, many studies on privacy only include perceptions and attitudes of users and no actual privacy-related behavior. By conducting the second survey, we are able to determine that relatively many Pokémon Go players act in a privacy-friendly way. By merging all the insights of both studies, we suggested that the majority of the Pokémon Go players are well aware of privacy risks and measures, but willingly trades-off benefits of the game against a higher level of privacy. Third, this research is one of the first to investigate privacy issues related to AR applications.

These insights indicate that users will abandon the protection of their privacy, if smartphone applications provide a level of utility that is high enough to outweigh the concerns. This conclusion is indepedent of the knowledge about and usage of privacy-preserving measures.

Future work should consider to include questions about privacy concerns and privacy measures in one questionnaire to include all three dimensions. First, the actual use behavior of the application. Second, the privacy concerns. Third, the actual privacy preserving measures undertaken by each participant (cf. Appendix B). In addition, our research on Pokémon Go and privacy could be conducted in other countries with different cultural values. This is especially interesting for the case of privacy perceptions and privacy preserving behavior. Another interesting dimensions is the investigation of this topic along different points in time. It could be investigated whether differences in the perception about Pokémon Go and associated privacy dimensions occur over time.

Acknowledgments. The authors wish to thank the Faculty of Economics and Business Administration of the Goethe University Frankfurt am Main for supporting this work with a grant within the funding program "Forschungstopf". This research was also partly funded by the German Federal Ministry of Education and Research (BMBF) with grant number: 16KIS0371. In addition, we would also like to thank Harald Zwingelberg for his valuable feedback with regard to the privacy measures.

A   Questionnaire I

Collection

Coll1. It usually bothers me when companies ask me for personal information.

Coll2. When companies ask me for personal information, I sometimes think twice before providing it.

Coll3. It bothers me to give personal information to so many companies.

Coll4. I am concerned that companies are collecting too much personal information about me.

Errors

Err1. All the personal information in computer databases should be double-checked for accuracy – no matter how much this costs.

Err2. Companies should take more steps to make sure that the personal information in their files is accurate.

Err3. Companies should have better procedures to correct errors in personal information.

Err4. Companies should devote more time and effort to verifying the accuracy of the personal information in their databases.

Unauthorized Secondary Use

USU1. Companies should not use personal information for any purposes unless it has been authorized by the individuals who provided the information.

USU2. When people give personal information to a company for some reason, the company should never use the information for any other reason.

USU3. Companies should never sell the personal information in their computer databases to other companies.

USU4. Companies should never share personal information with other companies unless it has been authorized by the individuals who provided the information.

Improper Access

IA1. Companies should devote more time and effort to preventing unauthorized access to personal information.

IA2. Computer databases that contain personal information should be protected from unauthorized access – no matter how much it costs.

IA3. Companies should take more steps to make sure that unauthorized people cannot access personal information in their computers.

Use Behavior

Please choose your usage frequency for Pokémon Go:

- Never
- Once a month
- Several times a month
- Once a week
- Several times a week
- Once a day
- Several times a day
- Once an hour
- Several times an hour
- All the time

The frequency scale is adapted from Rosen et al. [36]. All other items are measured with a seven-point Likert scale, ranging from "strongly disagree" (coded as 1) to "strongly agree" (coded as 7). Male participants are coded as 0 and females as 1.

B   Questionnaire II

Which of the following options are you using while playing Pokmon Go?

M1. If possible, I turn off services that can be used to collect location data.

M2. I have a separate e-mail address, which I only use for games.

M3. I use different e-mail addresses for games and social networks.

M4. I review, which apps are authorized to access my other accounts (Twitter, Google, Facebook).

M5. I reset the advertising ID on my smartphone at least once per month.

M6. I forbid Pokémon Go to have access to my smartphone camera and use it without the Augmented Reality functionality.

The participants were able to answer the questions with "yes" (coded as 1), "no" (coded as 2), "sometimes" (coded as 3) and "I don't know" (coded as 4). In addition, the same questions as in Survey I were asked with regard to users' demographics and use behavior.

References

1. Acquisti, A., Grossklags, J.: Privacy and rationality in individual decision making. IEEE Secur. Priv. Mag. **3**(1), 24–30 (2005)
2. Albao, M.G.: Ingress: A Game, Lifestyle and Social Network in One! (2014)
3. Apple App Store: Pokémon Go (2017)
4. Azuma, R.T., Baillot, Y., Feiner, S., Julier, S., Behringer, R., Macintyre, B.: Recent advances in augmented reality. IEEE Comput. Graph. Appl. **21**, 34–47 (2001)
5. BBC: Pokemon and the power of nostalgia (2016). http://www.bbc.com/news/world-asia-36780797
6. Bélanger, F., Crossler, R.E.: Privacy in the digital age: a review of information privacy research in information systems. MIS Q. **35**(4), 1017–1041 (2011)
7. Belanger, F., Hiller, J.S., Smith, W.J.: Trustworthiness in electronic commerce: the role of privacy, security, and site attributes. J. Strateg. Inf. Syst. **11**(July 2016), 245–270 (2002)
8. Bellini, H., Chen, W., Sugiyama, M., Shin, M., Alam, S., Takayama, D.: Virtual & augmented reality: understanding the race for the next computing platform. Technical report, Goldman Sachs Equity Research (2016)

9. Berendt, B., Guenther, O., Spiekermann, S.: Privacy in e-commerce. Commun. ACM **48**(4), 101–106 (2005)
10. Culnan, M.J.: How did they get my name?: an exploratory investigation of consumer attitudes toward secondary information use. MIS Q. **17**(September), 341–364 (1993)
11. Culnan, M.J., Armstrong, P.K.: Information privacy concerns, procedural fairness, and impersonal trust: an empirical investigation. Organ. Sci. **10**(1), 104–115 (1999)
12. Dienlin, T., Metzger, M.J.: An extended privacy calculus model for SNSs: analyzing self-disclosure and self-withdrawal in a representative U.S. sample. J. Comput. Mediat. Commun. **21**(5), 368–383 (2016)
13. Dienlin, T., Trepte, S.: Is the privacy paradox a relic of the past? an in-depth analysis of privacy attitudes and privacy behaviors. Eur. J. Soc. Psychol. **45**(3), 285–297 (2015)
14. Dinev, T., Bellotto, M., Hart, P., Russo, V., Serra, I., Colautti, C.: Internet users' privacy concerns and beliefs about government surveillance: an exploratory study of differences between Italy and the United States. J. Glob. Inf. Manag. **14**(4), 57–93 (2006)
15. Dinev, T., Hart, P.: An extended privacy calculus model for e-commerce transactions. Inf. Syst. Res. **17**(1), 61–80 (2006)
16. Dinev, T., Hart, P.: Privacy concerns and levels of information exchange: an empirical investigation of intended e-services use. e-Service J. **4**(3), 25–60 (2006)
17. Evans, I.: Pokémon Go May Not Truly Be Augmented Reality, and That's OK (2016)
18. Fitzgerald, B.: Concrete Steps to Take to Minimize Risk While Playing Pokémon GO (2016)
19. Grubert, J., Langlotz, T., Zollmann, S., Regenbrecht, H.: Towards pervasive augmented reality: context-awareness in augmented reality. IEEE Trans. Visual. Comput. Graph. **PP**(99), 1–20 (2016)
20. Gstoll, A.: A love letter from augmented reality to Pokémon Go, August 2016
21. Harborth, D.: Augmented reality in information systems research: a systematic literature review. In: Twenty-Third Americas Conference on Information Systems (AMCIS), pp. 1–10. Boston (2017)
22. Harborth, D., Pape, S.: Exploring the hype: investigating technology acceptance factors of Pokémon Go. In: 2017 IEEE International Symposium on Mixed and Augmented Reality (ISMAR), pp. 155–168 (2017)
23. Helsper, E.J., Eynon, R.: Digital natives: where is the evidence? Br. Educ. Res. J. **36**(3), 503–520 (2010)
24. Henseler, J., Fassott, G.: Testing moderating effects in PLS path models: an illustration of available procedures. In: Esposito Vinzi, V., Chin, W., Henseler, J., Wang, H. (eds.) Handbook of Partial Least Squares, pp. 713–735. Springer, Heidelberg (2010). https://doi.org/10.1007/978-3-540-32827-8_31
25. Hyman, P.: Augmented-reality glasses bring cloud security into sharp focus. Commun. ACM **56**(6), 18–20 (2013)
26. Ryan, Kh.: Augmented Reality Gets Boost From Pokemon Go (2016)
27. Lang, B.: 'Pokémon Go' is Where I Draw the Line on "Augmented Reality" (2016)
28. Mason, W.: Pokemon Go or: How I Learned To Stop Worrying About The Definition And Love Augmented Reality (2016)
29. Milgram, P., Takemura, H., Utsumi, A., Kishino, F.: Augmented Reality: A class of displays on the reality-virtuality continuum. In: SPIE Proceedings on Telemanipulator and Telepresence Technologies, vol. 2351, pp. 282–292 (1994)

30. Nedelcheva, I.: Analysis of transmedia storytelling in Pokémon GO. Int. J. Humanit. Soc. Sci. **10**(11), 3744–3752 (2016)
31. Niantic Labs: Official Website of Niantic Labs (2017)
32. Nicas, J., Zakrzewski, C.: Augmented Reality Gets Boost From Success of Pokémon Go (2016)
33. Norberg, P.A., Horne, D.R., Horne, D.A.: The privacy paradox: personal information disclosure intentions versus behaviors. J. Consum. Aff. **41**(1), 100–126 (2007)
34. Palfrey, J., Gasser, U.: Born Digital: Understanding the First Generation of Digital Natives, vol. 13. Basic Books, New York (2008)
35. Prensky, M.: Digital natives, digital immigrants. Horizon **9**(5), 1–6 (2001)
36. Rosen, L.D., Whaling, K., Carrier, L.M., Cheever, N.A., Rokkum, J.: The media and technology usage and attitudes scale: an empirical investigation. Comput. Hum. Behav. **29**(6), 2501–2511 (2013)
37. Schmitz, C.: LimeSurvey Project Team (2015)
38. Sheehan, K.B.: An investigation of gender differences in on-line privacy concerns and resultant behaviors. J. Interact. Mark. **13**(4), 24–38 (1999)
39. Jeff Smith, H., Dinev, T., Xu, H.: Theory and review information privacy research: an interdisciplinary review. MIS Q. **35**(4), 989–1015 (2011)
40. Smith, H.J., Milberg, S.J., Burke, S.J.: Information privacy: measuring individuals' concerns about organizational practices. MIS Q. **20**(2), 167–196 (1996)
41. Spiekermann, S., Grossklags, J., Berendt, B.: E-privacy in 2nd generation e-commerce: privacy preferences versus actual behavior. In: EC 2001 Third ACM Conference on Electronic Commerce, pp. 38–47. ACM, Tampa (2001). Humboldt University Berlin
42. Stewart, K.A., Segars, A.H.: An empirical examination of the concern for information privacy instrument. Inf. Syst. Res. **13**(1), 36–49 (2002)
43. Swan II, J.E., Gabbard, J.L.: Survey of user-based experimentation in augmented reality. In: 1st International Conference on Virtual Reality, pp. 1–9 (2005)
44. Swatman, R.: Pokémon Go catches five new world records, August 2016
45. Tang, Z., Hu, Y., Smith, M.D.: Gaining trust through online privacy protection: self-regulation, mandatory standards, or caveat emptor. J. Manag. Inf. Syst. **24**(4), 153–173 (2008)
46. Tschersich, M., Kiyomoto, S., Pape, S., Nakamura, T., Bal, G., Takasaki, H., Rannenberg, K.: On gender specific perception of data sharing in Japan. In: Hoepman, J.-H., Katzenbeisser, S. (eds.) SEC 2016. IAICT, vol. 471, pp. 150–160. Springer, Cham (2016). https://doi.org/10.1007/978-3-319-33630-5_11
47. Venkatesh, V., Thong, J., Xin, X.: Consumer acceptance and user of information technology: extending the unified theory of acceptance and use of technology. MIS Q. **36**(1), 157–178 (2012)
48. Warren, S.D., Brandeis, L.D.: The right to privacy. Harvard Law Rev. **1**(5), 193–220 (1890)
49. Weidner, J.B.: How & Why Google Glass Failed (2015)
50. Yu, H.: What Pokémon Go's Success Means for the Future of Augmented Reality (2016)
51. All websites. Accessed 20 July 2017

mHealth Applications for Goal Management Training - Privacy Engineering in Neuropsychological Studies

Alexander Gabel, Ina Schiering$^{(\boxtimes)}$, Sandra Verena Müller, and Funda Ertas

Ostfalia University of Applied Sciences, Wolfenbüttel, Germany
{ale.gabel,i.schiering,s-v.mueller,f.ertas}@ostfalia.de

Abstract. The potential of digitalisation in healthcare based on mobile health, so-called mHealth applications, is considerable. On the other hand these solutions incorporate huge privacy risks. In the context of goal management training, a neuropsychological training used for the cognitive rehabilitation of executive dysfunction after a brain injury, the use of mHealth applications is considered. Privacy requirements of this scenario are modelled based on methodologies as privacy protection goals and privacy design strategies. Measures to realize the requirements are proposed and discussed in the context of a study. The focus in privacy engineering is on pseudonymity of patients, data minimization and transparency for patients.

Keywords: mHealth · Privacy · Data minimization · Pseudonymity
Transparency · Privacy protection goals · Privacy design strategies
Goal management training · Executive dysfunctions

1 Introduction

Based on recent technological innovations as the Internet of Things (IoT) and smart devices, the potential of digitalization is also utilized in healthcare. Especially the widespread use of smartphones and broadband internet access fosters the trend of mobile applications in healthcare which has the potential to overcome structural barriers, allow for scalability and address the need for interdisciplinary research [4]. These so called mHealth solutions allow "real-time monitoring and detection of changes in health status" [32].

On the other hand 44 % of data breaches happen in healthcare alone [8,49]. In an evaluation of mHealth solutions and corresponding studies McKay et al. [37] point out the "lack of information in any of these studies about readability, privacy or security". The privacy risks of connected health devices and the importance of approaches as privacy by design are stated by Allaert et al. [1]. But in the literature about mHealth solutions privacy is often reduced to informed consent in combination with an ethical approval [47]).

© IFIP International Federation for Information Processing 2018
Published by Springer International Publishing AG 2018. All Rights Reserved
M. Hansen et al. (Eds.): Privacy and Identity 2017, IFIP AICT 526, pp. 330–345, 2018.
https://doi.org/10.1007/978-3-319-92925-5_22

Although there exist a broad range of reviews and assessments of mHealth solutions stating deficits especially in the area of privacy and information security, in mHealth solutions which are used in clinical studies, privacy and information security are not in the focus of the consideration. Hence this paper presents a case study about privacy engineering in the context of the mHealth solution presented in Sect. 2. In this context both privacy and data protection as differentiated by the Charter of Fundamental Rights of the European Union [16] in Article 7 and 8 are considered [31].

The aim of this paper is to realize privacy by design by privacy engineering methodologies in the context of an mHealth project and the accompanying studies. The feasibility of a structured privacy by design approach [23,25] for an mHealth solution and accompanying study is evaluated.

In this context an mHealth solution to realize the so-called goal management training (GMT) is considered. GMT is a neuropsychological training used for cognitive rehabilitation of executive dysfunction after a brain injury e.g. after a stroke or an accident [35]. The realization of GMT as mHealth solution has the potential to integrate rehabilitation measurements in the daily life of the patients instead of using it solely during therapy sessions as in the traditional approach. To cope with the accompanied privacy risks a privacy by design approach is applied. Privacy risks are identified based on the model of the seven types of privacy by Finn et al. [18] to cope with the variety of privacy aspects in the context of mHealth applications where devices are equipped with a huge variety of sensors as e.g. cameras and GPS localisation. Privacy requirements are modelled based on the concept of privacy protection goals [22,23]. These requirements are then detailed in in the architecture and data flow oriented context of privacy design strategies [25] where measurements are sketched if possible based on privacy patterns.

2 Background

2.1 Executive Dysfunctions and Goal Management Training

Executive dysfunctions are deficits of brain-damaged patients concerning "the selection and execution of cognitive plans, their updating and monitoring, the inhibition of irrelevant responses and problems with goal-directed behaviour usually result in disorganized behaviour, impulsivity and problems in goal management and self-regulation" [15, p. 17]. To address these disabilities an important therapy is the so-called goal management training (GMT) [35]. The main idea is to divide goals into subgoals and use the resulting list of subgoals to train multistep workflows. These trainings are typically realized based on standard tasks as e.g. proof reading or meal preparation with a pen and pencil approach during therapy sessions. The main steps of GMT are summarized in Fig. 1.

Typical study populations in the area of executive dysfunctions consist of 30 to 60 participants with acquired brain injuries, executive dysfunction which are at least 18 years old.

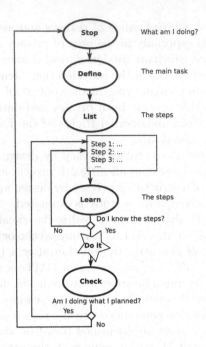

Fig. 1. Main steps of goal management training [35]

Recent studies which investigate variants of GMT [5,15] showed that the use of real-life scenarios based on individual tasks relevant to patients foster the motivation of patients. In the traditional paper and pencil approach the use and adaptation of individual tasks is time-consuming. Instead of checking the correctness of the steps after the "Do It" phase in Fig. 1 which could potentially lead to "learning errors", it is recommended to train the workflows based on a documentation e.g. realised by task cards. This approach is called *errorless learning*.

2.2   An mHealth Solution for Goal Management Training

An mHealth solution has the potential to simplify GMT with individual tasks in combination with errorless learning based on a workflow editor and the use of mobile devices for workflow execution. The roles in this scenario, the central process and screenshots of the GMT applications are summarized in Fig. 2.

The central roles are the neuropsychologist as *therapist* and the *patient*. The therapist develops and adjusts workflows based on individual tasks in cooperation with the patient using a workflow editor based on a specific customization of Google Blockly[1]. These individual workflows are transferred to a mobile device as e.g. a Smart Phone, Smart Watch or Smart Glasses by direct file transfer or via a server identified by a Quick Response (QR) Code. They are guided

---

[1] https://developers.google.com/blockly/.

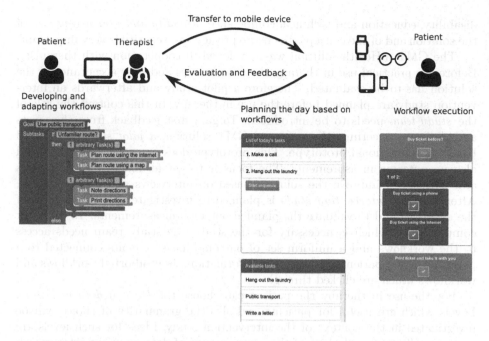

Fig. 2. Roles, process and screenshots of GMT mHealth solution

through daily tasks as e.g. taking public transport or preparing breakfast by predefined workflows which can also be combined to a daily schedule. During workflow execution the patient confirms the completion of a task by clicking it. The patient can provide direct feedback to the therapist about workflow usage and the impact.

At the moment the therapist only gains information about the time between two therapy sessions which is typically a week by the personal report of the patient. The GMT mHealth solution offers the opportunity to gain insight into this blind spot by collecting *outcome measurements* on the smart device. Examples are the number of cancelled workflows or workflows which are "clicked through" which means that a certain amount of tasks is clicked within seconds. Both measurements could give hints to problems in daily life to follow goals. On the other hand it is also possible that the patient was very confident about certain workflows and therefore skipped through the information for assurance. Combined with the personal conversation about the results during the therapy session the therapist gains more insight in the progress of the patient. Patients get training concerning GMT in general and the used GMT solution.

Hence behavioural data concerning the workflow execution as a basis for the therapy session is collected whereas typical mHealth solutions collect sensor data as e.g. blood sugar level, heart rate or movement data. Since the user group of people with executive dysfunctions is very diverse with respect to the level of disability, education and technical competence, *usability and user acceptance* of the solution and of the concepts to ensure privacy and security is very important.

The GMT mHealth solution was developed in cooperation with therapists. Before the practical use in therapy the effectiveness and user acceptance of the solution has to be evaluated. Therefore a pilot study and afterwards an intervention study are planned before the use in therapy. In this context the role of the *study team* needs to be introduced. To gain first feedback from therapists and patients concerning the proposed GMT solution, a *pilot study* is planned based on a functional prototype. This prototype does not collect any data and also no outcome measurements. The focus is to get feedback from therapists and patients to improve the solution based on interviews and questionnaires. Afterwards an *intervention study* is planned to investigate the effectiveness of the approach and to validate the planned outcome measurements. To allow for comparability, which is necessary for the study, the study team needs access to the workflows and a uniform set of outcome measurements connected to a pseudonym of a patient encompassing information about aborted workflows and workflows which are clicked through.

For the use in therapy the patient can choose the *level of data collection*. Levels which are useful for patients and also the granularity of choice will be investigated in the context of the intervention study. Ideas for such levels are no data collection, collection of the same amount of data as in the intervention study, collect only data about some workflows or collect only statistical data aggregated about all workflows.

3   Privacy and Legal Regulations in the European Union

Prior the review of mHealth solutions from the literature and privacy modelling of the case study which is the basis of the considerations of this paper, we summarise requirements for privacy based on legal regulations in the European Union. Since the mHealth solution used as a case study in this paper is not classified as a medical device, specific legal regulations for medical devices are not considered.

The basis for the consideration about privacy and data protection in the European Union is the Charter of Fundamental Rights of the European Union [16], which considers privacy and data protection in Article 7 and 8. The aspect of privacy is in the focus of Article 7 "Respect for private and family life" stating that "everyone has the right to respect for his or her private and family life, home and communications". Article 8 on "Protection of personal data" has the focus on data protection where in Article 8(1) it says "Everyone has the right to the protection of personal data concerning him or her" and in Article 8(2) this is detailed as "Such data must be processed fairly for specified purposes and on the basis of the consent of the person concerned or some other legitimate basis laid down by law. Everyone has the right of access to data which has been collected concerning him or her, and the right to have it rectified.".

Concerning data protection in the European Union compliance with the General Data Protection Regulation (GDPR) [17] is considered which applies from 25

May 2018. The central basis for data protection are summarised in the principles of data protection in Article 5 of GDPR as lawfulness, fairness, transparency, purpose limitation, data minimisation, accuracy, storage limitation, integrity, confidentiality and accountability.

For the lawfulness of the processing of personal data for an mHealth application and the corresponding intervention study, *informed consent* of the patients described in Article 6(1) and Article 9(2)(a) concerning health data is needed.

Section 3 details the rights of the data subject concerning *rectification and erasure*. According to Article 20 there is in addition the right to *data portability*, and Article 25 demands the realisation of *data protection by design and by default*. Concerning the security of processing in Article 32 beside the standard technical and organisational measurements the concept of *pseudonymisation* is mentioned which is an important concept in the context of the planned study. In Article 33, 34 regulations concerning data breaches are stated and Article 35 addresses the importance of a *data protection impact assessment*.

4   Privacy and Information Security in mHealth - An Overview

Based on the consideration of the legal requirements in the European Union, literature about mHealth is reviewed concerning the investigated aspects of privacy and information security. In the following an overview of scientific literature is considered including the description of mHealth solutions, studies and reviews.

In studies about mHealth solutions typically privacy aspects are only mentioned without further detail. In Volkova et al. [48] where a Food Label Trial app is investigated in a fully automated trial, it is only mentioned concerning privacy that "Ethical and security requirements have also been considered during the app development". Other studies as e.g. [28] focus solely on usability and do not even mention information security and privacy issues. Studies as [19,41,50] concentrate on the medical impact and mention at most the existence of an ethics approval. Vogel et al. [47] confirm this perception by stating that for legal compliance mainly informed consent and an ethical approval is needed, wheras Allaert et al. [1] point out the importance of privacy by design for mHealth.

A recent trend in mHealth are app ecosystems as e.g. Apple ResearchKit[2] and Google Study Kit[3]. Based on ResearchKit already studies as the mPower study concerning Parkinson disease [10] are performed where in addition the pseudonymised data is stored on Synapse[4], a general-purpose data and analysis sharing service. Mandl et al. [36] analyse the potential for innovation by standardised app platforms. There the need for regulation and certification especially concerning "accuracy, utility, safety, privacy, and security" is stated. A further analysis of such app ecosystems would be important, but is beyond the scope of this paper.

---

[2] http://researchkit.org/.
[3] https://studykit.google.com.
[4] https://www.synapse.org/.

Although in mHealth studies often privacy is not in the focus of the consideration, Peng et al. [40] mention in the context of a user study potential privacy issues of users concerning tracking behaviour and sharing of personal information. Prasad et al. [42] investigate user attitudes towards sharing of information and privacy. Evaluations of health apps [26] reveal several deficits concerning privacy and information security. Other evaluations [45] point out the lack respectively poor quality of privacy policies of mHealth apps, and furthermore the lack of regulatory guidelines and supervision [30,37,43,46].

5   Methodologies for Privacy Engineering

A central requirement of the GDPR [17] is to implement the principles of data protection by design and by default. *Data protection by design* respectively *privacy by design* was first introduced by Langheinrich [33] in the context of ubiquitous systems, where the intention was to develop guidelines for designing privacy-aware systems based on EU legislation and OECD guidelines. He proposes to investigate the seven areas notice, choice and consent, anonymity and pseudonymity, proximity and locality, adequate security, access and recourse.

In a more general approach Cavoukian [11,12] introduced *seven principles of privacy by design* as a holistic model for privacy integrated in the culture of organisations. The principles proposed there are proactive not reactive, preventative not reactive, privacy as the default, privacy embedded into design, full functionality - positive sum, not zero-sum, end-to-end lifecycle protection, visibility and transparency, respect for user privacy.

To realise the central ideas of privacy by design in a concrete mHealth project, we focus on methodologies in the context of privacy engineering. mHealth solutions encompass potentially various smart devices in combination with specialised apps connected to web applications and storing information in backend-respectively cloud services. Hence to start as a methodology for evaluating potential privacy risks of such a complex set of technologies, the model of *seven types of privacy* [18] is used, which differentiates the several types of privacy risks, as shown in Table 1.

Privacy requirements are modelled based on the description of privacy risks using the model of *privacy protection goals* [22,23]. As an extension of the security protection goals confidentiality, integrity and availability the privacy specific protection goals transparency, unlinkability and intervenability are introduced (Fig. 3). To realize the requirements modelled based on these protection goals in a system architecture, *privacy design strategies* [13,25] can be utilized in the system design process encompassing minimize, hide, separate, abstract, inform, control, enforce, demonstrate (Fig. 4).

This system design can be further detailed using *privacy patterns*. Privacy patterns are reusable solutions to recurring privacy problems [44]. These patterns often encompass security related aspects and they are proposed for different phases of the design process, such as requirements engineering, architecture, design and implementation or quality assurance [20,21,34]

Table 1. Seven types of privacy, as proposed by Finn et al. [18]

Privacy type	Description
Privacy of person	Right to keep body functions and characteristics (genetic codes, biometrics) private
Privacy of behaviour and action	Right to behave in (semi-)public/private space without monitoring or control of actions
Privacy of communication	Right to keep communications private, avoiding interception
Privacy of data and image	Right to keep indiviudals' data private and to exercise control over that data and usage
Privacy of thought and feelings	Right to keep thoughts and feelings private
Privacy of location and space	Right to move about in public or semi-public space without being identified, tracked or monitored
Privacy of association	Right to associate with whomever they wish, without being monitored

Examples include [34] patterns in privacy requirements engineering [29], architectural patterns such as the Data Abstraction or the Privacy Proxy pattern [7], as well as patterns for implementation and design such as privacy transparency patterns (Personal Data Table, Privacy Policy Icons) [44] or patterns regarding the protection goal hide (Cover Traffic, Anonymity Set, Layered Encryption) [20]. Furthermore privacy dark patterns are proposed, trying to "deceive and mislead" users for malicious purposes [9].

6 Privacy Engineering in the Context of an mHealth Solution

6.1 Privacy Risk Identification

The privacy engineering methodologies presented in Sect. 5 are applied to the GMT mHealth solution. The central basis for the consideration of privacy risks is the level of data collected for the intervention study described in Subsect. 2.2. For the use in therapy after the study the level of data collection can be controlled by the patients. There the patients can also choose not to collect any data. To consider the privacy risks especially in the context of smart devices, the model of seven types of privacy is applied (Table 2).

The central risk of the considered mHealth solution for GMT itself is the risk of behaviour tracking by outcome measurements as explained in Subsect. 2.2. In combination with names and descriptions of workflows which are associated with the outcome measurements, it is potentially possible to track behaviour and actions of patients. This is a typical risk of mHealth solutions in neuropsychology, because approaches for behavioural therapy are promising choices for digitalization. Since typical other mHealth solutions focus more on data collection with the help of sensors, the consideration differs in this point. The more general area of eHealth encompasses beside mHealth applications e.g. information systems as Electronic Patient Records which are difficult to compare.

Table 2. Types of privacy - privacy risk modelling

Privacy type	Risk in mHealth scenario		
	GMT risk by outcome measurements	General risk of smart devices[a]	Potential risk of extensions[b]
Privacy of person			
Privacy of behaviour and action	✗	✗	
Privacy of communication		✗	
Privacy of data and image		✗	✗
Privacy of thought and feelings			
Privacy of location and space		✗	✗
Privacy of association		✗	

[a]e.g. risks from third-party apps user tracking
[b]location-based workflows, progress documentation (e.g. photos)

Most of the other privacy risks identified here are associated with the use of smart devices in general. E.g. a personal smart phone of the patient where a broad range of apps is installed. In general it is difficult to control, limit and verify the behaviour of third-party apps on a patients device. An example of risks induced by those apps are the use of advertisement SDKs, which leak private data from the phone, such as call logs or location information, to track the users [3]. Furthermore in 2016 the browser plugin *Web Of Trust* (WOT) tracked users and sold their personally-identifiable information [38,39]. Since it is difficult to address these risks by technology, an important element of security and privacy measurements is user risk awareness and training which can be integrated in the general GMT training mentioned in Sect. 2.2.

Based on first feedback by therapists and job coaches there are possible *extensions* where workflows can also be triggered via location or additional markers such as QR codes. Also in some application areas for workflows it would be important to document the success of the whole workflow or certain steps by images respectively reporting of additional data. These risks are only mentioned here. Since these extensions will not be investigated further in the context of the GMT invention study which is in the center of the consideration here, these risks will not be considered further in this paper.

6.2 Modelling with Privacy Protection Goals and Privacy Design Strategies

In the privacy engineering process we model privacy requirements via the use of privacy protection goals (Fig. 3). The risk modelling is based on the risk areas identified with the model of seven types of privacy in Subsect. 6.1.

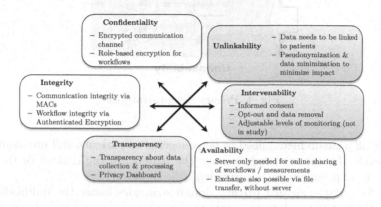

Fig. 3. Privacy protection goals in an mHealth scenario (MACs - Message Authentication Codes)

To address the modelled privacy protection goals in the system design process, we use privacy design strategies (Fig. 4). The privacy design strategies are considered in the context of the privacy protection goals with a focus on the privacy goals unlinkability, tranparency and intervenability. There the connection between privacy protection goals and privacy design strategies as proposed in Fig. 4 is used to structure the consideration. Based on the description of these strategies, possible measurements are discussed. If possible privacy patterns are proposed.

Unlinkability: In the context of this use case it is important for therapists respectively the study team to be able to get feedback in terms of outcome measurements linked to a specific patient. The aim to collect personally identifiable data in the context of the GMT mHealth solution, i.e. workflows and associated outcome measurements, is that therapists and the study team get insights in the progress of the therapy of a single patient. Aggregated data about several patients does not make sense to evaluate the progress of a single patient. Because of the number of participants in the intervention study, which is typically between 30 and 60 in the field of GMT [5], and data which is collected continuously over a time-frame of several months, full anonymisation would not be not achievable because of the risk of re-identification.

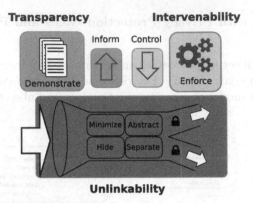

Fig. 4. Privacy design strategies

Since all measurements need to be connected to patients, full unlinkability is not possible. Therapists need to know the patient, in the context of the intervention study pseudonyms are sufficient.

The four, *data-oriented* privacy design strategies foster the unlinkability of personally identifiable data to a patient:

MINIMIZE: The collection and processing of personally identifiable data should be minimized as much as possible. Hence the modelling of outcome measurements must be restricted to necessary measurements and patients must be trained adequately. Outside of the intervention study patients can choose to store data only on the device of the user (pattern: Personal Data Store [14]).

HIDE: Strong pseudonymisation techniques should be applied in the context of the study. An option to share workflows between patients and therapists using the server, which is currently implemented, is to share a private link realised by QR codes. This is also known as the Private Link Pattern [14]. The intended encryption measurements are considered for the goal confidentiality.

SEPARATE: In the context of the intervention study it is intended to use a distributed pseudonym table, which is stored on the therapists sides. A similar approach, the so-called Pseudoynm Broker Pattern, which also avoids the use of a central pseudonym table by separation, was proposed by Hillen [24].

ABSTRACT: In addition to data minimization also the collected data should be abstracted as much as possible by data obfuscation [2] respectively statistical disclosure control [27]. Examples of these techniques are the choice of restricted granularity for time and location information, e.g. instead of storing a timestamp for every "click" of the user to detect clicked through workflows, only a specific feature, i.e. several tasks were clicked within a few seconds, is considered.

Transparency: Transparency is important since the user needs to be informed about the processing of personal data and the rights of the data subject concerning opt-out of the study, deletion, rectification and portability of data to foster trust in the mHealth solution and to comply with legal regulations (Sect. 3).

INFORM: An important pattern to realize transparency is a Privacy Dashboard [14, 44], which is a central place for privacy information in an application and allows the user in addition also to intervene, i.e. to modify, delete and stop processing of personal data, opt-out of the study. In addition the user needs to be informed about potential data breaches.

DEMONSTRATE: Measures as data protection impact assessments, privacy seals respectively certifications are important additional transparency measurements will be potentially considered.

Intervenability: Intervenability in connection with transparency is important to ensure the rights of the data subject.

CONTROL: To control processing of personal data and access to it a Privacy Dashboard is intended to be used. During the intervention study opt-out of the study is possible, which could be also stated to the therapist respectively the study team. When used in therapy, also the level of collection of personal data can be adjusted via this planned dashboard.

ENFORCE: Access to personally identifiable data needs to be restricted. Workflows are transfered with the help of the Private Link pattern. Access to outcome measurements should only be possible for the responsible therapist and during the intervention study also for part of the study team. This can be realized by role-based access control.

Confidentiality: Beside the restriction of access by role-based access control and the use of pseudonyms, information security measurements as encryption are important to ensure confidentiality of the information.

HIDE: To strengthen the role-based access control *attribute-based encryption* is planned to use. In general, this type of encryption needs an authority, which issues keys, certifying certain attributes to each user. In ciphertext-policy attribute-based encryption [6], a monotonic tree-access structure can be specified, such that a user has to satisfy a boolean formula of attributes to be able to decrypt a certain ciphertext. This concept could be combined with *authenticated encryption* to furthermore ensure authenticity and integrity. In addition the secrets involved in encryption and decryption should be kept on the client side (pattern: Encryption with User-Managed Keys [14]).

Availability: Standard measurements concerning availability of the server are applied, as e.g. backups, etc. As a work around if the server is unavailable, workflows and outcome measurements can also be exchanged via file transfer. The availability of the mobile device which belongs to the patient is not considered.

Integrity: Integrity of communication and data is ensured via TLS, using a profile which also provices MACs. Workflow integrity is ensured by authenticated encryption (cf. confidentiality). Integrity does not have an obvious representative in the design strategies, however one may argue that at least the data controller needs to be aware of data inconsistency to address the problem and inform the user. Hence this can be seen as connected to the process oriented strategies *INFORM, CONTROL*.

7   Discussion and Final Remarks

Privacy engineering methodologies proved to give helpful guidelines for the development of mHealth solutions in neuropsychology and the preparation of the accompanying intervention study. Therefore the chosen structured privacy by design approach was very helpful. The general approach as specified in Sect. 5 can be transferred to mHealth and eHealth projects in general, but as the risk modelling (Subsect. 6.1) showed, the risks in these areas differ.

Identifying privacy patterns which are applicable in a certain situation is still an intricate task: Pattern catalogues[5] and pattern languages [20] are an important first step, but still whole catalogues have to be checked to find the most appropriate pattern. There is a considerable variety concerning levels of abstraction of privacy patterns. Some patterns merely represent a general idea as the Pseudonymous Identity Pattern [7] whereas others focus on very special situations as e.g. the Pseudonym Broker Pattern [24].

In future work the focus will be the investigation and development of privacy patterns in areas which are important for the mHealth environment investigated here. These areas encompass data minimization including data obfuscation, pseudonymization techniques, key management and key exchange.

Based on these design considerations presented here a detailed system design needs to be developed and the usability of the mHealth solution needs to be investigated in depth encompassing measurements for privacy and security. Beside the mere technical design processes and additional organisational measurements to address the rights of the data subjects, also information and training for patients, therapists and the study team needs to be implemented.

Acknowledgment. This work was supported by the Ministry for Science and Culture of Lower Saxony as part of SecuRIn (VWZN3224).

References

1. Allaert, F.A., Mazen, N.J., Legrand, L., Quantin, C.: The tidal waves of connected health devices with healthcare applications: consequences on privacy and care management in European healthcare systems. BMC Med. Inf. Decis. Making **17**, 10 (2017). https://doi.org/10.1186/s12911-017-0408-6

---

[5] https://privacypatterns.org/.

2. Bakken, D.E., Rarameswaran, R., Blough, D.M., Franz, A.A., Palmer, T.J.: Data obfuscation: anonymity and desensitization of usable data sets. IEEE Secur. Priv. **2**(6), 34–41 (2004)
3. Bauer, A., Hebeisen, C.: Igexin advertising network put user privacy at risk, August 2017. https://blog.lookout.com/igexin-malicious-sdk
4. Becker, S., Miron-Shatz, T., Schumacher, N., Krocza, J., Diamantidis, C., Albrecht, U.V.: mHealth 2.0: experiences, possibilities, and perspectives. JMIR mHealth uHealth **2**(2), e24 (2014)
5. Bertens, D.: Doin' it right: assessment and errorless learning of executive skills after brain injury. [S.l. : s.n.] (2016). http://repository.ubn.ru.nl/handle/2066/149530
6. Bethencourt, J., Sahai, A., Waters, B.: Ciphertext-policy attribute-based encryption. In: 2007 IEEE Symposium on Security and Privacy (SP 2007), pp. 321–334, May 2007
7. Bier, C., Krempel, E.: Common privacy patterns in video surveillance and smart energy. In: 2012 7th International Conference on Computing and Convergence Technology (ICCCT), pp. 610–615. IEEE (2012). http://ieeexplore.ieee.org/abstract/document/6530407/
8. Bitglass: The 2014 Bitglass healthcare breach report (2014). https://pages.bitglass.com/pr-2014-healthcare-breach-report.html
9. Bösch, C., Erb, B., Kargl, F., Kopp, H., Pfattheicher, S.: Tales from the dark side: privacy dark strategies and privacy dark patterns. Proc. Priv. Enhanc. Technol. **2016**, 237–254 (2016)
10. Bot, B.M., Suver, C., Neto, E.C., Kellen, M., Klein, A., Bare, C., Doerr, M., Pratap, A., Wilbanks, J., Dorsey, E.R., Friend, S.H., Trister, A.D.: The mPower study, Parkinson disease mobile data collected using ResearchKit. Sci. Data **3**, 160011 (2016). http://www.nature.com/articles/sdata201611
11. Cavoukian, A.: Privacy by design: the 7 foundational principles. Implementation and mapping of fair information practices. Information and Privacy Commissioner of Ontario, Canada (2009)
12. Cavoukian, A., Taylor, S., Abrams, M.E.: Privacy by design: essential for organizational accountability and strong business practices. Identity Inf. Soc. **3**(2), 405–413 (2010)
13. Colesky, M., Hoepman, J.H., Hillen, C.: A critical analysis of privacy design strategies. In: 2016 IEEE Security and Privacy Workshops (SPW), pp. 33–40 (2016)
14. Colesky, M., Hoopman, J.H., Bösch, C., Kargl, F., Kopp, H., Mosby, P., Le Métayer, D., Drozd, O., del Álamo, J.M., Martín, Y.S., Gupta, M., Doty, N.: Privacy patterns (2012). https://privacypatterns.org/
15. Emmanouel, A.: Look at the frontal side of life: anterior brain pathology and everyday executive function: assessment approaches and treatment. Ph.D. thesis, Radboud University (2017). http://repository.ubn.ru.nl/handle/2066/166754
16. Charter of fundamental rights of the European union (2012/C 326/02)
17. Regulation (EU) 2016/679 of the European parliament and of the council of 27 April 2016 on the protection of natural persons with regard to the processing of personal data and on the free movement of such data, and repealing directive 95/46/EC (general data protection regulation). Official Journal of the European Union L119, pp. 1–88, May 2016. http://eur-lex.europa.eu/legal-content/EN/TXT/?uri=OJ:L:2016:119:TOC
18. Finn, R.L., Wright, D., Friedewald, M.: Seven types of privacy. In: Gutwirth, S., Leenes, R., de Hert, P., Poullet, Y. (eds.) European Data Protection: Coming of Age, pp. 3–32. Springer, Dordrecht (2013). https://doi.org/10.1007/978-94-007-5170-5_1

19. Gamito, P., Oliveira, J., Lopes, P., Brito, R., Morais, D., Silva, D., Silva, A., Rebelo, S., Bastos, M., Deus, A.: Executive functioning in alcoholics following an mHealth cognitive stimulation program: randomized controlled trial. J. Med. Internet Res. **16**(4), e102 (2014). http://www.jmir.org/2014/4/e102/

20. Hafiz, M.: A pattern language for developing privacy enhancing technologies. Softw.: Pract. Exp. **43**(7), 769–787 (2013)

21. Hafiz, M., Adamczyk, P., Johnson, R.E.: Growing a pattern language (for security). In: Proceedings of the ACM International Symposium on New Ideas, New Paradigms, and Reflections on Programming and Software, pp. 139–158. ACM, New York (2012). https://doi.org/10.1145/2384592.2384607

22. Hansen, M., Jensen, M., Rost, M.: Protection goals for privacy engineering. In: 2015 IEEE Security and Privacy Workshops, pp. 159–166, May 2015

23. Hansen, M.: The standard data protection model - a concept for inspection and consultation on the basis of unified protection goals, March 2017. https://www.datenschutzzentrum.de/uploads/sdm/SDM-Methodology_V1_EN1.pdf

24. Hillen, C.: The pseudonym broker privacy pattern in medical data collection. In: 2015 IEEE Trustcom/BigDataSE/ISPA, vol. 1, pp. 999–1005, August 2015

25. Hoepman, J.-H.: Privacy design strategies. In: Cuppens-Boulahia, N., Cuppens, F., Jajodia, S., Abou El Kalam, A., Sans, T. (eds.) SEC 2014. IAICT, vol. 428, pp. 446–459. Springer, Heidelberg (2014). https://doi.org/10.1007/978-3-642-55415-5_38

26. Huckvale, K., Prieto, J.T., Tilney, M., Benghozi, P.J., Car, J.: Unaddressed privacy risks in accredited health and wellness apps: a cross-sectional systematic assessment. BMC Med. **13**, 214 (2015). https://doi.org/10.1186/s12916-015-0444-y

27. Hundepool, A., Domingo-Ferrer, J., Franconi, L., Giessing, S., Lenz, R., Longhurst, J., Nordholt, E.S., Seri, G., Wolf, P.: Handbook on statistical disclosure control. ESSnet on Statistical Disclosure Control (2010)

28. Jenkins, A., Lindsay, S., Eslambolchilar, P., Thornton, I.M., Tales, A.: Administering cognitive tests through touch screen tablet devices: potential issues. J. Alzheimers Dis. **54**(3), 1169–1182 (2016)

29. Kalloniatis, C., Kavakli, E., Gritzalis, S.: Addressing privacy requirements in system design: the PriS method. Requir. Eng. **13**(3), 241–255 (2008). https://doi.org/10.1007/s00766-008-0067-3

30. Kao, C.K., Liebovitz, D.M.: Consumer mobile health apps: current state, barriers, and future directions. PM & R: J. Inj. Funct. Rehabil. **9**(5S), S106–S115 (2017)

31. Kokott, J., Sobotta, C.: The distinction between privacy and data protection in the jurisprudence of the CJEU and the ECtHR. Int. Data Priv. Law **3**(4), 222–228 (2013). https://doi.org/10.1093/idpl/ipt017

32. Kumar, S., Nilsen, W., Pavel, M., Srivastava, M.: Mobile health: revolutionizing healthcare through transdisciplinary research. Computer **46**(1), 28–35 (2013)

33. Langheinrich, M.: Privacy by design — principles of privacy-aware ubiquitous systems. In: Abowd, G.D., Brumitt, B., Shafer, S. (eds.) UbiComp 2001. LNCS, vol. 2201, pp. 273–291. Springer, Heidelberg (2001). https://doi.org/10.1007/3-540-45427-6_23

34. Lenhard, J., Fritsch, L., Herold, S.: A literature study on privacy patterns research. In: 3rd Euromicro Conference on Software Engineering and Advanced Applications (SEAA), Vienna, Austria, August 2017

35. Levine, B., Robertson, I.H., Clare, L., Carter, G., Hong, J., Wilson, B.A., Duncan, J., Stuss, D.T.: Rehabilitation of executive functioning: an experimental-clinical validation of goal management training. J. Int. Neuropsychol. Soc. **6**(3), 299–312 (2000)

36. Mandl, K.D., Mandel, J.C., Kohane, I.S.: Driving innovation in health systems through an apps-based information economy. Cell Syst. **1**(1), 8–13 (2015)
37. McKay, F.H., Cheng, C., Wright, A., Shill, J., Stephens, H., Uccellini, M.: Evaluating mobile phone applications for health behaviour change: a systematic review. J. Telemed. Telecare **24**(1), 22–30 (2016). https://doi.org/10.1177/1357633X16673538
38. heise online: Abgegriffene Browserdaten: WOT-Anbieter will Datenschutz-Vorwürfe prüfen, November 2016. https://www.heise.de/ho/meldung/Abgegriffene-Browserdaten-WOT-Anbieter-will-Datenschutz-Vorwuerfe-pruefen-3455466.html
39. heise online: Daten zu Surfverhalten von Millionen Deutschen als "kostenlose Probe", November 2016. https://www.heise.de/ho/meldung/Daten-zu-Surfverhalten-von-Millionen-Deutschen-als-kostenlose-Probe-3451556.html
40. Peng, W., Kanthawala, S., Yuan, S., Hussain, S.A.: A qualitative study of user perceptions of mobile health apps. BMC Public Health **16**, 1158 (2016). https://doi.org/10.1186/s12889-016-3808-0
41. Pfaeffli, L., Maddison, R., Whittaker, R., Stewart, R., Kerr, A., Jiang, Y., Kira, G., Carter, K., Dalleck, L.: A mHealth cardiac rehabilitation exercise intervention: findings from content development studies. BMC Cardiovasc. Disord. **12**, 36 (2012). https://doi.org/10.1186/1471-2261-12-36
42. Prasad, A., Sorber, J., Stablein, T., Anthony, D., Kotz, D.: Understanding sharing preferences and behavior for mHealth devices. In: Proceedings of the 2012 ACM Workshop on Privacy in the Electronic Society, WPES 2012, pp. 117–128. ACM, New York (2012). https://doi.org/10.1145/2381966.2381983
43. Ranchordas, S., Kaplan, B.: MHealth for Alzheimer's disease: regulation, consent, and privacy concerns. SSRN Scholarly Paper ID 2765976, Social Science Research Network, Rochester, April 2016. https://papers.ssrn.com/abstract=2765976
44. Siljee, J.: Privacy transparency patterns. In: Proceedings of the 20th European Conference on Pattern Languages of Programs, EuroPLoP 2015, pp. 52:1–52:11. ACM, New York (2015). https://doi.org/10.1145/2855321.2855374
45. Sunyaev, A., Dehling, T., Taylor, P.L., Mandl, K.D.: Availability and quality of mobile health app privacy policies. J. Am. Med. Inf. Assoc. **22**(e1), e28–e33 (2015). https://academic.oup.com/jamia/article/22/e1/e28/700676/Availability-and-quality-of-mobile-health-app
46. Tirman, V.J.: The current state of mHealth applications and the need for improved regulatory guidelines to protect the privacy of patient health information. Ph.D. thesis, Alliant International University (2016)
47. Vogel, M.M.E., Combs, S.E., Kessel, K.A.: mHealth and application technology supporting clinical trials: today's limitations and future perspective of smartRCTs. Front. Oncol. **7** (2017). http://www.ncbi.nlm.nih.gov/pmc/articles/PMC5346562/
48. Volkova, E., Li, N., Dunford, E., Eyles, H., Crino, M., Michie, J., Mhurchu, C.N.: "Smart" RCTs: development of a smartphone app for fully automated nutrition-labeling intervention trials. JMIR mHealth uHealth **4**(1), e23 (2016). http://mhealth.jmir.org/2016/1/e23/
49. Vrhovec, S.L.R.: Challenges of mobile device use in healthcare. In: 2016 39th International Convention on Information and Communication Technology, Electronics and Microelectronics (MIPRO), pp. 1393–1396, May 2016
50. Zmily, A., Mowafi, Y., Mashal, E.: Study of the usability of spaced retrieval exercise using mobile devices for Alzheimer's disease rehabilitation. JMIR mHealth uHealth **2**(3), e31 (2014). http://mhealth.jmir.org/2014/3/e31/

NFC Payments – Gaps Between User Perception and Reality

Poornigha Santhana Kumar[1]([⊠]), Michael Bechinie[1],
and Manfred Tscheligi[2]

[1] USECON, 1110 Vienna, Austria
{kumar, bechinie}@usecon.com
[2] University of Salzburg, 5020 Salzburg, Austria
manfred.tscheligi@sbg.ac.at

Abstract. Point of Sale (POS) terminals are used in almost all retail shops for commercial transactions by a wide range of users. The recent wireless payment method, Near Field Communication (NFC) is focused in this study. We aimed to study the experience gained by the user at POS terminals on privacy and security scales, while using NFC payments. The study revealed that the users have different mental models about NFC which hinders the success of the system. The results also portrays that the user experience gained from NFC payment system can be further improved. We suggest that designing/modifying the NFC payment system based on user experience will improve the privacy and security related experience gained by the user.

Keywords: NFC payment · User experience · Mental model

1 Introduction

Near Field Communication (NFC) payment is an emerging technology and it is currently being used for contactless payments in some countries [1]. The user can easily pay by holding either their NFC card or NFC enabled mobile phone against the payment terminal. It operates at 13.56 MHz and if the distance between the payment terminal and NFC card/NFC mobile is less than 4 cm a connection is established and payment is proceeded [2, 14].

We have rich literature which portrays that research is being conducted on NFC in various directions. To begin with, the advantages and possibilities of NFC technology have been well explored [2]. The main advantage pointed by various studies [2–4] states that NFC payment is faster than other payment methods (credit/debit card and cash payment) and reduce the hassles faced by the user. NFC payment also overcomes shoulder surfing attack as the user need not to input their PIN (Personal Identification Number) for purchases less than 25 euro. This transaction limit without PIN varies based on the country and the currency. The users can pay above this limit using NFC by providing their PIN. Given the above advantages, NFC payment seems to serve as a perfect alternative for existing payment methods.

Many existing NFC literature focuses only on NFC applications [5]. There are only few research studies in the direction of usability and user experience of NFC's payment

M. Hansen et al. (Eds.): Privacy and Identity 2017, IFIP AICT 526, pp. 346–353, 2018.
https://doi.org/10.1007/978-3-319-92925-5_23

in the literature. For example: Geven et al. [6] studies the usability and user experience issues related to NFC payment and suggests to improve the system such that proper feedback is delivered. Another usability study [7] in the field of NFC explores the usability of NFC based interactions. The study points out the existing usability issues such as visibility and accessibility in NFC based interaction and also states that there is not enough research in this direction.

As stated by [8] "technology is deeply embedded in our ordinary everyday experience". Each service, technology or product we use in our everyday life delivers us an experience which plays an important role in accessing that particular service, technology or product. Many existing literature [8, 9] highly recommends to design based on user experience. NFC payment system also lacks research and design in this direction.

2 Objectives

As usability and user experience play an important role in the success of any technology and to fill the literature gap in NFC, we decided to gain deeper insights in this direction. Any user would prefer to feel secured and privacy assured at any POS. We aim to capture and enhance the experience of felt security and privacy by the user at POS. As a first step we captured the user experience of NFC payments at POS. The methodology followed and the results of this study are summarized in this paper.

3 Methodology

We choose to work on retail shop checkouts as they involve a wide range of customers (age, gender and profession) and accept all types of payment (cash, credit/debit card, NFC in cards and mobile phones). We used 3 methods to understand the users and the existing mental model of the users on NFC payments. The methods used and their details are as follows.

3.1 Questionnaire

As a first step in understanding the users, we circulated the questionnaire to a wide range of users in Austria. The questionnaire was framed in such a way that it captures the mental model of the users and their knowledge about NFC payments (Appendix A). Questions like "When do you think the NFC transaction is initiated?", "What information do you think is transferred between the card and the payment terminal during the transaction?" were asked to understand the users' existing mental model about NFC payments. Questions about the feedback of the NFC payment were asked to understand if the users perceive the intended information from the NFC payment system. Finally questions like "What do you think is the limit (in EUR) of your NFC payment per transaction without entering the PIN number?" and "What do you think the limit (in EUR) of your NFC payment is per day?" were asked to test the users' knowledge about NFC payments.

The questionnaire was coded in "quest back" platform and was circulated via the USECON participant database. All participants above 18 years were allowed to answer the questionnaire. The questionnaire was online from 7th July 2017 till 30th September 2017. At the end of 3 months we received 247 completed responses. We had 148 (60%) male and 99 (40%) female participants with a mean age of 38.02 (SD = 12.25). The results from the questionnaire is summarised in Table 1.

3.2 Observation and Exit Interviews

The observations and exit interviews took place in 6 supermarkets located in 6 different districts in Vienna, Austria. The districts were selected based on average net earnings of the people living in those districts to avoid biases on their shopping behaviour. Given 100 to the standard average net income, districts with ±10 average net income was chosen for the study [13]. The study was conducted in the districts 2 – Leopoldstadt, 6 - Mariahilf, 9 – Alsergrund, 11 - Simmering, 14 - Penzing and 21 – Floridsdorf. In each supermarket, all customers were observed for 3 h and were asked for their willingness to give us a short exit interview. A 5 min interview was conducted with customers who were willing. The customers were questioned on their preferred mode of payment, feedback provided by the NFC payment system, the locations they use NFC payment and the information provided by their bank on NFC payments. The customers were also asked to rate the security of the NFC payment system on a scale of 1–7 (Likert scale), 1 being less secured and 7 being highly secured.

We received a total of 179 exit interviews from 6 supermarkets. We had 78 (44%) male and 101 (56%) female customers with the mean age of 41.69 (SD = 15.61). We also observed a total of 781 customers at the supermarket checkouts out of which 160 customers paid with card NFC. The customers were observed on the payment method used and customers who used NFC payment were observed for their behaviour. The NFC users were observed on how they scan their card against the payment terminal, if they receive the feedback delivered by the payment terminal and if they are aware of the situation where they have to input their PIN. The results from exit interviews are summarised in Table 2.

4   Results and Discussion

4.1   Mental Model

The questionnaire data portrayed 85 (34%) participants out of 247 did not have an idea about NFC. Some users also assumed NFC to be a very different technology. For example when question "what is NFC payment" users responded:

"As PayPal or similar?"

"Internet banking"

"Direct payment by means of 'moment' (identification via the iris) or "linguistic expression" (voice recognition) or personal handwriting (recognition similar to Fingerprint)... etc."

Table 1. Results from the questionnaire considering only the participants (n = 96 out of 247) who have experience with NFC payment.

Description	No. of participants
Aware of per transaction limit	68 (71%)
Aware of per day limit	12 (12.5%)
Participants who use mobile NFC	13 (13.5%)
Participants who think NFC payment is less secured than credit card payment	28 (29%)
Participants who think NFC payment is less secured than debit card payment	30 (31%)

Table 2. Results from exit interviews in 6 supermarkets (N = 179)

Description	No. of participants
Not aware of information provided by the bank	94 (52.5%)
Customers who feel NFC payment to be unsecured	65 (36%)
Participants who perceived the visual feedback from the payment terminal	24 (13%)
Participants who perceived the audio feedback	43 (24%)

"A finance centre or similar to PayPal?"

The interview and observation data also portrayed that users have a different mental model regarding "How NFC payment works". The mental model among the users doesn't match with the actual working model of NFC. The below responses from participants portray the gap between the mental model(s). When sharing their thoughts about NFC payment, customers mentioned:

"Can read data of card from distance"

"Shops could take more money than they show in the terminal"

"Technology without PIN? A PIN makes sure that money comes from me"

When questioned "why the user hasn't used NFC payment" in the questionnaire, the users responded:

"Technological concerns regarding safety"

"Is too uncertain for me, this can be very easily abused"

"Lack of security"

"Security aspect - after 40 years of computer experience"

"Data is too risky for me"

The above responses show us that the users have some misassumptions about the security of NFC payments. Also, when questioned about the security of NFC systems in our questionnaires, users mentioned that they do not feel secured while using NFC payments. 30 (31%) and 28 (29%) users mentioned that they feel less secured while paying with NFC compared to debit and credit cards respectively. Our interview data also supports that users do not feel secured while using NFC payments. 65 customers rated the security of NFC system under 4 on a Likert scale.

These assumptions may be due to the lack of knowledge about the security and the functional model of the system. We also observed that the banks fail to provide all necessary information to the user on "what NFC is about" and "how the NFC service works". The lack of information leads to above hesitations and misassumptions.

4.2   Lack of Information

Similar to the functional model of the system, details about the system were also not clear among the users. Some users were not aware about the transaction limit (with and without PIN) and the daily limit of NFC payments. During observation, we observed that the customers were unsure of when and when not to enter their PIN. Especially when the amount to be paid is 20 to 30 EUR the users were not sure if the terminal will ask them for the PIN. 12 customers had doubts about PIN at the terminal and out of which 10 customers the bill amount was between 20 to 30 EUR.

The participants who use NFC payment were also asked to input their per transaction limit without PIN number and per day limit in the questionnaire. The participants were aware of per transaction limit compared to per day limit of their NFCs. 68 participants answered the per-transaction limit correctly whereas only 12 (12.5%) of them stated their per day limit correctly.

As mentioned above, the banks do not provide transparent information about the usage of NFC on their websites. To further confirm the lack of information from banks, in exit interviews the customers were questioned if they received any information about NFC payments from their respective bank. Out of 179 customers 94 (52.5%) customers mentioned that their banks do not provide any information on NFC payment.

4.3   NFC Cards vs NFC Mobile

In our 6 day observation in supermarkets we did not have a single customer who paid with NFC enabled mobile phones. All the customers who used NFC used only their bank cards. When questioned about their preference in interviews, participants mentioned that they prefer cards over mobile. They also mentioned that they feel more secured with cards than with mobile.

Our questionnaire results also portray that only 13 out of 96 participants (13.5%) of the users uses mobile NFC.

This may be due to the fact that we are used to using cards such as credit and debit cards. As they are in use for a long period now, whereas mobile payment is a recent technology. As NFC improves in terms of technology and user experience the uptake will change over time and customers will adapt to mobile NFC's similar to other technologies.

5 Limitations

All the parts of the user study (questionnaires, observations and interviews) were conducted in Vienna, Austria. As it is evident from literature, NFC usage and acceptance differs greatly between various countries. For example the studies [10, 11] conducted in Korea and Malaysia respectively, predict and present different results as they were conducted in different countries. Given this, our results are geographically limited. To overcome this limitation we have planned to collect data through questionnaires from other countries and compare those results with the above obtained results.

6 Conclusion and Next Steps

To conclude, our study to capture user experience of NFC payment portrays that there are several misassumptions among the users. It is also evident that the users feel unsecure to use NFC payment due to lack of consistent information and different mental models on its functional model. We believe that there is still room for improvement in NFC on usability and user experience scales and further research is required in this direction.

We will be following the Human Centred Design process [12] to investigate the problem and to design and iterate different solutions. As a next step we aim to understand users in different location and develop (or modify) a new interaction design to provide users with privacy and secured enhanced experience. With the above stated interaction design being developed and evaluated with potential users, we will be able to bring new insight and possible recommendations for improving NFC commercial transactions.

Acknowledgement. The project leading to these first results has received funding from the European Union's Horizon 2020 research and innovation program under the Marie Sklodowska-Curie grant agreement No. 675730. We would also like to show our gratitude to Elisabeth Ettinger (USECON) for extending her support in conducting exit interviews.

Appendix A

1. How often do you use the following payment methods?

	Daily once	Several times a day	Weekly once	Several times a week	Monthly once	Several times a month	Never
Cash payment							
Debit card							
Credit card							
NFC payment							

2. Do you know about NFC payment?

- Yes
- No

3. Have you paid using NFC payment in any retail shop?

- Yes
- No

4. What type of NFC do you use?

- Cards
- Mobile
- Sticker

5. What do you think is the limit (in EUR) of your NFC payment per transaction without entering the PIN number?
6. What do you think is the limit (in EUR) of your NFC payment per day?
7. Does your bank provide any mobile app for managing your NFC payments?

- Yes (if yes, please enter the app name)
- No
- I don't know

8. Do you use any third party app for managing your NFC payments?

- Yes (if yes, please enter the app name)
- No

9. How secured is the following payments methods compared to NFC payment?

	Less secured than NFC	Equally secured as NFC	Highly secured than NFC
Cash payment			
Credit card payment			
Debit card payment			

10. When do you think the NFC transaction is initiated?
    - When I bring my card near the payment terminal
    - When I hold my card near the payment terminal
    - When I place my card on the payment terminal
    - None of the above

11. What information do you think is transferred between the card and the payment terminal during the transaction?
12. Which of the following payment terminal screen indicates you that the NFC payment is complete?

13. Which of the following sound from the payment terminal indicates you that the NFC payment is complete?

- Short beep
- Multiple short beeps
- Long beep
- Multiple long beeps

References

1. Leong, L.-Y., et al.: Predicting the determinants of the NFC-enabled mobile credit card acceptance: a neural networks approach. Expert Syst. Appl. **40**(14), 5604–5620 (2013)
2. Ok, K., et al.: Current benefits and future directions of NFC services. In: 2010 International Conference on Education and Management Technology (ICEMT). IEEE (2010)
3. Pasquet, M., Reynaud, J., Rosenberger, C.: Secure payment with NFC mobile phone in the SmartTouch project. In: 2008 International Symposium on Collaborative Technologies and Systems, CTS. IEEE (2008)
4. Massoth, M., Bingel, T.: Performance of different mobile payment service concepts compared with a NFC-based solution. In: 2009 Fourth International Conference on Internet and Web Applications and Services, ICIW 2009. IEEE (2009)
5. Coskun, V., Ozdenizci, B., Ok, K.: A survey on near field communication (NFC) technology. Wirel. Pers. Commun. **71**(3), 2259–2294 (2013)
6. Geven, A., et al.: Experiencing real-world interaction: results from a NFC user experience field trial. In: Proceedings of the 9th International Conference on Human Computer Interaction with Mobile Devices and Services. ACM (2007)
7. Tomitsch, M., Grechenig, T., Schlögl, R.: Real-world tagging in the wild: on the usability and accessibility of NFC-based interactions. In: Workshop on Future Mobile Experiences: Next Generation Mobile Interaction and Contextualization, Co-located with the Nordic Conference on Human-Computer Interaction, NordiCHI (2008)
8. McCarthy, J., Wright, P.: Technology as experience. Interactions **11**(5), 42–43 (2004)
9. Garrett, J.J.: Elements of user experience, the: user-centered design for the web and beyond. Pearson Education, London (2010)
10. Shin, S., Lee, W.-J.: The effects of technology readiness and technology acceptance on NFC mobile payment services in Korea. J. Appl. Bus. Res. **30**(6), 1615 (2014)
11. Tan, G.W.H., et al.: NFC mobile credit card: the next frontier of mobile payment? Telematics Inf. **31**(2), 292–307 (2014)
12. International Organization for Standardization: Ergonomics of human system interaction - Part 210: Human-centered design for interactive systems, ISO 9241-210:2010 (2010)
13. Lohnsteuerpflichtige Einkommen nach Bezirken 2014 Frauen und Männer (n.d.). https://www.wien.gv.at/statistik/arbeitsmarkt/tabellen/einkommen-gesamt-bez.html. Accessed 15 Nov 2017
14. NFC Forum: Home - NFC Forum (2017). http://www.nfc-forum.org. Accessed 15 Nov 2017

Real-World Identification
for an Extensible and Privacy-Preserving
Mobile eID

Michael Hölzl[1]([✉]), Michael Roland[2], and René Mayrhofer[1]

[1] Insitute of Networks and Security, JKU Linz, Linz, Austria
{hoelzl,mayrhofer}@ins.jku.at
[2] University of Applied Sciences Upper Austria, Hagenberg, Austria
michael.roland@fh-hagenberg.at

Abstract. There is a broad range of existing electronic identity (eID) systems which provide methods to sign documents or authenticate to online services (e.g. governmental eIDs, FIDO). However, these solutions mainly focus on the validation of an identity to a web page. That is, they often miss proper techniques to use them as regular ID cards to digitally authenticate an eID holder to another physical person in the real world. We propose a mobile eID which provides such a functionality and enables extensibility for its use with numerous different public and private services (e.g. for loyalty programs, public transport tickets, student cards), while protecting the privacy of the eID holder. In this paper, we present a general architecture and efficient protocols for such a privacy-preserving mobile eID that allows identity validation in a similar fashion as regular ID cards and makes carrying around various physical cards unnecessary.

1 Introduction

Many governments already provide their citizens with an electronic identity (eID) infrastructure to handle administrative tasks like doing taxes or applying for subsidies (cf. survey of European governmental eIDs by Lehman et al. [16]). However, they lack appropriate methods to allow eID holders to use the eID in a privacy-preserving manner. In our terms, such a privacy-preserving eID gives the prover (i.e. the eID holder) the capability to only reveal and prove the validity of certain attributes to a verifier. For example, an eID holder wants to prove to the bouncer at a disco that she is above 18 years old without revealing the name or even the actual date of birth. Furthermore, a privacy-preserving eID should also not leak any usage behavior to the verifier (e.g. how often does a specific eID holder enter the disco).

There are existing solutions for such a privacy-preserving eID, where the most recent ones are based on attribute-based credentials (ABCs) [7,8]. ABCs allow eID holders to prove a subset of their personal data attributes (e.g. age, name,

M. Hansen et al. (Eds.): Privacy and Identity 2017, IFIP AICT 526, pp. 354–370, 2018.
https://doi.org/10.1007/978-3-319-92925-5_24

citizenship) without revealing the full set. They have already been actively used for pilot studies in the ABC4Trust project [4,21] and have been implemented on smart cards [3,11,23]. Alpár and Jacobs [2] discuss the difficulties of such ABC systems (which applies to smart card-based identity systems in general):

- Controlling attribute access for verifiers requires either additional technical restrictions (i.e. let each verifier get a signed list of readable attributes from the identity manager), legal restrictions (i.e. in order to read attributes, verifiers must have valid contracts), or additional monitoring on the card.
- Verifying that the person presenting the smart card is the actual eID holder requires additional communication channels (e.g. picture on the card).
- The usage of PIN protection for smart cards ensures confidentiality, user consent and authentication, but adds additional complexity (e.g. the PIN may have to be entered in every verification on the card reader of the verifier).

One possible solution to these issues of smart card-based eIDs is the usage of a mobile eID. Although existing ABC technologies could already be ported to run on mobile platforms (e.g. Jensen's smart phone feasibility study of ABC4Trust [15]), there are additional challenges which have to be considered: (i) Mobile devices can easily be stolen and an adversary could attempt to take over the identity. (ii) The mobile device can run out of battery or (iii) has no online connectivity.

We envision a privacy-preserving mobile eID which addresses these challenges and allows eID holders to use it in a similar fashion as regular ID cards to prove their identity (we refer to this as *real-world identification*). Verification of an identity should even work with a turned-off prover device and in an offline setting, while the integrity of the eID should be protected with additional tamper resistant hardware. And finally, the mobile eID should be usable for multiple public or private services. We refer to these services as *domains* and use a loyalty program in a shop as an example use case throughout this paper (other examples would be public transport tickets, student cards, etc.) In this paper we describe the general architecture of such a mobile eID scheme and propose protocols to enroll to numerous domains and verify data attributes in an efficient way. The architecture allows to provide proofs of single eID attributes in a privacy-preserving manner and builds upon state-of-the-art technologies in that field.

2   Related Work

A specification for eIDs that has recently become famous is provided by the FIDO Alliance [9]. This consortium aims to improve the usability of user authentication on the internet by reducing the reliance on passwords. With one specification for biometric authentication and one for two-factor authentication, they provide schemes for secure identity verification to any online service.

Concerning governmental eIDs, the survey by Lehman et al. [16] about eIDs in the European Union shows that current systems do not provide sufficient privacy-preserving verification methods. Only the Austrian and German eID cards support notable features protecting the privacy of the user (i.e. generation of pseudonyms, selective attribute disclosure).

Nyman et al. [18] define a governmental and privacy-preserving eID architecture that is based on the use of so-called Trusted Platform Modules (TPM). They build upon version 2.0 of the TPM specification and evaluate its feasibility as an identity token on PC as well as mobile platforms. Similar to our concept, their system relies on additional tamper resistance hardware in computing devices. The mobile eID solution by Otterbein et al. in [19] also involves additional tamper resistant hardware. Their scheme uses a trusted execution environment on Android devices to enter secret information of the user and get access to the content of this additional hardware.

ABCs [5–7] build the basis for another field of research in the area of privacy-preserving eID schemes. In an ABC scheme, a credential is referred to as a cryptographic container for multiple attributes. An attribute, on the other hand, is a property about a person that some trusted authority attested. Most important technologies in that field are Identity Mixer (Idemix) [14], developed by IBM Research, and Microsoft's U-Prove system [20]. In addition, the ABC4Trust project defines a common, unified architecture that uses multiple ABC protocols for a privacy-preserving verification on any platform [4,21]. The benefit of ABCs is that besides ensuring authenticity and integrity of eID attributes, it also provides some privacy guarantees for credential owners. That is, it allows the eID holder to prove certain predicates of an attribute without revealing the actual content. Moreover, each verification of a single eID appears unrelated and can therefore not be linked by a verifier. In other related work, it has already been proven that ABCs can also be implemented on smart cards [3,11,23].

3   Threat Model

We consider two general types of adversaries in a privacy-preserving eID: (i) A malicious prover trying to forge or steal an identity. This would allow an attacker to adapt single data attributes for an attack (e.g. modify the age or place of residence), impersonate someone else, or even result in digital identity theft (e.g. take over mail and bank accounts). (ii) Malicious verifiers who try to compromise the privacy of an eID holder. We assume that this adversary has the capability to eavesdrop on all eID verification processes and attempts to:

- Misuse data. As information is processed digitally, users cannot be sure that the data they transmit to a verifier is adequately protected, only used for the claimed purpose (of identification), and not stored or passed on to other parties. Hence, in order to protect their privacy it is important that as little information as necessary is given to potentially malicious verifiers.
- Tracing identities. An adversary could use the digital information provided by the eID to trace activities of an eID holder. For example, the disco bouncer or the public transport system could track all identification processes and therefore trace all activities of a single user.

- Linking pseudonyms. A system that provides pseudonymity shall not allow verifiers to link single pseudonyms to each other. For example, a shop, where the user is enrolled in a loyalty program, should not be able to derive, link, or determine other pseudonyms of the user.

4 Extensible and Privacy-Preserving Mobile eID

We propose a privacy-preserving mobile eID that has the flexibility to be used as a regular identification document and for the use by numerous services. More specifically, besides protecting the privacy of the user, this eID provides:

- Real-world identification. The mobile eID can be used as a replacement for regular ID cards and can be used for identification and verification of attributes (e.g. age of the eID holder).
- Extensibility. The eID can also be used for numerous different services with the possibility to derive pseudonyms. A service provider can therefore easily and rapidly establish their own e.g. loyalty program on top of our eID system.
- Capable for offline and turned-off devices. The prover mobile device does not need to be powered on in order to verify the identity of the eID holder and no constant online connectivity to a central server shall be required.

4.1 Stakeholders

Figure 1 depicts the proposed eID architecture consisting of four stakeholders:

- The *eID issuer* is the central authority that controls the enrollment of new eIDs and provides an interface to acquire the public system parameters for eID verification (e.g. governmental authority in a nationwide eID).
- The *prover* is the actual owner of the eID and consists of a mobile device equipped with a secure element (SE). Communication to the SE can be done directly over near field communication (NFC) or through the eID management application (eID-MA) on the mobile device.
- The *domain manager* is responsible for controlling the enrollment of a prover to a specific *domain* (i.e. a service). A domain may have additional attributes associated to an eID or require a pseudonym for the prover.
- The *verifier* can be anyone who wants to verify attributes of the eID holder (e.g. disco bouncer). They can also be domain members (referred to as *domain verifier*) and read domain-specific attributes (e.g. loyalty card membership).

4.2 Building Blocks

Our architecture combines several techniques. That is, we make use of secure elements for the protection of sensitive data and use ABCs to verify the eID in a privacy-preserving manner as well as authenticate an additional secure channel:

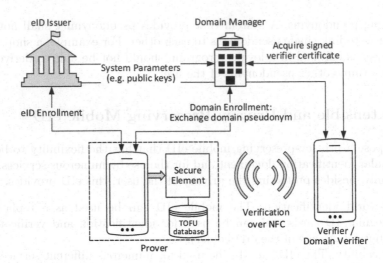

Fig. 1. General architecture of the proposed mobile and extensible eID system.

Secure Elements (SE). Our architecture assumes the existence of a trustworthy SE on the prover's device. An SE is usually shipped as an embedded integrated circuit in mobile devices together with NFC [17] (e.g. as a SIM card) and brings two main security advantages: (i) it protects against unauthorized access as well as tampering, and (ii) small applications (applets) can be executed directly on the card in the trusted execution environment. Another advantage of SEs is that they can be powered by the NFC field when the prover device is turned off (provided that the NFC controller in the prover device supports this feature).

In our eID scenario, the SE shall protect the identities of the eID holders as well as their attributes. All computations that require these data need to be performed within the SE. However, the constrained execution performance and memory on the SE have strong implications on the protocols and architectural design of the eID system (see performance evaluation in [12]). Our proposed architecture acknowledges these requirements and can be executed within this secure but constrained environment in reasonable time. That is, we assume that a user is not willing to wait for more then 2 s to finish a task.

Attribute-Based Credentials (ABCs). In our proposed architecture, we use ABCs for attesting the validity of the eID in a privacy-friendly way. We assume the following properties of ABC: (i) With a *selective disclosure* mechanism, the holder of the credential can reveal any subset of attributes and provide a validity proof of them (i.e. they have been attested by the trusted authority); (ii) Ownership of a credential can be proven without revealing the attributes itself; (iii) Verification of credentials are unlinkable to verifier and issuer.

In order to protect against replay attacks, the selective disclosure mechanism allows the verifier to send a random challenge. The prover responds to this with a non-interactive-zero-knowledge (NIZK) proof, which is also a signature of this challenge. Using this mechanism, we establish an authenticated secure channel as described in [1], and therefore introduce a simple notation for selective disclosure:

$$\pi = \text{SD}\,(\mathcal{A}, ch),\tag{1}$$

where $\mathcal{A}$ is the subset of disclosed attributes from a credential and ch is the random challenge.

The downside of ABCs is the higher complexity of issuing attributes and creating proofs. Although they have been successfully deployed on smart cards (i.e. execution on SE also possible) [3,11], they are still considerably slower than ordinary signature schemes and can become the bottleneck in a privacy-preserving eID system. For example, Vullers and Alpár report the results of a RSA-based 1024 bit smart card implementation of the Idemix technology in [23]. Disclosing and creating a proof for only one credential (with 4 attributes) takes already 1 s on the used MULTOS cards (incl. overhead). They also indicate that increasing the security level to a 2048 bit modulus would more than double the computation time. Furthermore, we assume that a regular transaction requires more than 4 attributes and that a user is not willing to wait for more than 2 s for the identification. Hence, for our use cases, the performance of an eID system solely based on ABCs is not sufficient. We therefore propose a system that only requires a single selective disclosure operation in any verification process.

4.3   Extensibility and Privacy-Preserving Mechanisms

A central component of our architecture is the potential usage of the eID for numerous services (e.g. loyalty card program). With simplicity as a major goal, it should thereby be easy for service providers to integrate with our system and for eID holders to control the data attributes that can be read by verifiers. We define three main mechanisms for that purpose:

Profiles. In order to give the user control over the data, we introduce the concept of profiles to the mobile eID architecture. A profile defines data attributes which are accessible for a specific purpose or a group of verifiers. For example, an age verification profile where only the date of birth and the portrait picture are accessible (for the disco bouncer use case). The management application (eID-MA) running on the mobile device of the prover maintains these profiles and stores them on the SE. It is also possible to associate one profile with a domain in a trust-on-first-use (TOFU) database. This enables the user to remember data attributes that can be retrieved by specific domain verifiers.

Trust-on-First-Use (TOFU). Each SE of an eID holder possesses a TOFU database with information about enrolled domains. The basic idea is that the trust relationship between an eID holder and a domain manager is established at the first encounter. The eID holder then stores the public key of this domain in the TOFU database and only trusts verifications for that domain where the verifier can proof the possession of the private key or demonstrate a certificate signed with this private key. An entry in the database consists of the identifier (i.e. public key) of the domain D_{id} and a profile, which defines the attributes a domain verifier can query. In addition, there might be additional attributes stored for that specific domain (e.g. validity of loyalty program membership). As a positive result of this mechanism, it is relatively simple for domain managers to integrate with our eID scheme. That is, they do not require additional, and potentially complex, authorization by a central administration.

Domain Pseudonyms. An eID holder that enrolls to a number of domains has unlinkable pseudonyms for each of them. They are derived from the identity of the eID holder as well as the identifier of the domain manager and can be used for domain-specific identification (e.g. for bonus point system in loyalty programs). We use a mechanism that does not require additional space on the SE. It also provides the capability for multiple devices of an eID holder to derive the same pseudonym for a specific domain.

5 Protocols

The protocols in our scheme use profiles for easy attribute selection and build upon ABCs to validate the eID as well as authenticate an additional secure channel. This secure channel is used to efficiently transfer the data attributes of the profile to the verifier. In addition, we introduce a simple mechanism to derive domain pseudonyms, which do not require additional space on the SE, and a TOFU database to store domain-specific profiles and attributes on the prover device (i.e. the SE). The notation of the protocol is listed in Table 1.

5.1 Setup

During setup, every involved party receives the public system parameters of the used ABC system as well as the elliptic curve parameters. Every domain manager creates a public/private key pair $(d_{sk}, D_{id} := d_{sk} \cdot G)$, where the public key D_{id} also serves as the domain identifier, and defines a list la_d, which specifies the attributes they want to access from a user. Each verifier generates a key-pair $(v_{sk}, V_{pk} := v_{sk} \cdot G)$ and the TOFU databases of each SE are empty.

5.2 Prover Enrollment

There are two types of enrollment: *eID* and *domain* enrollment. The enrollment of the eID can only be done once for every SE while the domain enrollment is only limited to the available storage space for the TOFU database on the SE.

Table 1. Notation used in this paper.

id_u	Secret identifier of the user
da_u	Data attributes of the user
$\mathcal{C}_u$	ABC key credential of user u for eID validation
$N_{u,d}, n_{u,d}$	Derived domain pseudonym and the corresponding secret key
G	Elliptic curve generator point
D_{id}, d_{sk}	Public/private key-pair of domain manager d
la_d	List of attribute identifiers which a domain d wants to access
V_{pk}, v_{sk}	Public/private key-pair of verifier v
$ca_{v,d}$	Certificate of domain verifier v
$\mathrm{H}(m)$	One-way hash function over message m
$\mathrm{Enc}(K, m)$	Symmetric encryption of message m using key K
$\mathrm{Sign}(sk, m)$	Signature creation over message m with private key sk
$\mathrm{SD}(\mathcal{A}, ch)$	Create a NIZK proof of an attribute-set $\mathcal{A}$ in a given ABC, while using the random challenge ch

eID Enrollment. During the initial eID enrollment, the SE of the prover and the eID issuer communicate in a secure channel using GlobalPlatform card management [10]. The eID-MA acts as a proxy between them. The process is initiated by the eID holder and presumably involves an additional out-of-band identity verification (the detailed steps of this enrollment are out-of-scope of this paper). We assume that during this process the SE acquires the secret identifier id_u and the data attributes of the eID holder da_u. The SE also acquires an ABC key credential $\mathcal{C}_u$ from the issuer, which is used to validate the eID and authenticate an additional secure channel with the method described by Alpár and Hoepmann in [1].

Domain Enrollment and Pseudonym Derivation. An example scenario for this enrollment would be an eID holder who would like to join a loyalty card system. This enrollment process is performed by the manager of a domain, the prover's mobile device and the SE. The eID-MA running on the prover's mobile device acts as a proxy between domain manager and SE. In contrast to the eID enrollment, domain enrollment does not require GlobalPlatform card management. Hence, user approval is sufficient (e.g. through entering a PIN/password that is verified on the SE) to add domains to the provers' SE.

The protocol steps of the domain enrollment consists of establishing an authenticated and privacy-friendly secure channel with ABCs (based on the scheme in [1]). This secure channel is then used to efficiently transfer eID data attributes directly between the SE of the prover and the domain manager.

Additionally, during this process the domain manager and the SE authenticate the pseudonym of the user and the domain public key, respectively:

1. The process is initiated by the eID-MA, for example, when the user taps an NFC tag in the shop with a loyalty program. In this first step, the eID-MA sends the enrollment request to the domain manager.
2. The domain manager creates a new ephemeral key-pair $(a, A := a \cdot G)$ as well as a signature $\sigma_{i,d}$ over the public part A as well as la_d:

$$\sigma_{i,d} = \text{Sign}\,(d_{sk}, \text{H}\,(A \,\|\, la_d)) \tag{2}$$

The manager sends $(\sigma_{i,d}, A, D_{id}, la_d)$ to the eID-MA.
3. The eID-MA asks the user to confirm the enrollment and the attribute disclosure of la_d. If the user rejects, the enrollment aborts. Otherwise, he has to authenticate himself with a previously defined PIN/password and the enrollment message is forwarded to the SE. Note that the user may only confirm a subset of the attributes in la_d. The SE conceals the remaining attributes from the domain.
4. On successful authentication, the SE proceeds and verifies the signature $\sigma_{i,d}$ with the received domain public key D_{id}. Furthermore, the SE checks in the TOFU database if an entry with the domain public key D_{id} already exists. If the signature is invalid or an entry exists, the SE sends an error message to eID-MA and aborts. Otherwise, it derives a pseudonym $N_{u,d}$ for that domain:

$$n_{u,d} = \text{H}\,(id_u \,\|\, D_{id}) \tag{3}$$
$$N_{u,d} = n_{u,d} \cdot G \tag{4}$$

Note that the pseudonym does not have to be stored on the SE (i.e. no additional space required) and can be easily derived in each verification (see Sect. 5.4). Also multiple devices of a user will derive the same pseudonym for a domain (i.e. all SEs receive the same id_u during eID enrollment).
For the next step, the SE creates a new ephemeral key-pair $(b, B := b \cdot G)$ and a NIZK proof over A, B, and $N_{u,d}$, using the ABC key credential C_u. Furthermore, the signatures $\sigma_{i,N}$ and $\sigma_{i,B}$ verify the knowledge of the secret-key $n_{u,d}$ and ephemeral key b, respectively:

$$\pi_i = \text{SD}\,(C_u, \text{H}\,(A \,\|\, B \,\|\, N_{u,d})) \tag{5}$$
$$\sigma_{i,n} = \text{Sign}\,(n_{u,d}, \text{H}\,(A \,\|\, \pi_i)) \tag{6}$$
$$\sigma_{i,b} = \text{Sign}\,(b, \text{H}\,(A \,\|\, \sigma_{i,n})) \tag{7}$$

The SE sends $(N_{u,d}, B, \pi_i, \sigma_{i,n}, \sigma_{i,b})$ to the domain manager.
5. With the NIZK proof π_i, the ephemeral public key A, and the received pseudonym $N_{u,d}$, the domain manager verifies the eID validity. The signature verification ensures the validity of the pseudonym and the ephemeral key. If any verification fails, the manager aborts. Otherwise, she creates a signature $\sigma_{i,A}$ to verify the ephemeral key and computes the session key K_i with

$$\sigma_{i,a} = \text{Sign}\,(a, \text{H}\,(B \,\|\, N_{u,d})) \tag{8}$$
$$K_i = \text{H}\,(a \cdot B), \tag{9}$$

and outputs $(\sigma_{i,a})$ to the SE.

6. If the signature $\sigma_{i,a}$ is valid, the SE also computes the session key K_i:

$$K_i = \text{H}\,(b \cdot A) \tag{10}$$

7. The SE and the domain manager use the session key K_i for an authenticated secure channel and to exchange data attributes now. The domain manager can only request attributes which have been confirmed by the user. Additionally, the SE adds a new entry to the TOFU database, with the domain identifier D_{id} and the accepted attributes of the attribute identifier list la_d (i.e. as the profile for that domain). The domain manager might also send additional attributes (e.g. loyalty card validity period), which are also stored on the SE and linked to the TOFU entry.
8. The domain manager stores the pseudonym and the data attributes.

5.3   Profile Selection

Prior to the verification, the user selects a currently active profile within the eID-MA. This profile is then stored on the SE as the default profile and is also active if the mobile device of the prover is turned-off. An example of such a profile would be the birthday verification profile where only the birthday attribute is accessible for verifiers.

In the case where the verifier belongs to a domain, the profile will be automatically selected from the TOFU database after a successful membership verification of the verifier. This is part of the verification protocol.

5.4   Verification

Verification of the eID is done between verifier and prover over NFC. On the prover mobile device the communication is either transferred through the management application to the SE (using NFC host-card emulation) or directly with the SE (if the device is turned-off). Both communication paths use the same protocol steps described in this section. However, the host-card emulation enables the management application to display additional information of the verifier to the user (e.g. domain name, id, etc.)

The verifier can be any user who downloaded and installed the verifier application or can be a specific verifier of a domain. In the latter case, we assume the existence of a certificate $ca_{v,d}$, which is essentially a signature of the long-term public key V_{pk} with the secret key of the domain manager d_{sk}.

The protocol steps are similar to the domain enrollment protocol and mainly consist of establishing an authenticated secure-channel between the SE of the prover and the verifier. This channel is based on ABCs to validate the eID and allows an efficient data attribute exchange:

1. The process is initiated by the verifier, for example, when the phones of verifier and prover are tapped together and communication over NFC is established. The verifier creates a new ephemeral key-pair $(c, C := c \cdot G)$ and sends $(D_{id}, ca_{v,d}, V_{pk}, C)$ to the SE. If the verifier is not part of a domain, the domain public key D_{id} and the certificate $ca_{v,d}$ are omitted.

2. The SE also chooses a new ephemeral key-pair $(b, B := b \cdot G)$, creates a NIZK proof over B as well as C and creates a signature using the new secret key:

$$\pi_i = \mathrm{SD}\left(\mathcal{C}_u, \mathrm{H}\left(C \,\|\, B\right)\right) \tag{11}$$

$$\sigma_{i,b} = \mathrm{Sign}\left(b, \mathrm{H}\left(C \,\|\, \pi_i\right)\right) \tag{12}$$

The SE sends $(B, \pi_i, \sigma_{i,b})$ to the verifier.

3. The verifier proves the validity of the eID using the NIZK proof π_i and checks the signature $\sigma_{i,b}$ to ensure the validity of the ephemeral key. If any verification fails, the verifier aborts; otherwise proceeds by creating a signature using its own ephemeral key c and the long-term secret key v_{sk}:

$$\sigma_{i,v} = \mathrm{Sign}\left(v_{sk}, \mathrm{H}\left(B \,\|\, C\right)\right) \tag{13}$$

$$\sigma_{i,c} = \mathrm{Sign}\left(c, \mathrm{H}\left(\sigma_{i,v}\right)\right) \tag{14}$$

The verifier sends $(\sigma_{i,v}, \sigma_{i,c})$ to the SE and computes the session key K_i:

$$K_i = \mathrm{H}\left(c \cdot B\right) \tag{15}$$

4. If any signature $(\sigma_{i,v}, \sigma_{i,c})$ is not correct, the SE cancels the process. Otherwise, the SE computes the session key K_i:

$$K_i = \mathrm{H}\left(b \cdot C\right) \tag{16}$$

The SE also chooses the profile that defines the allowed attribute disclosure now. There are two cases:

   (a) The verifier is member of a domain and sent $ca_{v,d}$ and D_{id}: the SE checks in the TOFU database if the domain public key D_{id} is already known. If the domain is not in the database or if the certificate $ca_{v,d}$ does not properly validate the verifier key V_{pk}, the process is aborted. If the check is successful, the profile from the TOFU database is chosen.

   (b) The verifier is not member of a domain: the default profile is chosen.

5. The SE and the verifier use the session key K_i for the attribute exchange in an authenticated secure channel now. During this process, the verifier may request different attributes and based on the chosen profile, the SE decides if the attributes are disclosed or not.

6. If the verifier is a valid member of a domain, she may also request the domain pseudonym $N_{u,d}$. The derivation of it is the same as described in Eqs. 3–4. However, as the proposed system should not allow single verifiers to trace the activities of the prover, the pseudonym is not directly revealed to the verifier. That is, we assume that not all domain verifiers can be trusted and only the domain manager shall verify the prover's pseudonym. For that purpose, the

SE generates a random value r, encrypts the pseudonym following the elliptic curve integrated encryption scheme [22] (ECIES), and signs the message with the secret key of the pseudonym:

$$K_N = \mathrm{H}\left(r \cdot D_{id}\right) \tag{17}$$

$$\gamma_N = \mathrm{Enc}\left(K_N, N_{u,d}\right) \tag{18}$$

$$\sigma_N = \mathrm{Sign}\left(n_{u,d}, \mathrm{H}\left(\gamma_N\right)\right) \tag{19}$$

The SE outputs $(\gamma_N, \sigma_N, R := r \cdot G)$ to the domain verifier. As the message is encrypted with the public key of the domain manager, the domain verifier cannot acquire the pseudonym $N_{u,d}$. Hence, a single verifier can validate the eID and get domain-specific attributes but by default cannot link and trace the verifications. Even if domain verification of the same eID is requested multiple times, a domain verifier cannot link these verifications due to the randomness of r. Only the manager can decrypt that message, verify the signature and perform appropriate actions on that pseudonym (e.g. add bonus points to the loyalty program account). Note that disclosed attributes may still make verifications linkable to verifiers (see analysis in the next section).

6 Security and Privacy Analysis

Following up on our threat model, the proposed scheme prevents against:

- Forging identities. The security of our scheme relies on the security of the used ABC scheme as well as on the usage of an SE as a tamper-resistant storage for the credential and the identifier id_u. For that purpose, the SE on the provers' mobile device has a special security compartment (referred to as *security domain* [10]) that is under the control of a trusted eID issuer. Hence, a malicious prover cannot modify or forge sensitive data (i.e. identity, ABC, data attributes, etc.) without breaking the security of the SE. This is state-of-the-art technology for protecting sensitive information (e.g. SIM/bank cards) and also protects the integrity of the eID in cases where the mobile device gets stolen or malicious software is able to exploit the operating system of the prover device.

  A malicious prover could also try to establish a secure channel to the verifier and send invalid data attributes. Without the knowledge of an ABC key credential $\mathcal{C}_u$, the malicious prover cannot authenticate the ephemeral public keys in Step 4 of the domain enrollment protocol or in Step 2 of the verification protocol. Hence, without breaking the security of the SE or the used ABC scheme, it is infeasible for an attacker to forge an authenticated secure channel to the verifier and send invalid data attributes.
- Misuse data. The profiles as well as the TOFU database on the SE prevent uncontrolled attribute disclosure. The user stays in control of which data is sent to which verifier.

– Tracing identities. ABCs are designed to enable credential holders to attest the existence of certain signed attributes, without revealing the attribute itself. We make use of this mechanism to attest the validity of the eID without revealing any information about the eID holder. Hence, under the assumption that the used ABC mechanism protects against identity tracing, our proposed architecture is also secure against it.

  Note that the disclosed attributes may still make verifications of a user linkable and enable identity tracing. Additional privacy-preserving mechanisms, such as the attribute queries proposed in [13], could reduce the amount of revealed information in this case and further protect the privacy of the eID holders.

– Linking pseudonyms. Our pseudonym derivation relies on the usage of a secure one-way hash function. That is, a hash function that is resistant against preimage, second preimage and collision attacks. Under this assumption, we argue that it is not feasible to link or deanonymize the pseudonyms of the prover without knowledge of the random and secret identifier id_u.

7   Evaluation

In the evaluation we use a 256-bit hash function, 256-bit elliptic curves (EC) for the creation of ECDSA signatures and 128-bit AES encryption. We will focus on the extensibility of the proposed architecture in terms of computation time as well as the required storage space on the SE.

7.1   Required Storage Space

Persistent and volatile memory are highly limited on an SE and therefore a limiting factor for smart card-based eID schemes. Hence, we briefly outline the required storage space of our architecture:

eID. The SE of the prover has to store the identifier id_u (we assume a size of 128 byte), the ABC key credential C_u (size depends on the specific ABC implementation and the required security level), and the data attributes of the eID holder da_u.

TOFU Database. Each enrolled domain adds one entry to the TOFU database, consisting of the domain public key D_{id} (33 bytes if point compression is supported, 65 bytes otherwise) and a profile that describes the accessible attributes for verifiers of that domain (we assume 4 bytes to control the disclosure of up to 32 attributes). There might also be additional attributes stored for each domain, hence, the exact size depends on the domain and cannot be estimated. Nevertheless, with an overhead of 37 bytes (or 69 bytes without point compression) for each domain, we argue that our proposed system is very space efficient and allows the use of many services at the same time.

7.2 Computation Time

We implemented the involved steps of the domain enrollment and verification protocol and measured the computation time on a NFC SIM card and a Yubikey NEO (also a smart card based computing device), both with JavaCard version 3.0.1. The measurements for the NFC SIM where done on an OPPO N1 Mini with Android 4.3 using the Open Mobile API and the Yubikey NEO measurements where done with a Thinkpad T440s over the USB interface. Note that an evaluation of the used ABC functionalities in our scheme is out of scope of this paper and not included in the computational analysis (an evaluation of ABCs on smart cards can be found in [23]).

As the transfer speed between SE and other devices highly depends on the interface [12], we omit the transfer time in this evaluation. For that purpose, we send the required data in a preceding command, store it in temporary memory on the SE, and then execute and measure the actual command.

Domain Enrollment. The measurement of the domain enrollment protocol (see Sect. 5.2) comprises of the following commands:

- Step 4 involves one signature verification, the pseudonym derivation (one hash and an elliptic curve (EC) point multiplication), generation of a new ephemeral key-pair and two signature creations.
- Step 6 involves one signature verification and the creation of the shared secret key (one EC point multiplication and a hash).

Table 2 lists the median results of 25 measurements performed on the two test cards. Overall, the steps involving the SE took 2053 ms for the NFC SIM and 1021 ms for the Yubikey NEO.

Verification. The evaluation of the verification protocol comprises of:

- Step 2 involves the generation of a new ephemeral key-pair and the creation of one signature.
- Step 4 involves two signature verifications and the creation of the shared secret key (one EC point multiplication and a hash).
- Step 6 is executed for domain verifiers and involves the creation of a public/private key-pair, a domain pseudonym derivation (one hash and an elliptic curve point multiplication), one AES encryption with a newly created secret key (one EC point multiplication and a hash) and a signature creation.

Table 3 lists the median computation time of 25 measurements on the test cards. Establishing the secure channel (Step 2 and 4) took overall 1402 ms on the NFC SIM and 315.5 ms on the Yubikey NEO. The derivation and encryption of the domain pseudonym (Step 6) took 1048 ms and 437 ms, respectively.

Table 2. Median computation time of the domain enrollment on the SE.

	NFC SIM	Yubikey NEO
Step 4	1432 ± 3 ms	672 ± 1 ms
Step 6	620 ± 5 ms	349 ± 1 ms

Table 3. Median computation time of the domain enrollment on the SE.

	NFC SIM	Yubikey NEO
Step 2	432 ± 13 ms	163 ± 0 ms
Step 4	970 ± 5 ms	153 ± 1 ms
Step 6	1048 ± 7 ms	437 ± 1 ms

7.3 Discussion

Based on these results, we argue that our proposed architecture and the protocols are efficient for the user and can be performed on a computationally restricted device in reasonable time (below 2 s). Especially the verification protocol, where two people (e.g. disco bouncer and the guest) are directly interacting with each other, should not exceed this limit. The evaluation shows that the channel establishment on the SE is below this time limit with some time left for the selective disclosure protocol and the data transfer (further communication to the SE uses symmetric encryption and is therefore rather efficient). Only the enrollment on the NFC SIM took more than 2 s. However, this protocol does not require direct human interaction and can be performed in the background.

Compared to other systems that use ABCs (e.g. the ABC4Trust project) for a privacy-preserving verification, our system has the downside that we do not provide a cryptographic proof for every transferred eID attribute. However, we argue that creating proofs for different attributes within multiple credentials becomes very slow in ABC systems and many use cases do not require these security guarantees. For example, a loyalty card program might not require such strong assurances and a simpler approach (which requires less storage and computation on the smart card) is sufficient. In addition, our scheme also benefits from a simple mechanism for service providers to integrate with the eID architecture (no authorization by central administration required).

One limitation of our proposed scheme is the requirement of an SE on the prover side as well as NFC on both involved devices. Due to the heterogeneous landscape of the mobile device market, it is therefore not provided that our proposed scheme can be deployed on every device.

8 Conclusion

In this paper we proposed an architecture and protocols for a privacy-preserving and extensible mobile eID system for real-world identification. The scheme combines attribute-based credentials with additional mechanisms (TOFU, profiles, privacy-preserving secure channel) to be implemented on computationally constrained hardware (NFC secure elements) in an efficient way (only one selective disclosure operation required). We evaluated the proposed architecture and protocols in terms of computation time as well as storage space and demonstrate that it can be executed in reasonable time on a computationally constrained device, such as smart cards. In future work, we will further analyze the security of our proposed scheme as well as evaluate the computation time on the verifier mobile device. Another part of future work will be to investigate possible solutions for an efficient and privacy-preserving revocation in our mobile eID system.

Acknowledgments. This work has been carried out within the scope of *u'smile*, the Josef Ressel Center for User-Friendly Secure Mobile Environments, funded by the Christian Doppler Gesellschaft, A1 Telekom Austria AG, Drei-Banken-EDV GmbH, LG Nexera Business Solutions AG, NXP Semiconductors Austria GmbH, and Österreichische Staatsdruckerei GmbH.

References

1. Alpár, G., Hoepman, J.-H.: A secure channel for attribute-based credentials: [short paper]. In: Proceedings of 2013 ACM Workshop on Digital Identity Management, DIM 2013, pp. 13–18. ACM (2013)
2. Alpár, G., Jacobs, B.: Credential design in attribute-based identity management. In: 3rd TILTing Perspectives Conference on Bridging Distances in Technology and Regulation, pp. 189–204, April 2013
3. Bichsel, P., Camenisch, J., Groß, T., Shoup, V.: Anonymous credentials on a standard Java card. In: Proceedings of 16th ACM Conference on Computer and Communications Security, CCS 2009, pp. 600–610. ACM (2009)
4. Bichsel, P., et al.: An architecture for privacy-ABCs. In: Rannenberg, K., Camenisch, J., Sabouri, A. (eds.) Attribute-Based Credentials for Trust, pp. 11–78. Springer, Cham (2015). https://doi.org/10.1007/978-3-319-14439-9_2
5. Bjones, R., Krontiris, I., Paillier, P., Rannenberg, K.: Integrating anonymous credentials with eids for privacy-respecting online authentication. In: Preneel, B., Ikonomou, D. (eds.) APF 2012. LNCS, vol. 8319, pp. 111–124. Springer, Heidelberg (2014). https://doi.org/10.1007/978-3-642-54069-1_7
6. Camenisch, J., Lehmann, A., Neven, G.: Electronic identities need private credentials. IEEE Secur. Priv. **10**(1), 80–83 (2012)
7. Camenisch, J., Lysyanskaya, A.: An efficient system for non-transferable anonymous credentials with optional anonymity revocation. In: Pfitzmann, B. (ed.) EUROCRYPT 2001. LNCS, vol. 2045, pp. 93–118. Springer, Heidelberg (2001). https://doi.org/10.1007/3-540-44987-6_7
8. Camenisch, J., Lysyanskaya, A.: A signature scheme with efficient protocols. In: Cimato, S., Persiano, G., Galdi, C. (eds.) SCN 2002. LNCS, vol. 2576, pp. 268–289. Springer, Heidelberg (2003). https://doi.org/10.1007/3-540-36413-7_20
9. FIDO Alliance: FIDO UAF Protocol Specification v1.1. Implementation Draft, February 2017
10. GlobalPlatform: Card Specification v2.3. Public Release, October 2015
11. Hajny, J., Malina, L.: Unlinkable attribute-based credentials with practical revocation on smart-cards. In: Mangard, S. (ed.) CARDIS 2012. LNCS, vol. 7771, pp. 62–76. Springer, Heidelberg (2013). https://doi.org/10.1007/978-3-642-37288-9_5
12. Hölzl, M., Mayrhofer, R., Roland, M.: Requirements for an open ecosystem for embedded tamper resistant hardware on mobile devices. In: Proceedings of International Conference on Advances in Mobile Computing & Multimedia, MoMM 2013, pp. 249–252. ACM (2013)

13. Hölzl, M., Roland, M., Mayrhofer, R.: Real-world identification: towards a privacy-aware mobile eID for physical and offline verification. In: Proceedings of 14th International Conference on Advances in Mobile Computing and Multimedia, MoMM 2016, pp. 280–283. ACM (2016)

14. IBM Research: Specification of the Identity Mixer Cryptographic Library v2.3.0. Research Report, April 2010

15. Jensen, J.L.: Smartphone feasibility analysis. Deliverable D4.4 (2014)

16. Lehmann, A., et al.: Survey and analysis of existing eID and credential systems. FutureID Deliverable D32.1, April 2013

17. Madlmayr, G., Langer, J., Kantner, C., Scharinger, J.: NFC Devices: security and privacy. In: Third International Conference on Availability, Reliability and Security (ARES 2008), pp. 642–647. IEEE (2008)

18. Nyman, T., Ekberg, J.-E., Asokan, N.: Citizen electronic identities using TPM 2.0. In: Proceedings of 4th International Workshop on Trustworthy Embedded Devices, pp. 37–48. ACM (2014)

19. Otterbein, F., Ohlendorf, T., Margraf, M.: Mobile authentication with German eID. Extended Abstract for Presentation at the 11th International IFIP Summer School on Privacy and Identity Management (2016)

20. Paquin, C.: U-prove technology overview v1.1. Technical report, Microsoft Corporation Draft Revision, April 2013

21. Rannenberg, K., Camenisch, J., Sabouri, A. (eds.): Attribute-Based Credentials for Trust - Identity in the Information Society. Springer, Cham (2015). https://doi.org/10.1007/978-3-319-14439-9

22. Shoup, V.: A proposal for an ISO standard for public key encryption (version 2.1). IACR e-Print Archive 112 (2001)

23. Vullers, P., Alpár, G.: Efficient selective disclosure on smart cards using Idemix. In: Fischer-Hübner, S., de Leeuw, E., Mitchell, C. (eds.) IDMAN 2013. IAICT, vol. 396, pp. 53–67. Springer, Heidelberg (2013). https://doi.org/10.1007/978-3-642-37282-7_5

Author Index

Printed in the United States
By Bookmasters

Printed in the United States
By Bookmasters